THE NORTHWEST

GREEN HOME PRIMER

Kathleen O'Brien and Kathleen Smith

With a foreword
by Denis Hayes

TIMBER PRESS
Portland • London

Front cover photos by Michael Moore, Keith Peterson, Art Grice, Bruce Sullivan, Andrea Nelson, Aaron Blake, Stacy Crooks, Alan Scott, and George Ostrow courtesy of Velocipede. Plans courtesy of Robert Harrison Architects.

Back cover photos by Rob Harrison, Wayne Godare, and Mike Seidl courtesy of Fusion Partners LLC. Illustration by Christopher Gutsche and Kathleen Smith adapted from drawings by AHBL.

This book is intended to aid laypersons in the decision making involved in building, remodeling, or purchasing a green home. It offers basic guidelines and suggestions for the reader to consider. It's not intended to substitute for professional consultation on a given project, nor is it a design guide. Each site and each home design may have characteristics that may make any one or more of the suggestions in this book inappropriate. It's your responsibility to work with professionals to determine what's appropriate for your project.

Some jurisdictions don't permit some of the concepts presented in this book. Check with your local building and planning officials if you have any question about specific green building and site development strategies.

Guidance related to health and safety isn't intended to substitute for professional medical consultation. The book is written for the general population and presents ideas that may not be appropriate for an individual with multiple chemical sensitivities or other illness or condition.

We don't mention many products by name, but when we do it's intended as an example of something that's available, not a recommendation of a particular product. If we haven't mentioned a product by name, it's not because we don't think it's a worthwhile product but only because we don't want to be in the business of representing products in this book. A list of trademarks mentioned in this book appears on page 292.

Published in 2008 by
Timber Press, Inc.
The Haseltine Building
133 S.W. Second Avenue, Suite 450
Portland, Oregon 97204-3527, U.S.A.
www.timberpress.com

Printed in the United States of America.

Text printed on acid-free, recycled paper.

FRONTISPIECE: *The Cunningham-Pinon residence, Portland.* PHOTO BY ANDREA NELSON.

Library of Congress Cataloging-in-Publication Data

O'Brien, Kathleen (Kathleen Anne)
   The Northwest green home primer / Kathleen O'Brien and Kathleen Smith.
      p. cm.
   Includes bibliographical references and index.
   ISBN-13: 978-0-88192-797-9
   1. Ecological houses--Pacific states. I. Smith, Kathleen (Kathleen Frances) II. Title.
   TH4860.O27 2008
   643'.1--dc22

                                        2007027196

For our children and grandchildren:
Chris, Scott, Don, Fred, Matt, Alice, Oliver, Ellie, Zach, Tommy, and Stratton.

And for all the children of the world,

And for the earth that they will inherit.

① WEST ELEVATION

LANDING F.F.
WEST TERRACE F.F.

SET HEIGHT OF TOP OF CAP
AT 6" ABOVE FINISHED GRADE ON HIGH SI
MATCH THIS HEIGHT ON LOW SIDE (TYP)

6'-10"
8'-0"
8'-0"
8'-0"
6'-10"
2'-0"
TO GRADE
2"
2"

UPPER ATTIC SUBFLOOR

INTERIOR F.F.
DECK F.F.
PTD WOOD BELLY BAND
EXPOSED CONCRETE
3" THICK
CONC CAP

4'-8"
8'-0"
6'-10"
6'-10"
14'-8"
3'-0"
2"

② NORTH ELEVATION

③ SOUTH ELEVATION

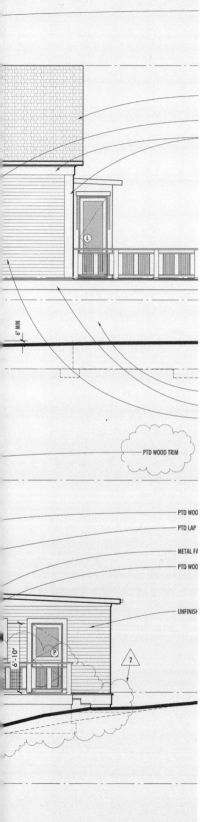

CONTENTS

FOREWORD

When we were organizing the first Earth Day in 1970, our hope was to shine a spotlight on several troubling environmental trends.

Earth Day's organizers had been born into a world where roughly 30 percent of the world's population lived in urban areas, and about 80 cities had populations of more than 1 million people. By 1970, the environmental impacts of separating living communities from their sources of food, energy, and water were becoming significant. Water and air pollution, loss of topsoil, and degraded landscapes were problems crying out for solutions. Over time, environmental agencies would be formed, federal regulations would be passed, and grassroots organizations would pound the pavements to raise public awareness and changes in behavior.

By 2000, when many of the students who'd organized Earth Day had become grandparents, they were living in a world where almost half of the world's population lived in urban areas and more than 400 cities had populations of over 1 million people. At the same time, some of the progress made in earlier years by environmental agencies and activist groups was being reversed.

Today, humans are triggering a wave of extinction unmatched since the last time a major asteroid hit the planet. We have laced all living organisms on the planet with complex, biologically-active, manufactured compounds with unknown consequences. Our clear cutting, bottom trawling, and massive hydroelectric projects have caused effects similar to those of massive earthquakes and volcano eruptions.

And, of course, we are changing the earth's climate.

As citizens, we must address these issues at the ballot box, in our businesses, and through local organizations. We can also play a significant role as homeowners.

The lighting, space conditioning, and appliances used in buildings now comprise the largest source of greenhouse gas emissions in the world. The good news is that the technical opportunities for dramatic reductions in building energy use—without any loss of amenity or productivity, and at little or no economic cost—are literally stunning. It is not particularly difficult (although it remains rare) today to build a carbon neutral building. This book will help those of us in the Northwest to get there.

Among the most important basic truths is that we must design with nature, adapting our structures to the conditions that surround them. It is idiotic to stamp out the same inane buildings in Seattle that we build in Miami or Anchorage. Cascadia has its own unique treasures and challenges. Wise buildings and green communities are informed by a regional ethos that permits them to rest lightly on the earth. Indeed, true "living buildings" have essentially no footprint.

In this pioneering book, Kathleen O'Brien and Kathleen Smith provide the sort of intelligent, thoughtful, experienced insights that—if followed—will ensure that we make the right choices. Certainly, anyone considering building, remodeling, or buying a green home should have this book. Those developing and redeveloping neighborhoods and communities should also take a look. And finally, it should be on the desk of every mayor, urban planner, and architect in the region.

Denis Hayes

Denis Hayes *directs the Bullitt Foundation, which is dedicated to making the Pacific Northwest a global model for sustainable development. An environmental visionary, Hayes was national coordinator of the first Earth Day. He has received the Jefferson Medal for Outstanding Public Service as well as the highest awards bestowed by the Sierra Club and many other organizations.*

PREFACE

When we started our professional careers in what is now termed *green building,* homes that saved energy were being called energy efficient, while homes designed with attention to air quality were called healthy. Homes that used efficient framing techniques or materials with recycled content were called resource efficient.

When the term green building was introduced in the early 1990s, neither of us really liked it. Too ambiguous, and meaning too many different things to different people. Still, it was important to come up with something that conveyed the idea of combining multiple strategies to make a home truly environmentally friendly. Calling a home environmentally friendly or environmentally sensitive was a mouthful, so in time we surrendered to the idea of simply calling it green.

That doesn't mean the term didn't confuse people at first. In the early days of the movement, we knew of builders showing up for seminars on green building thinking it was about building greenhouses or was geared to builders new to construction. Or they didn't show up at all, because they thought it was solely for fringe types.

Even folks who were directly involved in aspects of the movement tended to confuse the matter, as they would focus on their favorite aspect—for example, energy conservation, good air quality, resourceful materials, or water conservation—at the expense of other aspects, yet still call it green. All this has changed since the late 1990s. With consistent use of the term, and an insistence by many of us on a holistic application of the concept, *green* is now widely understood to refer to buildings that combine multiple environmental and health considerations.

In addition, it has been important to bring the realities of budget, performance, and schedule into any discussion of what is green. When undertaken with this understanding, green building becomes good practice or best practice rather than just an interesting philosophy. As such, green building, including your green home project, can truly contribute to creating a more sustainable future.

Both of us have been lucky enough to work professionally in the field of green building for some years. As often happens, though, just like the shoemaker with shoeless children or the carpenter whose home is never completed, we weren't able to enjoy the benefits of green building in our own households. That is, until recently.

In 1999, Kathleen O'Brien (whom we'll call by her nickname, Kate, from now on to avoid confusion) and her husband, John Cunningham, moved into their new green home on Bainbridge Island, a home that was the subject of a Home and Garden TV show on sustainable building and that has been visited virtually and physically by more than 40,000 curious seekers. In 2004, they remodeled the upper story of the garage to include a studio.

Also in 2004, Kathleen Smith, her husband, Chris Gutsche, and their daughter, Alice, moved to Bainbridge Island, into a duplex unit in Winslow Cohousing that they then remodeled. Now, joined by a son, Oliver, they all enjoy the benefits of living in a healthy green home that's part of a vibrant multigenerational community.

In chapter 2 we tell the tales of our personal journeys through our individual projects. These projects are priceless to us in that we now enjoy beautiful, green homes that we can safely say do contribute to a sustainable future. This last matter is no small thing to us as mothers (and in Kate's case as a grandmother). In addition, we've learned important lessons that we can carry into our work every day. These personal lessons, and the field experience we gain on a daily basis, are our gifts to you.

The book focuses on the Pacific Northwest, which is a hotbed of green building. We feel very lucky to live here. Throughout the book, local projects are highlighted, either in case studies or as examples of specific green building strategies. We relied heavily on our personal networks to identify projects for our first publishing effort together. We fully expect readers, including our working colleagues, to point out projects in other locations around the region that could have been included. We look forward to hearing from you—for our next book! We did try to diversify, so we have examples of new construction and renovation, historic and contemporary style homes, and homes located east and west of the Cascade Range to make sure we covered dry- and wet-country issues.

Further, sustainable building is a huge field. We've focused on some of our favorite ideas for the Northwest and provided just enough information—in our humble estimation—for you to meaningfully consider their application to your project. In addition, we feel very strongly that the process is as important to getting your job done right as choosing a particular material or technique, so we've devoted nearly equal time to managing your project as we have to technical strategies.

A stroll through the table of contents should reveal that this book applies to you whether you're building, remodeling, or purchasing a green home. We wish you the best in the pursuit of your dreams and a green home that

is built to last,
is comfortable and healthy,
saves you money and time over the long term,
    and
fits within our bigger home, the earth.

Who could turn that down?

Thanks for making us part of your experience!

ACKNOWLEDGMENTS

It takes a village to write a book. Thanks so much to all those who had a part in bringing this project to fruition. In particular, we wish to thank our intern, Andrea Nelson, without whom this book would simply not have been accomplished.

Thanks to staff members of O'Brien & Company who contributed to the book, especially Alistair Jackson, Sue Nicol, and Julia Zander—all LEED-accredited professionals and sustainable building hotshots, as well as those on staff who lived with us while we did it.

Thanks to case study contributors Jon Alexander, owner of Sunshine Construction; Kent Snyder; Alan Scott, architect with Green Building Services; Keith Peterson, scientist with Pacific Northwest National Laboratory; as well as sidebar contributors Chris Herman of Winter Sun Design; Dan Morris of Healthy Buildings, Inc.; and Sandy Campbell of 1Earth1Design.

Thanks to our technical advisors Chris Gutsche, architect with EcoSmith Design & Consulting on Bainbridge Island, who reviewed the chapters on site choices and building enclosure and assisted greatly with the illustrations; Greg Acker, architect with Portland's G-Rated Program, who reviewed the chapter on operating systems; and Kas Kinkead, landscape architect with Seattle's Cascade Design Collaborative, who reviewed the chapter on site choices. We'd also like to acknowledge Richard Knights, Blue Sky Testing in Seattle; Cheri Zehner, MPH, Certified Indoor Air Quality Investigator in Seattle; and Carl Magnison, Magnison Design and Building in Langley, Washington, for peer reviewing sidebars on mold prevention and treatment.

Thanks to the many who allowed us to use your photos and graphics. You're credited throughout the book, but we want you to know that we know how busy you are and how important your contribution is to the book.

Thanks to Eve Goodman at Timber Press, who thank goodness didn't warn us how much work this would really turn out to be and continued to be a source of optimistic "You can do this!" support throughout the process. Thanks also to Lorraine Anderson, who did a fabulous job of editing this tome.

Thanks as well to our husbands, John and Chris, and especially to our kids, Chris, Scott, Don, Fred, Matt, Alice, and Oliver, and Kate's grandkids, Ellie, Zach, Tommy, and Stratton. You inspire us daily to continue our work. This book is for you, in hopes of making a better, more sustainable world for you and all of us, one green home at a time.

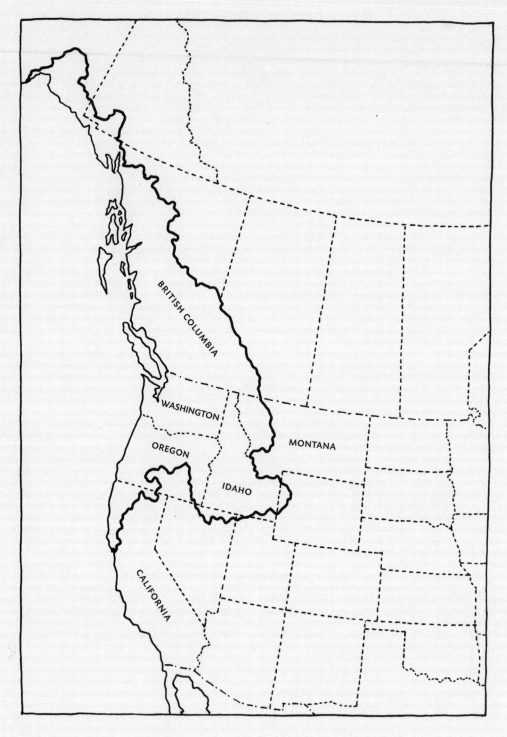

The Cascadia bioregion includes Oregon, Washington, Idaho, and parts of British Columbia, Montana, and northern California.

ILLUSTRATION BY
CHRISTOPHER GUTSCHE
AND KATHLEEN SMITH.

BRITISH COLUMBIA

WASHINGTON

OREGON

MONTANA

IDAHO

CALIFORNIA

> Green buildings do not poison the air with fumes nor the soul with artificiality. Instead they create delight when entered, serenity and health when occupied, and regret when departed.
>
> Paul Hawken, Amory Lovins, and Hunter Lovins, *Natural Capitalism*

1: The Case for Green Building

THE HOME SITS HAPPILY in a bustling urban neighborhood. Or it rests easily in an expansive rural setting dripping with coastal firs or dotted with dry brush. Or it nestles neatly into a close-knit suburban village. Regardless of its setting—and its style—the home seems to fit. It makes just the right use of its site, and as important, it does so without being overly greedy for resources. It takes the environment—near and far—into account. In broad-brush terms, this is what is meant by a green home.

Whatever a green home's surroundings, it will be judged on its performance by those who reside in it. Are the energy bills lower than usual? Is the indoor air fresher than provided in typical construction? Are the materials durable and long-lived? Does the landscaping require minimal water and maintenance once established?

AT HOME IN CASCADIA

For those who ponder larger issues, a green home in the Pacific Northwest will also be judged for its impact on the earth, and in particular on the Cascadia bioregion—an area encompassing an amazingly diverse set of climatic and cultural conditions related to variations in latitude and elevation, mountain ranges that sharply divide the east from the west, and large bodies of water that both divide and connect. It's an area that nonetheless shares one common and significant feature: the indigenous, iconic Pacific salmon. To some, this creature is the heart and soul of the Northwest.

In *The Good Rain* (1991), Timothy Egan writes that "the Pacific Northwest is any place a salmon can get to." If this is the case, the Pacific Northwest is shrinking in an alarming fashion. Though salmon are generally revered as beautiful creatures, good food, and a source of industrious livelihood, the fact is that wild salmon runs are decreasing drastically, both in numbers and geographic range, as a result of human activity. Pacific salmon—chinook, chum, coho, pink, sockeye, steelhead, and sea-run cutthroat trout— have disappeared from 40 percent of their former range in Washington, Oregon, Idaho, and California. Across the Northwest, at least 214 salmon runs are extinct, and more than 1000 are likely at risk (Northwest Environmental Watch 2002, 36).

Why is this significant? And what does it have to do with green homes? Consider salmon the canaries in the mine of our time and place. Their decline signifies degradation in a broad range of ecosystems, as well as a severe threat to a regional economy that relies heavily on environmental resources and natural appeal.

Salmon have been hardest hit where development is most intense. Ill-informed development activities can significantly affect both the quality and quantity of water available for fish and fish habitat. Some examples include poor erosion control during construction, permanent modifications of stream flows, removal of vegetation alongside waterways causing increased temperatures, and unnecessary expanses of impervious roof and parking areas.

As dams producing hydroelectricity fall out of favor as the regional power source of choice because of their negative impact on salmon runs, the effect of development activities on species health grows proportionately. To generate new power for our expanding human population, fossil fuels will be used, on-site or off-site. (We're already seeing a growing interest in expanding electricity generation from "clean" coal.) As development moves out into the hinterlands, car travel increases. Increased fossil fuel use means more CO_2 emissions, raising the region's contribution to global climate change.

Increasing flooding events in the Northwest resulting from development activities and climate change scour wild salmon habitat, dislodging eggs from the salmon bed or burying them in silt. Even hatcheries aren't safe, as illustrated by the hundreds of thousands of baby salmon that were killed in floods during one recent winter in the Puget Sound area (Mullen 2006).

Taking an environmental approach to development, therefore, is a direct response to the plight of salmon. Understanding that this problem represents perhaps only the most visible (and certainly the most culturally significant) aspect of human impacts on the bioregion, it's not an exaggeration to say that green homes, green remodels, and green communities developed on a broad scale can reverse the course of this degradation and preserve what matters to inhabitants of Cascadia.

TOWARD A SUSTAINABLE FUTURE

Green homes contribute to the overall sustainability of the region. *Sustainability* is a term that's widely misunderstood. The term originated as an ecological one, indicating a balance point (also known as carrying capacity) where a living species can be sustained

Cascadia is a richly diverse region with many large and small ecosystems providing natural services. An open field in Sisters, Oregon, with mountains in the distance (below) is counterpoint to a bog in Snoqualmie, Washington (far right).
PHOTOS BY ANDREA NELSON (RIGHT), NORA DALEY-PENG (LEFT).

by a given ecosystem. When the balance point is exceeded, the condition is called overshoot and the species' future is endangered unless something is done to reestablish sustainability.

The earth sustains us (and all life) by providing us with two primary services: resources we need to live, and the capacity to assimilate the by-products of life's activities (usually called waste). So, for example, our atmosphere provides us with oxygen to breathe and absorbs the carbon dioxide we exhale as waste. These life services provided by the earth have been characterized by leading environmentalists like Paul Hawken as natural capital. Natural capital includes resources (for example, water, minerals, trees, fish) as well as living systems (such as oceans, tundra, and wetlands). Not only do these make life possible, they also make life "worth living on this planet" (Hawken, Lovins, and Lovins 1999, 2).

The problem occurs when resources, or physical forms of natural capital, are consumed more quickly than they can be replaced, and more waste is produced than can be assimilated over time. An additional problem occurs when we create waste that can never reasonably be assimilated, meaning it would take many, many generations to break down, frequently harming our ecology in the process. Sometimes the harm can be local, such as lake pollution from nitrates released by lawn fertilizer products, or human illness caused by the release of chlorine into the air and water surrounding a vinyl siding manufacturing plant. Sometimes the harm can be global, such as ozone depletion from the use of hydrochlorofluorocarbons (compounds containing carbon, hydrogen, and fluorine) in equipment that heats or cools our buildings, or climate change from the use of fossil fuels to produce electricity.

Modern buildings use enormous amounts of natural capital; according to the most recent data available, as of 1995 they accounted for one-quarter of the world's timber harvest, one-sixth of the world's fresh water withdrawals, and two-fifths of the world's energy and material flows (Roodman and Lenssen 1995, 5, 23). Given the significant growth occurring globally, this data probably underestimates the problem. The present level of resource use has obvious significance for the natural world, but it would be extremely shortsighted not to see how we humans fit into this picture. If we continue on our current path, we seriously jeopardize our economic and physical health and our quality of life in general.

Yet if we stay within nature's limits through ingenious design and thoughtful planning, we protect our future. Just as with our personal savings, it's best

to live on the earth's interest (such as today's solar energy) rather than digging—literally—into our principal (such as the coal or oil that represents yesterday's solar energy). Interest can easily be built back up. Principal isn't so easily replaced.

As members of the biosphere (the physical sphere including all organic life), we humans are also part of the earth's natural capital. When human health is undermined, our society and our planet lose. The U.S. Environmental Protection Agency (EPA) reports that illness resulting from sick building syndrome has cost millions of dollars in lost time and productivity, not to mention the disruption of lives it causes (1989, 1). Projected gains from addressing sick building syndrome as well as other conditions aggravated by poor indoor air quality are impressive: $10 to $30 billion for reducing sick building symptoms, $6 to $14 billion for reducing respiratory disease, and $1 to $4 billion for reducing allergies and asthma (Fisk 2000).

Primary health risks in homes include mold resulting from moisture problems, dust mites stored in finishes (such as carpets) and furnishings, and sensitization related to exposure to a variety of chemicals found in building materials, products, and furnishings. These circumstances can lead to discomfort even for healthy individuals, but for people with serious allergies or suffering from asthma—which affects 20 million Americans, including 6.2 million children (American Lung Association 2005, 4)—they can trigger expensive if not deadly episodes.

THE NORTHWEST, NATURALLY

Given these universal circumstances, green building makes sense anywhere. It's not surprising, though, that the Pacific Northwest has enthusiastically embraced adoption of this environmentally friendly approach. For one thing, the natural beauty of the environment is never far away. Magnificent mountain ranges, shimmering waterways, emerald green forests, and spacious high desert terrain are in abundance. Even in urban centers, such as Portland, Seattle, and Vancouver B.C., inhabitants and visitors are daily treated to extravagant natural vistas. It's why most of us live here, yes?

Meanwhile, growing environmental concerns are as prevalent as the pretty views. Waterways suffer from pollution; mountaintops no longer boast snowcaps year-round because of changes in climate patterns; water tables are threatened. A haze of pollution blurs the air and tests the breathing capacity of the most vulnerable members of our society— our children and our elderly. Soil, the nutrient base that feeds our forests and our crops, continues to erode at an alarming rate. The increasing fragility of our environment is hard to ignore, and nearly daily, we read or hear stories on this topic.

No surprise, then, that most major northwestern cities (and many small cities and towns) have adopted policies that encourage green building in their jurisdictions. Nor that the first state to pass legislation requiring state-funded buildings to meet green building requirements is here in the Northwest. Washington State's stunningly successful 2005 bipartisan campaign (the final Senate vote was 32–16; House vote 78–19) to pass the groundbreaking legislation is expected to spur similar activities elsewhere in the region. Oregon is likely to be next. Meanwhile, nonlegislative state and provincial policies in British Columbia and California support using green building standards for public and in some cases private-sector projects. While green building still isn't an everyday occurrence in the Pacific Northwest, it clearly is a choice that forward thinkers and policy makers are coming to for the good of all.

MORE GAINS FROM GREEN BUILDING

It's a good guess that if you live in the Pacific Northwest, you hold the environment in high regard, whether you rely on it to enjoy a hike, fish for a living, raise crops, sail for fun, or harvest timber. For that reason alone, you might want to apply green building concepts to your new home construction or remodeling project. You needn't leave your yard to reap some very significant benefits. For example, drought-tolerant landscaping and durable building materials can reduce maintenance requirements. Efficient fixtures and appliances can lower energy and water consumption (and save you dollars). A single mature tree protected in place can provide nearly $300 in energy and resource value as a result of cooling, erosion and pollution control, and wildlife shelter (Akbari et al. 1992, 28).

Low-toxicity, easy-to-clean finishes and good moisture-control details can reduce health risks. If you're one of the many individuals in the Northwest suffering from asthma—current prevalence in the region ranges from 7.9 percent of the population in Idaho and Montana to 9.3 percent in Oregon, with Washington close behind at 9.1 percent (American Lung Association 2005, 22)—using green building techniques that emphasize indoor air quality is one way to manage your condition.

Reduced maintenance, longer service life, lower utility consumption, better moisture control, and healthier indoor air are all benefits that can be directly related to green building design and that you can enjoy while living in your home. If you plan to sell your home, green building can be a good deal as well, as research shows that specific aspects of green building, as well as green building overall, can increase market resale value. In both the Seattle/King County and Portland metropolitan areas, the Multiple Listing Service (MLS) used by realtors to list existing homes for sale has added energy efficiency and green building certification categories to the searchable database as recognition of the value these bring to the market. This is likely to occur elsewhere in the region as green building takes hold.

McStain Enterprises, based in Boulder, Colorado, one of the country's first developers to practice green building, conducted research on a subdivision of green homes it built in a development near Denver. When originally built in 1997, these homes sold faster and for slightly more than homes built by other developers in the surrounding area. Five years later, McStain found the homes reselling at prices 4 to 11 percent higher than those commanded by more conventionally built homes nearby (personal communication, 2002). In our region, it's too early to tell regarding resales, but initial interest is definitely high. The first weekend the Idea Home in Issaquah Highlands was open to the public, a thousand visitors marched directly from the home to the builder's information office! Everyone—even the builder—had underestimated the market for green building.

Mature trees can add significantly to your property value. More than 50 percent of 1350 real estate agents surveyed by Bank of America Mortgage thought that trees have a positive impact on potential buyers' impressions of homes and neighborhoods. A whopping 84 percent felt that a home with trees would be as much as 20 percent more salable. Studies in some regions of the country have found trees add as much as 30 percent to the selling price of lots (National Association of Home Builders 2004a, 17).

Other aspects of green building rated very highly by homebuyers in national and regional surveys include energy efficiency, healthier indoor environments, durability, and preservation of sensitive natural features, such as streams, wetlands, and topography.

HOW GREEN CAN YOU BE?

The realities of your situation will determine how aggressively you can apply green concepts to your home project. In practice, projects range from light to dark green, with dark green projects defined as those achieving the deepest long-term benefit for the owner and the lightest environmental impact. The final result has to do with your project budget, of course, but includes other considerations as well, including your schedule, product performance and availability, and where you're starting from.

No matter what your constraints, you'll achieve the darkest shade of green—and the maximum personal benefit—if you use a process that does two important things: integrates your green building goals from the beginning and all the way through to completion, and looks at the home as a system. Non-systems thinking looks at the house as a sort of box (an important box that keeps the elements out, but a box nonetheless) that you then throw stuff into to heat, cool, or provide fresh air and water. Paint it pretty colors for curb appeal, furnish, landscape the yard, and you're good to go. Not.

Using a process focused on green systems thinking from the start will provide you with better results, whether you're building from scratch or working with an existing home. With remodeling, you'll want to be sure the project is planned within the context of existing house systems rather than ignoring or discounting them. As an example, if you plan even a "simple" project such as enclosing your porch to create a sunny winter sitting area, you can leverage opportunities and avoid problems by considering how this change will affect the rest of the building. Among other things, you'll want to make sure that when you tie into the existing house you don't introduce moisture traps, that you don't remove the deciduous tree located next to the porch if it's needed for shading in the summer, and that if the porch is planned to be an important source of heat (and not just light) it doesn't overdo its job.

WHAT'S IT GOING TO COST YOU?

You're probably wondering what it's going to cost you to build green. The question may also be: What's it going to save you? Choosing Energy Star appliances and lighting fixtures is a smart move when energy prices have nowhere to go but up. An Energy Star refrigerator will use roughly 40 percent less electricity to operate than a conventional model, an Energy Star dishwasher 25 percent less. (The latter will also reduce your water consumption.) Recessed can lighting hardwired for the new improved compact fluorescents means you'll use two-thirds less electricity to light your work surfaces.

In many cases, an energy-efficient choice will mean better overall performance as well. For example, the reason a motor in an appliance runs more efficiently is that it's manufactured with better components that don't wear as quickly. So service life will be longer, and the motor will run more quietly. The extra insulation in Energy Star dishwashers is

another reason they run more quietly, something we really appreciate when our families are trying to have a meaningful conversation at the kitchen table after dinner. Good-quality compact fluorescents aren't just efficient, they also run ten times cooler than their incandescent counterparts. As a result, they last a lot longer.

You may be thinking that the cost of making a green home will correlate directly with the hue of green you strive for. Not necessarily so. If you use a comprehensive, integrated approach to design your home or remodeling project, you can actually achieve dark green results with no increase in your budget, or with only a small one, perhaps 1 to 2 percent more than the cost of the same project using a conventional approach. The typical premium for green projects certified in green building rating systems at the highest levels generally lands between 2 and 4 percent, with the upper range correlating with the overall market value of the home.

Consider two examples. The O'Brien-Cunningham residence achieved top rating in the local Built Green program while being well within financial reach of most homeowners in the region. In contrast,

An Energy Star label on your appliance is a green choice. PHOTO BY ANDREA NELSON.

The O'Brien-Cunningham residence (right) achieved the highest rating in the local green building program; the Living Homes prototype green modular home (below) achieved Platinum in LEED for Homes. Both are excellent examples of a thoughtful approach to green building. The O'Brien-Cunningham residence represents a significantly more modest investment. PHOTOS BY JOHN CUNNINGHAM (RIGHT), TOM BONNER, COURTESY OF LIVING HOMES (BELOW).

the Living Homes prototype green modular home, which achieved the first Platinum rating from the U.S. Green Building Council's LEED for Homes program and included many green innovations and a luxury feel, represents a significant financial investment.

If you focus on techniques and systems that reduce the long-term operational and maintenance costs of the home, you can factor in significant long-term savings as well, thanks to lower consumption, reduced replacement and repair fees, and lower maintenance costs. If family members struggle with sensitivities or allergies, using a green, healthy approach to your project should result in fewer medical bills. With emergency room visits for asthma costing roughly $130 each and with the average per capita cost of dealing with asthma in the U.S. at $1096 in 1994 (the latest data generally available), this is no small thing (Smith et al. 1997, 789).

Of course, there's no outside limit to how much you *could* spend on your project. We know of situations where owners have spent oodles of money on a green home or remodeling project without getting dark green results. The point is that the approach you take will affect the choices you make and when you make them, which in turn affects how dark a green you're able to achieve within your budget. Our intent with this primer is to focus on smart choices, not extravagant ones. Whether your budget is modest (as both of ours were) or not so modest, careless use of fiscal resources is no more justifiable than careless use of natural capital. To put it succinctly, it's dumb.

For our own homes, thinking about the long haul allowed us to make some choices we might not have made if we'd just been thinking first cost. For example, the O'Brien-Cunningham residence has a metal roof, which cost when installed a full 40 percent more than a conventional three-tab asphalt roof would have. However, its warranty is more than three times as long. In addition, if rainwater catchment is added to the project, the smooth metal roof will provide a cleaner surface for the rainwater to run off of. This implies something else: that good-quality dark green projects incorporate synergies. Every project, green or not, requires trade-offs, usually between less or more expensive options, but not always. With green projects, these trade-offs involve looking at options from multiple perspectives. It actually gets to be quite fun, thinking about how many benefits one strategy (such as a metal roof) can provide. In addition to guaranteeing longer life and providing a better surface for rainwater catchment, the metal roof satisfies the three Rs (reduce, reuse, and recycle)—the roof contains a healthy amount of recycled content (25 percent) and will be easy to recycle at the end of its life.

It's also fun to figure out how to make multiple strategies work together (even when they seem to conflict) to create an even bigger (and better) benefit. For example, it is possible to have a solar array generate electricity for your green home *and* use shade trees to reduce your home's summer heat gain. Of course, because the solar array needs as much sun as possible to maximize its output during the year, it will take careful site planning to make this work.

For those who argue that green buildings cost too much, one only has to look at low-income housing projects that have done an excellent job of

The Kerby Street affordable housing project in Portland managed to provide creative details such as the garage door living room window while enabling residents to harvest solar energy and rainwater. PHOTOS BY AARON BLAKE.

incorporating green features. If it makes sense for affordable housing, surely it makes sense for housing in the general market. Affordable housing advocates recognize the long-term benefits both to residents

The New Columbia project in Portland located affordable rental units off an attractive commons and installed rain gardens in the planter strip to manage storm water. Note the solar panels on the roof of the unit on the right. PHOTOS BY JUAN HERNANDEZ, COURTESY OF MITHUN ARCHITECTS.

looking to improve their lives and to agencies looking to reduce the cost of managing capital assets over the long haul. We personally know of efforts to build green low-income housing (either as an entire development or as part of a mixed-income development) in Portland, Spokane, Seattle, and Vancouver B.C., and we would guess there are others in conceptual stages throughout the region.

The Kerby Street and New Columbia projects (both in Portland) are good examples of affordable housing projects incorporating green features. Among other things, the 700-square-foot private stand-alone Kerby Street units are prewired for photovoltaics and solar hot water, harvest rainwater to flush the toilets, are hydronically heated (hydronic systems use water to distribute heat around the home in narrow-gauge pipes), and include special details to keep rainwater out. New Columbia located affordable rental units off an attractive commons and installed rain gardens in the planter strip to manage storm water. The Energy Trust of Oregon donated equipment to harness the sun to preheat water going to each unit's water heater, which provides both space and water heating; the agency will be monitoring energy usage for twelve months and comparing it to that of a similar unit that doesn't include solar preheat.

GREEN MONEY FOR GREEN HOMES

Many lending institutions recognize the value of

energy efficiency and offer energy-efficient mortgages (EEMs) around the country. In the Northwest, where energy efficiency has been valued for some time (and energy standards are in general more rigorous than in much of the rest of the United States), most new homes are automatically seen by lenders as energy efficient, so EEMs aren't really promoted here. EEMs have been more useful as a way to finance changes to existing homes where significant (and subsequent) upgrades to the current energy code have taken place. However, the availability of Energy Star Northwest certification options along with increases in fuel costs will make going beyond the energy code more attractive and may make lenders more interested in promoting EEMs in the region.

As of 2007 Fannie Mae has plans to offer lending packages to homes certified under the U.S. Green Building Council's LEED for Homes program and is piloting the Location Efficient Mortgage (LEM) in Seattle and San Francisco. The LEM offers a low down payment, competitive interest rates, and flexible qualification criteria to homebuyers looking to buy homes in convenient neighborhoods where residents can walk from their homes to stores, schools, recreation, and public transportation. In Washington State, Countrywide offers discounts on construction loans to builders constructing homes enrolled in the Built Green program. Individuals seeking mortgages in British Columbia for energy efficient and green homes or green remodeling projects can take advan-

Since the mid-1990s programs have proliferated in the Northwest to help promote green building to builders and to provide the public with a clearer definition of what makes a home, remodeling project, or development green. In Washington State, this effort has been led by homebuilding associations working with local jurisdictions. By 2006 there were eight green building programs in the state, most of which were called by the name Built Green and were participating in Built Green Washington.

Although the Oregon Building Industry Association (OBIA) has promoted green building, local cities and utilities have been more successful in developing and promoting guidelines in Oregon. For example, the City of Portland's G-Rated Program provides technical support and assistance regarding financial incentives. Earth Advantage, developed by Portland General Electric but now an independent nonprofit, offers a program that certifies new construction and remodeling projects that meet its requirements.

In California, the effort has come from multiple directions. The California Building Industry Association (CBIA) has a statewide Green Building program; Alameda County has spearheaded the Build It Green program, which it hopes will be picked up by the state; and local contractor groups have created their own programs—for example, Santa Barbara Built Green.

There are also programs focused specifically on greening affordable housing, such as SeaGreen, developed by the Seattle Office of Housing. Global Green in the Bay Area, the BuildSmart program of the Greater Vancouver Regional District in B.C., and Portland's Office of Sustainable Development all offer green building guidelines for low-income housing.

Meanwhile, Energy Star and IAQ Star Homes are national programs offered by the U.S. EPA. Energy Star signifies that a home exceeds a minimum standard for energy performance, similar to the Energy Star designation on your laptop. IAQ-Star (a much more recent development) assumes Energy Star requirements have been met as a minimum and has a number of additional mandatory items to prove performance in the indoor air quality realm. Because climatic conditions and existing energy codes differ from region to region, Energy Star has worked with the Northwest Energy Efficiency Alliance (NEEA) to create Energy Star Northwest for NEEA's territory (Idaho, Montana, Oregon, and Washington). IAQ Star may undergo similar adaptation.

State energy code requirements in the Energy Star Northwest territory vary, so the percentage by which homes with the Energy Star label must exceed these requirements also varies:

Idaho	30 percent or more
Montana	20 percent or more
Oregon	15 percent or more
Washington	15 percent or more

LEED for Homes is a national program of the U.S. Green Building Council (USGBC). LEED stands for Leadership in Energy and Environmental Design and is a trademark for a variety of systems developed by the USGBC that rate neighborhoods and nonresidential buildings and developments as well as homes. Many regional green building experts participated in the development of Energy Star Northwest and IAQ Star as well as of LEED for Homes.

At the core of these programs is a checklist of actions, some of which are required and most of which are optional. The optional actions, when taken, earn points; ratings are granted based on the total number of points earned. There are several levels of ratings, with each higher level representing greater challenge and, ideally, better performance. For higher levels in local programs, and for national programs such as LEED for Homes and Energy Star, some form of independent third-party verification is required. Although this brings costs with it, it also provides assurance to the homeowner that the work was done, and in some cases is used to justify incentives and mortgage breaks. You can find more details on these programs and organizations in "Resources" at the back of the book.

tage of a Canada Mortgage and Housing Corporation (CMHC) program that offers a 10 percent premium refund on its mortgage loan insurance premiums and a much longer amortization period, reducing monthly payments significantly (Environment Canada 2006). These programs are only the tip of the iceberg, as lenders and Wall Street observers begin to view green building as a means of risk reduction and a good investment (Walker 2006).

Municipalities and utilities in the region, faced with the rising cost of providing services to a growing population, run campaigns to promote the use of more efficient equipment and fixtures. These frequently include financial incentives, which can range from rebates on large items (such as an Energy Star washer or gas heater) with proof of purchase, to coupons for or even free samples of smaller items (such as compact fluorescent lightbulbs and low-flow showerheads). Incentive programs are generally temporary. When you're considering a new construction or remodeling project it pays to check in with your local water and energy providers to make sure you don't miss out.

With the urge for energy independence holding sway, there are also regional and national financial incentives for using renewable energy–related technologies. More information on these incentives is provided in chapter 5.

> Build a third less square footage than you think you need, then spend just as much money as you would have to build the larger building, but spend it on character. It isn't about square footage, it's about proper scale and function.
>
> Sarah Susanka, keynote address, 2006 Built Green Conference

2: Starting Out with Green in Mind

PROPER PLANNING OF A GREEN HOME—or any kind of home, for that matter—means keeping in mind that each planning choice you make will have implications for other choices. Every decision has the potential to work either with or against another decision. In the industry, this phenomenon is called making a trade-off. Typically, these trade-offs are based on one single factor—a first-cost budget—outweighing other important factors, such as long-term operational savings or qualitative benefits. Or even worse, the trade-off is made unconsciously, without any awareness of what has been surrendered in the process.

When the O'Brien-Cunninghams directed the builder of their new home to spend $100 more on the garage door with windows (as opposed to without), they made an aesthetic choice. Meanwhile, they didn't catch that the budget-conscious builder had chosen a standard fan for the whole-house exhaust system. Later they rued the decision—which they didn't realize they were making at the time—not to spend that $100 on a quieter, more energy efficient, and better running fan. They upgraded the fan when the original died, which it did sooner rather than later, since standard fans aren't actually built to be used in the way even the Washington code intends—at least eight continuous hours a day. (Most people don't notice because they turn the noisy fans off, extending the life of the fan but creating other problems.) Unfortunately, replacing the standard fan wasn't as easy as it sounds. The space was tight to work in, as the fan was located in the eaves, and the drywall had to be cut in situ to fit the shape of the replacement fan.

Thus even small trade-offs can become pretty significant. However, there are three big decisions that will affect all the others, and as such your ability to fulfill your goal of living in a green home. If you're considering remodeling an existing home, these decisions have already pretty much been made. Even so, we think it's important to understand the significance of your answers to three questions:

Where is your home?
How big is your home?
What type of housing is it?

We'll take these one at a time, although like everything else when it comes to green, they're connected. To help you understand why your answers to these questions matter, we'll first introduce the idea of your home's ecological footprint.

YOUR HOME'S ECOLOGICAL FOOTPRINT

As you start planning for your green home, consider a concept called Ecological Footprint Analysis developed by Mathis Wackernagel and his colleagues and promoted by the organization Redefining Progress. Footprint analysis calculates a given population's consumption and waste production expressed in acres of biologically productive land and ocean areas needed to maintain these services. The national ecological footprint measures the land area required to support a nation for one year, providing for its needs and absorbing its wastes. It's a complicated calculation, but it uses very conservative assumptions to evaluate energy consumption, as well as areas used for grazing, agriculture, fisheries, development, and timber harvest.

By calculating how much a given population consumes and how much waste it produces, and comparing this to how much natural capital is actually available, Ecological Footprint Analysis tells us just how far off the mark we are. And we in North America are well off the mark. According to Redefining Progress, the United States has the world's largest footprint at 23.7 acres (9.57 hectares) per person. The organization calculates that a sustainable footprint would be more like 4.6 acres (1.88 hectares) per person. To put this in perspective, developing countries like Bangladesh and Mozambique have footprints of 1.3 acres (0.53 hectares) per capita. Looking at human activities worldwide, footprint analysis reveals an overuse of the earth's natural resources by 15 percent (Venetoulis, Chazan, and Gaudet 2004, 12).

In other words, we would have to increase our efficiency very significantly (and very quickly), or find another planet or two to borrow from, just to serve the earth's current population in the way that U.S. residents are currently served. This gets even scarier when you realize that the global population continues to grow rapidly, and that the peoples of most developing countries want to experience the same quality of life we do. Some of those countries are making great progress in that direction. Witness China's explosive economic growth and infrastructure development. How do we equitably accommodate all of us in a sustainable fashion?

WHERE IS YOUR HOME?

Your home's location affects your household's ecological footprint significantly. This is primarily because fossil fuel used for transportation is a huge contributor to resource consumption and waste production (in the form of air pollution that must be assimilated). So when you reduce your transportation needs by locating your home near services and where you work, you reduce your footprint quite a bit. The easiest way to do this, of course, is to live in a more urban location. In addition to reducing your transportation requirements, choosing an urban or higher density location tends to reduce your household's footprint by providing efficient land use

In planning to make your home a green one, you'll want to use some basic guiding principles to serve as a framework for your effort. Joel Schurke introduced four beautifully simple principles at an EcoBuilding Guild workshop in 1996:

Build less. A green home is no bigger than it needs to be to provide you with the space you need to have a satisfying life without compromising the future choices of your children and your children's children's children's children's children. (If you don't have biological children, borrow your neighbors'.)

Build to use less. A green home conserves energy and water. It relies more on nature's "free" services than on nonrenewable sources for heating, cooling, and irrigation. And it's situated to make use of local services, such as grocery stores, the library, the post office, and alternative modes of transportation.

Build with less. A green home doesn't waste materials, either by requiring significantly more raw materials than necessary (with the overage serving no real purpose in the structure or being landfilled) or by not being built to last a very long time. A dark green home will be there for those children last in line—at least seven generations.

Build for health. A green home is a safe and healthy place for you to be. It also doesn't cause harm to natural systems in your backyard or in places that supply the raw materials for your project.

You might be surprised that the principle that applies to health is listed last. Shouldn't that be first? The list isn't intended to indicate importance as much as suggesting an ordering for the thinking process. If you apply the first three principles, you'll have a smaller home, with a thoughtful approach to your energy and water use, and you'll have a long-lasting one. In essence, you'll have made decisions that reduce the health risks to consider. For example, if you decide to build a smaller home, with fewer materials, you'll have reduced the amount of surface that's traditionally finished with products that might cause problems. If you build an airtight home with good energy performance, you'll be required to provide a consistent supply of fresh air to the home. You'll also be looking for ways to reduce the use of electric light by introducing natural light, another important ingredient of a healthy home. If you've built in a location where you and yours can walk safely to local services, you'll avoid the increasing risk of being overweight, which researchers are now tying directly to the sprawling nature of most new developments (Ewing et al. 2003, 54).

Issaquah Highlands in Issaquah, Washington, is one of a new breed of Northwestern communities being developed with green ideals in mind.
PHOTO AND PLAN COURTESY OF PORT BLAKELY COMMUNITIES.

and infrastructure. That's because it allows green, undeveloped fields—known as greenfields—to stay green and makes more effective use of land that has already been disturbed to build roads as well as lines for water, sewer, power, and phone. It also makes energy-conserving concepts such as district heating and cooling (a concept practiced in most of Europe and in some of our largest cities) cost effective.

If the thought of locating in an urban downtown core gives you the hives, you'll be happy to know that new developments such as Issaquah Highlands in Issaquah, Washington, are incorporating sensitive treatment of the land, clustered homes, walking and biking trails, and new local services you can walk to. These exurban developments appeal to householders who want to provide a more serene life for their kids but don't want to trash the environment while doing it. And in between city life and brand new villages built in suburbia are established towns that at one time eschewed density but have changed their tune to protect open space and still accommodate growth. Infill developments including cottage housing and mixed-use projects including condos or apartments are the result.

We've mentioned the health benefits of living where you can walk to your local services. Reducing your footprint in this way can provide financial benefits as well by reducing wear and tear on your car (not to mention on you), the insurance costs related to driving, and the gas you use to get places. And living in community can provide significant quality-of-life returns that come from knowing your neighbors. Both of our families reside in Winslow, a village on Bainbridge Island (total island population approximately 21,000) that serves as the island's main commercial and social hub and connects by way of a 35-minute ferry ride to downtown Seattle. Winslow has a definable center where it's easy to run into friends in the local grocery store, be recognized at the post office or bank counter, stop off at the gym for a workout, or pick up organic vegetables at the farmer's market held Saturdays during the summer at the sustainably built Bainbridge Island City Hall.

Density is one aspect of green development, but not the only one. As a result municipalities are starting to link density bonuses to other green attributes. For example, the City of Portland provides developers such density bonuses, allowing them to build more units than typically allowed, for incorporating green roofs. The City of SeaTac provides density bonuses for developments incorporating energy conservation beyond code requirements, and the City of Ashland provides density bonuses for developments incorporating renewable energy.

Even if you choose to build on a single lot (and not in a green development), you can still make a difference by locating your home so you don't have to jump in the car for everything you need. A nearby park for playing basketball with your kids, a church you can walk to, a (truly convenient) convenience store for the requisite early morning latte can all serve to reduce your household's footprint. Also, if you locate a new home in an infill lot—that is, an undeveloped lot in an existing development—you help avoid digging into a greenfield to create infrastructure items. Infill lots can be created by subdividing larger lots (although this usually requires rezoning) or by replacing a home destroyed by fire or other natural disaster. (We're not suggesting tearing down a perfectly good home to build your home; that wouldn't be green. Nor are we suggesting building on the edge of a cliff or on an earthquake fault line.)

HOW BIG IS YOUR HOME?

Right after location comes house size. By building small, you can reduce the footprint of your house significantly, first because it requires less natural capital to build, and second because the home will use less natural capital—energy, water, and replacement materials—during its lifetime. On the personal benefit side, it can use less of your household's capital—money and time—as well.

Although cost per square foot can be higher for a smaller home than for a huge rambling home, the overall (first) cost to construct the smaller home is generally less. You can pocket these first-cost savings or, as Susanka suggests at the outset of this chapter,

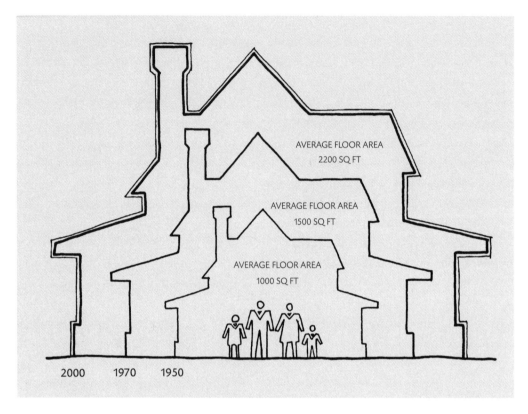

Since 1950 home sizes have more than doubled in the United States, while average household size has decreased. ILLUSTRATION BY CHRISTOPHER GUTSCHE AND KATHLEEN SMITH, ADAPTED FROM ORIGINAL DATA BY WILSON AND BOEHLAND (2005).

AVERAGE FLOOR AREA
2200 SQ FT

AVERAGE FLOOR AREA
1500 SQ FT

AVERAGE FLOOR AREA
1000 SQ FT

2000   1970   1950

invest them in your new home to achieve proper scale and functionality. In a truly green home, this money can be well spent on a more livable design, well-performing systems, and durable materials.

It's no secret that homes have been getting bigger. It's been considered a sign of our prosperity. Since 1950 home sizes have more than doubled in the United States, while average household size has decreased. Recent data reveals that the average single-family unit is now 2349 square feet (National Association of Home Builders 2006a, 14). Whether that increase in house size has meant an increase in true value is highly questionable. The term *McMansion,* which has become something of a cliché, refers

both to size and to predictability. Some green designers call these big homes "houses on steroids." The bulked-up effect is especially apparent when the homes are squeezed onto small lots. We haven't been immune to this trend in the Northwest.

Oversized homes are design failures. During the last two decades, as homebuyers have asked more from their new homes, the easy response has been to add more square footage rather than function to scale. Lazy design isn't the only explanation for the ballooning house size, but it's probably the one we can most easily correct.

Fortunately, interest in more manageably sized homes is on the rise. The most obvious evidence of this is the growing popularity of cottage-type developments such as Ericksen Cottages on Bainbridge Island. In this development, eleven two- and three-bedroom stand-alone units, roughly 1000 square feet in size, share a central courtyard and a common building for entertaining, meetings, and projects. The fact that combined sales of Sarah Susanka's books on the "not-so-big" house have hit the one million mark is also proof that the public is truly hungry for better design—not more house.

So what, exactly, can you accomplish by building small, besides having a smaller place to maintain? In "Small Is Beautiful: U.S. House Size, Resource Use, and the Environment" (2005), Alex Wilson and Jessica Boehland report on research into the differences in energy and raw material consumption related to house size. Energy modeling of two homes built to the same level of energy efficiency and experiencing identical climate conditions, one 1500 square feet and the other 3000 square feet, showed that the smaller home would use half as much energy to heat and two-thirds as much energy to cool as the larger home. This is similar to Wilson's conclusions in an earlier article where he compared large and small versions of similarly designed homes in two different climates (Wilson 1999, 11). In both cases, the research was focused primarily on efficiencies in enclosure construction. Small homes can also reap energy savings from fewer losses along (shorter) domestic hot water pipes and ducting. Other factors, such as amount of surface area, will affect the energy efficiency of even a small home. The O'Brien-Cunningham residence is basically a square, so surface area losses were minimized.

The Ericksen Cottages on Bainbridge Island are roughly 1000 square feet in size. Affordable and attractive, they weren't on the market long.
PHOTO BY ART GRICE. PLAN AND PHOTO COURTESY OF WENZLAU ARCHITECTS.

Wilson and Boehland also compare the materials use of large and small homes, citing estimates from the National Association of Home Builders (NAHB) that a 5000-square-foot home will use three times the material inputs of a 2082-square-foot home. In an unpublished white paper on the subject, Vermont designer Michael Horowitz (2006) reports a simple comparison of two sample homes using Chief Architect, a residential computer-aided design (CAD) program. Although he doesn't confirm the NAHB estimates exactly, he does show "significant reductions in structure and envelope materials" for a 1650-square-foot home as compared to a 4000-square-foot home.

The NAHB estimates that more than 13,000 board feet of lumber are typically used to build a 2272-square-foot home (Wilson 1999, 7), reflecting a wood use per square foot similar to Horowitz's projection. Reducing the lumber used to build a home is no small matter. In addition to reducing stress on limited forest resources, it can make a home more affordable. Ask any builder who has been in the business for more than a minute and he or she will tell you that the price of lumber in the Northwest has gone through the roof and continues climbing. The cost of lumber and wood products actually accounts for about one-third of the total cost of materials used to build a home, according to the NAHB (2006b, 30). Lots of other materials used to construct a home can also be reduced in quantity if you build small; concrete, siding, roofing, ducting, drywall, windows, and floor coverings are all good examples.

By reducing the amount of materials you use, you also limit vulnerabilities to cost spikes and lapses in availability. Oriented strand board (OSB) used for sheathing nearly disappeared during initial reconstruction efforts in Iraq in 2003. Projects can come to a standstill when concrete workers strike, as they did in 2006. Supply chokes shoot up the price. In addition, interruptions and delays in your project can cost money as well as aggravation, especially if you're paying interest on a construction loan.

House size is also a factor in how much impervious surface—surface that doesn't allow rainwater to infiltrate naturally—is created. For us in the Pacific Northwest, this is an important consideration. Poor hydrological function and storm water runoff are considered two of several major factors threatening the health of salmon and other species living in or near our waterways. Ironically, Cascadia contributes far more than its share to total surface runoff. Although its area is less than 10 percent of the continent, Cascadia contributes 20 to 25 percent of the total surface runoff (Go Northwest! 2006).

So bottom line, if you plan to build or purchase a small home (or perform a remodel that doesn't significantly increase your overall square footage), you start out on the right foot. You've already made a commitment that will save energy resources and tons of raw materials, and will significantly reduce

REDUCTION IN HOUSING MATERIALS RELATED TO HOUSE SIZE

MATERIAL	4000 SQ. FT. HOME	1650 SQ. FT. HOME	REDUCTION
Concrete	60 cu. yds.	35 cu. yds.	42 percent
Wall framing lumber	11,484 bd. ft.	5419 bd. ft.	53 percent
Roof framing lumber	5498 bd. ft.	2886 bd. ft.	48 percent
Wall sheathing	130 sheets	70 sheets	46 percent
Roof sheathing	108 sheets	50 sheets	54 percent
Roofing	3466 sq. ft.	1585 sq. ft.	54 percent
Siding	4093 sq. ft.	2100 sq. ft.	49 percent

NOTE: Finishes weren't included in Horowitz's study because they vary from house to house, regardless of overall size. Source: Adapted from Horowitz 2006, 2.

IDEAS FOR CREATING SMALL HOUSES THAT WORK

Don't include extra rooms or rooms that go unused most of the time.

Make rooms do double and triple duty.

Provide an open plan for kitchen/dining and living areas.

Avoid single-use hallways.

Combine functions in other spaces.

Provide built-in furnishings and storage.

Provide adequate storage.

Make use of attic space.

Don't turn bedrooms into living rooms.

Provide acoustic separation between rooms.

Provide connections to the outdoors.

Create outdoor living space through thoughtful landscaping.

Provide a variety of ceiling heights.

Provide natural daylight and carefully placed artificial lighting.

Provide visual, spatial, and textural contrasts.

Use light colors for large areas.

Keep some structural elements exposed.

Make use of interior windows.

Design spaces for visual flow.

Provide a focal point for each room or space.

Provide quality detailing and finishing.

Design for flexibility and change.

SOURCE: Susanka 2006; Wilson 1999, 11.

The Higgins residence in Portland is a compact but livable home that's also an award-winning infill project, built on a tiny lot in an established neighborhood. Loft spaces and built-ins are just a couple of space-saving ideas used in this home. PHOTOS BY BRYAN HIGGINS (TOP), ANDREA NELSON (MIDDLE, BOTTOM).

The Olivé-Mortola residence in Seattle is another award-winning compact infill project. PHOTOS BY ANNA STUECKLE.

your home's impact on the natural environment. To make a small house work, however, it's imperative that you use good design techniques. We include a few ideas here; also check out "Resources" at the back of the book.

WHAT TYPE OF HOUSING DO YOU LIVE IN?

Finally, housing type can make a big difference in environmental impact. Multifamily residences, such as attached townhomes, multiplexes, and condominiums, because they share walls, tend to be more efficient in the use of fossil fuel, and because they provide greater density, tend to better support local services and job creation, thus making long commutes to shops and work less likely.

Of course, given the significance of fossil fuel consumption in the calculation of your ecological footprint, it helps to own an efficient car, too. Accord-

ing to Mathis Wackernagel, "Living in a multi-unit condominium or apartment of similar market value to a suburban house, and using a compact, energy efficient car rather than a standard-sized vehicle, can reduce a household's transportation and housing footprint by a factor of three" (1996, 103.) So even if living in a multifamily residence doesn't work for you, purchasing one of the new hybrid vehicles (and using it only when you really need to) is an important step toward reducing your household's footprint.

THE CHOICE TO REMODEL, BUILD, OR BUY NEW

Wrapped up in the big decisions regarding location, size, and housing type is another major decision. To make your home green, will you emulate the Gutsche-Smiths and remodel? Or will you build new as did the O'Brien-Cunninghams? There are some obvious environmental benefits from reusing an existing structure, chief among these being the possible reduced use of virgin raw materials and the energy and water used to convert them into building products (although this isn't automatic—some remodeling projects aren't very efficient with materials, especially those that double or even triple the original house size without a correlating increase in household size). With remodeling, the planet also benefits as it would from a new home constructed on an infill lot, in that an undeveloped location doesn't need to be disturbed.

Many factors are involved in deciding what's best for you, however, and a household isn't really green if it doesn't provide a good fit for its inhabitants. For if your current situation isn't a good fit (and a careful analysis shows it won't ever be), several things are likely to happen: you'll feel unhappy (not fun for you nor anyone who has to live with you), you might try another go at remodeling (meaning more money, more resource use, and more disturbance), and you might end up moving anyway. In the case of the O'Brien-Cunninghams, changes to the building exterior where they lived to allow more daylight in were prohibited. This proved to be a deal breaker.

So how do you determine whether you can remodel your home and achieve the dark green goals of maximum personal benefit and lightest environmental impact or whether, for you, building or buying a new green home makes more sense? An initial needs analysis is the answer. Among other things, such an analysis means asking yourself how your current residence works for you and how it doesn't, and responding to these questions in detail. It's best to include all of your household members in the process, so that the end result works for and is valued by everyone. Household members will have different views of what works and how important various aspects of the home's performance are for them, so you'll have to weigh all of the data to come to a conclusion that works for all, hopefully through to consensus.

You'll need a tape measure, a camera, a pencil, paper, and a library card to complete this analysis. An initial needs questionnaire is provided here for you to use. Note that a few questions might best be answered in consultation with a designer or remodeler. One way to keep the cost of this consultation down is to complete this questionnaire as much as you can before you call in a professional. Here we aren't talking yet about getting a detailed breakdown of costs (called a takeoff); our experience is that any estimate of cost this early in your process will be too low. However, a from-the-hip estimate by a knowledgeable builder or remodeler will be invaluable to your decision making, and most seasoned builders or remodelers would be willing to provide you one, as long as you don't hold them to it when things actually get going.

In chapter 4 we discuss the process of selecting a qualified team for your project, and you can certainly use it to select the individual for this consultation. However, you needn't commit to the entire project at this point, and frankly, if you have the patience, you might want to get a couple of opinions before you decide whether to remodel. You might also want to think about whether you have the stamina for remodeling. A few books are available that discuss the remodeling process in detail; this is where the library card comes in handy. There's an old joke that most marriages don't last through a remodeling project, so you might want to take that into consideration.

Initial Needs Questionnaire

Questions that might best be answered in consultation with a designer or remodeler are marked with an asterisk (*).

Gut check

What's wrong with where you live? Brainstorm:

_____

_____

_____

What's right with where you live? Brainstorm:

_____

_____

_____

Convenience

How convenient is your home to useful services, such as your bank, the post office, your place of worship, a grocery store, mass transit stops?

Very inconvenient   1   2   3   4   5   Very convenient

NOTES:

_____

_____

_____

How convenient is your home to places you go daily, such as to work or school? Can you get there without driving in a single-occupancy vehicle? What would moving do to your commute in terms of time, cost, other factors?

Very inconvenient   1   2   3   4   5   Very convenient

NOTES:

_____

_____

Windows

Do you have enough windows you can open?   Yes   No

Can you open your windows comfortably? (Does opening them mean you suffer from too much noise, polluted air, or insecurity at night?)   Yes   No

NOTES:

_____

_____

_____

Do you have enough natural light?

Not enough   1   2   3   4   5   Plenty

Do you suffer from overheating as a result of too much solar gain from windows?

Overheating   1   2   3   Comfortable

Would it be feasible to change out windows or alter window layout if you wanted to? *   Yes   No

NOTES:

_____

_____

_____

Function

Do you have enough space for what you do in your home?   Yes   No

Do you have enough storage space? Enough places to display art, photos, or other things important to you?   Yes   No

How much storage / display space do you need? How much of this must happen in your own home? Brainstorm:

_____

_____

_____

Measure your rooms, closets, and floor and solid wall space, and describe what you use them for:

_____

_____

_____

If you don't have enough space, or the space doesn't provide the right mix, is it practical to get it through remodeling?

Yes   No

Weather protection

How well does the envelope (the building enclosure) perform? *

Very poorly   1   2   3   4   5   Very well

NOTES:

_____

_____

_____

Is it drafty, moldy, or cold in your home?   Yes   No

If you wanted to upgrade the envelope with better insulation, better moisture protection, and improved airtightness, is it feasible to do so? *   Yes   No

Budget

How much money are you now spending to operate your home? Consult your utility bills and calculate as a percentage of your income.

Very little   1   2   3   4   5   A lot

Is there potential to make meaningful improvements to energy and water efficiencies, thereby achieving significant operational savings, through remodeling

Yes   No

NOTES:

_____

_____

_____

If you're willing to spend more now to reap some long-term operational savings, do you have access to funds to do so?

Yes   No

NOTES:

_____

_____

_____

Would it cost more to remodel, or to buy or build new? *

How much more would it cost for the more expensive alternative?

Is there a green production or spec (prebuilt) home that meets both your functional and budget requirements? (With more and more builders signing on to local green building programs, this isn't out of the question.)   Yes   No

Once location, size, and housing type are firmly set and you've decided whether to remodel, build, or buy new, you'll still have many, many decisions to make regarding the likely biggest expenditure of time and money you'll ever make in your life. As long as you take the view that life is an adventure, it can be lots of fun. However, if you're like us, you may have a few other things on your plate, such as your job, the kids, and maybe getting out there to enjoy the planet we're hoping to protect. In chapters 3 through 7 we cover in a general way the process of building, remodeling, or buying a green home; in chapters 8 through 11 we get down to the specifics of implementing green choices in each phase of home building or remodeling. You'll notice in the latter chapters that we've scoped the choices down to our personal top green home picks for the sake of simplicity. You may come up with ideas that we haven't included or build on the ones we have. In the next few chapters, we also provide five case studies of projects (not our own) that illustrate the incorporation of many green ideas. To begin with, however, let us share our stories with you.

Case Study:
The O'Brien-Cunningham

It started with the bathtub. Early in 1997, after five years of my husband's trying to squeeze his 6-foot-2-inch frame into the small tub in our condo bathroom, John and I spent several frustrating months trying to figure out how to get a bigger bathtub into the bathroom.

Then there was the carpet. The 1200-square-foot unit was carpeted wall to wall, making a marvelous home for dirt, dust mites, and other irritants. Not good for John, who seemed to be suffering more and more from allergies. This, of course could be remedied by pulling the carpet and laying down a new hardwood floor on the concrete floor beneath it.

More problematic was the lack of natural light. I suffer from SAD (seasonal affective disorder); the condo was a long, narrow flat located on the second, middle floor, sandwiched above and below and on either side by other units. The only daylight we enjoyed was provided at the front and back, and the natural light landing on the back end was obscured for much of the year by the garage. I was constantly trying to turn lights on, only to realize the lights *were* on. The $200 SAD light I bought from EnviResource (a former incarnation of the Environmental Home Center) and the short brilliant Northwest summers just weren't enough to counteract the impact of living in a grim interior environment for most of the year.

I spent many nights lying in bed (since one of my symptoms is difficulty sleeping) scheming how to solve this problem, including secretly rigging a light tube with reflective mirrors up the outside of the condo back wall while not breaking codes and covenants! While I could fix the carpet and ignore the tub most of the time, the lack of light wasn't something I could live with, nor do anything about.

Then there was the fact that daily I was leaving my home to train and consult with others on the benefits of naturally lit, well-designed, good-for-the-planet homes. In some very important ways, our condo was green in that it was located in a three-story, mixed-use complex, with residential units atop retail stores and offices. We lived within walking distance of the grocery, the post office, the bank, and the hardware store, not to mention the coffee shop and my office; the Bainbridge Island ferry to Seattle's downtown was an easy twenty-minute walk. We enjoyed village life and especially liked not getting into the car. Eventually, however, we couldn't ignore the fact that although our home might be good for the planet, it wasn't working for us.

Even so, we couldn't build a green home and ignore the fact that we were increasing our impact by building a new stand-alone structure (actually two, including a detached garage). So before we found our lot, the two most important decisions we made were to build small and to build in a location that wouldn't require us to drive a car to get a quart of milk.

In the end, we did even better. Our real estate agent called to notify us of an infill lot on a dead-end street in a neighborhood about a twenty-minute walk from the center of Winslow (the main business district on Bainbridge Island). It was ten minutes from my office, and even closer to the ferry dock. There was one small problem. The agent called us particularly because he knew only an especially environmentally sensitive home would be allowed on the site. Although it was deemed buildable, only one-third of it really was, and that was the buffer for the Class III wetland that made up most of the lot. (On the scale of sensitivity, Class III is third from the top, with Class I being the most sensitive.) We had earlier told our agent of our desire to build small, and small was all that *could* work on this lot.

The O'Brien-Cunningham home is tucked into a wetland buffer that takes up a third of the property. This view from the east shows how the house looks from the wetland, which primarily occupies the northern and eastern parts of the property. PHOTO BY JOHN CUNNINGHAM.

So with the purchase of the lot, John and I became stewards of a fairly degraded and semi-functioning wetland that to this day is home to lots of birds and raccoons, the occasional otter, skunk cabbage, red-tipped dogwood, and a seasonal stream. Our commitment to the city's Wetland Advisory Committee (which approved a "reasonable use exemption") was to build as lightly as we could on the land and maintain it in a sensitive way. We also promised to explore ways we could restore the wetland that was already a haven for invasive Himalayan blackberries and morning glory—a battle we're still fighting.

Building small and using green materials

As I noted earlier, regardless of the site, we had decided to build a small home; the site's sensitivity only served to underline this goal. We had originally thought we would use a predrawn plan from a book, bumping it up slightly from 1500 square feet to 1600 square feet. Our builder, Doug Woodside of Woodside Construction, recommended that we forgo this route and hire an architect when our site with its idiosyncrasies presented itself, and we're very glad we did. The site-specific plan helped us take advantage of a wonderful southeastern exposure and offshore breezes that flow uphill to our street, and gave us privacy exactly where we need it.

Our architect, Jim Musar (Aspects, Inc.), used several techniques to create a space that works well for us, including a series of eight skylights (we probably overdid it, but my serotonin levels are just fine, thank you!); light surfaces with contrasting wood tones; varying orientations, degrees of privacy, and

ceiling heights; built-ins; and multiple-function spaces. Although at 1650 square feet our house is considerably smaller than conventional homes being built today, most visitors comment that the home "seems much bigger."

We also planned ahead for a studio apartment by installing windows and skylights in the garage during the original construction project. These now provide natural light to the upper-story one-level apartment we completed in 2004 and rent out as a supplement to our income. Grace Huang of Ming Architects, a student of mine, designed the studio to fit neatly into the existing garage structure. Because it, too, is well below the size of average living quarters, Grace incorporated many of the same techniques (such as built-ins, light surfaces, and lifted ceiling) we used in the home to create a sense of space and livability. She took the position that the tiny studio called for a boatlike design. The result is a highly functional nest that looks far more spacious than its 400 square feet.

Building small (and doing it well) was just the beginning. The remaining green choices had to do

The design Jim put together included a central shaft along the open staircase where fresh air travels between the operable windows below and operable skylights above, making for a very refreshing space even at the height of summer. The natural light from the skylights is okay too. PHOTO BY JOHN CUNNINGHAM.

with what went into building the structure itself. We looked for actions that provided multiple benefits. For example, the wood polymer decking on the front porch uses material that would normally be tossed into the landfill. It also doesn't need to be stained or painted and is highly durable. The deck was also part of our goal to build a fifty-year exterior (modest when compared to European buildings but not when compared to U.S. homes). With fiber cement siding products and metal roof (both having fifty-year warranties) covering most of the exterior, we thought we had come pretty close to achieving our goal. The exception was cedar we used for trim and a bellyband, and it seems to be holding up pretty well.

Low-E windows and an energy-efficient envelope are actually par for the course in Washington, where a fairly rigorous residential energy code drives those choices. However, we went further by using a hydronic heating system that uses our water heater as a heat source, not a separate boiler or furnace, and doesn't require ducts, which are notorious for losing heat as it's transported through the system. As a result we insulated ourselves somewhat from rising energy prices. We also reduced our water consumption by roughly 40 percent by employing Energy Star washers (for clothes and dishes) and landscaping with drought-tolerant plantings. We have a home that's very comfortable for us and hospitable to individuals with chemical sensitivities (CS). I know this because three individuals with serious CS visited during a home tour soon after construction was completed; all three were thrilled to be in a new home that didn't seem to trigger reactions. We have landscaping that's easy to care for, even through the droughts we've been experiencing in recent years. We can feel good about the materials we used.

Our green goals and results

For both our new home and the more recent remodeling project, we had some overall goals, all of which we think we've met:

- to provide a healthy, comfortable, and highly functional living space
- to build in a way that reflects our environmental ethic to "build less and build light"
- to provide a model of cost-effective, practical green building techniques
- to promote participation in voluntary green building programs

GREEN FEATURES IN THE O'BRIEN-CUNNINGHAM RESIDENCE AND STUDIO

FEATURE	RESIDENCE	STUDIO
Concrete	Concrete mix with 15 to 20 percent fly ash	No addition to foundation
Metal roofing	Metal with a minimum of 25 percent recycled content	No roof changes
Siding	Fiber-cement	
Framing	Advanced framing, with recycled-content drywall clips, finger-jointed studs, and Parallams (engineered structural beams)	All nonstructural framing minimized
Drywall	Drywall with 12 percent recycled gypsum and 100 percent recycled paper	Same
Insulation	30 percent recycled glass	30 percent recycled glass, formaldehyde-free, blown in for extra efficiency; fully insulated and sealed off from garage
Resilient flooring	Sheet vinyl with postindustrial recycled content	Linoleum, biodegradable
Ceramic tile	None used	Recycled glass tiles for accents in shower
Carpet	Minimized; carpet pad includes 100 percent recycled content	No carpet
Hard floors	Bamboo and biocomposite	Salvaged wood, remilled for floors
Built-ins	Modular components from Enviro-Star manufacturer; leftover bamboo and biocomposite discard used for shipment protection	Modular components from Enviro-Star manufacturer; leftover flooring for built-in desk
Decks, porch	Wood polymer decking for one porch	Wood polymer decking for stair and landing, metal cable to minimize wood use
Paint	Solvent-free, low-VOC	Solvent-free, low-VOC
Floor finishes	Water-based floor sealer	Water-based floor sealer and nontoxic wax
Appliances	Models listed in *Consumer Guide to Home Energy Savings* (Wilson, Thorne, and Morrill 2003)	Energy Star appliances, including new microwave/fridge apartment model
Fixtures	Conventional fixtures, with compact fluorescents where they fit	Energy Star fixtures and ceiling fans with dedicated compact fluorescents
Fans	Standard	Energy Star model combining light and fan
Heating	Hydronic radiant, in-floor, two-zone system; includes water heater	Electric space heater; 6-gallon electric water heater
Toilets	Standard low-flush (unintentional two-flush) model	Better-performing standard low-flush model (a true one-flush model)
Landscaping	Drought-tolerant, mulched with compost	
Skylights	Natural light and operable for ventilation	Natural light

Green materials lend themselves to creative uses. The biocomposite flooring (left) produced from sunflower hulls was actually being sold as a countertop finish; it's one of the conversation pieces in our home. Leftover salvaged flooring was used to create a built-in desktop for the studio (right). PHOTOS BY JOHN CUNNINGHAM.

The house and the studio were certified through the Built Green program (formerly the Build a Better Kitsap program) of the Kitsap Home Builders Association. In both cases, the projects earned points well above the number required to achieve the highest rating possible for each project type—three stars for a single-family home and two stars for a small remodeling job (less than 500 square feet). Not surprisingly, we had many more choices when it came time to design the studio in late 2003 than we had when we designed the house in 1998. Some of the more interesting materials and systems we were able to incorporate into our construction and remodeling projects are listed in the table.

The green premium for construction of our house, which cost a little under $115 per occupied square foot, was roughly 1 to 2 percent—that is, slightly above what it would have cost to build our home more conventionally. Most of this was due to two high-ticket items—the metal roof and the hydronic heating system. The green premium for construction of the studio, which cost a little under $138 per occupied square foot, was probably more like 4 percent. These figures aren't exact, however. In both cases, some of our "expensive" choices, such as the metal roof and a custom-built tiled shower in the studio featuring recycled content glass tile accents were as much aesthetic as environmentally friendly. We can hope that even a conventionally built home is aesthetically pleasing. One other factor pushed the studio cost per square foot higher (besides the obvious inflationary forces): John took on the role of owner/contractor to learn firsthand what it's like to do that kind of work, and taking on this role while working a full-time job made for a very steep learning curve.

Bottom line, though, our energy and water savings are working to offset our initial investments, while flexibility in the overall design and space offers more value for the money we spent. And we've learned so much. Of course, in addition to our successes, we've identified those things we wish we'd done differently. Since most people who tour our home want to know what works and what doesn't, we think it only fair to reveal our bloopers:

Energy efficiency. A closed-loop hydronic system with heat recovery would have been a good idea (our system is open-loop with no heat recovery). Besides cutting down on the oil we burn to run our water heater (natural gas wasn't available), this would more easily facilitate a move to preheating the water used in the hydronic system with a solar hot water system. We mentioned the whole house fan earlier; we've replaced the standard, noisy model with a much quieter, more efficient one.

Thermal comfort. We skimped on operable windows on the southeastern corner. As a result we don't get the full benefit of some fabulous breezes that come off the shore below. In addition, a ceiling fan in the master bedroom would make the little difference we need on the hottest nights of summer.

Materials. We used wood polymer on the front porch but not elsewhere. During the studio remodeling, we replaced our home's back steps with the same material and would love to do the same for the other wood deck. We've paid for this choice many times over trying to keep the decks free of mold and mildew. Also, a bellyband made of high-quality plywood with a thin cedar veneer was installed about midway up the exterior wall. It's pretty but doesn't truly meet our goal of a fifty-year exterior. We could have achieved the same architectural break with a different fiber-cement shingle pattern.

Some of these would have been costly to do, some not. All of them are more difficult to do after the fact. We firmly believe that a more deliberate, integrated process (such as the one we present in the book) will help keep your bloopers to a minimum. Good luck! ■

Case Study:
The Gutsche-Smith

In 2003 our lives changed for the better. Really the changes started in 2002 when I became pregnant with our daughter, Alice. This launched us on the odyssey of questioning what we wanted for our family, our quality of life, and our future. We were living in Berkeley, California. I had been living there for sixteen years (my entire adult life) and my husband, Chris, had been there for thirteen years. We loved where we lived, in an 800-square-foot apartment downtown—walking distance to everything, in the heart of a vibrant, diverse, mostly sunny, environmentally and socially progressive community where we had close friends, neighbors, and colleagues, and family living only an hour and a half away.

As we pondered our future and what we wanted for our family, however, we decided what we wanted most was time together, time to be a family—to raise our kids, to explore this amazing world and the process of growing up together. When we sought to expand our living quarters we realized that pursuing this vision of our future would not work in the Bay Area, for many reasons. So in late 2002 we made a painful decision—to leave our loving community of friends and family in California and venture north to Bainbridge Island.

It was the leaving that was painful, not the venturing north. We were very excited about the prospects that lay ahead. The area in general wasn't new to us, since Chris had lived here earlier in his life and we had been visiting some of his family here at least once a year since we met. However, Bainbridge Island was. We'd only been here once before (other than to drive through), and that was to visit Winslow Cohousing when it was brand new in the early 1990s. Little did we know then that Winslow Cohousing would be our future home.

Choosing cohousing

The decision to move was really a decision to move to Winslow Cohousing. We didn't look anywhere else in the region or at any other houses on Bainbridge Island. We were making a lifestyle choice and not a house choice per se. Cohousing is a type of collaborative housing where residents actively participate in the design and operation of their own neighborhood and are consciously committed to living as a community. The physical design encourages both social contact and individual privacy. Private homes contain all the features of conventional homes, but residents also have access to and share responsibility for common facilities such as open space, courtyards, a playground, gardens, and a "common house."

Cohousing communities are usually designed as attached or single-family homes along one or more pedestrian streets or clustered around a courtyard. The common house is the social center of the community. Typically it includes a large dining room and kitchen, living room space, recreational facilities, children's spaces, and often a guest room, a workshop, and a laundry room. Communities usually serve optional group meals in the common house at least two or three times a week. The need for community members to take care of common property builds a sense of working together, trust, and support. Because neighbors hold a commitment to a relationship with one another, cohousing communities use consensus as the basis for group decision making.

My husband and I were both very familiar with cohousing. We had studied it in school, and I had worked professionally in the world of cohousing and community housing for several years. In 1995, I co-authored a book about cohousing and other forms of shared-living communities, affording me the opportunity to talk to lots of people about cohousing and visit many communities, including Winslow Cohousing.

Winslow Cohousing (WCG) was the second cohousing community built in the United States. (The first was Muir Commons in Davis, California.) The first residents moved in during the spring of 1992. We moved in during the fall of 2004—twelve years later—to a well-established, vibrant community of instant friends and neighbors. WCG consists of thirty houses on just over five acres of land three blocks from the heart of downtown Bainbridge Island. We're walking distance to stores, galleries, restaurants, gyms, the library, the pool, schools, the kids' museum, city hall, parks, the water, and, as we like to say, downtown Seattle itself, since the ferry is walking distance also.

WCG itself has many amenities to keep us occupied. There are gardens; an orchard with apples, pears, peaches, and plums; compost bins—a worm bin and a retrofitted Clivus Multrum composting toilet; chickens; a wood shop; a pottery studio; a play structure and playfield; a patch of forest; bike sheds; a basketball hoop; a courtyard; and a 5000-square-foot common house. The common house contains a commercial kitchen, a dining room, a living area, a play space for little kids, a recreation room with pool tables and such, a guest room, a laundry room, a reading nook, mailboxes, and a teen loft. Dinners are served here five nights a week and many informal and formal gatherings and events (large and small) take place here. Partaking of meals is a lot like being a kid again—someone else plans the meal, cooks, and cleans up, and all we have to do is show up (and of course take our turn at cooking or cleaning about once for every six meals we enjoy). The parking is located at one corner of the property, leaving the rest of the property for people on foot. When our daughter runs out the front door onto our path we don't worry about the street or cars or strangers for that matter. There are some great gardeners here, and the community is a lush, beautiful, safe place to live.

Cohousing residents in general aspire to "improve the world, one neighborhood at a time." At WCG part of our vision is to have "a minimal impact on the earth and create a place in which all residents are equally valued as part of the community." WCG was designed to be environmentally responsible. The basic philosophy and layout of the community embodies this with shared (not duplicated) resources and amenities. More recently, this commitment to the environment took the form of placing more than an acre of our forest (the maximum possible based on layout) into a land trust so that it will forever be forest. As Bainbridge rapidly grows, this stand of forest may be the last in the downtown area.

It was into this context, community, and neighborhood that we moved. We were off to a great start in creating a place for us to live out our dreams of a sustainable family life. We bought our house on April 1, 2003, and on April 15 I gave birth to our beautiful daughter, Alice. Nothing like two big changes all at once, so we decided to add a third—remodeling, acting as our own general contractor. Our house is a two-story duplex unit with three bedrooms. It's roughly 1150 square feet, which means 287.5 square feet per person in our family. We're living in less space per person than the average family in 1950.

Our green goals and results

When we bought it, our house needed a lot of work inside to make it livable and comfortable. The interior had seen twelve years of wear on low-quality finishes. The walls were a dingy white; the flooring was stained gray carpet in the living areas and gray vinyl in the baths and kitchen. We had planned to stay in Berkeley until the fall, so that gave us time to plan and design our remodel and adjust to parenthood. Since we were both architects with a passion for sustainability and this was the first place we had to call our own, we had lots of ideas. What we didn't have was a lot of money. This posed a good challenge to us as homeowners and architects to determine the most important things to do, the things that would have the biggest positive impact for us and the environment. These were our main goals:

- to create a place that we would love to be in—that would truly be our home
- to provide a healthy, comfortable, highly functional and efficient small home
- to build in a way that would reflect our values, our love of the natural world, and our commitment to sustainability and sustainable living
- to make the best use of the resources we had available—our skills, our budget, and what the local environment offered
- to use this as an opportunity to dive into the world of green design and construction in the Northwest and to find out what was available, who could serve as resources, and so forth

Despite the house's need for repair and upgrading, the basic layout was mostly good. The open floor plan worked well, with views to abundant trees and good access to soft northern light. The main problem with the layout was that a small outdoor porch covered by the floor above was carved out of the back corner of the house on the ground floor, creating an awkward corner jutting into the living-dining space. The porch was dark as well and cut off light to the window and door facing it. We decided that capturing this corner as interior space would do the most to improve the quality of our living space within our modest budget. This added only 64 square feet, but the difference it makes in the way the house feels and the flow of space is enormous. We also gained a great deal of light by adding French doors on the north side and a window seat on the west side.

To minimize cost we kept the design straight-

forward by working with, not changing, the existing structural support system of the house. We also kept it small—the window seat is the only element that extends beyond the original footprint of the home and adds only 14 square feet. We also took this as an opportunity to create what we call a "gem," a special place within a home that's full of character and life. Our window seat is the heart of our home. It's a beautiful sunlit place where we spend countless hours reading books, playing games, napping, drawing, and watching the birds play and the breeze blow.

Inside where the corner was removed we installed three exposed columns and two exposed beams made of Douglas fir that was salvaged from a century-old warehouse just east of Seattle. The wood is absolutely gorgeous. The quality, density of grain, and richness of color are remarkable and like nothing available now with new wood. This is a

Our window seat is the heart of our home. We designed it to be big enough in length and width for a six-foot-tall person to sleep (making it an extra guest bed when needed) and three to four kids to play. PHOTO BY ART GRICE.

We used salvaged Douglas fir selectively in the main living areas to add warmth and character. Some of the wood's character markings are visible in the corner above the window seat, as well as in the built-in shelves that frame the seat and house treasures from travels and friends. PHOTO BY ART GRICE.

This close-up of the junction between two beams and a column show handmade brackets which add a personal touch to the beams that support the "heart" of the house. PHOTO BY ART GRICE.

feature that everyone comments on. The wood has some of what are called "character markings" (nail holes, blackened areas where the nails rusted, and other minor blemishes), which we chose to leave so as to use as much of this wood as possible and also to let the wood tell the story of its life.

All of the wood left over from making the posts and beams was used somewhere in the house. We used it for the window seat, built-ins, and bookcases. Using salvaged wood offers rewards in terms of habitat preservation, performance, strength, and beauty, but it also poses certain challenges, two of which are finding a source and allowing the lead time that may be needed to acquire it. We had to search a bit to find a good supplier and plan ahead to get this lumber ordered. Even so, it came just in the nick of time.

Other improvements we made that had great impact were to finishes—floors, walls, and trim.

There was no question when we first saw the house that the carpets and vinyl would have to go. Not only were they worn out, but also we didn't want wall-to-wall carpet in our home for health reasons. We chose bamboo for all of the living areas, including the kitchen, because of its strength and beauty, because it's a rapidly renewable resource, and because it's fun to walk on "grass" floors. We used linoleum in the upstairs bathroom, tile in the downstairs bathroom, and river rock in the small entryway. One very important decision we made, which we're thankful for every day, was choosing a light color of bamboo. Bamboo tends to come in two colors—a natural blond color and a darker caramel color. We had originally selected the caramel color because it most closely resembled the amber hues that we associated with hardwood flooring. One day sitting in our empty house contemplating paint colors after the

carpeting had been pulled up, we had an epiphany that we should use the lighter natural color to reflect more light. The lighter color makes our small house feel larger and brighter even on cold, overcast days.

The wall and ceiling colors we chose also help make the house feel warmer and brighter. We knew we wanted color but didn't know where to begin. We hired a color consultant for a little more than an hour and got a quick tutorial on color theory for homes. We choose a neutral or base color to use throughout the living room that has a slight yellow undertone—very cheery. Then we used some bolder colors in the other rooms that play off of and complement the base color. In the kitchen and dining room a caramel color adds warmth to the house. On the very tall stair landing wall a bold blue-green adds accent. It reminds us of the ocean and forests around us. Warm and light reflecting surfaces have made us feel much more at home here in the sometimes less-than-sunny Northwest. In our bedroom on the north side of the house we used a light green that we thought would feel relaxing and calm, but for my husband feels dreary against the northern light. We plan to repaint with something warmer and brighter.

Another simple yet important thing we did was replace the front door. The existing door was an insulated metal door that was poorly framed and sealed. We could feel the breeze coming in beneath it. We replaced it with a better-insulated, properly fitted and sealed wood door with glazing on the top half. The front of our house faces south. On the ground floor there are only two windows on that side—one into the downstairs bedroom, which we use as a home office, and another into the kitchen. The glaz-

We brought a little of the outdoors in by using wood from salvaged trees with a live edge (meaning with the bark still on it) for windowsills, a cap rail, and the top of a bookcase in the main living spaces of our house. PHOTO BY ART GRICE.

ing in the front door brings in twice as much light as was there before as well as views of the garden.

Graced by the new door, our entryway is small (3 feet by 5 feet 10 inches) yet efficient. Built-ins (made with salvaged wood) make space for jackets, hats, scarves, mittens, bubbles, chalk, kites, and a myriad of other things. A bench above shelves gives people a place to sit to take off their shoes. Mats inside and outside add another line of defense against dirt and particulates entering the house. The new front door brings sun, light, and views into our house, making the entryway and our house feel larger. A river rock floor brings a bit of nature indoors and prompts lots of "oohs" and "ahs."

Since the houses in the community were originally designed with green in mind, there were many things we didn't have to consider in order to improve the environmental performance and health of our house. These were some of the green features, materials, and equipment already in place:

- compact fluorescent fixtures with stab-in lamps
- double-pane windows
- radiant in-slab heat on ground floor and in base-boards on second floor
- operable skylight
- exhaust air heat recovery system
- rainwater harvesting system for irrigation
- dual-flush toilets
- low-flow sinks and shower
- well-insulated envelope
- durable siding
- laundry in the common house (so we could use the utility closet in our home for storage and not bring appliances and the associated energy use and indoor air quality issues into our home)
- native and edible landscaping (pesticide free)
- small pond (home to many frogs and visited by heron on occasion) with a small waterfall powered by a photovoltaic panel

The process of remodeling our home offered us many lessons. Here are a few new lessons learned and old lessons reinforced:

Variation in ceiling height helps makes a small house feel bigger. The ceiling over the kitchen is double height on one side and slopes down to about ten feet on the other wall. This volume adds variety to the open plan of the first floor and makes it feel much larger and more open.

Paint color matters—brighter is better. Choosing light colors with bright undertones as well as warm colors accented with a few greens and blues added variety and richness to our home as well as making it warmer, brighter, and livelier on cold overcast days than white walls ever could.

Take room use and your lifestyle into account when choosing finishes. We used water-based and/or low-VOC finishes everywhere, including a natural wax on the bamboo floor. They have held up well except in the kitchen. We opted for bamboo throughout the ground floor because a continuous floor surface makes the space feel bigger. Although we love the soft quality of the finish we wonder if a more durable water-based low-VOC finish might have been a better choice on the ground floor given the heavy use that occurs in the kitchen, especially with two kids and lots of kid friends.

Skylights in the right place really work, especially operable ones. We have one skylight in our home on the west slope of a very steep roof, above the kitchen and dining area on the ground floor and directly in front of the second floor landing between the two bedrooms and one bathroom upstairs. Before we moved in, we imagined remodeling our house sometime to add a third bedroom upstairs (the four-bedrooms units at WCG have the fourth bedroom over the kitchen and don't have a skylight). About a week after moving in we realized we could never lose the skylight. It brings a tremendous amount of direct and indirect light into both the downstairs and the upstairs. It provides views of the moon and stars at night and helps ventilate the house. We love our skylight and would never give it up now.

In remodeling projects it's okay to live with things awhile. We were in the position of remodel-

GREEN FEATURES OF THE GUTSCHE-SMITH REMODEL

FEATURE	COMMENTS
Concrete	Reused all concrete from demolished patio foundation on-site for garden retaining walls
Siding	Fiber-cement panels and FSC (Forest Stewardship Council)–certified lumber. (Existing house has vinyl siding, not what we would have chosen, and frankly, we're a bit loath as environmental architects to be living in a house with vinyl siding, but a key advantage to vinyl is its long life, so we realized that at this point the most environmentally responsible thing to do was to leave it in place.)
Framing and structure	FSC-certified wood, century-old salvaged Douglas fir, engineered shear panel (used smaller dimensional lumber)
Drywall	Recycled content
Insulation	25 percent recycled content, encapsulated fiberglass batts, formaldehyde-free
Heating	None added; we chose not to heat the slab under the new section of floor but rather to rely on the radiant heat from the rest of the house
Windows and French doors	Energy Star rated for the Northwest, double-pane low-E2 glazing; salvaged the existing door and window
Front door	New insulated wood door with double-pane glazing; lets in south sun; salvaged old door
Resilient flooring	Linoleum—rapidly renewable and biodegradable
Ceramic tile	Locally produced; recycled content was outside of our budget
Carpet	None used
Hard floors	Bamboo
Cabinets	Painted existing cabinets in bathrooms with low-VOC paint instead of replacing
Built-ins	Salvaged century-old Douglas fir, some left over from addition; off-the-shelf modular components from local manufacturer
Paint	Solvent-free, low-VOC
Sinks and showers	Flow regulator on kitchen sink; others were already low flow
Floor finishes	Hard wax floor sealer
Lighting fixtures	Salvaged antique fixture and two new conventional fixtures

ing a house we'd never lived in, so we had to imagine how we would be occupying the space and what our patterns of use and life would be. We considered remodeling the kitchen when we were moving in but decided it wasn't in our budget. In retrospect I'm glad we waited. With the passage of time we've been able to see what works and what doesn't in the kitchen and could now design it much more effectively and efficiently.

Start looking early for the right people to help you. Sometimes it can be hard to find someone who will take on a small project. Often contactors take on small projects to help fill in between bigger jobs. This means that you have to get on their schedule far in advance. We started talking to contractors before we started designing. Also, we made sure to find a contractor and a finish carpenter who were passionate about green design and who were specifically interested in working with salvaged wood and using every scrap to its full potential.

Allow more time than you think you could ever possibly need. What started out as a lot of time turned into a mad dash at the end. With the core of the remodeling complete we started moving in on December 21, two days before ten members of my immediate family were arriving to celebrate the holidays in our new home with our new baby. Our first night in our house was on December 23—surrounded by family, lots of boxes, and a few projects yet to do.

Now as I write this almost three years later, almost all of our projects are complete (we still need an exterior light fixture in the back). We've also been happily joined by our beautiful son, Oliver, born on May 11, 2006. People ask us what it's like living in a small house and how long we plan to stay here, especially now that we have two kids. The question always surprises me. It's not something I even think about. We're completely happy with the size and scale of our home. Living in a well-laid-out house full of character and charm that resonates with our life and our family creates more than enough space for what we need and want. I can honestly say that we love our house and we love where we live. It fills our souls with happiness. What could be more sustainable or sustaining than that?

In listing our goals earlier, the first one I mentioned was "to create a place that we would love to be in—that would truly be our home." This was a key driver in every decision we made. It was important to us that our home be infused with spirit and life and that it be a place that we love and feel joyful in. Longevity, durability, and reuse are touted by many, including us, as key aspects of sustainability. One way to help ensure that people make the best use of a building and the materials and energy that went into it is to create a place that they can love. No one would dream of tearing down the cathedrals of Europe. I hope that once you're done with your home or remodeling project, no one, most especially you, would think about tearing it down and that instead it sustains you and your spirit by reflecting you, your values, and your care for the world around you.

> When just 1 percent of a project's up-front costs are spent, up to 70 percent of its life cycle costs may already be committed. When 7 percent of a project's costs are spent, up to 85 percent of its life cycle costs have been committed.
>
> Joseph J. Romm, *Lean and Clean Management*

3: Managing Your Green Home Project, Part 1

CONSTRUCTION AND REMODELING projects (green or not) tend to take on a life of their own and can get away from you if not properly managed. This chapter begins to provide basic information on the design and construction process, and in particular points out ways to make sure that the result of your effort is a green home.

What the startling quotation from Joseph J. Romm boils down to is that the decisions you make early in your project will have a profound impact on what it costs both to build and especially to operate the home *over its lifetime.* This isn't to say that once these decisions are made, things will go just as you've planned. In addition to up-front planning, achieving a truly green home requires a continued focus on priorities, good communication among all parties involved, and a willingness to stay the course right to the end.

One way to frame the process for your project is to use the pertinent Ps—purpose, people, and place. In the realm of purpose, your process should help you clarify your project goals, identify specific design and construction strategies to achieve them,

budget for them, communicate them, and verify you've achieved them. As important is the P for people, both those you select to design and/or build your project and those you interact with to get your project done. Your process should make sure you have the right folks on the job and provide ways to manage them and deal with others who can affect the project's success. The final P, for place, has to do with making sure the project responds to the site—both its opportunities and its challenges.

This chapter helps you think about purpose. Chapter 4 continues with a focus on people and place. As you think about managing your green home construction or remodeling project, it helps to realize that you'll make literally hundreds of decisions during the project from start to finish. Starting out by knowing where you want to get to will make it much more likely that you'll arrive there.

PROGRAMMING: WORKING OUT WHAT YOU WANT AND NEED

In building design lingo, the programming phase is where you (generally with the help of an architect)

Qualified green architects make a point of learning what clients need and creating plans that apply green design principles to fulfilling those needs.
PHOTO COURTESY OF ROBERT HARRISON ARCHITECTS.

work out what you want and need. For the O'Brien-Cunningham residence, we performed an initial needs analysis to create a wish list, which we provided to our architect at our first working meeting. Based on this list and additional ideas that came up at the meeting, our architect then created a simple three-page document that became the substance of the program for the project. He also used the discussion as a basis for drafting a conceptual drawing for us to review.

Many designers use a questionnaire to kick-start the programming process. Ideally they'll provide you with this before your first working meeting so you'll have some time to complete it in relative quiet. It's likely to include questions like those you encountered in the initial needs analysis in chapter 2, in which case you've already done some of your homework. The questionnaire should also ask you to begin outlining

for the architect your green building priorities.

In addition to formulating your goals early on, a key to getting a dark green home is integrating your personal green building goals with other goals for your home. By integrating your goals, you'll uncover opportunities (or challenges) you might have missed otherwise. For example, you might be fortunate to have a beautiful view available from one or more elevations of your home. In considering how to access this view, you should also review goals for natural lighting, energy efficiency, and thermal comfort. Windows providing views and natural light can also, if well thought out, reduce your electric lighting needs, your heating load by providing solar gain, and if operable reduce the temptation for air conditioning by providing good cross-ventilation. The opposite can occur as well. Poorly laid out windows or minimally efficient options—those that just barely meet your state's energy code—may provide a view but can also let in unwanted noise, local air pollution, and too much heat. If the latter occurs, you may actually end up using shades—and electric lighting—during the day!

A good place to start your discussion of green building goals is to review the broad spectrum of possible strategies. If your budget permits, a green building consultant can facilitate a brainstorming session with you and your project team called an eco-charrette. An eco-charrette generally reviews possible ideas, formulates project priorities, and provides the basis for a report summarizing overall project goals and specific green building strategies to consider. In general, the report will identify sure things as well as maybes that call for further evaluation of concerns about cost, availability, or applicability to your project. The benefit of using a consultant is that doing so allows you and others on the project team to really focus on goal development rather than on facilitating a meeting; you get the benefit of deeper green building experience; and you have a written record of your decisions. In residential projects, participants in the eco-charrette should minimally include the architect, the general contractor, and the owner(s). Complex projects may benefit from including additional design professionals such as a landscape designer or a mechanical engineer.

You can also achieve a lot by a simple conference with your designer and/or builder/remodeler. The key will be making sure that you allot enough time (at least two hours) and don't allow the discussion to get sidetracked. Using a list of accepted green building strategies as the framework for your discussion should keep the conversation focused. Also, make sure you keep a written record of all decisions. It's easy to lose details and remember them down the road when it's too late to retrieve the idea—like when the project is nearly done and you no longer have the option to alter the design, or if you did it would be ridiculously expensive and stressful.

To create your green building wish list, you can use the recommendations outlined in chapters 8 through 11, or, if you prefer, you can use a checklist from one of the several green building certification programs that have been developed around the region and nationally. Green building program checklists are typically organized around several environmental categories that add up to a green approach:

- site development and surface water management
- energy efficiency
- water conservation
- materials efficiency
- indoor environmental quality

As you pursue strategies, you should also identify synergies—that is, action items that will provide your project with multiple benefits. This is one way to get the most bang for your green buck. For example, you may choose to employ a green or vegetated roof over all or part of your home. This one strategy, if done well, provides a more thermally protective roof (keeping heat in or out of your home's interior), reduces storm water runoff, reduces the heat effect that your home has on the microclimate surrounding it, provides a habitat for birds, and adds a pleasing aesthetic element to your home's exterior.

You'll also notice conflicts—actions you could take that would exclude other choices. For example, if you choose to restrict your product purchases to materials harvested or extracted locally, there may be some options (such as bamboo flooring) that, at least today, aren't available to you. In another example, if you're chemically sensitive, you may want to make sure that 100 percent of your interior finishes are nontoxic and non-emitting. This may eliminate some recycled products from your shopping list.

The other thing you must know in a building or remodeling project is that although it's very important to keep your goals firmly in place, the strategies to meet them are likely to morph a bit. Most of this should occur before you finalize project plans, but sometimes a builder/remodeler will make a snazzy in-the-field suggestion that's a minor tweak but significantly improves the overall livability and green performance of the home. Builders and remodelers are excellent problem solvers so it's good to hear them out, while keeping the budget in mind—as change orders can be costly.

Goals should be fairly encompassing, although the techniques to achieve them will be specific. The best goals are framed in a way that make it easy to tell when you've actually achieved them, while providing maximum flexibility in achieving them. For example, the O'Brien-Cunninghams were interested in durability and easy maintainability. We could have simply set the goal "to build a durable home." Instead, we aimed for the exterior of our home to have a life of fifty years. This goal gave us something precise to aim for; we could tell if we hit the mark. (In retrospect, we give ourselves an A-minus on this particular goal—not perfect, but pretty darn good.) The goal, of course, had various implications for material choices and construction details as well as cost, which in turn determined how we actually achieved it.

Here are some other examples of measurable—and quite attainable—goals you might consider:

- Build (or retain) a home that's smaller than the average house built today, less than 2349 square feet. Keep in mind that this is still a pretty big home, so you can easily attain good livability with a lot less square footage, depending on your household size.
- If you're remodeling, don't increase your overall building footprint.
- Aim for a fifty-year service life for materials.

- Beat the water usage of average households in the region—figure on roughly 75 gallons per person per day but check with your local jurisdiction. Seattleites use an average of just under 100 gallons per person per day, including indoor and outdoor use (Seattle Public Utilities 2004).
- Use resources on-site, such as the sun's energy and rainwater, to help operate the home. Aim for a certain percentage that makes sense on your site.
- Operate a carbon-neutral home: reduce energy demand by at least a third, replace fossil energy sources with renewable power sources, and purchase carbon offsets to mop up what's left.
- Aim for a particular certification level in your local green building program or the LEED for Homes program. For example, the Built Green program for King and Snohomish counties awards up to five stars for the highest level of green.
- Meet or exceed the requirements for an Energy Star Northwest certification.
- Design an interior that's pollutant-free and easy to keep that way.
- Design your home so that it can be taken apart (this isn't as far-fetched as it sounds; see "Design for Disassembly").

You may also want to create some additional goals that reflect a sense of responsibility beyond your lot line. One of our clients wanted an unostentatious home for future generations that would educate both their children and the neighbors, and serve as a catalyst for convening neighbors and friends around social issues and to promote creative thought. In a well-to-do area where older homes were frequently being replaced with megamansions, the client's remodeling project actually reduced the size of the home's footprint and today serves as an excellent example of environmental stewardship and green living to neighbors and visitors.

APPLYING PURPOSE TO PAPER: DRAWINGS AND SPECS

Once the programming process is complete, it will be important to make sure you've clearly communicated what you want conceptually. The designer or architect should provide you with simple drawings to review. These conceptual drawings may go through some iterations, but once there's agreement, the next step is developing drawings (plans) and specifications (specs). The drawings communicate the requirements of the work—including the building's size, location, materials to be used, and the way things fit together—to the builder.

For a simple house or remodel the drawing set need not be more than five or six 24-by-36-inch sheets. The more information the drawings contain, the more accurate the builder's estimate can be. The trick is finding the balance. Draw every little detail and the design fee is high. Don't draw enough and there may be serious and/or expensive mistakes. For every project you should minimally have drawings that show the site plan, floor plans, exterior elevations, building sections, wall sections, important construction details, and schedules—essentially lists—of materials, plumbing fixtures and appliances, and lighting and electrical fixtures. Information (in graphic or text form) can be included right in the drawings.

DESIGN FOR DISASSEMBLY

Design for disassembly (DfD) is a growing topic in the manufacturing realm, especially in European countries where manufacturers of durable commodities have extended producer responsibility, which means they have to take the products back at the end of their service life. Building innovators are now applying this idea to housing, since homes are generally a combination of preassembled components and components assembled on-site. The EPA has estimated that 92 percent of all construction-related waste produced annually in the United States is the result of renovations and demolitions, with only 8 percent from new construction (Franklin Associates 1998, ES-2). This represents a tremendous amount of lost resources.

If homes can be built to be disassembled in part (for remodeling) or in whole (when being replaced), those resources can be used again pretty much as is instead of being disposed of in a landfill or, in a better scenario, converted to a lower-value material, such as when construction wood is chipped up for mulch. According to the U.S. Census Bureau (2004), the average age of residential buildings is thirty-two years. What will happen to your home when it reaches this threshold? Because you don't really know, a precautionary goal to design using the principles of DfD might be in order. Specific DfD techniques are mentioned where they apply throughout this book, but you might also want to consult *Design for Disassembly in the Built Environment: A Guide to Closed-Loop Design and Building,* an entire guide devoted to this topic produced in a unique partnership between regional jurisdictions in the Seattle area and the Hamer Center for Community Design at Pennsylvania State University (see "Resources").

GREEN HOUSE PLANS: WHAT SHOULD YOU BE LOOKING FOR?

PLAN ELEMENT	DESCRIPTION	EXAMPLES OF QUESTIONS
Site plan	View of the site, showing where and how the house is located on lot, adjacencies, vegetation, sensitive spots	Do the site layout, building location and orientation, amount of landscaping, and amount of area to be disturbed conform to your personal green building goals? For example, are you taking advantage of solar access and natural breezes, and avoiding sensitive spots on the site?
Floor plans	Dimensions and layout for , each story looking from above	Does the floor plan conform to your overall green building goals? For example, does the floor plan indicate that standard dimensions are used to minimize material waste? Does the room layout match how you live so there won't be dead, wasted spaces? Where are operable windows located relative to each other and doors?
Exterior elevations	Views of the home from north, south, east, and west	Do the exterior elevations conform to your personal green building goals? For example, are windows at appropriate heights for light, views, and breezes? How much glazing is allotted to each elevation? Are overhangs adequate? Is the appropriate siding or other exterior material called out?
Building and wall sections	Building and wall components as if cut in half and viewed from the side	Do the sections contain details you would expect given your personal green building goals? Is the wall assembly properly detailed and does it meet your goals for scale? Does the wall section show appropriate insulation and moisture details?
Construction details	In-depth details of specific aspects of construction, usually those differing from conventional practice or requiring special care	Do the plans contain details of special green features or quality details that require special care, such as a green roof, stack/advanced framing, or rain screen?
Schedules	Various lists, usually including materials (such as glazing and finishes) and lighting fixtures	Do the lists include the materials, lighting, or other items you specifically want in your home? Are the descriptions precise enough even in the case of a substitution? (This is especially important if your designer uses the drawing set and notes as the entire construction document.) For example, if you want lighting fixtures to be Energy Star, do the lighting fixtures listed include this modifier? Are fixtures adequate and have they been selected for good color rendition based on use?

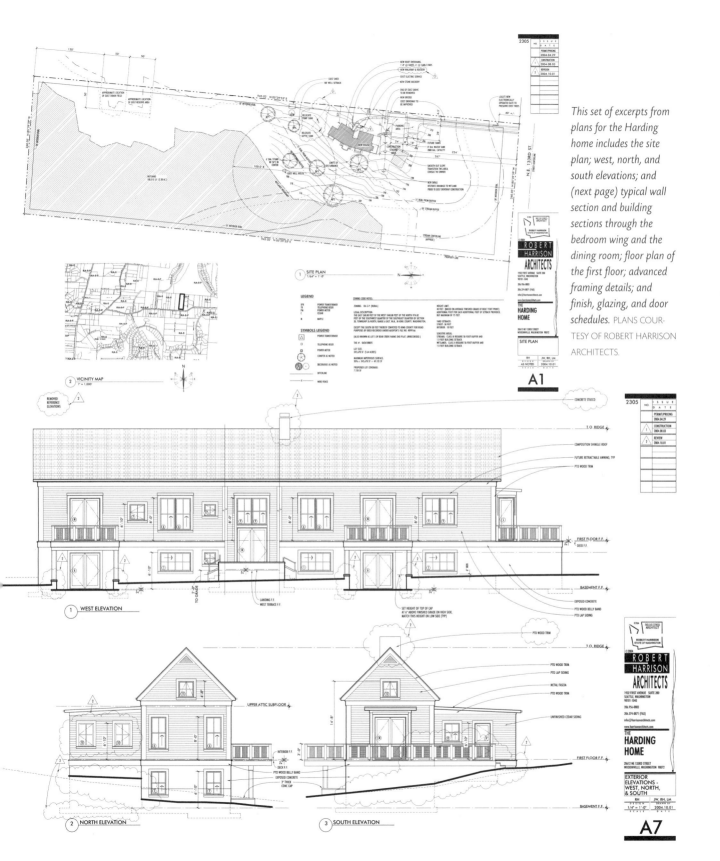

This set of excerpts from plans for the Harding home includes the site plan; west, north, and south elevations; and (next page) typical wall section and building sections through the bedroom wing and the dining room; floor plan of the first floor; advanced framing details; and finish, glazing, and door schedules. PLANS COURTESY OF ROBERT HARRISON ARCHITECTS.

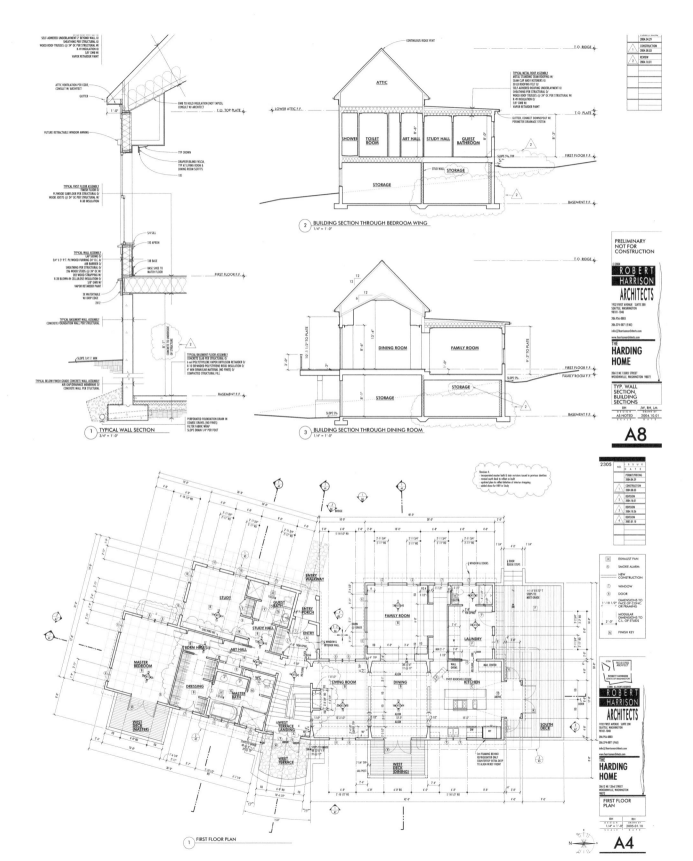

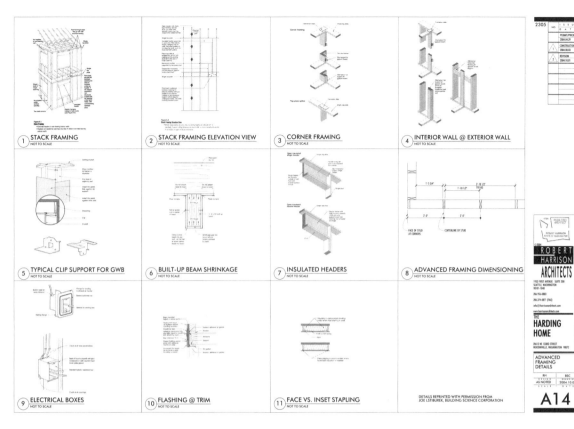

STACK FRAMING — 1 — NOT TO SCALE

STACK FRAMING ELEVATION VIEW — 2 — NOT TO SCALE

CORNER FRAMING — 3 — NOT TO SCALE

INTERIOR WALL @ EXTERIOR WALL — 4 — NOT TO SCALE

TYPICAL CLIP SUPPORT FOR GWB — 5 — NOT TO SCALE

BUILT-UP BEAM SHRINKAGE — 6 — NOT TO SCALE

INSULATED HEADERS — 7 — NOT TO SCALE

ADVANCED FRAMING DIMENSIONING — 8 — NOT TO SCALE

ELECTRICAL BOXES — 9 — NOT TO SCALE

FLASHING @ TRIM — 10 — NOT TO SCALE

FACE VS. INSET STAPLING — 11 — NOT TO SCALE

DETAILS REPRINTED WITH PERMISSION FROM
JOE LSTIBUREK, BUILDING SCIENCE CORPORATION

2305

ISSUE DATE
PERMIT/PRICING — 2004.04.29
CONSTRUCTION — 2004.08.03
REVISION — 2004.10.01

ROBERT HARRISON ARCHITECTS
1932 FIRST AVENUE, SUITE 200
SEATTLE, WASHINGTON 98101-1040
206.956.0883
206.374.0871 (FAX)
info@harrisonarchitects.com
www.harrisonarchitects.com

THE HARDING HOME
20612 NE 133RD STREET
WOODINVILLE, WASHINGTON 98072

ADVANCED FRAMING DETAILS

RH — BSC
AS NOTED — 2004.10.01

A14

FINISH SCHEDULE

Finish Key	Floor	Trim	Walls	Ceiling	Doors	Hardware	Cabinets	Countertops	Backsplash	Shower	Crown Mldg
A	12x12 slate OTM #634G	PTD WD	PTD GWB	PTD GWB	clear finish douglas fir	oil-rubbed bronze	clear finish douglas fir				PTD WD
B	character-grade madrone	PTD WD	PTD GWB	PTD GWB	clear finish douglas fir	oil-rubbed bronze	clear finish douglas fir	TBD			PTD WD
C	character-grade madrone	PTD WD	PTD GWB	PTD GWB	clear finish douglas fir	oil-rubbed bronze	clear finish douglas fir		Ceramic Tile TBD		PTD WD
D	12x12 slate OTM #634G	PTD WD	PTD GWB	PTD GWB	clear finish douglas fir	TBD	clear finish douglas fir	TBD	Ceramic Tile TBD	Ceramic Tile TBD	PTD WD
E	concrete	-	3	-	1	-	-	-	-	-	-
F	2	PTD WD	PTD GWB	PTD GWB	clear finish douglas fir	oil-rubbed bronze	Plastic Laminate TBD	Marmoleum w/clr fin fir edge	PTD WD	Ceramic Tile	
G	12x12 slate OTM #634G	PTD GWB/CLR FIN FIR PANELS	PTD GWB	PTD GWB	clear finish douglas fir	TBD	clear finish douglas fir	TBD	Ceramic Tile TBD	Ceramic Tile TBD	PTD WD

NOTES
1 Clr fin douglas fir on both sides of doors B, C, D and F.
2 Marmoleum tile in checkerboard pattern, colors TBD.
3 PTD GWB at insulated walls, otherwise no finish.

GLAZING SCHEDULE

Mark	Qty.	Mfr/Model No.	Type	Glazing	Rough Opening W(inches) x H(inches) Total (TGA)	Window Area W(inches) x H(inches) Total (TGA)	Door Daylight Opening W(inches) x H(inches) Total (TGA)	Glazed Area	U-Value	Tested TGA x U	Remarks
BASEMENT (unheated)											
1	3	Milgard Ultra	Horizontal Slider	dbl, low-e, arg	70.5 x 42 = 61.69				0.34	20.97	3
2	2	"	Vertical Slider	"	35 x 52 = 25.28				0.34	8.59	3
14	1	"	Casement	"	26 x 26 = 4.69				0.34	1.60	1,3
FIRST FLOOR											
3	1	not used			x						
4		not used			x						
5		not used			x						
6	14	Milgard Ultra	Vertical Slider	"	35 x 64 = 217.78				0.34	74.04	5
7	2	"	Casement	"	35 x 36 = 17.50				0.34	5.95	1
8	1	"	Vertical Slider	"	35 x 48 = 11.67				0.34	3.97	
9	1	"	Vertical Slider	"	35 x 60 = 58.33				0.34	19.83	
10	4	"	Casement	"	35 x 52 = 50.56				0.34	17.19	
11	2	"	Vertical Slider	"	35 x 36 = 17.50				0.34	5.95	2
12	1	"	Awning	dbl, low-e, arg	35 x 36 = 8.75				0.34	2.98	
13	2	"	Awning	"	42 x 29.5 = 17.21				0.34	5.85	
17	1	"	Casement	"	26 x 26 = 4.69				0.34	1.60	1, tempered glass
ATTIC (unheated)											
15	1		Awning	"	35 x 36 = 8.75				0.34	2.98	
SKYLIGHTS											
16	1	Velux	VSE 104	trpl, low-e, arg	21.5 x 39 = 5.82				0.22	1.28	
GLAZED DOORS											
A	2	Milgard Ultra	Full Light French Dr	dbl, low-e, arg	72 x 82		72 x 82 = 123.00		0.35	43.05	3
L	1	"	Full Light French Dr	"	36 x 96		36 x 96 = 24.00		0.35	8.40	3
M	4	"	Full Light French Dr	"	72 x 96		36 x 96 = 96.00		0.35	33.60	
N	1	"	Full Light French Dr	"	36 x 96		36 x 96 = 24.00		0.35	8.40	1
P	1	Simpson	Half Light Dutch Dr	"	36.5 x 82.5		27 x 34 = 6.38		0.35	5.83	1
					Window Glazed Area 405.11		Door Glazed Area 273.38			99.28	

REMARKS
1 Hinge right
2 Hinge left
3 Not included in glazing area calculation
4 Two of total quantity shall be triple glazed for master bathroom
5 Two of total quantity shall be tempered glass for master bathroom

GLAZING PERCENTAGE CALCULATION:

Glazing Area / Cond. Floor Area = Glazing Percentage
678.5 (SF) / 2279.0 (SF) = 29.77 %

DOOR SCHEDULE

Room	Door	Width x Height	Thickness	Manufacturer	Type	Hand	Hardware Set	Finish	Remarks
BASEMENT									
Hall	B	2'-8" x 6'-8"	1 3/8"	TBD	2-panel		Passage		
Under Stair Storage	C	2'-8" x 6'-8"	1 3/8"		2-panel		Closet		2
Mechanical Room	D	3'-0" x 6'-8"	1 3/4"		2-panel		Passage		2,4
Storage	E	3'-0" x 6'-8"	1 3/8"		2-panel		Passage		
Basement Hall	F	3'-0" x 6'-8"	1 3/8"	TBD	2-panel		Passage		
Storage	G	3'-0" x 6'-8"	1 3/8"		2-panel		Passage		2,3,4
Crawlspace	H	3'-0" x 6'-8"	1 3/8"		SC flush access		Closer		2,3,4
FIRST FLOOR									
Entry	I	3'-0" x 6'-10"	1 3/4"	TBD	Fiberglass Decorative Entry		Entry		4,5
Entry	J	4'-0" x 6'-8"	1 3/8"		2-panel french pair		Closet		
Audio Tech Room	K	3'-0" x 6'-8"	1 3/8"		Bookshelf Door			custom cabinet face	
Kitchen	L	2'-8" x 6'-8"	1 3/8"	TBD	2-panel Pocket		Pocket		
Laundry Room	M	3'-0" x 6'-10"	1 3/8"		Dutch		Entry		4,5, upper half glazed
Hall 1	N	3'-0" x 6'-8"	1 3/8"		2-panel french pair		Closet		
	R	x						not used	
Hall 1	T	2'-8" x 6'-8"	1 3/8"		2-panel Pocket		Privacy		
Hall 1	U	2'-8" x 6'-8"	1 3/8"		2-panel Pocket		Privacy		
Hall 2	V	2'-8" x 6'-8"	1 3/8"		2-panel		Privacy		
Hall 2	W	2'-8" x 6'-8"	1 3/8"		2-panel Pocket		Closet		
Study	X	4'-0" x 6'-8"	1 3/8"		French Pair		Closet		
Bedroom Hall	Y	2'-8" x 6'-8"	1 3/8"		2-panel Pocket		Pocket		
Dressing	Z	2'-8" x 6'-8"	1 3/8"		2-panel Pocket		Pocket Privacy		
Master Bathroom	AA	2'-8" x 6'-8"	1 3/8"		2-panel Pocket		Pocket Privacy		

REMARKS
1 Minimum 1/2" throw on dead bolt or dead latch for doors.
2 20 minute Fire Rating
3 Self-closing Mechanism
4 Provide weatherstripping for sound insulation
5 Tempered Safety Glass
6 Solid Core Wood

2305

ISSUE DATE
PERMIT/PRICING — 2004.04.29
CONSTRUCTION — 2004.08.03
REVISION — 2004.10.01

ROBERT HARRISON ARCHITECTS
1932 FIRST AVENUE, SUITE 200
SEATTLE, WASHINGTON 98101-1040
206.956.0883
206.374.0871 (FAX)
info@harrisonarchitects.com
www.harrisonarchitects.com

THE HARDING HOME
20612 NE 133RD STREET
WOODINVILLE, WASHINGTON 98072

SCHEDULES

RH — JW,RH,LM
NO SCALE — 2004.10.01

A15

As you review the plans, your concerns should be to check drawing elements against the goals you've set and specific strategies you and your designer have discussed. If you don't think you see what you want in the plans, say so. It may be there but not recognizable to a layperson. A good designer won't mind the questions.

In addition to communicating job requirements to the builder, drawings show the local jurisdiction how the project intends to meet the applicable building and zoning code requirements. It's vital that project drawings include information your local planning and building department needs to review for this purpose. Many jurisdictions provide "client assistance memos" or something similar on

more challenging building or site details. The more forward-thinking municipalities and counties in the Northwest provide guidelines specific to green building innovations, such as green roofs or rainwater catchment, detailed on drawings. These can be very helpful.

Besides drawings, many designers, especially for more complex projects, provide detailed narrative specs that describe the materials and techniques to be used in the project. The specs are often provided in a separate book or as a full drawing-size page of notes in the drawing set. When in book form, specs are generally provided in a conventional format using Construction Specifications Institute (CSI) divisions. In addition to general introductory sections,

This excerpt from the narrative specs for the Harding home in conventional CSI format includes the first page of the table of contents and a page from the General Conditions section that discusses project requirements for product usage, project closeout, air leakage control, and construction waste management.
COURTESY OF ROBERT HARRISON ARCHITECTS.

HARDING HOME

Robert Harrison Architects 206.956.0883
REVISION 2: OCTOBER 1, 2004
SPECIFICATIONS

HARDING HOME Specifications   Revision 2: October 1, 2004   8
© 2004 Robert Harrison Architects 206.956.0883

01035 PRODUCT USAGE

1.   Materials containing chloroflourocarbons (CFC's), urea formaldehyde, benzene, toluene, carbon tetrachloride, styrene-butadiene, or trichloro-ethylene shall not be installed in the work or used on the job site.

2.   Materials containing asbestos shall not be used.

3.   Coatings having a lead content over 0.06 percent by weight of nonvolatile content, and coatings containing zinc-chromate or strontium-chromate shall not be used.

4.   The use of any pesticides, herbicides, or noxious cleaning products is prohibited anywhere in the building or on the job site.

5.   Smoking shall not be permitted anywhere in or within 25 feet of the building at any time.

6.   The use of petroleum fueled generators, heaters, or other appliances in the building or within 25 feet of the building is prohibited.

01040 PROJECT CLOSEOUT

1.   **Project cleaning:** clean glass and remove labels from windows; HEPA vacuum all surfaces (HEPA filter in Shop Vac); clean ducts; wash floors.

2.   **Equipment testing:** test lighting; heating equipment and controls; fans, dampers, audio equipment, etc. Submit record of tests to Architect.

01420 AIR LEAKAGE CONTROL

1.   Integrity of the building envelope will be controlled for the purpose of maintaining optimal indoor air quality, energy efficiency and comfort, and preserving the structure.

2.   The building shall be pressure tested for air leakage by a specialty contractor who is a member of the Affordable Comfort Home Performance Association. The test will be conducted after completion of the interior building envelope, but before installation of cabinets, casework, electrical and plumbing fixtures and insulation. The maximum allowable air leakage will be seven (7) air changes per hour at 50 Pascal's (ACH@50), based on a single-point depressurization test and guidelines developed by Washington State Department of Trade and Economic Development for their Low-Income Weatherization Program. Contractor will provide a test report. (Alternative: Air flow at 50 Pascals (CFM50) shall not exceed 35% of the building envelope nominal surface area, per specifications by Engineered for Life Program. Contractor shall submit a test report to the Architect.)

01505 CONSTRUCTION WASTE MANAGEMENT

1.   The Owner has established that this Project shall generate the least amount of waste possible and that processes that ensure the generation of as little waste as possible due to over packaging, error, poor planning, breakage, mishandling, contamination, or other factors shall be employed.

2.   Of the inevitable waste that is generated, as many of the waste materials as economically feasible shall be reused, salvaged, or recycled. Waste disposal in landfills shall be minimized.

3.   List of materials to be recycled, reused or returned to manufacturer shall include, at minimum, the following materials:
     a. Cardboard, paper, packaging

spec divisions describe job requirements to various tradespersons who will work on your project.

With drawings and specs, it will be important for your designer or general contractor to clearly communicate deviations from conventional practice to those who are actually doing the work. Narrative specs are a helpful communication tool because you can (and should) get pretty specific about products and systems, and how you want them installed. Frequently product suppliers will provide specs for working with their product, because it's in their best interests to make sure the product is installed or prepared properly. A good example is the set of instructions provided by its manufacturer for applying OSWax, a natural sealer for wood, bamboo, and cork floors. Such instructions should be included in the specs. Other specifications are available from independent sources—for example, the American Society for Testing and Material Standards (ASTM) provides a standard spec for using coal fly ash as a replacement for portions of cement when producing concrete.

Drawings and specifications are considered contract documents or CDs. Your contract with the builder should specifically reference each of the drawings and the specs. The builder, then, is obligated by your written agreement to provide the design exactly as shown, with all of the materials you've chosen. Of course, as noted earlier, the process of construction by nature includes a fair amount of improvisation, so it's good to be open both to opportunities that arise that might not have been apparent on paper (like, "If we move this window two feet this way it will perfectly frame this view") and to letting go of some of the things you really wanted (if say, the recycled glass tile you picked out is going to be six weeks late). Do keep in mind that deviations from the specs or plans—especially those you initiate—can result in a change order, and you want to avoid doing too many of those.

Details *are* sometimes lost on jobs even when they are in the drawings and specs. But if a detail isn't included in the construction documents (CDs), you can be assured it won't magically find its way into the completed project. This is where your good record keeping and vigilance pay off. Before you finalize your project drawings and specs, we suggest you have a meeting to review them, referring line by line to the list of green building strategies you initially agreed upon and asking for clarification as to where each action item shows up in the project documents. It's also an excellent time to review the overall goals. Do the documents as drawn and written appear to meet them? This is the time to speak up. If you have any doubts that proper documentation of your green project elements will occur, this is a point in the process where you might bring in a green building consultant to perform a quick and independent review of the paperwork and provide comments.

Frequently, the product named in your plans or specs may not be available from the suppliers your contractor (or the subcontractors, such as the plumber or electrician) generally uses, or it has simply gone out of production. Product names change. Manufacturers go out of business. The subcontractor does some research and finds a more cost-effective product that seems to do the same thing. You can plan for these possibilities in two ways: by relying on performance specs rather than naming a preferred product or type of product, and by having a policy in place (usually in the specifications but it can also be included in your general contract) that allows for the substitution of approved equivalents but doesn't compromise your project goals. As an example of the former, your designer would specify some amount of VOCs (volatile organic compounds—the stuff that smells and gives you headaches) per liter that's allowable for interior paints, in addition to naming some products that meet the criteria. For the latter, responsibility for approving the substitution should reside with the project team member—usually a designer or a designer/builder—best able to interpret product literature and compare the substitution to the original product you'd hoped for.

The matter of substitutions points to the need for being clear on the rationale for choosing the original product in the first place and recording that in your project notes. It's too easy to forget why something was important at one time and in the fray of a fast-paced project make a decision that effectively contradicts your original intent. This isn't to say that substitutions don't sometimes represent an improvement; they certainly can. Frequently, however, they don't, so this is a place to be hypervigilant.

It may perhaps be superfluous to mention it, but regardless of how simple or complex your project is (and the shade of green you hope for), your agreement with your contractor(s) and/or designer should be a matter of written record. Don't work without a written contract that specifies timeline, payment schedule, and general working arrangements. As noted earlier, the CDs should be incorporated (as

exhibits) into the contract. See *Building Your Home: An Insider's Guide* by Carol Smith (listed in "Resources") for its helpful tips on contracts and agreements.

SELECTING MATERIALS

In conventional building, issues of performance, availability, and cost are the criteria for choosing a material. With a green home, these factors are still very important, but you're adding the factor of environmental impact.

All building materials have an environmental impact when they're produced. This varies significantly from material to material, so your choices can make a difference to the environment at large. The impact occurs as the raw material is converted to a usable building material through extraction, transportation, and manufacturing processes. Each product represents a certain amount of embodied energy, the amount of energy used to take a raw material from its original location and condition to your doorstep. By buying locally made products (ideally manufactured with locally sourced raw materials) you reduce the amount of energy used to transport them to you, so that's a good start. In addition, materials can have significant impacts when they're installed and when they operate over their service life.

The ideal to aim for—although difficult to achieve—is to choose materials whose use results in either a neutral or a beneficial impact. This gets especially challenging when you're dealing with complex assemblies, composite materials, and equipment made with a variety of components. Still, it's a goal worth pursuing. In general, you're looking for products and materials that can be described with these terms:

Resource efficient. Materials are resource efficient when they include recycled content, are reusable or recyclable, are salvaged from another building or your original building, and/or save raw materials by virtue of the way they're manufactured or installed. Note that there's a difference between postindustrial and postconsumer recycled content. Postconsumer recycled materials have served their intended use and have been collected from the end user and reprocessed. In contrast, postindustrial recycled material is usually derived from manufacturing waste or substandard products that haven't been used. For this reason, postconsumer material is considered a bit greener than postindustrial, but both are better than using virgin materials. Many examples of resource-efficient products are provided in later chapters; one example might be wood flooring remilled from beams removed from a building being demolished or from old cedar railroad ties.

Healthy. Healthy materials don't include or emit levels of problem substances (such as volatile organic compounds or VOCs) that are linked to illness or health risk in the people who produce them, install them, or live with them. This mostly applies to interior finishes (such as carpet and paint) and furnishings (like your sofa or drapes) but can be more broadly considered, especially if you share our concerns about those individuals who must deal with the results of manufacturing or disposal of the given building material.

Energy efficient. When you use the product, it doesn't use as much energy as a conventional product (one that just meets code) would.

Water efficient. Water-efficient products save water over conventional practice. An example is a low-flow showerhead beyond code.

Site friendly. When you use site-friendly materials, they either improve site conditions or don't harm them. An example is using an organic compost berm rather than polyethylene silt fences to manage storm water during construction.

Other factors in material selection include durability (length of service) and maintenance requirements. For example, when choosing wood for your new deck, you're committing to regular refinishing and maintenance to keep wood healthy and safe (not slippery). What will you use to treat the wood? Alternatively, plastic lumber lasts forever and requires no refinishing.

What makes material selection fun (and challenging) is that all materials have advantages and disadvantages. You'll discover that there's no perfect material; all decisions will involve compromise or trade-offs. (That durable plastic lumber won't biodegrade.) In the end you'll be making decisions based on what's important to you. This may include looking at impacts beyond your particular project. If this is the case, you'll want to home in on products that are available locally, address the environmental and health issues you're passionate about, directly address the big environmental issues in your community, and provide multiple benefits. Fortunately, we in the Northwest are relatively blessed with a high level of responsiveness by building materials' manufacturers to the public's desire for more environmentally sensitive options, so there are a lot of green products

Some building materials, while offering major advantages, include chemicals that are controversial and have stirred up enough concern that leading green materials researchers and government agencies (such as the EPA) have suggested we avoid them as a precautionary measure. Neither of us is a materials scientist and we haven't tested products (other than to observe them in our homes), so we don't have the firsthand knowledge that would allow us to condemn a product outright. However, we would be remiss if we didn't point out materials of concern. Two examples used in many common building materials are polyvinyl chloride and form-aldehyde.

Polyvinyl chloride, commonly known as PVC, is a common and versatile synthetic material. "Vinyl" as a product description—except when used in relation to paints, glues, and certain plastic films—almost always means made of PVC, according to the Healthy Building Network (HBN). Some resilient flooring, such as linoleum, is not vinyl, although it's frequently, but mistakenly, called that. The HBN advises, "When in doubt about the use of the term vinyl, ask if it is PVC." The concern with PVC is its chlorine component, which according to the HBN results in "the generation of dioxin, a highly carcinogenic chemi-cal produced in both the manufacture and disposal of PVC" (Healthy Building Network 2005, 1).

According to the HBN, roughly 75 percent of all PVC manufactured is used in construction materials (Healthy Building Network 2006, 1). Vinyl siding makes up a signifi-cant portion of that. The award-winning documentary *Blue Vinyl* (Helfand and Gold 2002) raised serious questions about the potential upstream and downstream environmental and health impacts associated with the use of vinyl siding.

The HBN claims that PVC is an environmental health disaster on a global scale since dioxin is persistent (it travels long distances without breaking down) and bio-accumulative (it concentrates as it moves up the food chain in humans). In addition, a commen-tary provided to the U.S. Green Building Council on the use of the material for buildings concludes that the data shows that "PVC poses serious threats at every stage of its existence" (Steingraber 2004, 21). The HBN promotes using PVC-free alternatives to serve many of the functions the chemical now serves. For exam-ple, for piping, the organization suggests using cast iron, steel, concrete vitrified clay, copper, and HDPE (high density polyethyl-ene) (Healthy Building Network 2006, 2).

Formaldehyde is an important chemical widely used to manu-facture building materials as well as other household products. It's also a by-product of combustion and other natural processes. Thus it can be present in substantial concentrations both indoors and outdoors. At the low concentrations generally found indoors you can't smell it, but that doesn't mean it doesn't affect you. According to John Bower, author of *The Healthy House,* "Form-aldehyde exposure . . . has been shown to be a potent sensitizer [which] means exposure to formaldehyde can cause an individual to become sensitive to other chemicals that were previously not problematic" (2000, 21). At higher concentrations, the chemical itself can produce symptoms ranging from burning eyes, tight chest, and headaches, to asthmatic attacks, depression, and even death. The Natural Resources Defense Council (2005) lists formaldehyde as one of its "Most Wanted" common household contaminants.

According to the U.S. Environmental Protection Agency (2006b), the most significant sources of formaldehyde in the home are likely to be pressed wood products made using adhesives that contain urea-formaldehyde (UF) resins. Pressed wood products include particleboard, hardwood plywood paneling, and medium density fiberboard (MDF). The agency notes that MDF contains a higher resin-to-wood ratio than other UF pressed products and is therefore "generally recognized as being the highest formaldehyde-emitting pressed wood product." There are alternatives, including formaldehyde-free MDF, and pressed wood products produced for exterior use. The latter contain phenol-formaldehyde (PF) resin and according to the EPA "generally emit formaldehyde at considerably lower rates than those containing UF resin."

to choose from.

The job of selecting materials—even those that are noncontroversial—to use for your green home project can be quite challenging. Getting consistent and clear information from suppliers regarding environmental attributes (including both advantages and disadvantages) can be difficult. Several resources can make it easier, including eco-certifications, independent product directories, and life-cycle assessments.

Eco-certifications

When you do your product research, check if the product is qualified through one of several existing eco-certification processes, such as GreenGuard for meeting air quality standards or Energy Star for meeting energy standards. Scientific Certification Systems (SCS) is a leading third-party evaluation and certification firm; environmental claims they have verified relevant to building products include recycled/recovered content, biodegradability, and forest management. Products that meet SCS standards bear a Green Cross label.

An eco-label helps protect you from falling prey to greenwashing. Some claims made about products' green attributes can be quite ridiculous. The value of the eco-label, even in cases where there are different certifications for the same type of product, is that you know the product has undergone some scrutiny and meets a specified threshold. Still, eco-labels are just a start. It's important to understand what the label actually stands for. For example, Energy Star sets a minimum efficiency threshold. *All* products that meet this threshold get the Energy Star label. If you want to make sure you get the model with the *high-*

est energy efficiency available or at least a very high efficiency, use the bright yellow energy efficiency labels to compare actual projections of energy use. You can also check the Energy Star Web site, which lists energy use projections for specific models.

In addition, there are in the wood product world several eco-certifications to choose from, each with a different level of rigor. The Forest Stewardship Council (FSC) provides, in addition to high standards for the sustainable growth and harvest of wood products, a chain-of-custody process that tracks the wood from harvesting through milling, distribution, and retail. Forests in the FSC system are certified by a third party. As of November 2006, the FSC is the only sustainable forestry management system with a complete chain-of-custody verification process in the United States. FSC accredits independent certification agencies to do its work; SCS is one of them, so you'll often see a Green Cross on FSC-certified wood. There are three other sustainable forestry certification systems in North America:

The Sustainable Forestry Initiative (SFI), a program of the American Forest and Paper Association, doesn't require third-party certification nor provide chain-of-custody verification.

CSA International (CSA), an independent nonprofit accredited by the Standards Council of Canada, does require third-party certification but provides chain-of-custody only on a limited scale.

The American Tree Farm System, a program of the American Forest Foundation, requires third-party certification but doesn't provide chain-of-custody verification.

While none of these currently offers complete chain-of-custody verification, the market for certified wood products is rapidly growing, and the demand for certainty may result in their adoption of this standard. For these certifications, you'll frequently see the certification advertised in signage at the point of sale but not actually stamped on the wood.

Independent product directories

One of our favorite resources for researching products is the GreenSpec Directory, published by BuildingGreen, the same folks who produce *Environmental Building News.* Both print publications take no advertising or sponsors and provide good-quality, considered information. The publisher uses consistent criteria to screen products for inclusion in the directory; the criteria are listed in the front of the document. The sixth edition includes information on nearly two thousand green building products in more than 250 categories. Included are product descriptions, environmental characteristics and considerations, and manufacturer contact information with Internet addresses. Many of the products listed in the directory have distributors in the Northwest. Another resource from the same group is the Building Green Suite; it's available through subscription and pricier, but a great tool for your architect or designer/builder to use regularly as a decision-making resource for your project.

Although it originates from the City of Portland's Office of Sustainable Development (OSD), the relatively new online Northwest Green Directory promises to provide information on green building products and services throughout the Pacific Northwest. Other product directories may become available as the movement gains momentum. Since this is definitely one of those areas of change, it's worth doing an Internet search under the word string "green building products, Northwest" to find them. If you do turn up a product resource, make sure the publishing source is a credible one, the criteria used to screen products are provided, and the geographic area covered applies to you.

Life-cycle assessments

The results of life-cycle assessments (LCA) that some of the more committed manufacturers are conducting on their products will be more available in the future as a decision-making tool. Conducting an LCA is an expensive process, but it's probably the most detailed analysis of the environmental impact of a given material and product. According to BuildingGreen's GreenSpec Directory, "Product LCAs typically consider the extraction or harvesting of the raw materials, the refining and manufacturing processes that turn those raw materials into useful products, transportation of those products, their use, and their eventual disposal or reuse. This scope of analysis is often called 'cradle to grave' or, including the reuse potential, 'cradle-to-cradle' LCA" (Wilson and Malin 2003, xxix).

Software programs are available that compare the environmental impacts of products (BEES, free software available from the National Institute of Standards and Technology) and building assemblies (Athena: Environmental Impact Estimator), but because not all manufacturers have conducted LCAs, the databases for these programs are incomplete and thus limiting. In addition, BEES in particular muddies the water by throwing in cost as a factor, so that questionable products can offset environmental impact if they're made cheaply.

We suggest you ask manufacturers for a copy of any LCAs they may have conducted on products they're claiming as environmentally friendly that you're concerned about. They may have actually conducted an analysis for the product. Even if they haven't, your question will get them thinking about it.

BUILDING THE BUDGET

The budget is another place where your project's green goals should be reflected. A builder will typically create the budget from a detailed list (known as a takeoff) of materials he or she is responsible for purchasing, as well as from bids received from subcontractors performing discrete aspects of the project.

If the drawings and specs are complete and accurately convey all of the green strategies you're hoping for in your project, the budget should also be accurate, since both the general contractor and subcontractors should be referring to the paperwork to create their estimates. However, with Murphy's Law in place, it's fully possible that a subcontractor might not read all the fine print and might submit an estimate based on a typical project using products from his or her normal supplier. This might work if the supplier stocks the type of product you're looking for; if not, you might run into an upcharge for a product that requires going outside of the usual supply chain.

The key is to make sure the drawings and specs and other paperwork are accurate, kept up to date,

. . . .

HEALTHY BUILDING CHECKLIST FOR WORKERS

❑ Don't smoke anywhere on site, especially in the building.

❑ Don't wear anything that smells like anything but sweat.

❑ No clothes, shoes, or gloves that smell like oil, gasoline, creosote, paint thinners, varnishes, etc.

❑ No scented deodorant, soap, insect repellent, aftershave, etc.

❑ Cover the floors or ground when working with toxic things.

❑ Use care when handling fungicides, wood preservatives, glue, fixatives, varnishes, plumbing cement, paints, etc.

❑ Immediately clean up any spills.

❑ Never use gas-powered machinery inside the building.

❑ If you have a choice, use less-toxic materials.

❑ For example, use vegetable oil instead of concrete form oil.

❑ Double-check the toxicity of all substitutions with the architect.

❑ Check the label and MSDS for warnings like "use with adequate ventilation." Avoid using if possible.

❑ Use less-toxic cleaning supplies.

❑ Check warning labels and avoid cleaners with ammonia, bleach, chlorinated powder, disinfectants, and detergents.

❑ Protect porous building materials from weather and water.

❑ Cover all lumber, plywood, etc.

❑ Discard any materials that get wet. They grow mold.

❑ Use extra care to keep the job site clean.

❑ Remove all scrap building materials, especially if using those with formaldehyde like particleboard, plywood, etc.

❑ Don't allow anything to be buried on the site, including bits of glue, varnishes, and paints.

❑ Use buckets for washing out brushes and other applicators.

❑ Don't pour any dirty residue onto the site.

❑ Never use pesticides or herbicides on the job site.

and religiously referred to during development of the budget.

JOB SITE MANAGEMENT

In thinking about making your project a green one, you're most likely focused on the things about the project that are permanent—the structure itself—or at least long-lasting, such as landscaping and finishes. However, there's another aspect of the project that can have significant environmental impact that most homeowners don't really see—and that's how the job is managed during construction. Three main areas concern us here: construction waste management, air quality protection, and surface water management. For each area the best practice is to require that your contractor provide a management plan. This plan needn't be lengthy or complicated. Signage on the job communicating the plan to all who work on the site is a good start. The main thrust of the plan should be to avoid making a mess in the first place, and to clean up messes that do occur using an environmentally preferred method.

For construction waste management, you'll want the contractors to employ the three Rs (reduce, reuse, and recycle). To reduce wood waste, for example, some contractors will purchase framing in measured cutpacks based on a very careful takeoff of all the dimensional lumber required for the project. Or/and they might use a central cutting area to make sure cutoffs are easily accessed for use as blocks or backing. Contractors can reuse their wood forms (or better yet, use steel forms that last years and include recycled content). Finally, they can recycle any wood waste. Clean wood left over from a job can be offered as free firewood (okay) or recycled as hog fuel in mills (better); it can also be chipped and used for ground cover on-site (even better).

For air quality protection, you'll want contractors to avoid introducing through substitutions any materials that emit unwanted VOCs; the original specs should aim at excluding these problem substances. Because total exclusion of emitting materials is sometimes difficult, proper ventilation during application of interior finishes (such as paints or adhesives) should be required, and air flushing with 100 percent outside air for at least seventy-two hours at the end of a job is recommended. Preventing dust from entering the heating system and protecting stored materials from getting wet and possibly introducing mold into the home are also good ideas. For remodeling projects especially, the contractor's plan for dust control should be spelled out in the contract; you could be living with the problem for a long time.

Surface water management is one aspect of job site management that's regulated. However, we've seen too many job sites where required surface water management tactics have been poorly applied and have failed. For example, we've seen silt fences installed on the wrong side of the slope, or staked too far apart, or not inspected after a heavy rainstorm and so loaded with silt that any further rain will result in sheeting right over the top. Any job where the soil is going to be disturbed and left bare during the wet season should employ redundant measures so that if the first line of defense fails, the second is in place. In addition, a heavy rainfall (for example, when more than a half inch of rain falls in a twenty-four-hour period) should trigger an automatic visit to the site to make sure surface water management measures are still intact.

QUALITY MANAGEMENT

A good quality control and assurance program is an important aspect of any professional design or construction project, green or not. Most contractors have some form of quality management, in the form of a punch list that's basically a final list of items that need to be addressed (minimally nail pops, dings, and cleaning), and a final walk-through that assures they have been. This is generally tied to the final payment.

Since aspects of green building require contractors and their subs to do things differently it's important to consider how to ensure that those differences actually occur. Will the job site management plans described earlier actually be carried out? Will green products be installed as planned? Will your home's enclosure be durable? Will the home's operating systems perform as hoped? Four things that can contribute to the quality of a newly constructed or remodeled green home include crew training, performance testing and verification, commissioning, and final walk-through orientation.

Crew training

We've observed situations where framing contractors, even if provided plans that specify advanced framing techniques, will do it the way they've always done it. Now you have a building that's not framed the way you want it to be; your choices are telling the contractor to do it over (meaning a lot of time and

A sign at the job site laid out the management plan arrived at by O'Brien & Company for the Sound Health LLC project, a medical health services building aimed at clientele with multiple chemical sensitivities in Anacortes, Washington.

The Harding residence was built with stack framing techniques that saved 25 percent of the wood that would otherwise have been used. The crew was specially trained in the new technique by the architect and the general contractor. PHOTO BY ROB HARRISON.

material wasted, and likely a spoiled relationship) or giving up on your original plan.

Architect Rob Harrison of Seattle wanted to make sure that the stack framing techniques specified for the Harding residence were skillfully carried out. Harrison and the general contractor, George Piano, organized an afternoon workshop at Harrison's office for Piano's entire framing crew followed up by an afternoon on the job site where the crew built a section of stack frame wall including a corner and several types of openings. The latter gave them a chance to try out new flashing techniques as well. The crew went on to build the best stack framing Harrison has ever seen (Harrison, personal communication, 2006). Not only that, but Piano was also gracious enough to allow the structural engineer,

Andy Herrick, to bring two other contractors to visit the house during framing. According to Rob Harrison, "Following the visit, each was sufficiently convinced by the efficiency of the system to employ advanced framing techniques at two new housing developments including a total of forty-two houses. At 25 percent wood saved per house, you might say we saved all the wood used in the Harding residence ten times over" (Harrison 2005). Obviously, the Hardings benefited directly, but so did the larger community.

Framing and building enclosure details in general are two areas where we see a tremendous need for training, but there are other nonconventional techniques that would benefit from this approach. Remember that you're dealing with individuals who work with their hands. A hands-on training (such as just described) can be very valuable.

One way to organize this training cost effectively is to invite in building material or equipment suppliers or product manufacturers to put together the training. As noted earlier, it's in their best interest to make sure their product is installed correctly. And most contractors and subs should recognize the value this training will bring to their company and not charge the client for this time.

Performance testing and verification

In order to make sure your home is actually as green as your drawings and specs indicate it should be, you may decide to incorporate performance testing and verification into your process. This type of service has been available in other parts of the country for some time and is just becoming more popular in the Northwest. Performance testing looks at the home as a system and examines how the system performs. Verification looks at selected components of the home and confirms that they've been installed.

For the most part, performance testing in the housing industry has focused on energy performance, testing for air leakages that can translate into significant energy losses, through the building enclosure and if applicable from air ducts. A blower door test is a proven means to identify air leaks in a home. A blower door consists of a variable speed fan sealed into an exterior doorway and is used to blow air into or out of a house. When air is blown out of the house, the house develops a slight negative pressure (or vacuum) relative to outside. The pressure

A blower door test is used to identify air leaks in a home. PHOTO COURTESY OF THE ENERGY CONSERVATORY.

difference drives outside air into the house through any available openings in the enclosure. These leaks can be located by touch or with smoke, then sealed. The test yields an estimate of the leakiness of the home in square inches, as well as the approximate natural rate of air changes per hour (ACH) in the house. The aim is for enough air changes to occur while at the same time not jeopardizing energy efficiency. Blower doors can also be used to perform duct blaster tests to locate duct leaks.

Similarly, verification has until recently focused solely on energy components in the home and has included visually verifying that energy-efficient equipment, including appliances, fixtures, and heating and cooling systems, has been properly installed.

Energy Star Northwest requires that performance testing and verification occur at completion. That's nice, because you get to brag about being an

Energy Star Northwest home. However, we recommend at least one inspection and testing prior to drywall installation, when your contractor still has access to sources of concern and can correct problems. Our experience is that this both helps prevent serious heat losses and possible moisture problems in your home and helps the subcontractors learn to do their jobs better.

With green building becoming more significant, there has been a push to expand performance testing to include air quality testing, and to expand verification to include the visual verification of all types of green building strategies. Your local green building program or other green building organizations can put you in contact with individuals qualified to do this. In addition, HVAC contractors are beginning to perform tests specific to the equipment they install as a value-added service.

Commissioning

Commissioning (Cx) is a term borrowed from the shipbuilding industry to refer to making a determination that all systems are "go" and working well together. An example as applied to your home might be to check to make sure that installed daylight sensors or motion sensors work properly in conjunction with the lighting systems. Although commissioning isn't a common practice in the residential world, some level of basic commissioning is advisable, especially where innovative systems have been installed. This should take place as systems are installed and before the final walk-through.

There are certified building commissioners out there but their expertise is primarily with commercial buildings. We would recommend working with your designer or builder to create a simple Cx plan for your home. If you choose to go the route of performance testing and verification, you want to coordinate aspects of your Cx plan with that effort. In addition, your Cx plan should include your contractor checking in with you before the end of the first year of occupancy (and before any warranty in the contract expires).

Final walk-through orientation

Walk-throughs are a typical practice in the construction world. With a green project, the final walk-through should include time for homeowner orientation to any innovative systems installed as well as any special tips needed to maintain and operate a green home. A homeowner's manual summarizing this information should be provided.

As part of this final orientation, make sure you get contacts for service providers who can tune up and repair the systems in your home (innovative or not). You'll also want a record of how the systems and structure were actually built—known in the trade as "as-builts." This can be achieved by updated drawings, notations on the original drawings, photos of installations, or videos. This will be particularly helpful down the road when you need to make repairs, do maintenance, or do some remodeling. Product manuals and warranties should be a part of the package. These materials should be stored in a convenient place and passed on to new owners if you sell your home.

Of course, the solutions will vary strongly from place to place. It is a matter of listening to *what the land wants to be.*

Sim Van der Ryn and Stuart Cowan, *Ecological Design*

4: Managing Your Green Home Project, Part 2

ARTICULATING YOUR DESIRES with regard to your new home or remodeling project is extremely important, but if you don't have the right people helping you to bring your desires to fruition, it won't matter. This is true of any construction project but particularly true with green building, where integration of various concepts and techniques (some of which may be unfamiliar to your contractor) can make the difference between a cost-effective and high-performing project and one that misses the mark. In addition, your green project won't be successful if it's blind to its location.

This chapter provides information on the two management Ps referring to the people you work with and the place where your project is located. It also includes two case studies of new construction that neatly exemplifies all three management Ps—the importance of designing from a clear set of goals (purpose), having the right team (people) on board, and responding to the site (place)—as well as some other variables we've touched on. The Scheulen residence is located in an urban neighborhood in Seattle, Washington, subject to a fairly mild though

wet winter climate. The Scheulens hired a general contractor known for green building for their project (Jon Alexander, author of the case study). The Peterson residence is located in an established suburban development in Pasco, Washington, on the east side of the Cascade Range. The Petersons live in a climate that's harsher, with more radical seasonal temperature swings and large wind and dust storms. Keith Peterson acted as his own general contractor. Both homes are stellar examples of green building. The Scheulen project experienced a 9 percent cost premium; the Peterson house, no premium at all.

PUTTING TOGETHER A QUALIFIED PROJECT TEAM

If you're building a new home or remodeling your existing one, you'll get the best results—with the least pain—from a project team that will

- perform their work in a professional manner—that is, will communicate honestly and directly, be considerate of your budget and schedule, and be client-centered in their approach
- offer the skill sets and experience required to get

the job done, including design, construction, and project management expertise and practice

- support each other's efforts by working together, sharing information, and being accountable for fulfilling individual responsibilities; and, most relevant to this book
- support your project goals, and in particular your green goals, with practical green building expertise and a willingness to meaningfully explore the green building opportunities appropriate for your project

It's possible that you'll find all of these within a single company, as with a designer/builder with green building expertise. It's much more likely, however, that you'll need to hire design expertise separately. One key is remembering that in order to get that dark green home that functions well for your lifestyle, you'll want to have someone on your team who's capable of conceptualizing a home that works as a system. We strongly suggest that for new custom homes and for major remodeling projects and additions you use an architect or a highly qualified designer/builder with an architect on staff. It will be the best money you ever spend.

When it pays to hire a green building expert

Although more and more professionals are becoming knowledgeable in green building, it's still a relatively new movement, and in some communities you may not be able to find the breadth of skill and experience you'd like to see for your project. This is where supplementing your team with a green building consultant or specialist might be in order.

Most green building consultants will provide a range of services, from simply reviewing what your team is doing at predetermined checkpoints and providing some guidance, to providing complete green building project management, starting with setting goals at an eco-charrette and then seeing the project all the way through to completion. If you're hoping to install innovative systems, you'll probably need to bring in a specialist or two. A green building consultant can make recommendations for these specialists and can even manage their work. Specialized service providers include designers and installers of these systems:

- systems for capturing rainwater
- systems for treating wastewater on your site
- plumbing that uses both potable (drinking) water and gray water (such as rainwater or treated wastewater)
- systems that use solar energy to provide electricity
- systems that use solar energy to provide water heating
- specialized building systems (such as an alternative foundation type)
- landscapes that act as storm water management systems (for example, rain gardens and bioswales)

In addition, if someone in your household has serious health sensitivities and your designer and/or contractor doesn't specialize in healthy construction, you might consider bringing in a hygienist or indoor air quality expert for advice on the project.

Here are ten questions you can ask designers and contractors to determine if they have the capacity to make your green project a successful one:

1. Have you had any projects where you've used sustainable building concepts? What role did you play in making the project green? Listen for: "Yes!" (or "No, but I'm willing to learn more about it and work with you on that.")

2. Are you active in the green building movement? What relevant organizations do you belong to? What about your business is green? Listen for: "I'm a member of Built Green" (for Washington residents) or "I belong to the Cascadia Region Green Building Council" (and/or the Northwest EcoBuilding Guild). Also listen for participation in committees in professional associations such as the AIA Committee on the Environment. Also, "I use waste reduction measures, alternative fuel vehicles, an environmentally friendly printer for our promotional materials. I live in a green home myself and my business is located in a green building."

3. Do you have any green building credentials? Listen for: "I'm a LEED Accredited Professional" (or a Certified Sustainable Building Advisor, an Energy Star Performance Tester or Verifier, and/or a Built Green Verifier, or other credentials).

4. Are you familiar with green building programs that apply to homes? Do you participate? Listen for: "Yes, I know about Built Green [or other local green building program], LEED for Homes, Energy Star Northwest, and/or Environment for Living, and I participate."

5. What measures do you take to protect the site and water during and after construction? Listen for evidence of a specific knowledge base—for example, "I make sure the site is protected from erosion, and I inspect the site after major rainstorms."

6. What measures do you take to conserve water? Listen for evidence of a specific knowledge base—for example, "I've installed ultra-low-flush toilets" or "We landscape with drought-tolerant plants."

7. What measures do you take to improve energy efficiency? Will you build an Energy Star qualified home? Listen for evidence of a specific knowledge base—for example, "I performance-test my homes" or "I make it a practice to provide extra-efficient windows beyond code."

8. What measures do you take in design and construction to ensure good air quality and health? Listen for evidence of a specific knowledge base—for example, "I try not to use products that off-gas and cause health problems."

9. What measures do you take to conserve natural resources through designing in materials efficiency or through waste management practices including materials handling and selection? Listen for evidence of a specific knowledge base—for example, "I like to use techniques that keep waste down, such as in-line framing" or "I recycle all of our waste."

10. What kind of training and information will you provide on the green building features to help me maintain them and keep my home operating green? Listen for: "I provide a homeowners manual on the major products and appliances so you know what the cleaning and maintenance requirements are. I provide the names and contact information for installers and service companies relevant to all of the systems in your home. I provide a final and up-to-date record of the project 'as-built' in case you need to make repairs or for future renovations. I provide an orientation to your green operating systems as part of the final walk-through."

Finding the right designer and contractor for you

For new custom construction it's frequently the designer or architect who you contract with first, who then finds a contractor for the job. However, the finding and hiring process can vary depending on your situation. For the O'Brien-Cunningham residence it was the contractor who suggested the designer for the job. For the garage remodel, we hired the designer and the contractor in completely separate processes. One thing that may be obvious to you but wasn't to us is to make sure you hire a remodeling contractor for remodeling jobs. Contractors used to new home construction won't necessarily have the temperament and proper experience base to handle remodeling, which requires a different approach to scheduling and a greater capacity for handling surprises in the field.

In looking for the right designer and contractor you'll want to follow the usual guidelines, including asking for references and following them up. Talk to past clients and visit projects, if possible. Check on contractors' licenses, bonding, and insurance. If you have any concerns, call the Better Business Bureau. Ask questions and listen not only for specific responses but also for how well they listen to you and are able to communicate with you. After you interview prospects, ask yourself: Did they try to talk me out of wanting green features or did they seem receptive to exploring and evaluating options and trade-offs with me? Were they able to give specific answers or only vague assurances? Do they seem open to working with specialists? Or do they dismiss such ideas out of hand?

Don't be intimidated when you interview designers and contractors for your project. It's the best way to determine how deep their green knowledge base is—and whether they seem open to being your partner in learning about green building and green living. Green building is by nature a learning opportunity, even for the most experienced of us. That's what makes it fun.

Keep your radar tuned for greenwashing, either of projects your prospective team members are referencing as experience, or of design and construction abilities. Are your prospects exaggerating the positive environmental attributes of their work? Look for thoughtful yet optimistic individuals. Don't even bother with the builder who responds to all of your questions about green building with the "It's tough to be green" mantra: it's too pricy, it takes too long, and it can't be done. Ask for particulars; it's your right. Besides, everyone (including those you hire) will be much happier if the match is a good one.

Managing the project and keeping it green

The general contractor is usually responsible for managing the project. Project management (PM) can in fact be done by anyone on the team with scheduling, budget management, and communication skills, including yourself if you have the time and the inclination to learn and if the professionals you're working with are willing to let you. If you do take on the PM role and this is new to you, expect to pay a price in time and/or money in exchange for your on-the-job education.

No matter who does it, someone on the team must take the role of green building champion. This is certainly a role you as the owner can take—again, if you have the time and the inclination. The green building champion keeps an eye on the prize and makes sure the team and the project don't lose their green focus. The role can range from cheerleading to persistent reminding (aka nagging) and can include performing supplemental research to find green products, resources, and services. For example, when the plumbing contractor for the O'Brien-Cunningham garage-studio remodeling job couldn't seem to locate the water-conserving showerhead with the special Venturi effect to make the flow seem stronger, it took Kate a five-minute surf on the Internet to find a supplier (five minutes, go figure).

Working with the trades

If you're acting as owner–general contractor, you'll be working directly with tradespersons. As noted earlier, written agreements and records of discussions of preferred methods and materials are critical to getting what you want. It's absolutely amazing how dramatically memories of a conversation can differ. Even if you're not acting as contractor, encourage your builder to make written agreements with subcontractors (subs), especially calling out materials or methods that may be a change from the subs' current practices.

Assertiveness training is also a good idea. No kidding. In general, tradespersons are pursuing a craft, are proud of what they do, and would like to keep doing it the way they've been doing it for as long as they do it. Practice saying: "This is what I want" in the mirror with a kind and generous smile. Then repeat with your subs, as often as required. (They'll think you're a bit goofy, but never mind about that.)

If a reluctant subcontractor provides a reasonable justification for his or her position, such as real cost data (since prices do vary) or researched lead times that don't work with your schedule, you'll probably want to back off. Don't antagonize needlessly. Just don't assume that the first negative response is where you have to stop. It's your project, your home, and our planet, after all.

The other real factor in any interactions with your tradespersons (or your general contractor if you hire one) is an extremely tight labor market that's not going to loosen up in the near future. Be nice.

Finding product suppliers

When selecting materials, you're implicitly choosing to work with specific manufacturers and suppliers. Our preference is to use products from manufacturers who are local and who treat the environment and their employees well during the manufacturing process. In addition, we prefer to deal with manufacturers and suppliers who have the capacity to stand by their product if we run into a problem with it, and to be reliable and honest in their dealings with us.

When choosing carpet for the O'Brien-Cunningham residence, we ran into incredible resistance from the supplier to provide recycled-content carpet. After we'd made several trips to the showroom, the vendor offered a carpet that didn't have recycled content but implied that it was a new product on the market that did. It wasn't until the product was installed and visitors were touring the house that the truth came out. You can imagine the fireworks! In the end, we negotiated a deal where the profit on

any special hoops you may have to jump through or even some incentives you may not know about. It pays to find an ally in the planning department who is sympathetic to green building. This isn't that tough, especially as many jurisdictions now have policies that support green alternatives. They won't make it possible to do something outside the law, but they may be able to facilitate the process and remove time- and money-burning roadblocks. Some jurisdictions—for example, Portland and Seattle—have identified individuals on their planning or building department staff to help folks who want to build green.

The most successful consultants we know of who design and install innovative systems have cultivated excellent relationships with local jurisdictions. In addition to your local planning and building department, jurisdictions that can have a significant effect on what you want to do include the local health department (which frequently reviews applications for composting toilets, use of rainwater for toilet flushing, or use of a Living Machine, a proprietary system for biological wastewater treatment) and the fire department (which may review the ability to run a fire truck to your property).

the sale was turned over to the local green building program as a donation, and the vendor promised to provide more accurate information about environmentally friendly selections.

Working with your jurisdictions

If you have your heart set on doing something innovative in your project, it pays to meet with your county or city planning department early to identify

Finding sympathetic lenders

We're assuming you're like us and will need to borrow the money to build, remodel, or purchase your home. In chapter 1 we discussed the emerging practice of lenders offering green construction loans and mortgages. These may or may not be available in your location. Even if such an option isn't explicitly advertised, it doesn't hurt to ask. If nothing else, it encourages your favorite lender to get educated!

Case Study:
The Scheulen Remodel (Seattle, Washington)

*by Jon Alexander,
Sunshine Construction*

Bob Scheulen and Kim Wells chose their new home's location because they could walk to the grocery store as well as other local services including a bus stop, and because it had good solar potential—although not perfect, as the lot's shape (and zoning laws) prevented ideal solar orientation along the east-west axis. They were also good friends with the next-door neighbors. In fact, the backyard is landscaped to allow easy access between the households.

The home is located in a middle-class neighborhood called Hawthorne Hills in northeast Seattle, primarily populated with single-family residences. Lots in the neighborhood are typical city-sized lots, ranging from 5000 to 10,000 square feet (the Scheulen lot measures 5033 square feet). However, the block the home is located on is perhaps not so typical. It has a strong sense of community, with most neighbors knowing each other and getting together from time to time. The Scheulens felt it likely that this neighborhood would embrace what they were doing, potentially adopting some of their methods.

The project, also dubbed "The Sensible Home," consisted of deconstructing an existing 900-square-foot home and replacing it with an 1800-square-foot home accompanied by a 650-square-foot accessory dwelling unit (ADU). We began the project in June 2003; it took ten months to complete. The project cost about $200 per square foot, typical for custom homes in Seattle at the time. We probably spent an extra 9 percent or so on green features. The residence was awarded an Innovations in Conservation BEST Award by Seattle Public Utilities and Resource Venture, Inc. in 2005. The home also won the City of Seattle's Built Green design competition.

This project was about bringing green building to a new level. The owners wanted an affordable, attractive, comfortable, functional, healthy, and environmentally friendly home that would be something almost everyone would want if only they knew it was available and had a chance to experience it. The project provided me, as the contractor, with a unique opportunity. Although I've been specializing in building green homes for fourteen-plus years, the Scheulens' commitment to demonstrating green

The 1800-square-foot Scheulen residence incorporates numerous green features in a "just the right size" house that aimed to be something almost everyone would want if only they knew it was available. PHOTO COURTESY OF NORTHWEST PROPERTY IMAGING.

had both worked, together and separately, on numerous green homes over the years. I was able to rely on an extensive network of suppliers and subcontractors knowledgeable about (or at least sympathetic to) green building, which I've developed over the years. And the owners were very engaged—Bob did an extraordinary amount of research for the project and was involved hands-on with the construction.

We pushed the limits in nearly all areas of green building, but I'd like to highlight a few things in particular: the overall fit of the design, energy-efficient features, water efficiency, and materials management.

Just the right design

The home was designed with the "not-so-big house" principles promoted by Sarah Susanka, tweaked into what we call a "just the right size" house. Care was taken in the design of the house to build only rooms the owners would use day to day, making those rooms a functional size and no bigger.

When I visit the owners now that the project is complete, they talk about how well this house works for them. They talk about things like how beautiful the morning light is coming in through their windows. How the heat wasn't needed until well into the cold season. How well protected the inside of the house is from street noise with its superinsulated walls and triple-glazed windows. How being out on their front porch and working in the yard they've met so many neighbors. And most of all, how this house feels like it really has soul.

The design included "feel good" spaces and gathering places such as the kitchen (above) and nook bench (right) as part of a plan to build a highly functional home. Both the kitchen and nook have large windows, connecting the spaces to the outdoors and providing lots of quality lighting. PHOTOS COURTESY OF NORTHWEST PROPERTY IMAGING.

building *without compromise* meant that I was able to incorporate more green features in this project than in any other single project I've ever been involved with in my entire career. It also meant that I was dealing with materials and processes new to me, making it both rewarding and challenging.

As with any building project, getting the owners what they wanted depended on having a good team in place. In this case, the architect, Ted Granger, and I

Energy efficiency

The home has qualified for both Energy Star and platinum-level Engineered for Life certifications. It was rated at 90.6 on the Home Energy Rating Standard (HERS) scale. (Just to provide a reference, you need 86 on the HERS scale of 100 to meet Energy Star performance standards.) Engineered for Life calculations estimate the house will produce 10,287 less pounds of carbon emissions per year than the average home of its size, based on an estimated annual heating bill of $174.

The house has a very energy-efficient shell that includes these features:

- nine-inch-thick double-framed 2 × 4 walls insulated with cellulose to R-33
- double walls using advanced system framing with a two-inch air gap between them
- a twelve-inch R-48 structural insulated panels roof system
- R-43 floors
- triple-glazed U.20 fiberglass windows

A final blower door test showed .14 air changes per hour (ACH) at natural pressure, meaning the house is much tighter than the average home.

The heating system is a hydronic coil system that includes a vacuum tube solar water collector, a heat recovery ventilator, a design that optimizes passive solar collection, and a 3-kW photovoltaic installation.

Water efficiency

The house is expected to use 115,340 fewer gallons of water per year than the average four-person household in Seattle. This was accomplished

Surprise: The stamped concrete patio (above) sits on top of a 7000-gallon cistern that stores captured rainwater. A filter at the drainpipe (see the black sloped attachment on the white drainpipe, left) removes twigs, leaves, and similar gutter debris from rainwater on its way to the cistern. The brick used for the wall along the edge of the patio was salvaged from deconstruction of the original house. PHOTOS BY JON ALEXANDER.

by adding these details:

- a rainwater collection system with a 7000-gallon cistern
- drought-resistant landscaping with no turf grass and a drip irrigation system using rainwater from the cistern

- toilets that are filled by rainwater from the cistern (making this the first residence in the city of Seattle to obtain permission to use rainwater for toilet flushing)
- low-flow faucets and high-efficiency fixtures
- 3/8-inch inside dimension PEX (cross-linked polyethylene) supply lines used in the house to reduce water wastage when hot water is turned on

The house has a patio that's actually part of the rainwater capture system. Water is drained off the roof and directed into a 7000-gallon cistern installed under the patio, where the water is stored until it's needed. Filtration happens at three places—at the drainpipe (where prefiltering removes twigs, leaves, and similar gutter debris), at the intake pipe for the cistern, and inside the house before going to a pump.

Smart and sustainable materials use

We elected to deconstruct the existing house instead of remodeling to most cost effectively reach our energy and healthy house goals. Our original plan included preserving the existing foundation and first floor framing. Estimates from concrete contractors and from subs revealed not only that it would be cheaper to start from scratch, but also that it would be faster, safer, and surprisingly would use less new concrete! So we ended up taking it all down. Through careful planning, we were able to salvage most of it. Many of the materials were reused in this home including flooring, framing, trim and stair treads, brick walls, and door and light fixtures. Other materials were salvaged for resale. The remaining materials were sorted for recycling. Very little material was sent to the landfill; in fact, the project had a recycling rate of more than 85 percent. Much of the new wood bought for flooring, interior trim, and framing was FSC-certified.

Using long-lasting materials—such as forty-year roofing, fiber-cement siding, fiberglass windows, quartz-composite countertops, and wood polymer decking and railings—and not using carpeting or vinyl flooring contributed to the home's green design as well. It was further enhanced by protecting against moisture damage by providing large roof overhangs and metal-clad exterior trim, by paying careful attention to flashing details, and by installing a rain shield system for siding. ■

PLACE: GETTING ACQUAINTED WITH YOUR SITE

As mentioned earlier, location is a very significant factor in a home's ecological impact. What you do on your lot can be nearly as significant. If your project, whether new construction or remodeling, responds to the site itself, you'll be capturing opportunities to more sustainably light and condition (heat, cool, and refresh) your home.

In general, your project should begin with an inventory of existing conditions. (If you used the questionnaire in chapter 2 to perform an initial needs analysis, those answers should be helpful as part of this inventory.) An inventory of existing conditions is sometimes called a site analysis, although it frequently goes beyond the site itself to look for circumstances that could affect what you do on your lot. The inventory should look at these aspects:

- natural systems
- built structures, on-site and adjacent
- codes, zoning, or other restrictions and standards
- neighborhood and beyond

The site analysis should help identify the ideal orientation of your home on the site to optimize solar and natural ventilation benefits. Orient for solar gain first, with the longer side of the home running along an east-west axis if possible to get the most out of the sun for heating in winter and daylighting year-round. Designing with the longer side running directly north-south provides the least solar benefit and, in fact, may lead to overheating and glare from low western sun. In many cases, especially in an infill situation or with challenging topography, you won't

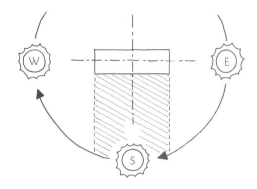

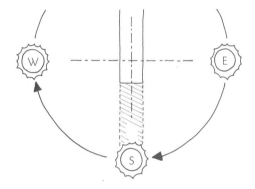

be able to orient exactly to the ideal, but the closer you can get the better. If summer breezes are in sync with an ideal solar orientation, that's super, but it's hardly typical. You can mitigate this by using vegetation and building extensions to scoop breezes and redirect them back toward openings in the building enclosure. Keep in mind that if your "breezes" translate into stiff winds from the north in winter, you'll want to mitigate this with smaller, energy-efficient windows. In an ideal situation, a site assessment takes place over a long enough period to experience the range of seasonal conditions; more often, however, you'll have to base climate analysis on historic

It's best but hardly typical for summer breezes to be in sync with an ideal solar orientation (top). If your situation is less than ideal, you can use vegetation and building extensions to scoop breezes and redirect them back toward openings in the building enclosure (bottom). ILLUSTRATIONS BY CHRISTOPHER GUTSCHE AND KATHLEEN SMITH.

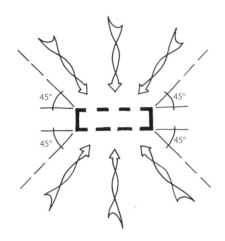

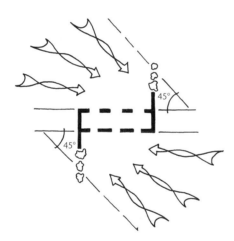

weather data and reports from the neighbors.

We provide a questionnaire here that you can use to identify opportunities (and problems) that will affect your new construction or remodeling project. Some conditions are observable; other information you may have to dig for. Records on your lot—which may be very detailed or not—are probably available at your town planning desk. You might need to hire a consultant to investigate some aspects, such as a geotechnical engineer to investigate geological conditions. If you're remodeling, an additional questionnaire in chapter 6 will help you gather information about the existing structure you intend to modify.

Site Analysis

Use this questionnaire to perform a site analysis for your new construction or remodeling project.

Natural systems

What would your site look like if no human had ever touched it? What would be happening there?

What biological activities are occurring there now?

Plant and animal communities: _____

Pattern of plant cover: _____

Wooded areas: _____

Specimen trees: _____

What biological activities off-site could affect your project?

Types, size, and area of vegetation: _____

Plant and animal communities: _____

What regional climatic conditions may influence the site?

Temperature: _____

Precipitation: _____

Humidity: _____

Cloudiness: _____

Sun angles: _____

Wind direction and speed: _____

What microclimate conditions exist on the site?

Breezes: _____

Solar access: _____

Air quality (outdoor): _____

Acoustics: _____

Precipitation patterns, including drifting patterns (for snow): _____

What does it feel like to be on the site?

Character and relationship of the space: _____

Special spots: _____

Viewpoints and vistas: _____

Odors: _____

Quality of the light: _____

Sounds: _____

What geological conditions exist on the site?

Soil types and depths: _____

Underlying geology: _____

Areas of fill or ledge: _____

Proximity to earthquake fault lines: _____

Rock character: _____

Aquifer recharge areas: _____

Site Analysis (continued)

What topographical conditions exist on the site?

Patterns of landforms: _____

Slope: _____

Unique features: _____

Wetlands: _____

What topographical conditions of adjacent land could have an effect on the site?

Trees and vegetation: _____

Slope: _____

Wetlands: _____

What water-related conditions apply?

Water bodies: _____

Drainage patterns: _____

Water table: _____

Water supply: _____

Floodplains: _____

Built structures

What human-made structures exist on the site? What is their condition and use?

Existing buildings: _____

Road and path networks: _____

Utilities: _____

Fences or walls: _____

What adjacent human structures have an effect on the site?

Existing buildings: _____

Road and path networks: _____

Utilities: _____

Fences or walls: _____

Coding, zoning, or other restrictions and standards

What uses are allowed on the site?

Are there special conditions that apply as a result of sensitive site conditions?

Are there height and bulk regulations?

Are there any easements or ownership issues?

Must you meet design standards and undergo a design review?

Does your jurisdiction have policies that preclude or encourage green alternatives?

- ❏ rainwater for household use
- ❏ composting toilets
- ❏ constructed wetlands
- ❏ Living Machines
- ❏ rain gardens
- ❏ bioswales

❏ active solar

❏ other

Does your jurisdiction provide incentives for green alternatives?

❏ expedited permitting process

❏ financial incentives

❏ credit for pervious surface

❏ credit for downspout disconnection

❏ other

Do local utilities provide financial incentives for energy or water conservation?

Is there a local program that sets voluntary green building standards for your project? Does your jurisdiction recognize this program in any way?

Neighborhood and beyond

Are there any positive or negative feelings the neighborhood might have about development of your lot (if it's not currently developed)?

What's the character of the neighborhood?

❏ mixed-use buildings

❏ mixed housing types

❏ rear alleys for cars

❏ number of garage stalls per home:

What's the typical market and appraised value for most homes in the area?

How easy is it to leave your car at home?

❏ walking/biking distance from mass transit

❏ walking/biking distance from grocery store

❏ walking/biking distance from bank

❏ walking/biking distance from library

❏ walking/biking distance from post office

❏ walking/biking distance from place of worship

❏ pedestrian/bike paths that connect to the outside community

How safe is the neighborhood?

❏ traffic-calming devices

❏ porches or "eyes" on the street

❏ safe and easy-to-use bike and/or walking paths

Is there any evidence of community support for sustainability?

❏ community garden

❏ nature trails

❏ interpretive signage explaining natural features

❏ active environmental group

❏ community center or outdoor gathering space (stage or plaza)

❏ parks/landscaping

Case Study:
The Peterson Residence (Pasco, Washington)

Our home is located in a semirural neighborhood in the Tri-Cities area of the Columbia Basin, at the convergence of the Columbia, Yakima, and Snake rivers. The region is arid, averaging less than 8 inches of rain per year, and is subject to extreme weather conditions, with weeks of 100-degree-plus temperatures in the summer, and subzero temperatures and some snow in the winter. We typically have more than three hundred days of sunshine a year. There's little native vegetation in the region, but since the large hydroelectric dam projects of the New Deal, this area has been cultivated into productive farming and agriculture. The relative lack of trees in the region, along with extreme temperatures, promotes large wind and dust storms, especially in the spring and fall. Sustained winds of 30 to 40 mph for twenty-four hours at a time aren't uncommon.

We chose our lot because it offers an economical view of the river, easy access to the park and boating on the river, and proximity to schools. Because of careful forethought by the subdivision's developer in the early 1950s, we enjoy an established, quiet neighborhood with little risk of sub-par construction coming in. Moreover, our lot was one of the last remaining undeveloped lots, so we could evaluate the quality of the neighborhood. As far as the potential for green building goes, the half-acre lot provided enough flexibility for us to capture river views, a good solar orientation, and an optimal relationship to prevailing winds on the property. We planned to build a 2400-square-foot single-story residence with a full basement. (The subdivision's sixty-year-old covenants prohibited two-story construction, as well as any outbuildings.)

This view of the 2400-square-foot Peterson home from the southwest shows the deep overhangs and covered porches used to minimize solar heat gain. The garage was sited at the left to buffer the house from the noise and views of a busy arterial. PHOTO BY KEITH PETERSON.

Although I work as a scientist at the Pacific Northwest National Laboratory, I chose to act as general contractor for the project, primarily so I could test the sustainable design theory I use at work in the real world of home building, as well as to address the fact that at the time there were virtually no local contractors specializing in green building. The cost of the project was less than $100 per square foot, comparable to conventional construction costs in Pasco at the time. We began construction in March 2003, and it took nine months to complete the project. Our goal was pretty straightforward: we wanted to prove that green construction could be available to everyone, not just the wealthy. Our theory was that through careful integration of the design we could achieve a truly green home that we could afford, and that proved to be the case.

A rule of thumb is that green construction will cost between 2 and 5 percent more than traditional construction. This might be true if green building means simply upgrading to environmentally preferred technologies and materials. However, our project proves that these cost upgrades can be reduced or even eliminated through integrated design. We did have to let go of some ideas that didn't fit into the integration scheme or our budget; a ground-source heat pump, for example, would have required a premium we weren't prepared to pay. In our case, integration began with site selection and continued through to the home furnishings. The result was a highly energy-efficient, comfortable, durable home with an Energy Star rating of 90.2 (out of 100, with 86 as the minimum required for Energy Star status), built by local contractors within conventional budgets. Integrated design principles were adopted in four aspects of the project: site and building design, construction technology, finish material selection, and function.

Site and building design

It's tempting to find a favorite house plan and try to adapt the site to the house. However, the wrong house plan can prevent large and essentially free energy efficiencies, as well as miss ways to connect the functions of the house with the community and the natural setting. Our design made possible these gains:

- maximized natural daylighting of interior spaces with skylights and solar tubes into central rooms and closets
- minimized solar heat gain by orienting the narrow side of the house to the south, locating all skylights on the east pitch of the roof, and providing deep overhangs and covered porches on the south and west faces
- maximized views from the living spaces
- used the garage as a visual and sound buffer against a busy arterial road

Construction technology

Many exciting new construction technologies are

Using ICF construction for the exterior walls of the house from the basement up (top) ensures that the hydronic radiant heating system (bottom) won't have to compensate for the air leaks that are more likely with traditional stick-frame wall systems. PHOTOS BY KEITH PETERSON.

available that can reduce environmental impact and save energy. The challenge is to select technologies that accommodate installation of the other building systems, are familiar to contractors, and won't put the building inspectors in a spin. For example, straw bale construction provides an excellent thermal and acoustical building enclosure but requires special adaptation for installing electrical systems and interior drywall, and permit approval is hard to obtain for this type of construction. These challenges can be overcome but they add cost, which we were trying to avoid.

We found insulated concrete forms (ICFs) to be one of the most integration-friendly, sustainable construction technologies being used today. ICFs are forms for poured concrete walls that are made of rigid foam. Typically ICFs are preformed interlocking blocks or separate panels connected with plastic ties. The forms are left in place to act as a continuous double-sided insulation of the concrete wall assembly. The ICFs also act as an excellent sound barrier, as well as a backing for drywall on the inside and for virtually any exterior finish of choice on the outside. The 2½ inches of foam on each side of the concrete wall is deep enough to accommodate plumbing and electrical lines without any special tools or hardware. The benefits of ICF construction grow when integrated with other green building technologies. High-efficiency windows and hydronic radiant heat provide energy savings on their own, but when integrated with ICF, the technologies work even better because they're not compensating for the built-in leaks of traditional stick-frame wall systems.

Another construction technology used in our project is PEX (cross-linked polyethylene) plumbing. PEX plumbing replaces traditional copper or PVC piping with a high-density, heat-and-cold-resistant, continuous and flexible plastic tubing. Using PEX plumbing means fewer fittings and hard corners in the plumbing system, allowing for faster installation, quieter water flow with less pressure drop, and fewer places inside the walls where the plumbing can fail and leak. PEX tubing is less reactive with the minerals in the water supply as well, providing for less scale buildup in the lines and cleaner, healthier water.

Finish material selection

With the many advances in technology and material supply networks, the most exciting thing about incorporating green materials is the growing number of choices that are comparable in price and quality to the less sustainable options. In many cases we found that the environmentally preferred choice was also the more durable and cost-effective choice and thus a perfect fit for our integrated, cost-conscious design. Cork flooring in the kitchen, for example, provides a highly durable and resilient, stain-resistant, warm, and comfortable surface underfoot and is a rapidly renewable harvested product. We also selected bamboo hardwood flooring, natural fiber carpeting, medium density fiberboard (MDF) for the baseboards and trim, fiber-cement exterior lap siding, and plastic lumber decking.

Function

Optimizing the function of a building requires integrating across all phases and aspects of the construction project. By designing multipurpose living spaces, sizing heating and cooling equipment to efficiently meet the typical demand, selecting low-energy dimmable lighting, and installing water-conserving fixtures and Energy Star appliances, we ensured that all aspects would work together to reduce the physical and environmental footprint of the building.

One last thing

The cost premium is often the primary reason cited for not using green building concepts. We wanted to prove that cost need not be a barrier

PEX plumbing allows for faster and easier installation, quieter water flow with less pressure drop, and cleaner, healthier water. PHOTO BY KEITH PETERSON.

to green building, and we did. But our project also demonstrated that there may be other challenges to overcome when you approach your own green building project, depending on your location. In our case, we had to make a special effort to find tradespersons knowledgeable about and willing to use green construction technologies. Also, given that the City of Pasco has a progressive building department that supports—even promotes—innovative construction technologies such as ICF wall systems and PEX plumbing technology, it surprised us to find that the city has an ordinance on the books that essentially requires large areas of lawn. This seems in conflict with a xeriscape (drought-tolerant) landscaping approach that would make better sense given the increasing reality of water restrictions and drought concerns.

The bottom line is that although building a green home is very achievable for a family on a budget, it still takes intent. For us, and probably for anyone else hoping for a truly green home, this means being alert to the opportunities as well as potential barriers. Now as we're living in our new home with the added comfort, quiet, security, and durability gained through green features, we can say it's worth it. ■

5: Green Energy Choices for the Northwest

REGARDLESS OF HOW WELL YOU DESIGN your home to reduce its energy requirements, some energy will be needed to fuel its operations. What form of energy will you use? If you're reading this book, no doubt you're already aware of the potential ramifications of this choice.

In your heart of hearts you may aspire to becoming completely energy independent using benign energy sources today, but most of us will have to work toward that goal in steps. Most obviously your financial resources will come into play to determine how fast you get there, but so will external forces over which you have little control. These forces affect not only the cost of a fuel but also whether it's even available. For the O'Brien-Cunningham residence, natural gas would have been the most efficient fossil fuel choice to fire the hot water heater, but it wasn't an option owing to the lack of natural gas infrastructure on Bainbridge Island.

If you can't go completely green today, the trick is to make fuel, design, and system choices now that allow progressively more benign choices in the future—a form of futureproofing your home. Because

energy independence may be the most significant benefit of a green home, we've devoted this chapter to a discussion of fuel choices to guide you in your thinking about design and systems.

WHAT ARE YOUR ENERGY OPTIONS?

Your energy choices for your home include generating power on-site from renewables (solar, wind, biomass, geo-exchange), importing fossil fuels (gas and oil), and importing electricity (which may be produced from renewables or not). Choosing what you actually use is an interactive process. The fuels practically available to you will influence the systems you install, and to some degree, your system preferences will influence the fuels you use. You also have the option of conserving, which is where we'll start.

Generating negawatts

Negawatts, a term coined by energy guru Amory Lovins, refers to the amount of energy you gain by not using energy, or by conserving. Forget the image of spending uncomfortable, damp winters wrapped in a heavy cardigan. That's not what this means. You

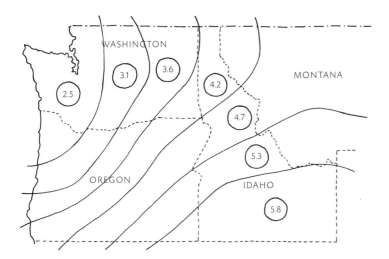

Although some locations in the Northwest gather more solar radiation than others (rated by the numbers shown on the map, with larger numbers indicating more radiation), there are no bad solar sites, according to Northwest energy planners. ILLUSTRATION BY CHRISTOPHER GUTSCHE AND KATHLEEN SMITH BASED ON DATA FROM THE RENEWABLE NORTHWEST PROJECT (1999).

can live quite comfortably by reducing your heating (or cooling) loads through an efficient building enclosure, providing some of your heating and cooling through good passive design, and installing reasonably energy-efficient operating systems to supplement what you gain passively. Regardless of what fuel you use to operate your household equipment, conservation is the greenest form of energy you can buy, and because you're investing in it today, you don't have to worry about price escalation.

Generating power on-site

The beauty of solar and wind energy—also a form of solar energy, since the sun's energy as well as the earth's rotation powers global and local wind patterns—is that the energy itself is free and has little or no negative environmental impact when you use it. Another benefit is that it's generally delivered right to your doorstep. The challenge with solar and wind energy is that they're not available all the time (with daily and seasonal fluctuations), so you need ways to store the energy or supplement it when neces-

sary. Solar and wind energy can be used directly as heat (passive solar heating, solar thermal collectors) or cooling (natural ventilation), or converted into electricity using photovoltaic (PV) panels or wind turbines. Now, before you assume that solar energy isn't really an option in the Northwest, think again. The Northwest receives more than enough sunlight to meet its entire annual power needs; even the cloudiest locations receive almost half as much solar energy as the deserts of California and Arizona (Renewable Northwest Project 1999).

Wood and other biomass is actually a stored form of solar energy—trees and plants store solar energy by using it to convert carbon dioxide and water into cellulose. Burning wood releases that solar energy as heat. Wood is a renewable energy source, since it can be replaced in a reasonable time, can be sustainable if it's harvested and used at the same rate as it's replaced, and is often available very close to your home, minimizing the impacts of transportation and transmission losses. It isn't the most user-friendly source of energy since it has to be cut, hauled, and split and is generally fed manually into the combustion chamber (woodstove) where the heat is generated. However, modern woodstove designs use compressed wood pellets fed from a hopper. Older woodstoves were considered a significant source of particulate air pollution with negative effects on both human and environmental health. In contrast, modern woodstoves, particularly those using compressed wood logs or pellets, can be a fairly efficient and clean source of heat.

Geo-exchange uses the naturally constant temperature of the earth (or in some cases, the

Until recently, storing electrical energy generated from the sun and the wind for later use meant homeowners had to install a bank of (generally toxic) batteries in the garage. Then along came the concept of net metering. Instead of storing surplus energy in batteries, you can let it flow through your main electrical connection into the grid for others to use—like making a deposit in a community bank account. When you need more than you can produce, you "withdraw" an equivalent amount of electricity from the grid at no charge. When you push energy into the grid, your meter literally turns backward; when you pull from the grid, the meter turns forward. You pay only if you use more than you produce, and you get credit at the end of the billing cycle for any net excess you produce—hence "net metering."

In Washington State, utilities are required to offer net metering on a first-come first-served basis until the input volume reaches 0.25 percent of the utility's peak demand in 1996. So far that hasn't been an issue, but with the growing interest in renewable energy systems, expect to see changes in these rules before long. Oregon has a similar law (with a "potential" cap at 0.5 percent of a utility's single-hour peak load), and utilities in Idaho and Montana offer similar programs.

bottom of a large body of water) as the primary energy source. It's accessed using a ground-source heat pump that uses electricity to move the heat from surrounding ground or nearby water into the house (or vice versa). The equipment uses a gas condensation/vaporization cycle, just like a refrigerator. This source of energy is more or less renewable as long as the system is properly designed; if the loops are too small for soil conditions, the surrounding ground can heat up or cool down to the point that the system loses its effectiveness. The renewable aspect of geo-exchange also depends on how the electricity is sourced, although electricity consumption is typically highly efficient. Ground-source heat pumps have a coefficient of performance (COP) greater than 1, meaning they put out more heat energy than they consume; this is because they use electricity to *move* rather than *generate* heat. The U.S. Department of Energy (2001) recommends using a ground-source heat pump with a minimum COP of 3.3; such a system would produce more than three times as much heat as a conventional electric resistance heater for every kilowatt hour of electricity consumed.

In a green urban remodeling project O'Brien & Company consulted on, the client chose to combine a geo-exchange system with a hydronic radiant heating system. The geo-exchange system has six loops—each 600 feet long, 300 feet down and 300 feet back up—drilled into the ground. The loops are filled with water, which in the winter circulates and picks up heat from deep in the ground and brings it into the house. The geo-exchange heat transfer process is reversed in summer, taking heat from the house and

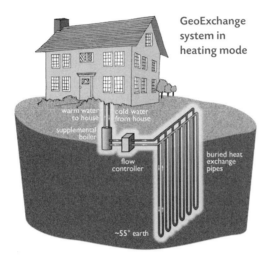

GeoExchange system in heating mode

This geo-exchange system has six loops—each 600 feet long, 300 feet down and 300 feet back up—drilled into the ground. The loops are filled with water, which in the winter circulates and picks up heat from deep in the ground and brings it into the house, and in the summer takes heat from the house and exchanges it for coolness in the earth. Supplemental heat is provided by a natural gas–fired boiler. GRAPHIC COURTESY OF O'BRIEN & COMPANY, INC.

exchanging it for coolness in the earth. While the system is in the heating mode, supplemental heat is provided by a natural gas–fired boiler, which does double duty as the source of hot water for showering and baths.

A newcomer to the fuel mix is biodiesel. This is a fuel oil product made from either recycled fryer grease—yes, the kind you find on your fingers after you eat french fries at your local burger joint—or vegetable oils from oilseed crops, such as soy, rapeseed, and hemp. While primarily being used as a transportation fuel at this point, it can be used as a replacement for fossil heating oil.

Importing fossil fuels

Nearly all the energy we have available to us to run our systems comes from the sun, the only source of energy for our otherwise closed global system. (Nuclear energy is an exception, as it's produced by splitting or fusing atoms to release energy.) Even coal, oil, and gas are a form of solar energy, but

they're not renewable. That's because they're the result of thousands of years of rich organic growth, followed by millions of years of heat and intense pressure, which is why they're called fossil fuels. They're compressed forms of energy in that they produce lots of Btus (heat value) per unit of material and are highly portable and inexpensive to extract. These are a few of the emerging problems with the use of fossil fuels:

Supply. Because we've made little effort to replace the fossil fuel we consume, many industry observers believe that we've reached, or are about to reach, the peak in production of oil, the most energy-rich and convenient of the fossil fuels; global oil reserves are 50 percent depleted and what remains will be increasingly difficult and more costly to extract (EnergyBulletin.net 2006). In addition, where we get our fuel from has become an increasingly significant issue. The United States is a net energy importer. In fact, we import almost 30 percent of our total energy demand (Werner, Lyman, and Jones 2005, 7), and because of its high portability all of our imported energy is fossil fuel. A lack of energy independence has been justifiably linked to an insecure present and an even more insecure future.

Cost. As supplies become constrained and demand continues to rise with growth, prices go up. Some forecasters say the price of oil, which as we write is around $70 a barrel, may reach $100 a barrel by 2010 (Lowry Miller 2006).

Side effects. We're only beginning to understand the environmental and associated human implications of taking billions of tons of carbon, stored over millions of years, out of the ground and releasing it back into the atmosphere (in the form of carbon dioxide) over a span of two centuries. Using the precautionary principle, which is the idea that it's better to be safe than sorry, it makes sense to look for alternatives.

There was a time when coal was a popular fuel for home heating. It was cheap and plentiful. It was also bulky to store and dirty to manage, and the pollutants resulting from inefficient combustion caused dramatic air pollution problems and enormous impacts to human and environmental health. Coal still provides significant amounts of energy in the Northwest, but you don't see it because it's combusted at coal-fired electric power stations. Nearly 40 percent of the energy delivered by Oregon's utilities is produced through coal combustion (Oregon Department of Energy 2003, 1); nearly 18 percent for Washington's utilities (Washington State Department of Community Trade and Economic Development 2006). This reliance on coal is expected to increase to service growing populations in the region.

Once oil was discovered and became widely available, it became the heating fuel of choice, but its appeal has also diminished because of storage, distribution, and combustion concerns, as well as its greater value as a transportation fuel and feedstock for plastic production. The fossil fuel of choice for home use is now gas—either natural gas delivered to the home via a pipeline or, where no distribution network is installed, bottled gas such as propane delivered by truck and stored on-site in a pressurized tank. Gas is clean burning and efficient. Costs vary by type; natural gas prices are regulated and natural gas

currently still offers more Btus per dollar than most other fuels, whereas propane is unregulated so price fluctuates with demand and can be expected to be at least equivalent to the price of electricity in the winter.

Importing electricity

Electricity is energy that has been converted or generated from another form, renewable or nonrenewable. Renewable forms of electric power include:

Hydroelectric power—electricity generated by turbines that are driven by water, which releases its energy as it falls under the influence of gravity.

Wind power—electricity generated by turbines that are powered by the wind, which is powered by solar income. At the time of this writing (2006), wind is among the most cost-competitive energy sources, renewable or nonrenewable, per megawatt of generation capacity.

Solar power—electricity (photovoltaic or PV) generated through a physical reaction that occurs when light from the sun hits photovoltaic materials such as silicon crystals.

Biomass energy—electricity generated through the combustion of biomass (wood, straw, and such) that grew by absorbing solar energy. This includes gasification, where organic materials are heated in an oxygen-free environment to prevent combustion, producing a hydrocarbon fuel in gas or liquid form.

Biodigestion power—electricity generated from the combustion of methane gas released as a by-product of the natural process of decay of organic materials that grew by absorbing solar energy.

2005 Washington State Electricity Utility Fuel Mix

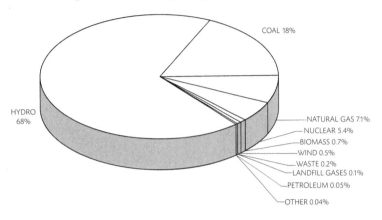

COAL 18%

HYDRO
68%

NATURAL GAS 7.1%
NUCLEAR 5.4%
BIOMASS 0.7%
WIND 0.5%
WASTE 0.2%
LANDFILL GASES 0.1%
PETROLEUM 0.05%
OTHER 0.04%

While it varies from state to state in the Northwest, the percentage of renewable hydroelectric energy available is generally greater here than in the rest of the country. The pie chart shows data on the electric fuel mix in Washington State in 2005 (Washington State Department of Community Trade and Economic Development 2006). Similar reports are available for most states in the region, although they may be based on different calculation methods.
ILLUSTRATION BY O'BRIEN
& COMPANY.

Nuclear fission, the current viable nuclear technology, splits uranium atoms to release energy, depleting a finite global supply of uranium. However, newer reactor technology known as fast breeder reactors can actually produce new reactor fuel (or nuclear weapons–grade material) while generat-

ing electricity, making it at least quasi-renewable. Increasing concern about climate change and looming energy deficits in many countries are stimulating new interest in nuclear energy, and the renewable label is being attached to it as a way of defining it as different from fossil fuels, with their associated climate impacts. However, the long-term threat of radioactive releases and the problem of disposing of waste that will remain highly toxic to life for millions of years are the as-yet-unresolved legacy of nuclear energy.

Nationally, the majority of electricity comes from nonrenewable fossil fuels. In the Northwest, a majority of our electricity comes from hydroelectric power stations. Due to regulatory mandates and/or self-interest, groups like the Energy Trust of Oregon and the Northwest Energy Efficiency Alliance are also taking steps to increase the percentage of renew-

GREEN POWER TO THE PEOPLE

Many electrical utilities are now offering "green power" programs, which enable you to ensure by paying a premium that all or part of your electricity effectively comes from renewable sources. Signing up for a green power program doesn't make any difference in the actual electrons that enter your home and power your appliances, but the premium you pay contributes to the development of new renewable generating capacity (such as wind farms and photovoltaic arrays) equivalent to the electricity you consume. This is a convenient

way to access renewable energy, costing only a few dollars a month for the average household. For many, it just takes a phone call to your local utility. Or you can buy Green Tags (which means paying your premium to a Green Tag broker rather than to your utility company) by contacting the Bonneville Environmental Foundation (see "Resources"). Green Tags cost about $25 per megawatt hour (1000 kilowatt hours)—that's between one and two months' worth of electricity for the average household.

able generation capacity through investment in wind farms, solar electricity, and other renewable methods.

From an environmental standpoint, electricity can be a good choice, but there are efficiency and economic questions to consider. Electricity is clean, healthy, and 100 percent efficient as a heat source at the point of use—1 kW of electricity used provides 1 kW of heat energy. Electrical systems generally have a lower first cost since there's no combustion equipment to install and distribution is by wiring, which is quick and easy to install. But electricity isn't cheap, because while it's efficient at the point of use, it's very inefficient from the point of generation. A fossil-fueled electric generating plant converts only about 33 percent of its feedstock energy into electrical energy. A new generation of gas-fired power stations using combined gas turbine and steam turbine technology can achieve as high as 65 percent to 90 percent fuel efficiency, but these represent a small percentage (6 percent) of U.S. generating capacity. Furthermore, as the electricity is transmitted over cables, more energy (approximately 9 percent in 2001) is lost as heat. So the electricity that comes out of the outlet in your home represents only about 31 percent of the energy that was available in the gas or oil or coal that was burned to generate it (U.S. Department of Energy 2006). By comparison, if you burn natural gas in a 90-percent-efficient gas furnace in your home, you get 90 percent of the energy in that gas as heat. From that perspective, using gas as your energy choice for space heating would seem to be a smarter choice economically and environmentally.

TO GRID OR NOT TO GRID

If your home is located in an urban or suburban area, it's likely to be hooked up to the grid, with access to utility-supplied electricity and/or natural gas. In general, living off the grid has been relegated to those building in remote rural locations, where the cost of connecting to a distant utility line is prohibitive. But now an increasing number of households are choosing to go off the grid even if they don't have to, to gain energy independence.

If your home is to be unhooked, your fuel choices will be driven by how much solar and wind potential you have on-site, and if you need to import energy, what you have available. Wood will most likely be less expensive but also less convenient, requiring more hands-on management. (And to maintain your green goals, you'll want to make sure it's coming from a sustainably maintained woodlot.) Propane and fuel oil will be more costly but more convenient, giving you access to systems and controls that will greatly decrease your level of active system management. Propane and fuel oil suppliers aren't regulated, however, so their prices are market-driven and fluctuate significantly with seasonal supply and demand, with generally painful implications for your pocketbook. On the other hand, most fuel oil systems can burn biodiesel, providing a renewable and almost carbon-neutral energy alternative, and one that's somewhat immune to the fluctuating fortunes of the fossil fuel business.

It's the nature of green design to think a little farther into the future. Let's take a look at the two most popular fuel choices in the Northwest as of 2006: natural gas and electricity.

Natural gas is an efficient, convenient energy source for domestic and commercial/industrial use. Consequently, demand for it is increasing rapidly. Reserves of natural gas are finite and not evenly distributed geographically. As demand increases and/or supplies diminish or become unavailable for geopolitical reasons, the price of natural gas will increase. In 2005, the Northwest experienced a 25 percent increase in the retail price of natural gas, resulting in a retail price of around $12 per MBtu (million Btus). Natural gas is supplied by regulated utilities, with pricing and security of supply and distribution controlled by regulators who are accountable to the public, not to the utility's shareholders.

Electricity is clean and efficient at the point of use, but the generation and transmission losses associated with a centralized generation and distribution system make it less efficient overall and more costly per unit of energy than natural gas. (In the Puget Sound region, electricity retails for about $20 per MBtu.) This makes natural gas look like a good economic choice in the near term. Electricity generated by burning fossil fuels will feel the same price increases as natural gas as fossil fuel production peaks and demand outstrips supply, and because grid electricity is less efficient than natural gas, its price may increase faster.

On the other hand, the rising cost of fossil fuels will increase the economic appeal of alternative, renewable forms of electricity generation, resulting in a shift toward more environmentally benign forms of electricity. This may give electricity both an economic and an environmental advantage over natural gas in the long term—but when will that happen? If you choose electricity as your energy source now, how long will you be paying higher electricity prices before the shift takes place? Good question! No one seems to have a good answer, though there are lots of opinions. Note that as of 2006, the cost of energy from electricity (in dollars per MBtu) was about equal to the higher wintertime cost of propane. The shift may be closer than you think.

Bottom line, we want to encourage you to move toward an energy independence founded on the use of renewables and, if necessary, the sensible use of nonrenewables. Here's a good, better, best scenario to use as you work your way to a dark green lifestyle:

Good. Start with conservation through good design and energy-efficient equipment utilizing the most efficient form of nonrenewable fuel available to your site. Design your home for future conversion to renewable forms of energy. Purchase green power through your electric utility or buy Green Tags.

Better. Do all of the above but supplement with supply from on-site renewable sources. The type of on-site source you use will depend on conditions specific to your site, and you should consult with a professional to determine which type is cost effective for you. (See "Resources" for wind mapping and renewable energy resources for the Pacific Northwest.)

Best. Your home uses on-site renewable sources to produce the same amount of energy it consumes over the course of a year, making it a net zero home. You might have to import energy at times, but your ability to export surplus energy balances the bottom line. Even better is to power your home entirely with on-site renewables. While you're at it, you might switch your gas-powered vehicles (cars, lawnmowers, and powerboats) to carbon-neutral alternatives as well.

FINANCIAL INCENTIVES FOR INSTALLING RENEWABLE SYSTEMS

Net metering, described earlier, gives you a financial incentive to install a renewable energy system. Other financial incentives that can help you offset the cost of installing your renewable energy system are also in place. These aren't likely to be permanent, so check with contacts provided in "Resources" to determine what's current. For example, benefits have included:

Federal. Systems brought on line in 2006 and 2007 received a 30-percent tax credit with a cap of $2000 for homes and no cap for businesses. The credits may be used in both years and solar hot water systems are also eligible. Most observers expect these incentives to be extended if budget resources allow.

Green Tags. When you install a solar photovoltaic system you can sell green tags. You can earn $0.05 per kWh from Cascade Solar Consulting for everything your PV system produces, which Cascade Solar will then sell as Green Tags. The program is expected to be available through 2010.

Canada and British Columbia. Canada offers

CARBON NEUTRAL: WHAT DOES IT MEAN?

A carbon-neutral home doesn't contribute to climate change, because it offsets CO_2 emissions in one or more of these ways:

Planting trees. Trees absorb carbon dioxide from the atmosphere and store the carbon for the life of the tree, a process known as carbon sequestration. Since trees grow rather slowly and can burn or die (especially as the climate changes and tree species find themselves in hostile environments), planting more trees isn't a solution we should rely on entirely. (It's not a bad thing to do, just not the whole enchilada.)

Purchasing off-site green power. If you support the purchase of a utility wind turbine or solar photovoltaic array that wouldn't otherwise have been installed, replacing the use of fossil fuels, this will reduce CO_2 emissions that would have been released by those fuels. This is a good thing to do and it's a little more efficient than planting trees, but, again, it takes a while to get green power infrastructure up and running.

Choosing on-site energy efficiency and renewables. You can do this right now. First, reduce the amount of energy needed to operate your home dramatically—by at least 50 percent. Then install renewables (solar hot water and/or photovoltaic panels) to supply your remaining energy needs, and then some. To actually offset carbon emissions you need to install more solar photovoltaic panels than you need so that the surplus can be run back into the grid.

---

several incentive programs for renewable energy systems. EnerGuide for Houses provides incentives based on the level of energy improvement of the home. Solar installations typically recoup from $50 to $100. British Columbia (BC) offers several programs as well. The Provincial Sales Tax Exemption allows for solar electric and thermal systems to be exempt from provincial sales tax when sold as a system. The

SolarBC Hot Water Acceleration Program can help homeowners obtain grants of up to $700 from Natural Resources Canada, as well as an additional rebate of $20 per gigajoule (GJ) from BC. (Only the first fifty applicants in BC qualify for the additional rebate.) A goal of the BC 100,000 Solar Roofs Initiative is to encourage the installation of solar heating panels on 100,000+ rooftops in the province.

California. Many California public utilities have rebate programs in place for residential and commercial PV systems. Contact information for all of them can be found in the Database of State Incentives for Renewables and Efficiency (DSIRE); see "Resources." It's worth mentioning two California State rebate programs: the Emerging Renewables Program (ERP) and the Self-Generation Incentive Program (SGIP).

The ERP provides incentives for several types of grid-connected renewable energy generating systems: PV systems ($2.60 per watt for systems less than 30 kW), solar thermal electric systems ($3 per watt for systems less than 30 kW), fuel cells using renewable fuels ($3.00 per watt for systems less than 30 kW), and small wind turbines ($2.50 per watt for the first 7.5 kW and $1.50 per watt for increments greater than 7.5 kW and less than 30 kW). The funding cap is $400,000 for any one site. Rebates for eligible renewable energy systems installed on affordable housing projects are available at 25 percent above the standard rebate level up to 75 percent of the system's installed cost.

The budget for the Self-Generation Incentive Program (SGIP) was increased by $300 million in December 2005. In addition, the California Solar Initiative (CSI) was approved in January 2006 to provide incentives for solar development of $2.8 billion over eleven years. The SGIP offers incentives for these technologies using renewable fuels: PV (Level 1), $2.50 per watt; wind turbines (Level 1), $1.50 per watt; fuel cells (Level 1), $4.50 per watt; microturbines and small gas turbines (Level 3-R), $1.30 per watt; internal combustion engines and large gas turbines (Level 3-R), $1.00 per watt. These incentives are offered for technologies using nonrenewable fuels: fuel cells (Level 2), $2.50 per watt; microturbines and small gas turbines (Level 3-N), $0.80 per watt; internal combustion engines and large gas turbines (Level 3-N), $0.60 per watt.

Idaho. Through 2011, Idaho will waive the sales tax on purchase and installation of PV equipment. The Idaho credit is available as long as the installed system produces at least 25 kW. The state also allows an income tax deduction of 40 percent of the cost of solar and other energy devices used for heating or electricity generation. Taxpayers can apply this 40-percent deduction in the year in which the system is installed and can also deduct 20 percent of the cost each year for three years thereafter. The maximum deduction in any one year is $5000 and the total maximum deduction is $20,000. In addition, the Idaho Department of Water Resources administers low-interest loan programs for energy-efficiency projects including solar. The interest rate is 4 percent with a five-year repayment term.

Montana. Montana gives a tax credit equal to the cost of purchase and installation of the alternative energy systems, not to exceed $500. The tax credit may be carried over to the next four taxable years. The state also offers low-interest loans for system installations and upgrades. Once a loan is approved, the applicant is told whether funds are currently available, and if not, when new funds are anticipated.

Oregon. Oregon gives tax breaks for a variety of solar applications. PV systems are eligible for a credit of $3 per peak watt with a maximum limit of $6000, up to 50 percent of the installed cost. (The maximum credit was increased from $1500 as a result of SB 31, enacted in September 2005.) However, the amount claimed in any one tax year can't exceed $1500 or the taxpayer's tax liability, whichever is less. Unused credits can be carried forward for five years. Solar space and water heating systems, wind systems, and fuel cells are eligible for a credit of $0.60 per kWh saved during the first year, up to $1500. Oregon's property tax exemption specifies that the value added to any property by the installation of a qualifying renewable energy system not be included in the assessment of the property's value for property tax purposes.

Washington. Through 2011, Washington will waive the sales tax on purchase and installation of PV equipment. The state also passed a bill in 2005 authorizing utilities to pay $0.15 per kWh for every kWh a solar and/or wind system produces from July 1, 2005, to July 1, 2014. This is voluntary on the part of the utility. If you buy an inverter manufactured in Washington, the $0.15 is boosted to $0.18 per kWh. If you buy PV panels manufactured in Washington, you can add $0.36 per kWh to the previous $0.15 or $0.18 per kWh. As of 2007 no PV panels are manufactured in Washington, but that could soon change. Check with your local utilities about additional offers; for example, Puget Sound Energy offers customers an up-front rebate for the cost of installation of $525 to $600 per kW depending on what county you live in, and Chelan PUD's SNAP program offers assistance to customers installing renewable systems.

> Greening your home is a process. The goal is not creating a perfect home, but creating a better home. Small steps and the right attitude can lead to big changes. Learn a little, do a little, laugh a lot, don't beat yourself up over what you can't get done.
>
> Jennifer Roberts, *Good Green Homes: Creating Better Homes for a Healthier Planet*

6: Planning a Green Remodel

HOW GREEN CAN YOUR HOME remodeling project be? The answer is very, very green. To start with, remodeling, by its very nature, generally represents a greener approach than building new, as it avoids consumption of the raw materials used to build an entire new home, as well as the land upon which it's built. On top of that, green gains can be realized by remodeling to increase energy efficiency, improve indoor air quality, and reduce water consumption. Making smart use of the existing structure is a dark green option.

Your remodeling project may be large or small. At one end of the spectrum, some who hope to shorten their permitting process will essentially call a teardown a remodel and will be able to do this thanks to idiosyncratic permitting regulations in some jurisdictions. If you're removing most of a structure (leaving perhaps a wall standing), you can take a green approach by deconstructing rather than demolishing; you'll find tips on that in this chapter. You get additional green points if you resist the temptation to expand your footprint when you rebuild.

At the other end of the spectrum, if you're plan-

ning a very small remodel, you might wonder if your project will have any impact at all on the environment, and if it's worth going the extra mile to make a bathroom, a utility room, or a porch green. We believe it is, not because any one project is going to by itself save the planet, but because each green project adds to the impetus for change. In the same way that one hybrid vehicle whirring quietly up the road won't stop the buildup of greenhouse emissions but lots of hybrid cars will, your effort will contribute to the greater good.

Whatever their size, remodeling projects are notorious for their surprises, so you'll want to ensure that you don't lose your green focus in the midst of an unanticipated crisis. This chapter discusses two major areas related to crisis prevention: budget planning and analyzing the existing structure. To demonstrate how green you can go with a remodel, the chapter also includes two case studies. Both are located in Portland, but they present very different circumstances. The Snyder residence is a fairly ordinary fifties ranch updated to a more contemporary look; the project was substantial and performed in

The Ziophirville remodel won Seattle's 2005 Built Green design competition. The owner, Ophir Ronen, is shown talking on his cell phone in front of the original building (left). The remodeled home (right) is designed to produce 75 percent of its energy in summer, 50 percent in winter. PHOTOS BY JIM BURTON (LEFT) AND MICHAEL MOORE (RIGHT).

one fell swoop. The Rivas-Scott residence is a historic home; improvements have been made over time, with its young householders living in it and performing a lot of the work.

PLANNING YOUR REMODELING BUDGET

Earlier we mentioned the axiom about remodeling being hard on relationships. There's another saw that most folks laugh at until they live it—that once you've figured out how much money you want to spend on your remodel and how much time you think it will take, you should double both numbers.

We can hear you thinking, "Ah, but my case is different; we'll plan so well that that doubling effect won't happen!" With a remodel, we can tell you that planning well includes doubling your initial budget and timeline. If you can't live with the new number, you need to look at what you really can afford. No matter what, if you go forward with the remodel,

we recommend that you include a healthy contingency line item in the budget (even if you just have it in your brain, but it's best to have it in your bank account).

Why so? Remodeling jobs can be planned well, but much more than with new construction they have a terrible tendency to suffer from scope creep. This is because with a remodel you deal with the constraints of an existing structure, as well as with the unknowns lurking within that structure, behind walls, above ceilings, and underground. We know of several cases where a remodel turned into a teardown because the frame of the house turned out to be rotten. The only original element used was the foundation.

With regard to setting a budget, conventional thinking is to avoid investing money you may not get back if you have to sell. According to the

National Association of Home Builders (2004b), real estate experts recommend limiting your remodeling investment to no more than 10 or 15 percent above the median sales price in the neighborhood. Yet homeowner Ophir Ronen reports he had no problem selling his remodeled home in the Capitol Hill neighborhood of Seattle for a price well above the neighborhood's typical market value one year after completion. This probably speaks for the selling power of both good-quality green design and "techie" features the Seattleite market appreciates. Ronen works in the information technology industry and invested approximately $175 a square foot for an energy-efficient, modernistic home that boasts green materials and showcases many sustainable building technologies, including whole systems monitoring, a solar array (PV and solar hot water), and wastewater heat recovery. Bottom line, if the home stands out in the neighborhood, it needs to stand out in a way that appeals to future buyers, so do your homework.

When you crunch the numbers, be sure to figure in the fact that moving to a new home costs money, too—about 8 to 10 percent of the value of your current home, not to mention closing costs and broker commissions, line items that have no direct impact on the greenness of your home, or the quality of the home at all (National Association of Home Builders 2004). You can also compare the intangibles of moving versus remodeling. If remodeling can cause enough stress to fracture relationships, so can moving. And beyond avoiding the environmental impact of building new, remodeling means that you don't have to give up a familiar

WHAT IF YOU RENT?

Understandably, there's far less incentive to make permanent improvements to your rented home or apartment than to one you own. However, if you have a fairly long lease, pay your own utilities, and have a good relationship with your landlord, you might be able to work creatively with the landlord to take these steps toward green:

- Identify energy improvements that are cost effective, including replacing old appliances and inefficient heating and/or cooling equipment with Energy Star models. (Actually, if the landlord pays the utilities, this might be an easy sell, but your benefit will be less tangible.)
- Identify cost-effective opportunities to replace old water fixtures with newer, more efficient ones.
- When you begin a new lease or renew an old one, negotiate upgrading interior finishes, such as carpet, paint, and resilient flooring, using healthier, resource-efficient choices.
- Replace outside landscaping with drought-tolerant options; instigate an integrated pest management program.
- If you live in a multi-unit building, negotiate a spot for a recycling center that includes a food composting option. Start a building-wide educational program with and for tenants in the building.
- If you live in a fair-sized apartment building with generous parking, negotiate a parking spot for a shared car or work on a policy of preferred parking for hybrid or electric vehicles and bikes.
- Even without the cooperation of your landlord, employ green cleaning products and equipment to maintain your home's interior. Educate your neighbors to do the same.

If you see additional ideas in this book that might make sense in your situation, don't hesitate to suggest them to your landlord, especially if you think he or she has a yen to go green.

Here are some things to look at when analyzing an existing home for a green remodel:

KEY STRUCTURAL ELEMENTS. What's the physical condition of key structural elements of your home? Is there evidence of major cracks, serious leaks, termite damage, and/or rot in the foundation, framing, attic, and/or roof? A building inspector will have a much more detailed checklist to assess these elements.

MAJOR SYSTEMS. What's the status of the major systems and features that determine your home's resource use and efficiency? Performance tests, such as the blower door and duct blaster tests mentioned in chapter 3, can also be useful in identifying common discomforts in an existing home.

Insulation—Are the walls, ceiling, and floor adequately insulated? Is the foundation insulated properly?

Air leakage—Does the envelope leak air where it shouldn't? Feel for drafts and look for damp spots where moisture might be condensing behind the wallboard. A blower door test by an experienced home performance contractor is the best way to check for air leakage.

Heating and cooling equipment—How old is the equipment? Is it cycling on and off frequently? What's the energy efficiency rating? If combustion appliances, are they drafting properly?

Air distribution (ducts and fans)—If you have a ducted system, how easy are the ducts to maintain? Are they leaky? Do they deliver enough heat where you want it? Can you feel pressure when you open a bedroom door when the furnace/air handler is running? Are the exhaust fans in the house so noisy you use them as little as possible? Do they seem to clear up steamy rooms effectively (in a few moments)? What's the energy-efficiency and sones (a measure of loudness) rating for the fans in the home?

There are ways to test the flow through a forced-air or exhaust register—check with your home performance contractor.

Appliances—How old are your kitchen and laundry appliances? Are they Energy Star qualified?

Fixtures—Do you have low-flow faucets, showerheads, toilets? Do they meet current standards? How old are they? How well do they operate? Are there wet spots around tubs, sinks, or washing appliances?

Windows and doors—Are they in good physical condition? Do you feel drafts near windows and doors? How much window area do you have on each side of the home? Could remodeling help open the home to a passive solar design?

FUNCTIONALITY. Does the home fit the way you live your life, providing sufficient functionality?

Room layout—Note the rooms you live in and the ones you hardly use, and consider why your life in the home takes that particular pattern. There may be rooms you don't need at all, such as that formal dining room you use maybe once a year. Does your pattern of use vary from season to season due to warm or cold spots, drafts?

Circulation—Take a few days to observe how you and your family travel around your home. Are there corridors you avoid? Are there rooms you don't use but would if you could get there easily?

Storage options—Are your closets so filled to the brim as to be useless? Alternatively, do you have half-filled closets? You might actually need the same amount of closet space in your remodel, just allocated a bit differently so that it can be used more efficiently. How much stuff do you have and how often do you have to access it? If access is seasonal, can you simply alternate between a more (closet) and less (attic) convenient storage space?

Privacy versus open space—Do you have sufficient hidey holes for you and members of your household? Are there places where household activities naturally blend and it would be fine if a wall didn't formally divide up by function? For example, does most of your visiting actually happen in your kitchen?

Display and furniture placement—Is the space arranged in such a way that you can't display your favorite art or piece of furniture and so it's sitting in a closet or the garage?

HEALTH CONSIDERATIONS. Is the home conducive to your health?

Natural light—Do you have to turn on the light during the day most of the year? How far does natural light penetrate into the home? (Do you see a connection between that and the areas you use the most?)

Views—Do you have any natural or distant views from your home? Either will lend a sense of well-being to household members.

Fresh air—When you come into the house after being out for a while, does it smell stale? Are there odors? Does it feel stuffy at night? During the heating season?

Asbestos and lead—Do you have any materials that could contain asbestos and lead?

Mold—Are there stains that indicate long-time leaks? Is there a mildewlike odor? Do people with allergies react after being in your home for a while?

neighborhood and familiar schools.

And one more thing. If you can avoid penetrations in your enclosure when you remodel, it generally keeps costs down (and can also avoid potential construction challenges).

ANALYZING WHAT YOU'VE GOT

If you filled out the initial needs analysis in chapter 2 and the site analysis in chapter 4, you've made a good start toward determining whether you can remodel your home and achieve the dark green goals of maximum personal benefit and lightest environmental impact, or whether, for you, building or buying a new home makes more sense. In the case of a remodel, the site analysis should be extended to include a very exacting analysis of your existing home. This analysis will help you identify problems as well as opportunities, and will provide you with a much better idea of what it would take to attain your green goals. The important thing to remember is that there will be problems; after all, remodeling is inherently a problem-solving activity. The question is whether they're resolvable within your budget and time frame, and whether the result will be as green as you want.

Assuming you're not a building inspector, you'll need to draw on the services of an experienced building inspector to conduct aspects of this analysis, including in particular a thorough examination of the physical condition of structural, electrical, and plumbing systems of your home. A home performance contractor can help you with energy systems, including equipment and building enclosure efficiency. If you have special health needs, you might

Remodels are an excellent opportunity to creatively use green technologies to solve conventional construction problems. Pin foundation systems, a means of minimizing disturbance on a site, are frequently used for new construction in sensitive locations (such as a shoreline). Here the system is used to support a deck addition. PHOTO BY GRACE HUANG.

also want to hire an indoor air quality specialist, sometimes called a hygienist, to look for conditions that might indicate a potential health problem and determine whether they're resolvable. (If they aren't, continuing to live in this home may not be appropriate for you.) Also, if you're planning an addition and the only way to do that is to go up, you'll need to ask a designer or engineer whether the home's existing structure would support such a change. Certain aspects of the analysis could require you to poke behind walls and under floors so may be appropriate only if you think you have a serious problem or know for sure you'll be opening up walls or floors as part of the remodel.

A qualified green remodeling contractor can help organize this analysis as part of his or her contract.

(How to find such a contractor? The green building projects and professionals listed in "Resources" for chapter 4 are a good place to start looking.) Keep in mind you'll still have an important role in the analysis itself, in that your daily observations about what is and isn't working in your home are an important part of the equation.

THINKING DECONSTRUCTION INSTEAD OF DEMOLITION

If you intend to remove most or all of an existing structure, you can take a green approach to its removal by deconstructing rather than demolishing it. Deconstruction is just what it sounds like, a reversal of the construction process. It differs from typical demolition in that for the most part it keeps building elements whole so they can be reused. Even if your remodeling project is modest, it can make sense to deconstruct the area you're remodeling rather than demolish it.

In chapter 3, we discussed the concept of design for disassembly (DfD). If this concept is adopted wholesale by the homebuilding industry, it should be easier to deconstruct homes in the future. For today, it's still an ambitious approach to take but definitely doable. (Recall that the original structure was deconstructed in the Scheulen residence case study in chapter 4.)

Here are some tips from Dave Bennink, a deconstruction consultant who has been involved in more than two hundred deconstruction projects (including roughly a hundred homes) in Washington and Oregon:

Do an inventory of materials to be removed;

identify those that can be used in your own building project and those that can be sold. Keep in mind that some items can't (and shouldn't) be reused for their original function because of code constraints. Examples include old toilets, inefficient fixtures, and single-pane exterior windows. In contrast, wood trim, flooring, interior doors, casework, and cedar siding are frequently worth salvaging. Some building inspectors frown on reusing dimensional wood for structural purposes unless an engineer regrades it, but the wood in older homes can be better quality than you can find on the market today.

Sell or give away items before you actually remove them, using the Internet or local waste exchanges; this avoids issues with storage and gives you a real sense of the market value of the materials in your area.

Deconstruction takes more time than demolition (although the process of deconstructing a home can be done in a week if planned well), which can affect your project schedule negatively. Reduce the differential by careful staging. For example, exterior siding can be removed while you're living inside the home. If asbestos abatement is part of the project, time the deconstruction to coincide with the abatement.

For materials that you don't plan to use or sell, consider free-cycling or donating to Habitat for Humanity. Find a place for everything you deconstruct, but don't try to deconstruct 100 percent of the building. The law of diminishing returns dictates that the last 25 to 30 percent or so won't be worth it. (But don't trash the remaining material either!

Major steps in this deconstruction project included removing vegetation for replanting elsewhere, removing the deck in large pieces, stripping the home of valuable materials, and (next page) processing those materials and hauling them away. PHOTOS BY DAVE BENNINK.

BEST PRACTICES FOR DEALING WITH LEAD AND ASBESTOS

Buildings constructed before 1978 may have interiors treated with lead-based paints, and those constructed before 1980 are almost sure to contain some level of asbestos. Homeowners actually aren't required to remove asbestos-containing materials or abate lead-based paint found in private homes. However, you may want to remove and dispose of these materials to avoid potential future problems. Hire an experienced contractor who will follow the best practices suggested by the EPA for removal and disposal of these hazardous materials.

For lead, this will include these measures:
- careful preparation of the space to avoid circulating lead-contaminated dust into the environment, generally, and in particular through forced-air systems
- limiting access to the workspace to workers dressed in protective clothing and wearing appropriately fitted and filtered respirators
- not using blasting or high-temperature tools to remove the paint
- ventilating properly if using paint strippers to remove the paint
- careful cleanup to avoid leaving traces of the hazardous material
- testing for lead dust contamination after cleanup
- disposal at a hazardous waste facility in accordance with regulations

For asbestos, these measures should be taken:
- posting the site with asbestos warning signs
- preparing double barriers of plastic sheeting at entrances to and exits from the work area, so one barrier is always in place
- protecting surfaces and nonremovable items in the work area with taped plastic sheeting
- limiting access to the workspace to workers dressed in protective clothing and equipped with appropriately fitted respirators
- preventing spread of dust and debris and keeping the area clean with industry vacuum cleaners fitted with HEPA filters
- before beginning work, disposing of all used heating, cooling, and ventilation filters at approved waste disposal sites (replacing the filters after the work is done)
- properly exhausting air from the workspace through a local, filtered exhaust system
- disposing of the asbestos at a hazardous waste facility in accordance with regulations

Recycle as much as you can.)

Hire a deconstruction company. Bennink says there are "not enough deconstruction contractors, but probably a dozen in the region." He considers it his job to "convert demolition contractors to deconstruction contractors." Experienced deconstructors have learned how to make the work economically feasible for them even though it's labor intensive and requires more equipment. They keep costs to a minimum with efficient operations and offset any premium that does occur through sale of salvaged materials. Their bid will depend on how much of the material they can resell and recycle, rather than dispose.

Case Study:
The Snyder Remodel (Portland, Oregon)

For more than twenty years, I've had a goal of retrofitting passive solar space heat into an existing home. When Phyllis and I married in 1998, I found a partner who not only agreed with the idea but was willing to help make it happen. Given our love of Portland and my involvement with the Sustainable Develop-

ment Commission of Portland/Multnomah County, we wanted to stay in the city limits and on the west side of the Willamette River.

As we looked for a suitable house, the first thing I did with any good prospect was to pull out my compass to check the home's orientation. The fifties-era ranch-style home we ended up buying had good bones, a great price, and an ideal orientation—the house faces due south with the lot sloping gently up to the north away from the street. It's also only six miles from downtown Portland and a few blocks from Lewis and Clark College. With a bit of planning we can go anywhere we want by bus. My neighbors are generally well established in life, but there are also a number of homes rented by students at the college and law school. The area is lightly forested. Thus the neighborhood is a vital and attractive place for us to raise our children.

The remodeling job lasted fifteen months and included renovating the 1800-square-foot existing house as well as building an 1150-square-foot addition to accommodate a new sunspace and a master suite. Our cost for the project was roughly $130 per square foot, including some high-ticket items and a rainwater capture and filtration system that provides us with our drinking water. The home features many green materials selected for their durability, earth-friendly composition (no to toxins, yes to recycled content), or local origin. But here we'll highlight three of my favorite aspects of the home: the passive

by Kent Snyder, owner

solar design, the rainwater system, and the smart use of the existing structure. Each aspect is an example of harvesting free resources.

Passive solar design

Our goal was to create a carbon-neutral home, meaning no fossil fuels are burned to create global warming CO_2. Photovoltaic panels will be installed in the backyard in the future. The electricity they'll generate is supplemented by green power we purchase from our local utility. The house is heated with a combination of passive solar and hydronic radiant floor heat. A high-efficiency air-source heat pump makes the hot water for the radiant system as well as the home's domestic hot water. For the radiant system, the hot water is run through flexible pipes installed in the floor under about 70 percent of the home.

Heat from the radiant system is augmented by passive solar heat that's captured in the new sunspace added to the south side of the home and that's stored in the space's concrete slab and stone finish floor. The thermal mass of the floor slowly releases the heat as it's needed. The warm air is transferred to the rest of the home by opening the interior sliding doors or with a ventilating fan. We don't expect overheating in the summer because of cross-ventilation provided by high windows installed in the sunspace to provide night flushing.

The Snyder kitchen showcases Paperstone countertops made with recycled paper, and cork floor tile. Walls are textured with Aglaia, a natural wall finish. Cabinets and woodwork are made with plantation-grown Lyptus; cabinet boxes are made from wheatboard. PHOTO BY WAYNE GODARE.

Drinking rainwater

We collect all the rain falling on the roof, an area measuring slightly less than 4500 square feet. We calculate that an inch of rain will yield about 2800 gallons of water. Most of the rain that falls on the roof of the house collects in the gutters and flows through the downspouts into an underground pipe that leads to the cisterns. However, some rain that falls on the house roof drains onto the garage roof and then flows out of an open air scupper and cascades like a waterfall into a dry pond bed below, creating an attractive water feature in the yard. From there the water collects into a standpipe below the pond which connects to the same underground pipe that the downspouts feed into. Before reaching the two 3000 gallon underground cisterns, the water passes through a filter which removes the large particulates like needles and sediment. When we turn on a faucet in the house, the water is pumped from the cisterns through a three-stage filtration system (20 micron, 5 micron, and UV sterilization)

Rainwater is stored in two cisterns totaling 6000 gallons that are hidden underground. PHOTOS BY WAYNE GODARE (LEFT) AND ANDREA NELSON (RIGHT).

and into the home's plumbing system. Rainwater is turned into drinking water and it tastes great! When we turn on the irrigation system outside, the water flows directly from the cisterns to water the plants, bypassing the three- stage filtration system.

Given the amount of storage we have and all the water conservation features incorporated into the house—including dual-flush toilets, low-flow fixtures, hot water recycling, water-conserving washing

When the Snyders turn on a faucet in the house, water is pumped from the cisterns through this filtration system (20 micron, 5 micron, and UV sterilization) and into the home's plumbing system. PHOTO COURTESY OF PORTLAND OFFICE OF SUSTAINABLE DEVELOPMENT.

machine and dishwasher, and drought-tolerant landscaping—we may be able to live on rainwater alone. The challenge will be in the dry summer months. If needed, supplemental water is provided by the city.

When the cisterns are full, a pipe at the top carries excess water to an infiltration pipe buried deep in the soil along the back of the garage. There the water flows out and recharges the aquifer. Any remaining water flows into a daylit bioswale where it collects and slowly seeps into the soil and recharges the aquifer. Permeable pavers used in the driveway also allow rainwater to stay on-site and recharge the aquifer.

Harvesting materials

All the bones of the original house remain. We harvested materials and reused as much as we could. We took the nails out of the lumber, used the old shiplap siding for all sorts of things, and turned the old cedar siding over with the unfinished side out (which looks fantastic, by the way). We donated anything useful or of value to the ReBuilding Center. We estimate that at least 50 percent of the materials removed from the house were reused in the project and 25 percent were donated.

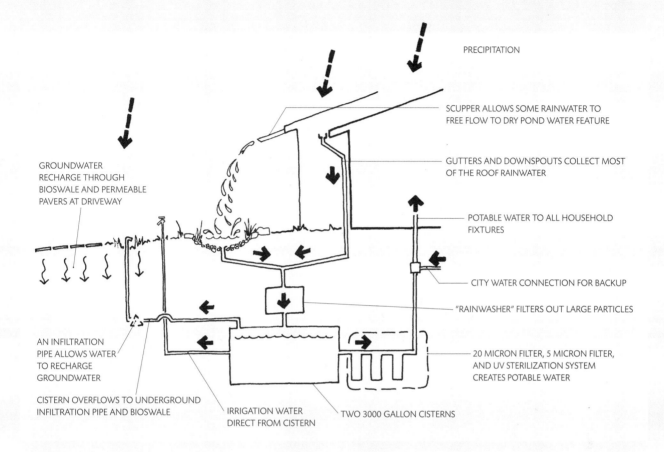

PRECIPITATION

SCUPPER ALLOWS SOME RAINWATER TO FREE FLOW TO DRY POND WATER FEATURE

GUTTERS AND DOWNSPOUTS COLLECT MOST OF THE ROOF RAINWATER

POTABLE WATER TO ALL HOUSEHOLD FIXTURES

CITY WATER CONNECTION FOR BACKUP

"RAINWASHER" FILTERS OUT LARGE PARTICLES

20 MICRON FILTER, 5 MICRON FILTER, AND UV STERILIZATION SYSTEM CREATES POTABLE WATER

GROUNDWATER RECHARGE THROUGH BIOSWALE AND PERMEABLE PAVERS AT DRIVEWAY

AN INFILTRATION PIPE ALLOWS WATER TO RECHARGE GROUNDWATER

CISTERN OVERFLOWS TO UNDERGROUND INFILTRATION PIPE AND BIOSWALE

IRRIGATION WATER DIRECT FROM CISTERN

TWO 3000 GALLON CISTERNS

Was it worth it?

It's always more challenging to work with an existing structure than to start with a clean slate. I don't think the costs of incorporating green features into a remodel are any greater than one would find in building a new house. The challenge was taking the time to think through how to incorporate systems into the structure so we would end up with an integrated whole.

The environmental challenges we face over the next few decades won't be solved by building new housing for our entire population. If we're really going to solve these problems, we must radically improve our existing housing stock. I wanted to see how practical it is to do so. So far, I remain optimistic. ■

This schematic diagram shows the rainwater catchment system in the Synder house. All rain falling on the garage and house roofs is collected either in downspouts or a dry pond bed in the yard. The water runs through a primary filter to remove large particulates and then is stored in two underground cisterns. When a faucet is turned on in the house, the water flows through a three-stage filtration system to become drinking-quality (potable) water. An infiltration pipe and a bioswale allow overflow from the cisterns to stay on-site and recharge the groundwater below. Permeable pavers at the driveway and abundant vegetated area throughout the yard round out the project's holistic approach to stormwater management by also allowing rainwater to stay on-site and recharge the groundwater. ILLUSTRATION BY CHRISTOPHER GUTSCHE AND KATHLEEN SMITH.

Case Study:
The Rivas-Scott Remodel (Portland, Oregon)

My wife, Ana, and I bought our first and present home in 1991, a little more than a year after we were married. It's a historic home located in southeast Portland, two miles from downtown in the Brooklyn neighborhood, surrounded by a mix of other historic homes and modern single-family houses, duplexes, and small apartment buildings. Our 870-square-foot Victorian cottage was built in 1904 and had suffered several previous remodels that compromised its historic features. But its long, skinny profile attracted us because of the quality and quantity of natural light available on cloudy winter days.

The home's 19-foot-wide front façade faces a tree-lined street to the west; its long sides face side yards to the north and south on a 40-by-100-foot midblock lot. Two bedrooms and a bath are located on the north side of the house, with the main living spaces along the south and west sides, all sitting atop a full unfinished basement accessed from the outside. Trees block the hot afternoon summer sun, keeping interior temperatures comfortable.

Like many remodels, ours has taken place as a series of improvements, some simple and small, some pretty significant, starting in 1993. The biggest change occurred in 2000, when we significantly remodeled 160 square feet and added 150 square

The Rivas-Scott remodel made the front façade more inviting and changed the roofline on the long side of the house to maximize southern exposure for solar hot water and photovoltaic systems. PHOTOS BY ALAN SCOTT.

by Alan Scott, AIA, LEED AP, Green Building Services, Inc.

feet, a covered back porch, and a new heating and ventilation system. We also made modifications to allow for the future installation of a photovoltaic system on the roof, and a rainwater cistern in the basement. This particular project took about five months and cost approximately $180 per square foot. We estimate it added at least 40 percent to the value to the home, so it was an excellent long-term investment.

We were able to take advantage of several financial incentives, including an Oregon state tax credit for 66 percent of the cost of the solar hot water heater that I installed myself, and a grant of approximately $3000 from the City of Portland Office of Sustainable Development in exchange for supplying information for a project case study and for participating in the city's Build It Green tours. We also received approximately $660 in incentives and tax credits from Northwest Natural (our natural gas supplier) and the State of Oregon toward the new gas water heater component of the radiant heating system (reducing the system cost by 8 percent); an approximately $11,700 incentive from the Energy Trust of Oregon and a $1500 tax credit from the State of Oregon paid more than 50 percent of the cost of the PV system.

As a family, we place a high value on the environment and on protecting the heritage and beauty implicit in a historic home. We want our two young daughters to grow up in and enjoy a home that's true to our values—not large by American standards, but comfortable, healthy, and beautiful. In addition, as an architect specializing in green design, I welcomed the opportunity to get hands-on experience with innovations that a growing number of my clients are interested in, and to do so within the constraints of a

A hydronic radiant heating system was installed under the existing wood floor. Copper tubing and heat transfer plates were stapled to the bottom of the subfloor. PHOTO BY ALAN SCOTT.

historic remodel. (To be sure, it wasn't all hands-on; we had some help with the 2000 remodel from Paul Gardner and Kris Charlson of Craftsmen Unlimited.)

Although we employed a range of green techniques, the bulk of home improvements have focused on improving the building's energy efficiency while improving air quality, reducing water consumption, and using wood wisely.

Energy efficiency and air quality

For energy efficiency and air quality, we started with simple things like buying compact fluorescent bulbs and adding cellulose insulation to the exterior walls, blown in through holes drilled in the shiplap wood siding. Later we installed insulated low-E

replacement sash in all the existing double-hung windows and replaced one window in the central room on the south side of the house with two new windows to increase daylight and sun tempering.

Although the shape and orientation of the house made it well suited for a passive solar retrofit, the small floor plan and our interest in preserving the historic character of the house presented challenges. To create a truly passive solar house, I estimated that I would have to double the number of south-facing windows and sacrifice limited floor space in the already small living areas to add sufficient thermal mass. So while I can't say the house is truly passive solar, I can say that we never need to turn on a light anywhere in the house during daylight hours, even for reading on a cloudy day, and on cold clear winter days (yes, we have some in Portland) the thermostatically controlled heat stays off from midmorning until after sunset.

As part of the 2000 project, we removed the old, noisy, inefficient gas furnace and ductwork and had a hydronic radiant heating system installed under the existing wood floor. The system includes PEX tubing for hot water supply and return with copper tubing and heat transfer plates stapled to the bottom of the subfloor and a 30-gallon, 94 percent efficient, condensing gas water heater that provides both space heating and domestic hot water.

We had radiant panels installed behind the wainscot in the bathroom, adjacent to the old claw-foot tub, to provide additional comfort. A solar hot water heater installed in 1995 on the south-sloping roof preheats water supplied to the gas water heater. The addition created more south-facing roof surface, allowing for the installation of a 3-kW grid-tied photovoltaic system in 2004. Over the years, we've systematically weather-stripped, caulked, and sealed the envelope of the house, significantly reducing unwanted infiltration and heat loss. In the 2000 remodel, an energy recovery ventilator (ERV) was installed in the attic to introduce tempered fresh air to the house while removing CO_2, pollutants, and moisture.

Saving water indoors and out

We also wanted to save water indoors and out. Indoor water consumption was significantly reduced in 2000 when we installed low-flow faucets and shower heads and dual-flush toilets. We're currently undertaking an ambitious landscaping project to further reduce our water consumption while getting some additional benefits such as habitat for urban wildlife and food self-sufficiency. As part of that project, we're removing existing invasive and water-loving plants from the yard and replacing them with native and drought-tolerant plantings.

We're also disconnecting our downspouts from Portland's combined sewer system and directing them instead to new swales where rainwater can be infiltrated and treated naturally. The new basement under the addition was designed to eventually hold a 2000-gallon rainwater cistern. Once this is installed, we'll use rainwater to irrigate our organic garden and fruit trees.

Treating wood like it's special

A goal for the project was to use as much salvaged wood as possible. This effort began with care-

ful deconstruction to preserve existing siding and studs for reuse. The contractor used the ReBuilding Center as a primary source for salvaged wood materials including concrete formwork, framing, and interior and exterior trim. We purchased salvaged cedar from a pier deconstruction in Tacoma and had it remilled as new siding to match the historic cladding of the house. In the end, more than 60 percent of the wood for the remodel came from salvaged sources.

The 2000 remodel was also an opportunity to employ advanced framing techniques for the new exterior walls, improving energy efficiency while reducing new wood consumption. Most of the new wood we purchased for the project was FSC-certified. ■

Where wood from the original structure could be reused, it was. Here, studs salvaged from the demolished exterior walls are being used to frame interior partitions. PHOTO BY ALAN SCOTT.

This thing called environmentalism is not new and not left-wing whacko. Though religious conservatives prefer to call it "creation care," it's the same thing. It is an apolitical extension of a very long progression—and the right thing to do.

Ray Anderson, keynote address,
Second International Conference on Gross National Happiness, 2005

7: Purchasing a New Green Home

IF REMODELING YOUR EXISTING HOME isn't appropriate and you can't afford to buy land and have a new home built, you still have options. Here in the environmentally minded Northwest, we're quite fortunate in that finding a green home on the market has become increasingly possible. Purchasing a green home still takes some care, however. This chapter provides some general guidance as well as tips specific to purchasing a spec, production, or existing home.

As an example of what you might find on the market, the chapter includes a case study of the Built Green Idea Home, a home built by production builder Bennett Homes in Issaquah Highlands, Washington. Because it was intended as an educational showcase, it's not exactly a standard model, but it isn't a custom home either. It's also an example of a home located in a community focused on providing "green living."

AN OVERVIEW OF GREEN HOME BUYING

If your choice is to buy a new green home or a home that has the potential to become green, you have these options:

Find a builder who builds green homes speculatively. Spec builders construct homes on land they own without a particular buyer in mind. Spec homes generally have a custom feel and include signature features the builder is known for.

Buy a home from a production builder who offers green features. Production builders also build without a particular buyer in mind. However, they tend to use stock plans, generally offering several plan choices with a variety of options.

Find an existing home that's been built or remodeled by its owner, or can readily be remodeled, to meet green standards.

Consider buying a green condo. Condo developments such as The Vineyards on Bainbridge Island, Washington, are cropping up around the Northwest. Although this was a speculative project, the developers believed there was enough market interest to include many sustainable features, including sensitive site development, green materials, energy efficiency, and solar power.

At The Vineyards, the cottages on the right and the townhomes on the left are Energy Star certified. Eight penthouses (center) have been wired for PV solar, and at least one penthouse buyer is installing a rooftop PV system. The entire project is qualified under the Built Green program in Kitsap County. PHOTO COURTESY OF THE VINEYARDS.

The starting point for thinking about purchasing a green home is the same as for building or remodeling: determine your needs and goals. A purchased home may not match your needs perfectly, but knowing what your needs are will help you determine what's a match and what's an acceptable compromise. Use the initial needs questionnaire in chapter 2 to give you a good foundation for house shopping. The discussion in chapter 3 about purpose can also provide help in setting your green priorities.

If you're thinking about buying a production or spec home, you'll be dealing with a builder or a builder's sales staff. Just as an increasing number of Northwest custom builders and remodelers are incorporating green into their building designs, a growing number of production and spec builders are building green. As with most things, however, some will do a better job than others. It pays to take a good hard look at green building claims and what's

behind them. You can adapt the project team questions from chapter 4 to interview spec and production builders regarding their level of interest and experience in green building.

When you get serious about a particular house, request a list of the green features installed in the project. If the home has been qualified in a green home-building certification program, a checklist of such features should be available. If the home's green features have been independently verified (a service offered by some builders), that's a very good sign of a serious commitment. Performance verification is available through some local green building programs, as well as LEED for Homes, Energy Star Northwest, and the building science–oriented Environments for Living. Find out how well the home scored in the rating system used.

If you're planning to buy in a subdivision and have a choice of lots or are purchasing an existing home, use the inventory of existing conditions in chapter 4 to determine if the site is suitable for things you have your heart set on—features that depend on lot orientation, solar access, soil types, and/or the way water behaves on (or under) the site. These circumstances could significantly affect the practical application of passive solar design, natural ventilation, and rain gardens, for example. It's a little-known fact that many builders "meter" the release of lots, with the worst lots being released first. If you want one of the best lots in a particular development, you may have to wait. Of course, lot pricing directly correlates with quality.

To gather some information, such as soil and water conditions or the location and condition of underground utilities, simple observations won't be enough. In the case of a production or spec home, you should be able to get details from the builder or sales rep. For existing homes, you might need to consult the as-builts (ideally the homeowner will have them on file) or any documented tests kept on file (if the home was permitted in recent years), or to hire someone to perform tests relevant to your particular green goals.

If you're planning to purchase a home in the hopes of adding green features some time later, keep in mind that some things will be harder to do as a retrofit than others. Swapping out an appliance is easier than replacing carpet; pulling up carpet and replacing it with ceramic tile is generally easier than upgrading insulation. If you have the option of including a hard-to-retrofit feature now, as might be true with a production home offering upgrades, it might be better to delay something else that can more easily be retrofitted. Be sure that the deferred modification you're hoping to make is even allowable. An existing (site) conditions inventory should turn up any restrictions (covenants, jurisdictional limits) that could prohibit your hoped-for modification.

When you get to the point of negotiating the purchase of an existing home, you should employ the same level of analysis suggested in chapter 6 for evaluating an existing home for a green remodel. If the current owner claims the home has been independently verified to meet green building standards, ask for documentation.

When you make the final walk-through before taking occupancy, be sure to get all the information available on any systems or features in the home, green or not, visible or invisible. Suggestions for what you should get in a walk-through are included in chapter 3.

WHERE CAN YOU FIND GREEN HOMES?

One way to more easily find new homes that are green is to look for new green communities. Essentially these are entire new developments that have employed techniques to create more walkable, livable townlike environments and have used more sensitive methods to create their lots and build their roads and other infrastructure. This generally means more clustered home sites, a variety of services on-site (such as a small grocery store, a coffeehouse, or a public school), wooded or otherwise vegetated open space, constructed wetlands (as opposed to a big detention pond) to treat storm water, bike paths or walking trails, and connections to mass transit. Truly committed developers may certify their project under a local program such as Built Green Communities or the national LEED's Neighborhood Development Rating System. Both programs evaluate developmentwide techniques and integrate with sister programs that evaluate residential buildings.

Another way to find a new green home is to take advantage of green home tours that are occurring more and more around the Northwest. Folks planning these tours—such as the Northwest EcoBuilding Guild, Solar Washington, the City of Portland, and home-building associations with local Built Green programs—tend to combine physical and virtual technologies in order to get as many examples out there as possible. Frequently homes on these tours

Nora Daley-Peng and Tien Peng found their new townhouse (on the right) when they went on a tour of winners in the City of Seattle's Built Green design competition.
PHOTO BY TIEN PENG.

are for sale, or at the very least provide an opportunity for you to see green homes in the flesh and learn about the builders who constructed them. For example, Nora Daley-Peng and Tien Peng put an offer on a new townhouse when it was on a tour as a winner in the City of Seattle's Built Green design competition. It was one of four units developed by Greenleaf Construction on a city lot previously occupied by a single-family residence. A move from the suburbs to the four-star Built Green home reduced the couple's ecological footprint (which they calculated using the ecological quiz at www.myfootprint. org) from 21 acres to 9.

A third way to find a green home is to contact organizations sponsoring green home-building programs in your area. Participating green home builders are usually listed on the Web sites of such programs and are often hot linked to such sites. See the list of green building program resources under chapter 1 in "Resources."

TIPS ON BUYING A SPEC HOME

A spec home is frequently a one-of-a-kind (or at least a limited edition) house. If it's dark green, it's highly responsive to the site and includes many of the features discussed in this book. It's the rare builder who will build a spec house that's dark green, though, as he or she is risking putting a house on the market that may not sell. Still, we do know of spec builders who have attempted this. In some cases, their homes were snapped up immediately; in other cases, the homes languished on the market.

In general, spec home builders who employ green measures are slightly more modest in their approach than they would be if they had a client demanding green. To determine what they've actually achieved and whether they're qualified, you can ask questions very similar to those suggested in chapter 3 for interviewing your designer or contractor. You'll want to cover the basics by checking with past clients, the Better Business Bureau, and the local contractors' association.

What you want to avoid is being a guinea pig. Is this the first green home they've built? If they installed innovative systems, did they rely on the help of experienced consultants? If so, who did they work with? If they've installed special systems or products, can they provide you with product information and company contacts you can interview? This is especially important if they're boasting about an expensive and innovative heating or cooling system—you'll want to talk to folks who've had those systems installed and have firsthand experience to share.

Depending on a production builder's commitment to green building, the line between what's offered as part of the standard package and what's offered as an option or upgrade will move. For example, a production builder might simply build homes to meet Northwest energy code minimums (which, when compared to minimums in most of the rest of the United States, aren't all that bad), offering higher insulation levels or more energy-efficient windows as an upgrade. A more aggressively green production builder might build homes beyond energy code minimums but pass on getting the homes certified under the Energy Star program, which requires verification and performance testing. A third, even more ambitious production builder might get all homes Energy Star certified. Frequently, green production builders will offer Energy Star appliance and heating equipment options, as well as material upgrades that include green alternatives.

As an example, Quadrant Homes, one of the top ten production builders in the Puget Sound region, participates in the Built Green program and is certified to build Energy Star–compliant homes. Quadrant offers energy upgrade packages including higher efficiency furnaces, extra insulation, and Energy Star appliances. The company is particularly known for its highly resourceful use of wood.

Minimally, you'll want a production builder who understands and complies with local green codes,

This three-star residence from Quadrant Homes is located in the Snoqualmie Ridge development in Snoqualmie, Washington, notable for its clustered layout, preservation of open spaces, and convenience to retail, schools, and other services. PHOTO BY SCOTT MANTHEY, COURTESY OF QUADRANT HOMES.

such as existing energy-efficiency, indoor air quality, and water-efficiency standards, and surface water management requirements. Although it's rare for a large production builder to attempt to skirt these standards, the fact is that these codes are sometimes not met. In a study of whole-house ventilation systems conducted in Washington State, fewer than half of the thirty-one homes evaluated met prescriptive or performance requirements. The study speculated that the requirements, particularly those having to do with systems integrated with forced-air heating, were "widely misunderstood" (Devine 1999, 1).

Municipal building inspectors expected to pick up errors in the field are strained to the limit with increased workloads and reduced staff. Builders must rely on a labor market that's tapped and frequently less skilled than desirable. Pressure to build quickly to take advantage of interest rates or other factors adds to errors in the field as well. If a production builder has a good quality assurance (QA) program in place, this is less likely to happen, so you might inquire about this.

A production builder who advertises a green approach should, besides meeting green building codes, meet these expectations:

- values durability and pays special attention to construction details that could affect the quality and longevity of the home
- doesn't use interior finishes that can make you sick, such as paints with high VOC levels
- installs a ventilation system that will perform satisfactorily in all seasons
- doesn't use exotic materials from far away when there are good local equivalents
- offers upgrades to increase the home's energy and water efficiency, healthfulness, longevity, and environmental sensitivity

A visit to the builder's sales center should reveal if the builder is participating in a green builder program. Ask for detailed information on the green features included in the homes as standards, and investigate offered options. Compare this list to the kinds of features described in chapters 8 through 11 of this book, or those on a green building program checklist.

You may be disappointed by the kind of information you get from home sales information centers. Although some of the more dedicated real estate professionals in the region have taken an interest in green building, many are intimidated by the topic and haven't educated themselves about the specific green features in the homes they're selling. We've seen communities where even though builders include selected green features as a matter of course, these features aren't adequately described by sales professionals nor even listed in sales literature. This is truly a missed opportunity, for the industry and for prospective homeowners. We believe this will change if homebuyers aren't afraid to ask questions. Don't rely on general claims that a home is "energy efficient" or "healthy." Press for more details to learn how the home was built to achieve these attributes. If consumers want to know, the home sales industry will respond. It's their business.

Don't hesitate to ask builder representatives to review model plans and specs with you, identifying green features in the documents. This can help you determine how well green building claims translate into design details. For example, a home may have natural light, but a plan will show you how much. Looking at the plans and specs can also help reveal whether the house design is adaptable and can be "greened up" with a future remodel.

If the builder's representatives are genuinely committed to serving you and to promoting green alternatives, they should be able and willing to work with your current budget to determine how green you can go now, as well as to point out opportunities for future upgrades that make sense and that are allowable in that location. When negotiating the budget with a builder's sales representative, make sure standard costs are deducted before adding in costs for an upgrade. If you choose linoleum over standard vinyl in the bathroom, for example, the price should reflect the difference. This seems obvious, but maybe not in the midst of negotiations on the biggest purchase of your life.

If you're looking at owning a home for the first time, or if locating in an established community appeals to you, you'll be looking at the existing home market. With green building gaining traction in the Northwest, we now have the happy phenomenon of finding green options in the resale market. Because green features tend to maintain value, this means the homes may cost a little more than their nongreen neighbors. If you do the math, however, you'll generally find that the additional cost is lower than if you were to custom build a comparable home and that long-term savings—as well as the prospect of a comparatively higher resale value if you need to move—makes the premium well worth it.

Interest among real estate professionals in supporting the green building movement is on the rise. As a result there are individuals within large regional agencies—as well as entire small agencies—who now specialize in brokering green homes. If you want to make sure this interest is soundly based, don't be afraid to quiz prospective agents as to whether they've gotten any training on the topic. The Sustainable Development Training Institute, a division of O'Brien & Company, offers training to real estate professionals who want to become knowledgeable in this area. In general, we find participants in the classes highly committed to green building for personal reasons, and that's the best kind of commitment there is.

An encouraging development in the existing home market is that real estate professionals and home lenders in the Portland and Seattle metro-

GREEN MODULAR HOMES

Modular homes are built in a factory. The modules are shipped to your site, bolted together on your foundation, and finished on-site. These factory-built homes must comply with local codes and regulations, unlike "manufactured homes" (the single- and double-wide homes that often come with their own wheels attached), which are built to the national Housing and Urban Development (HUD) code.

Building a home in a factory generally reduces site impacts, minimizes material waste, and can result in a tighter, better constructed home. The controlled environment of a factory keeps materials clean and dry, and eliminates climate, labor, and other variables that can lead to schedule delays. Several modular home designers and builders are leveraging the efficiency and controlled environment of factory production to incorporate more green materials and green features into their homes. (See "Resources.")

Because of these efficiencies, rather unconventional designs can be priced comparably to conventionally designed homes. Lead times can be long, however, as there are just a few companies combining modularity with green. If you want anything but the standard package offered, you can expect additions to your budget and timeline. Although no modular home companies in the Northwest are currently aimed at the "affordable" housing market, we know of at least one company that hopes to provide options for low-income households in the future.

Installation of modular homes can be quite efficient. Here the LEED Platinum modular home pictured in chapter 1 is being installed.
PHOTO BY STEVE GLENN, COURTESY OF LIVING HOMES.

politan areas successfully lobbied for inclusion of a checkbox on standard Multiple Listing Service (MLS) pages to signify if a home has been previously certified in a green building program, such as Built Green, LEED for Homes, and Energy Star, and if the home was independently verified. Additional lobbying for recognition by the appraisal industry of the value of green building or Energy Star certification is also occurring, and we anticipate it will be successful. Combined, this activity should make it lots easier to find (and finance) a green home on the existing home market.

If you're looking at existing homes with the idea of green remodeling, work with a real estate agency that specializes in brokering green homes, or with a green remodeling contractor. Either should be able to provide guidance as to whether the home you're looking at really has the potential you think it has.

Case Study:
Puget Sound Energy Buil

The Idea Home is located in Issaquah Highlands, a master planned community on the edge of the city of Issaquah, sixteen miles east of Seattle. Issaquah Highlands was the first certified Built Green community in the Puget Sound region. This means a great deal of attention was focused on minimizing environmental impact in the design and land development of the community.

Homes are clustered on smaller lots to maximize open space; 1400 acres of the total 2200 acres are permanent open space to provide habitat for wildlife.

Land is graded so storm water infiltrates naturally.

Narrow streets and other features reduce storm water runoff, which is collected in vegetated pond areas to filter vehicle oil, sediments, and other pollutants.

One hundred twenty acres of protected wetland help ensure a healthy ecosystem; prohibition of pesticides, copper, and galvanized metals preserves water quality.

The development will include retail and commercial space, providing shopping and employment on-site to reduce vehicle use.

A thousand-vehicle Park & Ride provides mass-transit convenience to all Metro bus services.

The goal of the Idea Home was to demonstrate how Built Green features could easily be incorpo-

by Alistair Jackson, LEED Home
Consultant, O'Brien & Company

rated into a production home environment and be competitive in today's market. The home wasn't a standard model. Bennett Homes, a production builder, commissioned Mithun Architects to design the Idea Home to take best advantage of the lot location and orientation, and to add extra pizzazz to what was, after all, an educational showpiece. Tremendous media coverage was generated for the Idea Home; articles, TV, and the Internet offered detailed information to Puget Sound residents about the feasibility and benefits of green building. More than eight thousand people visited and took guided tours of the home during open house weekends in the spring of 2004.

The Idea Home was priced at $560,000. The project team decided that based on consumer

Mithun Architects designed the Idea Home to take best advantage of the lot location and orientation, and to add extra pizzazz to this educational showpiece. PHOTO BY MIKE SEIDL, COURTESY OF FUSION PARTNERS.

Glazing on the long south side of the house lets a lot of sun into hallways and living rooms. Slate floors hold the solar heat and radiate it back to the house at night. PHOTO BY MIKE SEIDL, COURTESY OF FUSION PARTNERS.

research it would spend no more than $20,000, or less than 5 percent of the market price, over the builder's conventional construction budget to allow for innovation. The premium was to be spent only on things consumer research indicated the market was interested in, including substantial reductions in energy and water consumption, healthier indoor environmental quality, and durable, low-maintenance finishes and landscaping. The proof is in the pudding: the house sold for the asking price before the open house even started. Bennett Homes now offers some of the Idea Home concepts as standard and some as options in their homes.

Reduced size and good solar orientation

At 2800 square feet, this home may be seen as large by green standards, but in this price range and location, it's quite modest. Reduced size allowed more attention to design details while keeping the project on budget.

Although the house is situated on the west side of a north-south street, its orientation takes advantage of available free energy on-site, even with a snug lot and close-up neighbors, through passive solar design. Hallways and living rooms on the long south side of the house feature a lot of glazing to capture winter sun. Slate floors over a two-inch base of low-density concrete, and double layers of drywall absorb solar heat during the day. At night, that warmth is radiated back to the house and circulates naturally to the upstairs bedrooms through convection.

In addition, deep overhangs protect south-facing windows from the high summer sun. Unfortunately, the builder decided not to install trellis shades originally planned for above south-facing French doors. This omission was offset to some extent by the installation of glazing with a solar heat gain coefficient (SHGC) of 0.33, rather than the originally specified 0.60 (which would have maximized winter heat gain in the interior). As a result, the house doesn't fully capitalize on the passive solar design in winter and is probably warmer in summer than ideal. This is a good example of how attention to even small details can be significant in house design—lesson learned!

Energy efficiency

Energy conservation begins with an efficient envelope (roof, walls, and floors) to keep the heat in in the winter and out in the summer. The house is insulated beyond code requirements, with R-23 walls, R-38 to 48 ceilings with "energy heel trusses" to ensure full-depth insulation over the exterior walls, R-30 floors, insulated headers to reduce heat loss, and high-performance windows (R is a measure

of insulation value and is further explained in chapter 9). Special attention was paid to making the envelope as airtight as possible to reduce uncontrolled movement of air in and out of the house.

Because of the thermally efficient envelope and the fact that some of the wintertime heating load is addressed through passive solar design, the designers selected a smaller, more efficient heating system. Heating for both space conditioning and domestic hot water is provided by a single natural gas–fired on-demand water heater feeding individual wall-mounted fan coil heaters in every room. Heat is distributed around the house in small-diameter PEX tubing that runs through the walls inside the thermal envelope—more efficient in terms of both space and energy consumption than a ducted forced-air system. The wall-mounted heater units are individually zoned, allowing very precise control of temperatures to match patterns of use, solar heat gain, and other variables.

No air conditioning was installed; the energy-efficient enclosure, ceiling fans, and natural ventilation keep the home comfortable. Energy consumption was further reduced through the installation of compact fluorescent lamps in at least 50 percent

of the light fixtures, reducing lifetime energy and replacement costs by as much as $25 per lamp. Overall, energy modeling performed by the Washington State University Energy Extension Office demonstrated that the house uses approximately 20 percent less energy than a similar house built to code, saving around $300 a year in 2004.

Water efficiency

Indoor water consumption was reduced through the installation of low-flow faucets in the bathrooms, dual-flush toilets (providing a 1.6-gallon flush for solids, 0.8 gallons for liquids), and a front-loading Energy Star washing machine that uses around 15 gallons of water per wash (compared to 40+ for a similar capacity top-loader). These steps reduced indoor water consumption by approximately 35 percent (approximately 23,000 gallons), saving around $85 a year at local water rates, compared to a code-built home. (In this location, sewer rates are at

The natural gas–fired on-demand water heater (left) feeds individual wall-mounted fan coil heaters in every room for space conditioning and also provides domestic hot water. PHOTO BY MIKE SEIDL, COURTESY OF FUSION PARTNERS.

The Idea Home's landscape limits turf grass, emphasizes drought-tolerant native plantings, and conserves rainwater to cut outdoor water consumption by about 50 percent compared to a typical residential landscape in the area. PHOTO BY MIKE SEIDL, COURTESY OF FUSION PARTNERS.

a fixed monthly fee. In areas with a sewer rate tied to water consumption, savings would be greater).

Outdoors, soils were fully amended with compost to improve landscape health and moisture retention, turf grass was limited to 20 percent of the lot, and drought-tolerant native species were emphasized, all with the goal of minimizing irrigation and maintenance requirements. Rain barrels were installed on various downspouts to collect rainwater for irrigation purposes. In combination, these steps reduced outdoor water consumption by about 50 percent compared to a typical residential landscape in the area, or another 23,000 gallons. Since most of these savings come from higher summertime consumption rates, the dollar savings are higher—in the range of $120 to $150 per year.

Indoor environmental quality

Indoor environmental quality includes several areas of interest—air quality, light quality, thermal comfort, and aesthetics. In this home, indoor air quality was addressed first by minimizing the sources of potential pollutants, then by ensuring effective ventilation to dilute and remove any that remain. Materials and finishes were carefully selected to minimize off-gassing of toxic VOCs and other chemicals into the living space. Materials used included low-VOC paints and adhesives; formaldehyde-free, recycled-content cellulose insulation; and hard-surface, natural flooring materials including slate, cork, bamboo, hard woods (with water-based finishes), linoleum, and berber-style wool carpet (in the master bedroom).

For ventilation, the home features a continuous, dedicated heat-recovery ventilation system designed to remove moisture and stale or contaminated air from the house and replace it with fresh outside air. In the process, the system recaptures heat from the exhaust air and uses it to precondition the inbound fresh air before delivering it via small-diameter ducts to bedrooms and living spaces. Humidistats located in the bathrooms will boost exhaust ventilation when high humidity is detected.

The home features a higher-than-average amount of glazing (approximately 25 percent of the conditioned floor area compared to an average of around 15 percent for an average production home). This results in great natural light in most areas of the house.

Smart and sustainable materials use

In addition to its healthy, low-emitting, and environmentally friendly materials, the Idea Home also features other material choices that are environmentally preferable and that offer durability and low-maintenance benefits to the homeowner: fifty-year fiber-cement siding, permeable pavers on the driveway and patio, and nontoxic recycled timbers for landscaping. Ceramic tile with high recycled content was used in the bathroom.

Construction waste was reduced through good construction practices, and 85 percent of the waste generated was recycled instead of going to the landfill. ▨

> A thing is right when it tends to preserve the integrity, stability and beauty of the biotic community. It is wrong when it tends otherwise.
>
> Aldo Leopold, *A Sand County Almanac*

8: Site Choices

A TRULY GREEN HOME SEEMS to know where it is; its placement and design take site and climate conditions into account. The structure intentionally leverages the free services nature offers—heating, cooling, fresh air, and light—to provide comfortable shelter to the people within, while maintaining a small footprint on the land. There's also a deep sense of connection—a dialogue between inhabitants and their surroundings. This isn't just a happy accident. It comes from careful design flowing naturally from a site assessment process similar to the one presented in chapter 3.

It's also not new—examples from ancient indigenous or vernacular architecture around the globe demonstrate what it looks like to build in a place that's well understood. The necessity of conserving resources, the process of building slowly, and the norm of living in a place long enough to understand it has created unique forms suited to the specifics of climate and place, such as the cliff dwellings of the Southwest, the sod houses of the Northern Plains, the tent structures of the Middle East, and the longhouses of the coastal Northwest.

In this chapter we focus on how to work with a site. In particular, we look at lot layout, a critical first step in any project, as well as three other aspects of site planning and development: site preparation, site water management, and landscaping. Assume that the results of a site assessment are in hand as you begin planning. Major factors that influence your choices include the lot size, adjacencies, existing environmental conditions, and what's allowed by law or other restrictions. Thus, what you choose for your site may not be appropriate for someone else.

Here's a summary of the positive environmental impacts that can result from your site choices, and the general approach to achieving them:

Energy independence. Place the home to use solar energy and natural breezes.

Habitat health. Protect or restore soils, vegetation, and hydrology.

Water conservation. Reduce water needs and use nonpotable water in place of potable water for landscape uses.

Connection. Make choices that will help you deeply connect to the place.

Starting in this chapter, which marks the beginning of the series of chapters focused on the specifics of implementing green choices in the building or remodeling process, you'll encounter a number of questions designed to help you sort out what's most important in the major areas related to the topic under consideration. You'll see the questions listed in general order of importance in "What matters?" near the front of each chapter. You'll also see them repeated in **boldface** in the sections that follow, which discuss the questions in more detail and relate them to what we call our *top green home picks.*

LOT LAYOUT

What's the ideal location for your new home or addition? It would be nice if you could work entirely within the realm of nature's dictates to locate your

WHAT MATTERS?

These are the important questions to consider regarding lot layout, site preparation, site water management, and landscaping:

- What's the ideal location for your new home or addition?
- Can a smaller home with a smaller footprint meet your needs?
- Does a multilevel structure work for you?
- How carefully will you be able to monitor what happens during construction?
- Can you live in a house that looks different on the outside?
- How much time and energy can you devote to landscaping?
- Does your jurisdiction allow the use of nonpotable water for irrigation?

new green home or addition. However, that would ignore the practical reality of zoning constraints, existing infrastructure (utilities, roads, and such), homeowner associations, and environmental regulations. If the lot is small, there's considerably less latitude. The point is to optimize placement and orientation of the home or addition so your household benefits and the environment doesn't suffer unduly. The site assessment should tell you where you should and shouldn't locate new construction.

Different sites have different issues, as two examples will illustrate. A major factor in lot design for the O'Brien-Cunningham residence on Bainbridge Island, Washington, was the fact that nearly two-thirds of the lot was wetland. Although the wetland was highly degraded and not particularly functional according to regulatory standards—specialists rated the wetland a Category Three on a scale of one to four, with one being the highest quality—we wanted to do what we could to protect what was there. That meant limiting or offsetting changes in hydrology that could starve the wetland of surface and subsurface flows, as well as changes in solar exposure that would alter the environment for wetland plants. The home's small footprint (roughly 30 × 30 for the house and 20 × 20 for the detached garage) and placement were dictated by this circumstance. The home's orientation was further influenced by our desire to take advantage of a southeastern solar exposure and peekaboo view of Puget Sound. In comparison, a major factor in locating and orienting the Sullivan residence in Bend, Oregon, was the owner's desire to employ earth sheltering (using the earth to insulate portions of the home's exte-

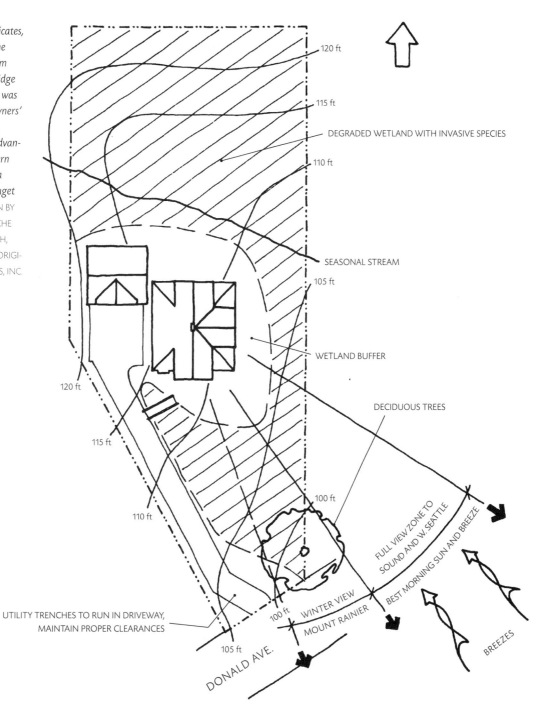

As this site map indicates, the orientation of the O'Brien-Cunningham residence on Bainbridge Island, Washington, was influenced by the owners' desire to protect the wetland and take advantage of a southeastern solar exposure and a peekaboo view of Puget Sound. ILLUSTRATION BY CHRISTOPHER GUTSCHE AND KATHLEEN SMITH, ADAPTED FROM AN ORIGINAL PLAN BY ASPECTS, INC.

120 ft

115 ft

DEGRADED WETLAND WITH INVASIVE SPECIES

110 ft

SEASONAL STREAM

105 ft

WETLAND BUFFER

DECIDUOUS TREES

120 ft

115 ft

110 ft

100 ft

FULL VIEW ZONE TO SOUND AND W. SEATTLE

BEST MORNING SUN AND BREEZE

100 ft

WINTER VIEW

MOUNT RAINIER

BREEZES

UTILITY TRENCHES TO RUN IN DRIVEWAY, MAINTAIN PROPER CLEARANCES

105 ft

DONALD AVE.

The site map for the Sullivan residence in Bend, Oregon, shows that the owner's wish to employ earth sheltering, passive solar strategies, and an active solar water heating system were major factors in locating and orienting the home. ILLUSTRATION BY CHRISTOPHER GUTSCHE AND KATHLEEN SMITH, ADAPTED FROM AN ORIGINAL PLAN BY JIM CHAUNCEY, SUNTERRA HOMES, INC.

rior); passive solar design strategies to maximize the potential for heating, cooling, and lighting with the sun; and an active solar water heating system.

Whatever your site's conditions, keep in mind that it's next to impossible to reproduce the soil and vegetative conditions nature creates over any length of time. It may be tempting to think you can just replant vegetation or replace soil, but it's far better to avoid disturbing sensitive or natural areas in the first place. Sensitive areas—often regulated as "critical areas"—can include wetlands, streams, wildlife corridors, shorelines, and steep slopes.

With that in mind, here are our *top green home picks* for lot layout, in order of their importance and/or impact:

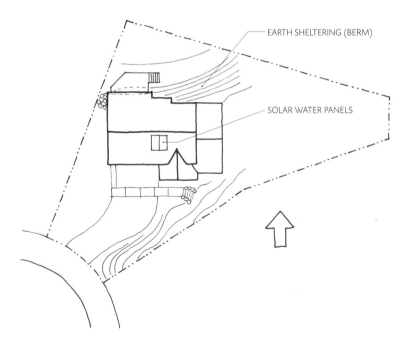

EARTH SHELTERING (BERM)

SOLAR WATER PANELS

- Conserve the best parts of the site.
- Use what's already been spoiled.
- Maximize passive solar design opportunities.
- Orient to breezes.
- Integrate existing vegetation into your home's comfort scheme.
- Balance access to the home with aesthetic and environmental considerations.

Conserve the best parts of the site.

Environmental regulations generally protect sensitive natural features such as wetlands, streams, and shorelines by disallowing building in sensitive areas or requiring mitigation if you do. Other natural features may be unregulated, such as a clutch of small-diameter trees. These natural areas may already have been compromised, in which case you should consider restoring them to health and vigor.

If your site is blessed with sensitive natural features, design the lot to provide maximum distance between developed areas and areas to be preserved. Also design so natural flows of water, sun, wind, and wildlife aren't interrupted and outputs from the home (such as storm water) aren't introduced into them in a way that could cause harm. Dividing intact natural areas has a big impact on habitat. Many birds and invertebrates will only inhabit areas that are of a certain size. Leaving islands of nature may be an aesthetic choice but not a good habitat choice. The more edge you create in a stand of forest, the more change you bring to that forest, allowing the invasion of nonnative birds (starlings and house sparrows, for example) that will compete with and displace native birds.

While significant trees, streams, and bluffs are

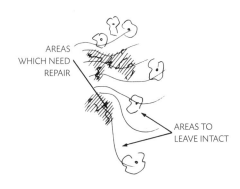

AREAS
WHICH NEED
REPAIR

AREAS TO
LEAVE INTACT

The beautifully written A Pattern Language *(Alexander et al. 1977) elaborates on Pattern 104, Site Repair: "The most talented of traditional builders have always been able to use built form, not only to avoid damage, but also to improve the natural landscape" (511).* ILLUSTRATION USED WITH PERMISSION.

obvious candidates for protection, the importance of protecting native soil itself is underestimated by most of us. Soil is the silent breeder of much native life, which we compact, cut up, or seal off when we develop a site. Make sure your site plan includes a map of the soils, so you know where the healthiest soils lie. (Even if damaged, the best soils for infiltration, such as gravelly sandy soils and sandy loam soils with high amounts of tiny particles, are worth protecting. Clay and silt, on the other hand, won't provide much if any infiltration capacity.)

Use what's already been spoiled.

As a corollary to avoiding the best parts of the site, try to build on spots already spoiled by human intervention. An exception would be if a site analysis shows that previous interventions occurred on a particularly poor place to build, such as in a low spot that floods. If this is the case, consider restoring it rather than building on it.

Maximize passive solar design opportunities.

Orient the building or addition on the site to optimize the home's ability to derive solar gain through south-facing windows and minimize solar gain and glare through east- and west-facing windows. Very simply, having the long side of the home face southward is generally ideal for passive solar heating, daylighting, and setting up active solar systems, such as photovoltaics or solar hot water. Many books have been written on passive solar design; a few of our favorites are listed in "Resources."

Also, plan landscaped areas with the sun in mind. Landscape architect Kas Kinkead says: "Here in the Northwest, sunny spots are a luxury. Awaken your inner rock lizard. Locate your patio, gardens, or other hangout spots outside a southern wall, so you can enjoy what sunshine we have, and benefit from reflected heat." Further, she says not to install lawn where it will be perpetually in shade. The turf won't do well, and people are less likely to use the space because it's cooler. A moss garden or plantings of other shade-tolerant ground covers are more appropriate choices for shady areas.

Orient to breezes.

Natural gentle breezes are a pleasant connection to the outdoors. Further, in the warmer areas of the Northwest, and as climate change warms the entire region, orienting the home to pick up on these breezes will help it stay comfortable in the warmer summer months. (Proper window design is critical for this to be meaningful; more on this in chapter 9.) Even in the cooler months of the year, using fresh outdoor air to ventilate can help create a healthy indoor space.

This isn't always the case, however. Some locations in the region, such as the Columbia River Gorge, are quite windy, making dust intrusion (and

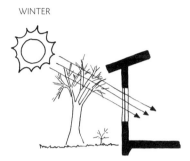

WINTER SUMMER

Deciduous trees are a useful way to shade windows in the summer and allow solar gain in the winter. ILLUSTRATION BY CHRISTOPHER GUTSCHE AND KATHLEEN SMITH.

howling noise) a serious problem. Another instance where relying on opening your windows for ventilation may be inappropriate is adjacent to an active roadway where tiny but multitudinous tire fragments, noxious fumes, and noise abound.

Your site assessment will tell you what's appropriate for your project. Even where outdoor conditions aren't ideal, you can mitigate by using native trees and hedges to screen and filter noise and pollution. Conifers are excellent for this purpose because of the amount of surface area of the needles (Spirn 1985, 3).

Integrate existing vegetation into your home's comfort scheme.

Vegetation can be used to modulate airflow, temperature, and daylight on the site. Ideally you'll be able to use existing trees and mature shrubs to do so; in more developed areas, you'll have to supplement with new plantings. Deciduous trees are especially useful as the shade is there when you need it in the summer and gone when you don't in the winter. Kinkead advises against bigleaf maples, though. She considers a species that provides light shade suffi-

cient in the Northwest. On a large site, properly locating a combination of deciduous and coniferous trees can protect against temperature extremes and direct airflow away or toward your home depending on the season.

Balance access to the home with aesthetic and environmental considerations.

The more deeply a driveway is built into the site, the more impact it will have environmentally and aesthetically. In addition, the placement of the garage has as much impact on views from your home (and of your home) as it does on the environment. Think about what you want to see when parking the car and approaching your door. Is it okay to walk a bit from where your car is parked? Consider the approach to your home as an important expression of your green values. Our friend Steve Loken, a longtime green builder based in Missoula, Montana, calls much of what we see out there "car-chitecture"—built around the automobile. Perhaps there's another way.

SITE PREPARATION AND SITE WATER MANAGEMENT

Your home's footprint has a large bearing on site preparation, with smaller footprints requiring less disturbance. Thus, thinking about site preparation should start with a consideration of house size. You also need to consider how carefully you'll be able to monitor what happens during construction, and how much it matters to you that your house will look different on the outside if you manage site water differently.

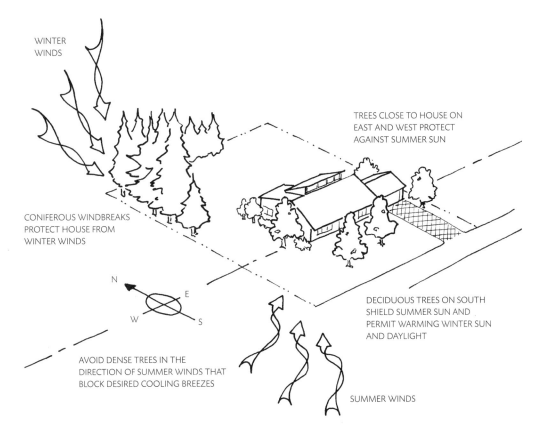

WINTER
WINDS

CONIFEROUS WINDBREAKS
PROTECT HOUSE FROM
WINTER WINDS

TREES CLOSE TO HOUSE ON
EAST AND WEST PROTECT
AGAINST SUMMER SUN

N
E
W
S

AVOID DENSE TREES IN THE
DIRECTION OF SUMMER WINDS THAT
BLOCK DESIRED COOLING BREEZES

DECIDUOUS TREES ON SOUTH
SHIELD SUMMER SUN AND
PERMIT WARMING WINTER SUN
AND DAYLIGHT

SUMMER WINDS

A combination of properly located deciduous and coniferous trees can protect against temperature extremes and direct airflow toward your home in the summer and away in the winter. ILLUSTRATION BY CHRISTOPHER GUTSCHE AND KATHLEEN SMITH.

Can a smaller home with a smaller footprint meet your needs? We can never say enough about house size. If the design uses square footage efficiently, the building footprint can stay small. This will reduce the amount of disturbed vegetation and soil, as well as reduce the quantity and flow of surface water runoff from the hard, impervious surface the house represents. With a remodel, maintaining the same size footprint while improving your home's functionality is a worthy goal.

Does a multilevel structure work for you? A home's footprint can be even smaller if you can tolerate stairs. The O'Brien-Cunningham residence is two stories, but we requested a plan that will allow us to live comfortably on the first level if we become incapacitated by illness or when hosting family members who are less mobile.

How carefully will you be able to monitor what happens during construction? Even with the best contractors, stuff happens on a job site. It's not unusual to "lose" a tree you were hoping to save because of a miscommunication or mistake during site preparation. When Kate visited a job site, she found a suspicious-looking bucket sitting adjacent to the wetland on the property. It had been used for applying colorized stucco to a retaining wall and had

The look of the New Columbia development in Portland deviates from the traditional monolithic suburban lawn, with a bioswale integrated into this corner unit landscaping and planter strip. Immediately after a rainstorm, there should be some standing water in the swale, but it will be drawn down fairly quickly. PHOTO BY JUAN HERNANDEZ, COURTESY OF MITHUN ARCHITECTS.

been rinsed. She could only guess where the rinse water had been emptied! There are ways to reduce these unpleasant surprises, starting with communicating to the contractor that you care about protecting sensitive site features (such as trees, wetlands, or streams), memorializing this by writing protective requirements into the construction contract, and erecting clear signage at the job site outlining expectations and restrictions. It also helps to be actively involved in your project. If you never visit the job site, it communicates a clear message that what happens there isn't important to you.

Can you live in a house that looks different on the outside? A green home needn't look odd. However, some aspects of green design can make a home's exterior or grounds look different from the neighbors'. Covenants may prohibit them as a result. For example, are you allowed to capture rainwater in aboveground barrels or cisterns, install solar panels on the roof or grounds, or allow rainwater to infil-

trate naturally and slowly in rain gardens? Your site assessment should have uncovered the existence of covenants or regulations that limit (or outright prohibit) use of one or more of these features. If regulations require installation of redundant measures, such as connecting to the municipality's storm water system even though you have an on-site storm water infiltration system, the economics can change significantly.

Answering the preceding questions will prepare you to deal with issues of site preparation and water management. Here are our *top green home picks* in those areas:

- Protect trees and sensitive areas.
- Handle removed or damaged vegetation on-site.
- Work with the excavator to limit the construction footprint.
- Plan a foundation system that requires less site disturbance.
- Use best practices for storm water management during construction.
- Keep surface water on-site for good.

Protect trees and sensitive areas.

During construction, set up reasonable, immovable, and obvious barriers around trees or sensitive areas you want to protect. Frequently, trees ostensibly saved during construction don't survive more than a few years because construction equipment and vehicles were driven or parked on top of roots hidden under the soil that extended beyond a minimalist construction barrier. Keep in mind that tree damage won't be evident for some time. Trees can fail from two to ten years after disturbance. Take special care to protect native cedars, hemlock, and dogwoods, as they're hardy species under natural conditions and support the entire native plant community.

The minimum protection recommended for trees is a barrier at the tree's drip line. A preferred location for the barrier, however, would be at the edge of a circle two or three times larger than the outline of the tree's drip line, since most trees have surface roots extending well out into the shallow soil surrounding them. If cutting into a tree root is absolutely necessary, require that any cuts the contractor makes be clean and that the ends be kept moist by covering them with burlap until the trench is filled in. Ripping through roots will harm more than cutting the root off cleanly.

For any sensitive natural area on the site, make sure the barriers actually stay in place and are observed throughout construction. This might take some ingenuity. We've known owners who, in addition to writing this into the construction contract, have posted signs on trees they wanted to preserve with the dollar value that would have to be paid were the trees damaged. (If you do this, don't use nails with copper in them. It will kill the tree.) A certified arborist can determine a tree's value by using the *Guide for Plant Appraisal* produced by the Council of Tree and Landscape Appraisers. It's as important to pay attention to this issue during a remodel as it is during new construction. In addition to setting up clear and adequate protective barriers, you'll want to designate parking and material lay-down areas as far as possible from the areas you want to protect.

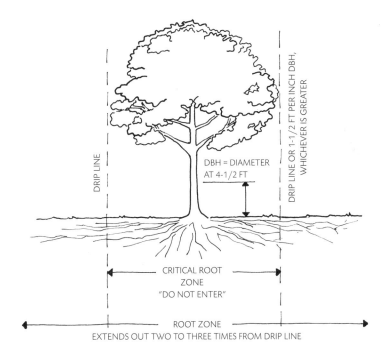

We don't encourage building homes in forested areas, but many people do build in such areas, removing a few trees at the time of construction only to find remaining trees falling during a storm. Obviously, this isn't sustainable. Trees that have grown up in a forest respond to environmental stresses as one unit. They support each other. When trees are removed from this support network, the remaining trees may not be able to stand up to wind and storm events. Hiring an arborist can help you make decisions when building around existing trees and can save you many thousands of dollars in the long run. The Pacific Northwest Chapter of the International Society of Arboriculture provides a list of certified arborists in communities throughout the Pacific Northwest.

A tree to be saved on a construction site needs to be protected by a barrier that at a minimum encircles the tree's drip line and ideally protects the entire root zone, which extends outward beyond the drip line. ILLUSTRATION BY CHRISTOPHER GUTSCHE AND KATHLEEN SMITH.

Handle removed or damaged vegetation on-site.

If significant vegetation needs to be removed from a location, try to keep it on-site by replanting it in another location. If you can't do this, find someone who can use it. If you have some damaged vegetation or vegetation it doesn't make sense to replant, have your contractor chip and leave it on-site. A mix of green and wood waste is perfect for mulching around existing trees, as long as the wood waste isn't pressure treated. Don't use it on new plantings until completely composted for two years, however; the carbon-to-nitrogen ratio should be less than 50:1 (the nitrogen portion will decrease as the material composts). For established plantings with deeper roots, it isn't as much of an issue. Wood chips are a fine material for informal paths through your garden, and during construction can be laid across nonvegetated soil areas to avoid muddy messes and to reduce compaction of subsoils.

Work with the excavator to limit the construction footprint.

Excavation is perhaps the most intimidating aspect of a residential construction project to those of us who aren't practitioners. It must be those big machines. This aspect of construction can be one of the most damaging environmentally, arguing for minimizing your home's footprint by building up rather than out. You can also limit the construction footprint, the area outside of which construction machinery and vehicles aren't allowed to go. This reduces the amount of soil compaction and vegetation damage during construction. Green building programs generally limit grading to 20 feet outside the building footprint. Some of the truly green-hearted can reduce this footprint further, although keeping it under 15 feet will probably add cost as it requires considerable effort on the part of the excavation crew, especially if this is their first green project. Site damage can also be minimized by setting up parking and staging areas in places that will eventually be (or are already) paved.

Permanent damage to the soil to a depth of 3 feet can be done by the passage of one truck tire, never mind all four or eight. Compacted soil has no air in it, so no place for water, nutrients, or roots. Require the contractor to disk, rip, deep-tine aerify, air excavate, or rototill to a depth of 12 inches and to add 4 inches of compost (not wood chips) wherever trucks have driven out of bounds. Having these requirements spelled out in advance helps everyone, even your contractor, especially when a rush order of concrete shows up with a new driver.

Plan a foundation system that requires less site disturbance.

Basements, which demand the most dramatic excavation, aren't typically built in the wetter parts of our region. But even slab-on-grade systems can be improved. Some alternatives being promoted in our region include pin or pier foundations, and for the more adventurous, stilts. We should point out that basements aren't inherently bad; they just require a lot of excavation. There may be good reasons for them, such as when a daylit basement can provide indoor nonconditioned shelter for household activities or storage, or where a garage is tucked under the home (because there's no space for a detached

garage), and it makes sense to provide basement storage as part of the garage excavation.

Use best practices for storm water management during construction.

Regulations for storm water management exist in every jurisdiction, and your job is to make sure they're met and even exceeded when appropriate. With construction activity high and jurisdictional budgets getting slashed, building officials are generally overbooked. It's not uncommon to find a job site where the erosion and sedimentation controls are poorly maintained and failing, water flows aren't sufficiently controlled, or soil stabilization techniques are inadequate. If you have a site where storm water runoff is an issue (which includes most rural or suburban sites with a slope), make sure the contractor has provided a single construction entrance stabilized with rock, installed sedimentation controls such as storm drain inlet protection or check dams, and stabilized soils with mulch, nets, or temporary seeding.

An erosion control plan makes clear the limits of land disturbance, where construction activities should take place, and where erosion control practices should be installed. On a particularly sensitive site, it's a good idea to have a plan in place to inspect all erosion and sedimentation control measures immediately if more than ½ inch of rain falls in a twenty-four-hour period.

A green choice is to use compost for erosion control; slightly coarse to coarse compost mixes are effective in holding soil in place even during heavy rainfall and can have a restorative effect. The compost application rate depends on degree of slope, soil type, and compost characteristics. As a rule of thumb, however, a 3-to-4-inch layer of compost will perform effectively on a slope of up to 45 percent for one to three years. Make sure the compost contains only yard trims, uncontaminated wood by-product based materials, and well-stabilized biosolids.

Keep surface water on-site for good.

For many years, the best practice for permanently handling surface water was to get it off-site and into an engineered municipal storm water system as quickly as possible. Thinking has evolved in the Northwest, however, and in suburban and rural areas, some method of slowing the water down and keeping it on-site as long as possible is preferred.

A pin foundation, such as this one used for a straw bale home in western Washington, reduces both the amount of land disturbance and the amount of concrete required for a home's construction and thus provides both environmental and economic benefits. PHOTO BY R. GAGLIANO, COURTESY OF PIN FOUNDATIONS, INC.

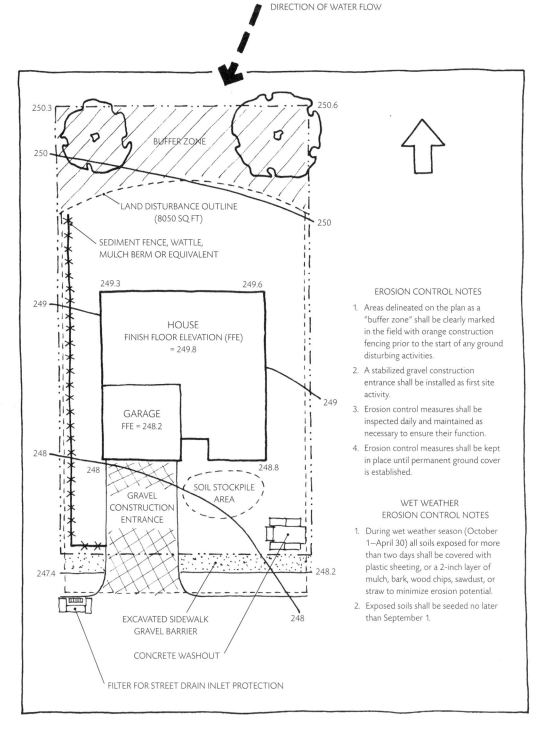

DIRECTION OF WATER FLOW

250.3

BUFFER ZONE

250.6

250

LAND DISTURBANCE OUTLINE
(8050 SQ FT)

250

SEDIMENT FENCE, WATTLE,
MULCH BERM OR EQUIVALENT

249.3

249.6

249

HOUSE
FINISH FLOOR ELEVATION (FFE)
= 249.8

249

GARAGE
FFE = 248.2

248

248

248.8

SOIL STOCKPILE
AREA

GRAVEL
CONSTRUCTION
ENTRANCE

247.4

248.2

EXCAVATED SIDEWALK
GRAVEL BARRIER

248

CONCRETE WASHOUT

FILTER FOR STREET DRAIN INLET PROTECTION

In this sample erosion control plan for a fairly tight lot, storm water would naturally flow from the highest northeast corner of the lot. Sediment control features (a silt fence, mulch berm, or equivalent) are to be located along the west side and the southwest corner of the lot. Further protection is provided at the street drain by installing a filter for street drain inlet protection. ILLUSTRATION BY CHRISTOPHER GUTSCHE AND KATHLEEN SMITH, ADAPTED FROM CITY OF CORVALLIS REQUIREMENTS (2005).

EROSION CONTROL NOTES

1. Areas delineated on the plan as a "buffer zone" shall be clearly marked in the field with orange construction fencing prior to the start of any ground disturbing activities.

2. A stabilized gravel construction entrance shall be installed as first site activity.

3. Erosion control measures shall be inspected daily and maintained as necessary to ensure their function.

4. Erosion control measures shall be kept in place until permanent ground cover is established.

WET WEATHER
EROSION CONTROL NOTES

1. During wet weather season (October 1–April 30) all soils exposed for more than two days shall be covered with plastic sheeting, or a 2-inch layer of mulch, bark, wood chips, sawdust, or straw to minimize erosion potential.

2. Exposed soils shall be seeded no later than September 1.

For some time, this has meant creating human-made structures (ponds aboveground; vaults underground) to hold water, either permanently or for a short time, to address the runoff from a subdivision or very large lots. These structures can be expensive, and permanent detention ponds have come under fire because of concerns about harboring mosquitoes that may be carrying the West Nile virus.

A more sustainable solution is to design a site that acts as it would if you hadn't built on it at all. An undeveloped site experiences a pattern of precipitation (rain), evapotranspiration (direct evaporation and transpiration of water through pores in leaves), infiltration, and flow to downstream waterways—a pattern that's significantly changed through conventional development. Techniques that slow down surface water flows across the site help increase evapotranspiration and infiltration. Such techniques are collectively called low-impact development (LID). Even if you can't take a full-blown LID approach, using one or more of these techniques to improve the hydrological function of your site is a worthy goal. The bottom line is you don't want to provide surface water with the opportunity to travel fast and far over hard surfaces, picking up sediment and impurities, such as oil from that spot under your car.

One simple technique for handling surface water that many jurisdictions are promoting is to disconnect your downspouts from the storm water system and use splash blocks to feed storm water into a gravel bed. Directing roof water into rain gardens around your house will do double duty—infiltrating rainwater back into the soil while supporting native plants most likely to be happy in our region. These

Jim Gleckler's demonstration rain garden on Bainbridge Island is open to the public (if the gate is open, you're welcome to enter). In the garden's first year, it took about three hours after a big storm for the water to drain completely. PHOTO COURTESY OF NATURAL LANDSCAPES.

Designing your driveway to provide a break in the surface water pathway helps achieve a greater level of infiltration. The country lane drive for a Vancouver, British Columbia, home (middle) and the combination gravel and open paver drive for a Seattle, Washington, home (bottom) are two examples. PHOTOS BY CURTIS HINMAN, WSU (TOP), AND ANNA STUECKLE (BOTTOM).

An undeveloped site (top) experiences a pattern of precipitation (rain), evapotranspiration (direct evaporation and transpiration of water through pores in leaves), infiltration, and flow to downstream waterways. The hydrological system is significantly changed through conventional development (bottom).
ILLUSTRATIONS BY CHRISTOPHER GUTSCHE AND KATHLEEN SMITH, ADAPTED FROM DRAWINGS BY AHBL.

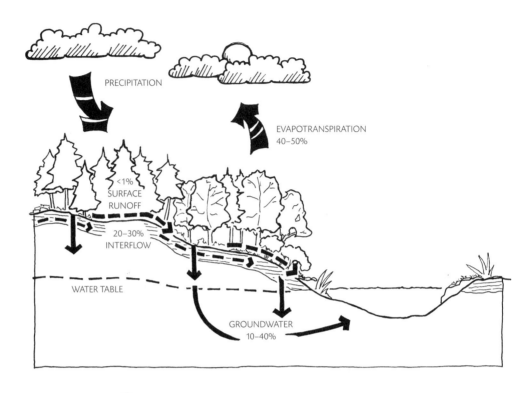

PRECIPITATION

EVAPOTRANSPIRATION
40–50%

<1%
SURFACE
RUNOFF

20–30%
INTERFLOW

WATER TABLE

GROUNDWATER
10–40%

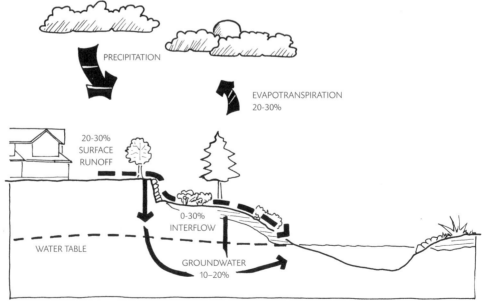

PRECIPITATION

EVAPOTRANSPIRATION
20-30%

20-30%
SURFACE
RUNOFF

0-30%
INTERFLOW

WATER TABLE

GROUNDWATER
10–20%

plants, which are well adapted to our droughty summers, will, once established, do quite well without watering in the summer. If properly designed, rain gardens can deal with long rain cycles without causing standing water. Demonstrating this idea is Jim Gleckler's rain garden on Bainbridge Island, Washington, which is open to the public. The soil mix used in Jim's rain garden is 40 percent native soil, 40 percent compost, and 20 percent sand to provide a good growing base for plants and proper drainage. In the garden's first year, Gleckler reported that it took about three hours after a big storm for the water to drain completely. This should improve as the garden matures.

LANDSCAPING

Very often, landscaping is an afterthought or even eliminated because of cost constraints as a project nears its end. The temptation can be to quickly finish the project up with a process an architect friend calls "shrubbing it up."

Green landscapes serve many functions, many of them hidden but important. When you preserve an existing landscape, you preserve a soil ecosystem, subsurface hydrology, and a complex web of interconnected systems of evapotranspiration, nutrient and air cycling, habitat, and natural storm water control. When you create a new landscape, it's important to emulate the functions that the landscape would perform naturally while creating a space that works for you. Thoughtful landscaping can also repair a site in the case of a remodel or lot redevelopment. With the right (and sufficient) plantings, you can restore hydrological function, encourage wildlife,

and provide yourself with an important connection to nature. A green landscape should offer a thriving and vital setting in which to dwell.

We've already discussed how vegetation can add to a home's interior comfort. In addition, a landscape can have significant implications for maintenance duties and water use. Many municipalities in the Northwest have led initiatives to reduce the amount of water used for domestic irrigation. Consumption for this purpose, however, is still significant, frequently doubling a household's water consumption. Meanwhile, the U.S. Geological Survey monitors for drought on its WaterWatch Web site and in the fall of 2006 it identified areas in Washington and Idaho as well as several locations in Northern California and Oregon as subject to drought. The cost of municipally supplied water is going up as supplies are threatened (U.S. Geological Survey 2006).

Healthier soil means you can establish planted vegetation more easily and be less tempted to rely

The backyard of the new Olivé-Mortola residence in Seattle, Washington, is designed for character and function, and proves you can enjoy privacy and connection to the outdoors even in a tiny urban space. Appropriate (including native) species newly planted in well-amended soil, no lawn, a birdbath to attract birds, artfully laid pavers, a simple wood polymer deck, and a set of Adirondack chairs are elements of this very affordable installation. PHOTO BY ANNA STUECKLE.

Low-impact development (LID) has many definitions. For our purposes, it's a strategy for storm water management and land development that emphasizes conservation and the use of on-site natural features. These are generally integrated with engineered, small-scale hydrologic controls to mimic natural or predevelopment conditions. The goal of LID is to prevent harm to streams, lakes, wetlands, and other natural aquatic systems that would receive the storm water (and anything it picks up) from your developed site.

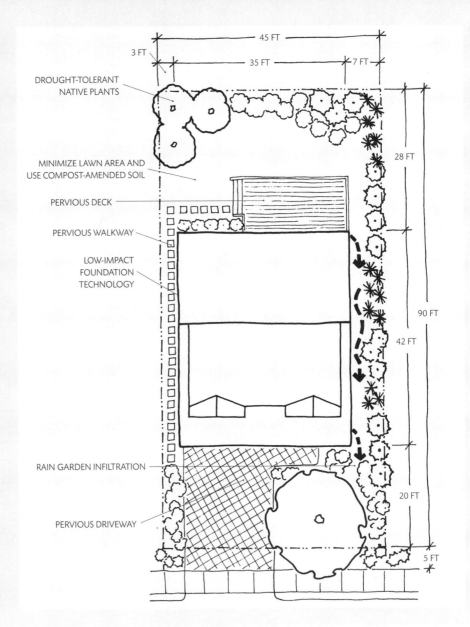

DROUGHT-TOLERANT NATIVE PLANTS

MINIMIZE LAWN AREA AND USE COMPOST-AMENDED SOIL

PERVIOUS DECK

PERVIOUS WALKWAY

LOW-IMPACT FOUNDATION TECHNOLOGY

RAIN GARDEN INFILTRATION

PERVIOUS DRIVEWAY

45 FT
3 FT
35 FT
7 FT
28 FT
90 FT
42 FT
20 FT
5 FT

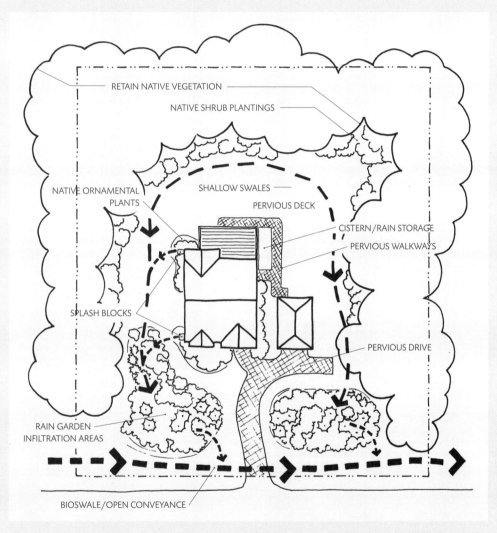

RETAIN NATIVE VEGETATION

NATIVE SHRUB PLANTINGS

NATIVE ORNAMENTAL PLANTS

SHALLOW SWALES

PERVIOUS DECK

CISTERN/RAIN STORAGE

PERVIOUS WALKWAYS

SPLASH BLOCKS

PERVIOUS DRIVE

RAIN GARDEN INFILTRATION AREAS

BIOSWALE/OPEN CONVEYANCE

The low-impact development (LID) approach needs to be adapted to your particular site to get the best results. So ideal LID strategies for a medium-to-high-density lot (left) will be different from those employed on a large or rural lot (right). ILLUSTRATIONS BY CHRISTOPHER GUTSCHE AND KATHLEEN SMITH, ADAPTED FROM DRAWINGS BY AHBL.

General guidelines for LID include these:

- Reduce building footprint.
- Orient building along topographic contours to reduce cutting and filling.
- Amend disturbed soils to regain storm water storage capacity.
- Use low-impact or minimal foundations.
- Transport storm water to places (rain gardens, splash blocks) where it can be dispersed and infiltrated on-site.
- Minimize hardscapes by using pervious or porous pavements or pavers.
- Drain rooftops to cisterns for nonpotable reuse within the house or garden.
- Install a vegetated roof to evaporate and transpire storm water.
- During construction, limit clearing and grading, and protect land from construction-related compaction.

More and more developments are employing LID strategies. For example, the City of Seattle worked with homeowners in a north Seattle neighborhood to retrofit an entire block with LID strategies as part of its SEA (street edge alternatives) Streets project. The result was a nearly total reduction of surface water flow into nearby street drains, water quality monitors found there wasn't even enough storm runoff to test. Similar projects adapting lessons learned from SEA Streets now dot the municipality. The New Columbia development mentioned earlier in the book uses bioswales as well as pervious pavement, which allows water to infiltrate the street while providing an adequate structural basis for neighborhood traffic.

After an entire block in Seattle was retrofitted with LID strategies (top), surface water flow into nearby street drains was reduced to nearly nothing. PHOTO COURTESY OF SEATTLE PUBLIC WORKS.

The New Columbia development (bottom) uses pervious pavement, which allows water to infiltrate the street while providing an adequate structural basis for neighborhood traffic. PHOTO BY JUAN HERNANDEZ, COURTESY OF MITHUN ARCHITECTS.

on chemicals to establish and feed wanted plants or eradicate unwanted ones. The simple act of incorporating good quality compost deep into your soil can drastically reduce irrigation needs, eliminate pesticides, and eliminate or reduce the needs for herbicides. In addition, you can expect as much as a 50 percent reduction in water use, if not more, by following best practices for soil amendment (MacDonald 2005).

How much time and energy can you devote to landscaping? Green landscaping alternatives don't magically plant and maintain themselves. Time and financial resources are required to establish and maintain a landscape. Even areas landscaped with pavers will require some weeding to avoid a scruffy look. Drought-tolerant plans take watering for the first year or two. When designing a landscape, keep in mind your interests, abilities, and energy. Plan for a significant investment of time in the first two or three years of plant growth, when weeding and irrigation needs will be most intensive. Careful attention during this period will pay off, as ensuing years will find plants healthier, better able to outcompete weeds, and better able to go without irrigation in their maturity.

Does your jurisdiction allow the use of nonpotable water for irrigation? It might surprise you to know that rainwater isn't considered potable. *Potable* is a legal term describing water from a source approved for drinking. Other types of domestic nonpotable water include gray water, or water that has been used in showers or for washing dishes and clothes, and black water, water that has been used to convey human waste. Unfiltered rainwater may

MULTIPLE FUNCTIONS OF TREES

A single, mature, properly watered tree with a crown of 30 feet can "sweat" or transpire up to 40 gallons of water a day, which is enough to remove all the heat produced in four hours by a small electric space heater (Lawrence Berkeley National Laboratory 1999). This cooling effect is just one of a multitude of environmental benefits that come from doing what you can to protect existing trees, or from investing in trees that will mature and be healthy in future years.

Here are some other important functions of trees:

- Leaves, twigs, and branches absorb sound and block erosion-causing rainfall.
- Branches and leaves provide shape and reduce wind speed.
- Evapotranspiration from leaves cools surrounding air.
- Leaves filter dangerous pollutants from the air.
- Roots, leaves, and trunks provide habitat for birds, animals, and insects.
- Roots stabilize soil and prevent erosion.

include impurities picked up from a roof, driveway, or other impervious surface. In general, health districts allow rain to be used for irrigation but suggest that you distribute it through an underground system. There's really nothing to stop you from capturing rain in a barrel, and many jurisdictions encourage this.

There's a law on the books in the State of Washington that's intended to prevent individuals and entities from grabbing inordinate amounts of rainwater, an issue in agricultural communities. Technically, Washington State doesn't allow rainwater to be captured on a systematic basis. However, the state's Department of Ecology recognizes the value of using rainwater rather than drinking water when appropriate and is working to change the law. In practice, more and more jurisdictions (even in Washington) are promoting rainwater catchment and storage as a way to conserve drinking water supplies. This is especially true in the case of small residential systems and for uses that don't really require drinking-quality water.

However, landscapers we know suggest considering gray water rather than rainwater for irriga-

tion. That's because in our region it rains the least when irrigation water is needed the most, during the warmer, drier summer months, whereas gray water is produced consistently all year long. Even so, many homes we reviewed for the book do use rainwater for some or all of their irrigation needs. An irrigation system dependent on summer rains can work if you reduce the amount of water you need in the first place. Amending soils to retain moisture and using plants that don't require a lot of water help you get there.

Rainwater harvesting for toilet flushing and even drinking is certainly an option and we discuss this in chapter 10. Of the five case studies presented in this book, two use rainwater for indoor, potable uses: the Scheulen residence in Seattle and the Snyder remodel in Portland.

Many books on sustainable landscapes elaborate on irrigation and much more; a few of our favorites are listed in "Resources." Here, then, are our *top green home picks* for designing a landscape to accompany your green home in the Northwest:

- Think ecosystem.
- Amend disturbed soils to restore or improve soil health.
- Use environmentally preferred choices for imported soil.
- Grow the right plant in the right place.
- Reduce lawn area.
- Use inert materials for landscape features.
- Irrigate only where and when you need to, and use nonpotable water.

Think ecosystem.

When creating your landscape plan, think about the soils you have, the rain that falls on your site, the vegetation that's already in place, and the wild and tame creatures that inhabit (or could inhabit) the site. Use what's right and healthy about your site and work with what's wrong to optimize the overall vitality of the site, as well as the connection to nature it provides for the two-legged inhabitants—that's you! Whether you bring in outside resources to help you will depend on the scale of your project and how far you want to go. If the lot is a small in-city lot and you simply want to create a drought-tolerant landscape, you can probably rely on plant lists and guidance from your local extension agent or Master Gardener program. If you want to create a permaculture landscape—an ecological landscape that produces food—or are developing or restoring a large site (1 acre and up), you might want to pull in a landscape architect with an ecological or sustainability focus.

If you decide to develop an edible landscape, dwarf apple and pear trees make great landscape trees. Edible shrubs such as blueberries or currants can be designed into a sunny shrub border. Grape and kiwi vines can be grown over backyard arbors and trellises. Edible groundcovers such as strawberries or lingonberries are easily grown as well.

Acres and acres of native habitats are converted to housing for humans every year in the Northwest. Planting native landscapes can be one of the most sustainable actions a homeowner can take. Native plants are easy to find at local nurseries. After a year or two of watering while they get established, they need little or no supplemental water and are well

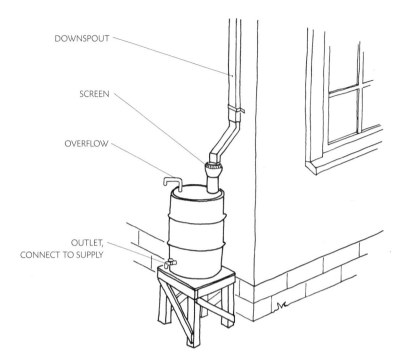

DOWNSPOUT

SCREEN

OVERFLOW

OUTLET, CONNECT TO SUPPLY

adapted to provide wildlife with food, shelter, and places to nest.

Amend disturbed soils to restore or improve soil health.

Again, the first step with soil is to recognize the incredible value native soils bring to a site and do what you can to protect them in place. Undisturbed topsoils typically contain from 6 to 10 percent organic content. Subsoils exposed during construction contain significantly less organic content, as little as 1 percent. Without healthy organic matter in the soil, newly installed plants (even native plantings) and lawns get stressed and frequently turn brown. Besides making establishment of plants more likely, healthy soil generally means better capacity to

This drawing shows how rain from the roof can be directed to a storage barrel that can be connected to a surface or subsurface irrigation system. In the case of a subsurface system, perforated pipes buried in the soil allow for a steady, controlled release of the water at root level. ILLUSTRATION BY CHRISTOPHER GUTSCHE AND KATHLEEN SMITH.

infiltrate surface water and reduced need for those dreadful weed-and-feed products that run off with surface water to set off chemical imbalances in our precious waterways. For topsoil that has to be excavated, stockpile (cover with a breathable tarp to protect from rain) and then amend it with compost when reapplying it to the site. Subsoils that end up being used as topsoil—that is, within the top 12 inches of your landscape—should be amended as well.

Adding compost to your soil improves soil structure, supplies nutrients slowly for root uptake, improves the soil's capacity to hold moisture, reduces erosion, and immobilizes and degrades pollutants that might come with storm water and other runoff. The compost you use should be good quality—that is, it should have the right amount of density, organic matter, moisture content, and carbon-to-nitrogen ratio, with minimal presence of heavy metals. Compost vendors can frequently supply this information; if not, an on-site analysis can be performed. A simple way to judge compost quality is to smell and examine it. The Washington Organic Recycling Council recommends these characteristics you can observe yourself (Puget Sound Action Team 2003):

- smell: earthy, not sour, sweet, or ammonia-like
- color: brown to black
- texture: mixed sizes and crumbly
- temperature: stable, and doesn't get hot when rewetted

The amount of compost you need to mix into the soil will depend on your site's soil conditions and the amount of organic content required, which in turn depends on the type of vegetation you're going to grow. In general, you'll need less organic content for turf areas than for other forms of vegetation. Application guidance is widely available, but the key is making sure you apply the right compost mix in the right quantities to the right depth. Skimp on any of these aspects and you won't get the benefits you're looking for. Proper ground preparation (scarification or tilling) after construction activities is an important aspect as well. Just make sure when you prepare the ground for amendment you don't violate the protection areas around trees discussed earlier; otherwise you'll cause root damage. And don't recompact the soil when it's installed. When you're done, it's worth testing the soil again ($50 soil tests are available from most plant and soil labs) before you actually plant anything.

If you're purchasing a new home or remodeling a relatively new home with existing landscaping, be aware that the layer of topsoil may be quite thin. With topsoil increasing in value, it's common for developers of conventionally constructed homes to remove the topsoil before building, reapply a very thin layer after the home is built, and sell the excess to other developers. The compaction of the subsoil isn't alleviated and long-term problems occur because rain and irrigation water can't soak in. Decompaction can be done with little risk to underground utilities if air excavation equipment is used. A deep-tine aerifier can also be used, but you must take care to stay away from areas with underground utility lines.

Use environmentally preferred choices for imported soil.

If the soil on your site is of poor quality or just

plain gone, you may have to import topsoil, preferably with the right amount of organic content for your use. If you have a large site it may be worth hiring a professional to develop a soil specification. Whether you go that route or not, have the actual soil batch you're buying evaluated before you have it delivered. In addition to the right stuff, you don't want the wrong stuff either (such as large pieces of plastic, stones, and weed seeds). Depending on its source, you might have to amend the topsoil once it gets to your site, in which case you would use tactics similar to amending site-disturbed soils. If you're working with an urban lot, structural soil specifically designed to provide breathing room for the roots of trees growing next to sidewalks in narrow lawn strips has been patented by the Urban Horticulture Institute at Cornell University and licensed to producers around the United States (Urban Horticulture Institute 2005, 3).

Whether you consider soil poor is a relative thing, according to Kas Kinkead, who says, "If you have rocky, dry, free-draining soil, you could use plants that are quite happy in that kind of soil, or with a little more patience you could seed with a cover crop and rototill in, or with even more patience you could plant a succession forest." The latter suggestion is made somewhat tongue-in-cheek since depending on how old you are, it might take the cooperation of your offspring. You start by planting an alder forest and letting it colonize the soil with nitrogen-fixing nodes, then interplant with Douglas firs, cut the alders in five years, replant with an understory of shrubs and small trees, and so on.

Grow the right plant in the right place.

Putting the right plant in the right place is standard procedure for the conscientious landscape architect. This means planting regionally appropriate species, preferably hardy ones, and preferably in zones based on sun/shade and water availability as well as soil type. The result of this approach, like that of amending the soil, is significantly reduced watering and supplemental feeding (fertilizing), as well as reduced vulnerabilities to weeds. Even with this approach, keep in mind that planting stresses plants as much as it does you; give the plants a little extra attention, including some water. If you can schedule planting to occur outside of the hot and dry months, you may be able to reduce or avoid watering altogether.

Reduce lawn area.

Turf is great in that it can take a lot of trampling while providing a flat play surface. To keep lawns green in the Northwest in the summer, however, you need to irrigate. And although lawns are better than pavement as far as infiltrating storm water runoff, they're not as good as forested areas or planting beds. So use turf judiciously. Establish outdoor rooms where you can entertain, stretch out a blanket, have a game of croquet. But if you can't identify how you'll use a lawn area, don't put it in. Kids need spaces to run, but they don't need a full football field. Use the local park for that. It's a great way to share in nature's wealth and meet your friends.

Don't plant lawns in heavy shade or in areas with saturated soils or steep slopes. And don't install turf on a shoreline—even if you won't use weed-and-

As part of relandscaping an existing home in Seattle, Washington, landscape designer Stacy Crooks removed a significant amount of lawn and replaced it with a more environmentally friendly and aesthetic landscape. The sod that was removed was given away free.
PHOTO BY STACY CROOKS.

feed, which could harm fish; the next owner may be tempted to. Plus lawn eliminates habitat and shade for wildlife and can potentially cause erosion.

When installing a new lawn, select a grass mix or sod that's suitable for the sun or shade conditions on your site and for the intended use. Locally adapted rye-fescue seed blends can resist drought if given a deep soil culture to root in. Shallow roots will mean more watering. If needed, use a slow-release, low-phosphorous fertilizer to help the lawn get established; such fertilizer is more efficient and has fewer negative environmental impacts than others. If you're planning to install an irrigation system (which we're not really encouraging), design a lawn shape that can be efficiently watered—that is, that matches the design of available irrigation systems, such as sprinkler sprays or pop-up irrigation sprays.

Use inert materials for landscape features.

It seems that wood treatments for outdoor land-scape features are either very effective at preventing rot and mildew, in which case they leach toxins to the environment, or they're benign to the environment but don't perform well. Recycled plastic lumber and plastic-wood composite lumber provide durable alternatives to treated wood for decks, bed borders, fences, docks, and outdoor benches.

Irrigate only where and when you need to, and use nonpotable water.

Many of the strategies we've suggested for landscaping have the effect of reducing irrigation needs. If you employ the strategies you may need only a temporary watering system to establish your landscaping. If you do need ongoing supplemental watering for a very small area, using rainwater is one option. (If you intend to hand water with a hose connected to a rain barrel, make sure you locate the barrel at a higher elevation than the watering area so gravity works for you—and make sure your hose isn't leaky.) Although it's not inexpensive, the most reliable nonpotable irrigation system for sizable areas is one that uses gray water, since this supply is available year-round.

WHAT WE DO TO OUR WATER, WE DO TO OURSELVES

Quick question: Do you know which watershed your home is located within? Your watershed represents the area of land over and through which water flows on its way to the streams, rivers, and lakes near you. As water makes this journey, it passes through vegetation and wetlands and is naturally cleansed.

In addition to providing this cleansing benefit, healthy wetlands are home to hundreds of plant and animal species and provide storage during times of high rainfall, preventing flooding. Commonly called marshes, swamps, or bogs, wetland areas are saturated or covered with water for at least some part of the year. They can be found throughout the Northwest along river corridors and shorelines as ponds and lakes and in shallow depressions. They can be found in high mountainous areas as well as lowlands, and in both wet and arid areas.

In the past, it was common practice for developers to fill in wetlands and basically "disappear" them. That's no longer true, but development can still have a negative effect on wetlands by interrupting natural flows and starving them—drying them up and killing the vegetation that requires saturated conditions. The Pacific States Marine Fisheries Commission estimates that at least half of the original wetlands in Oregon and Washington and

about 90 percent of California's wetlands have already been lost to diking, filling, and development (1991, 7).

Those of us who have the good fortune to live adjacent to a salmon-bearing stream in the Northwest have a significant responsibility to protect the species with which we so closely identify. Salmon and other Northwest fish species require cool, clean water. When vegetation along streams is removed as part of a development project, warmer temperatures result. In addition, stream banks erode, causing sedimentation. Water becomes unclear, streams become shallow, and temperatures go up further.

When you build your home or addition, it's important for you to treat protective buffers (undisturbed land that extends from the edge of a protected natural feature, such as a wetland or salmon-bearing stream) as sacred. Jurisdictions are now likely to prevent you from building in a buffer, but once you've built on the site, or if you purchase in a neighborhood where this is an existing condition, no one is likely to be looking. So it will be up to you to resist the temptation to landscape these areas or otherwise extend your household's activities into the buffer zone.

We all use solar energy. Without the sun, life on earth would be intolerable. Doesn't it make sense to go that last little bit to use the sun for comfort and conditioning our homes?

Christopher Gronbeck, Sustainable Building Advisor Course, 2006

9: The Building Enclosure

IN THIS CHAPTER, WE MOVE FROM SITE planning to the design of the building itself. We've located the building in the most appropriate spot on the lot; now what's it made of? The bottom line for any building is to adequately shelter its occupants and contents from the elements. With a green home, we ask for more. The service life of a truly green building will be longer than that of conventional buildings. Ideally it will require less material to construct, without compromising structural integrity. It will be easier to deconstruct in the future if that becomes necessary. When compared to conventional buildings, it will consume fewer nonrenewable resources to heat and cool and rely more on nature's free services (preferably coming mostly from the site itself) to fulfill the needs of its occupants.

We've discussed how important it is to consider life-cycle costs and benefits when making green building choices for your new home or remodeling project. In budgeting for your project, we hope you've been able to allow for some choices that may cost more initially but can be expected to reap long-term savings and provide quality. It can be tempting to spend this allowance on aspects of green you may find more exciting—a pretty countertop made with recycled material, perhaps, or a high-tech energy management system. We can't stress enough, however, that if there's any one place where it makes sense to invest more in your project, it's in a well-designed, highly durable, and efficient building enclosure.

Although we frequently focus on heating and air distribution equipment as the source of thermal comfort in our homes, it's the building enclosure that provides the basis for that comfort. In addition, having good indoor air quality depends in large part on designing the enclosure to prevent problems with moisture intrusion, and the mold that can result. Thus, a well-designed building enclosure is critical to achieving a truly green home. For those contemplating remodeling, this chapter includes strategies that can be employed to upgrade your existing enclosure. We'll point out things especially pertinent to remodels, as well as things you probably shouldn't try.

Special contributors Chris Herman and Dan Morris join us in this chapter. Chris, a passive solar

This solar-powered zero energy spec home built on Bainbridge Island by the Rolling Bay Land Company is designed to LEED Platinum standards. PHOTO BY KELVIN HUGHES, COURTESY OF LARRY SKINNER.

home designer and longtime active member of the Northwest EcoBuilding Guild, provides some basic information on how to take advantage of passive solar heating and cooling. Dan, an indoor air specialist, offers pointers on how to avoid mold growth. In chapter 12 he provides tips on dealing with mold if it occurs.

Here's a summary of the positive environmental impacts that can result from your enclosure choices, and the general approach to achieving them:

Energy independence. Construct an energy-efficient building enclosure to reduce your overall heating and cooling requirements.

Building longevity. Design in moisture control to extend the life of materials used to build the enclosure, and use more durable exterior materials.

Human health. Design in moisture control to reduce the risk to human health from mold and mildew.

Human comfort. Design in thermal comfort for occupants, without hot and cold spots or drafts.

Materials efficiency. Design the enclosure to provide sufficient structural integrity with less overall material use and less use of virgin materials.

Habitat health. Use building materials that don't significantly degrade the living environments where they're manufactured or disposed of, or contribute to climate change.

BUILDING IN DURABILITY

Aiming for durability with your enclosure choices is one of the two most important things you can do to build green, along with aiming for thermal efficiency. Durability (building longevity) has to do primarily with three factors: including construction details to keep rain out and to let it out when it makes its way into exterior walls, building in good mechanical ventilation to adequately deal with moisture created by occupants (and maintain good indoor air quality in the closed-up days of winter), and choosing long-lived materials (fifty-year goal) for those portions of the enclosure exposed to the weather.

What design tactics are you using to protect the integrity of materials exposed to the weather over the projected service life of your home? One of the biggest challenges to the integrity of the building enclosure is water. Building scientists say you should expect water to make its way into your home's façade, so plan for it. If it's allowed to stay there for any length of time, or worse, to migrate into the house interior, it can do significant structural damage while posing a health threat to your family when it gets mold and mildew started. Keeping water out as much as possible is important, but making sure it can get out once it gets in is just as important.

Here are our *top green home picks* for building durability into the enclosure:

- Keep rainwater out.
- Plan for water intrusion.
- Select all materials exposed to the elements, including the earth, with the goal of at least fifty years of service life.

Keep rainwater out.

Traditional architectural styles in this region feature significant overhangs for good reason—they deflect rainwater away from the walls, even when the rain is windblown. Roof design with skimpy overhangs and eaves (all too common in production housing) that direct rainwater toward walls and windows instead of gutters along with inadequate flashing at roof-wall intersections are major causes of wall assembly failure. When you look at roof flashing, think like water. Where are you going to flow as you roll off the roof? What opportunities for mischief can you see?

Water management starts at ground level. Many problems can occur in foundations and basements that aren't properly designed to deal with surface and subsurface moisture. The underlying principles are the same: keep moisture away from the founda-

The Sullivan residence, under construction in central Oregon (above), and a newly completed Cannon Beach residence on the Oregon coast (left) use earth berming to take advantage of the earth's core temperature to boost thermal performance. In addition, the beach residence has a vegetated roof, which extends roof life, provides habitat, and mitigates storm water runoff. PHOTOS BY BRUCE SULLIVAN (ABOVE), NATHAN GOOD (LEFT).

tion as much as possible and create pathways for it to drain away when it does get in. Start by choosing a site location where the seasonal high water table is below your foundation if possible. Otherwise you'll have to employ complicated drainage and sump pump systems, and you'll find yourself fighting nature rather than working with it.

Install a proper gravel drainage layer below and around your footings, with a tile or perforated pipe drain beside the footing to carry water away from the foundation to a rain garden or dry well down grade from your building. To further protect the

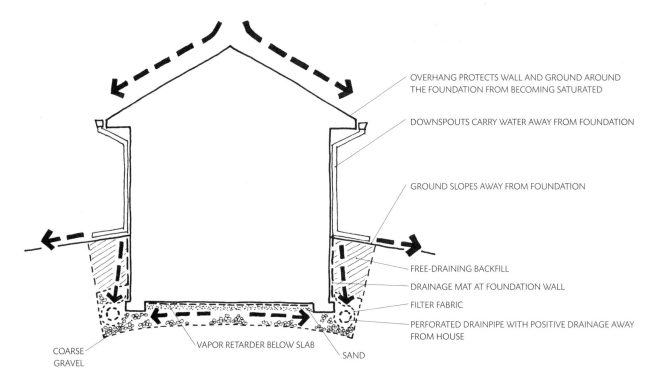

OVERHANG PROTECTS WALL AND GROUND AROUND THE FOUNDATION FROM BECOMING SATURATED

DOWNSPOUTS CARRY WATER AWAY FROM FOUNDATION

GROUND SLOPES AWAY FROM FOUNDATION

FREE-DRAINING BACKFILL

DRAINAGE MAT AT FOUNDATION WALL

FILTER FABRIC

PERFORATED DRAINPIPE WITH POSITIVE DRAINAGE AWAY FROM HOUSE

COARSE GRAVEL

VAPOR RETARDER BELOW SLAB

SAND

Properly sized overhangs can deflect a majority of the rain we experience in the Northwest away from house siding, even in coastal areas where higher winds often accompany rainfall. ILLUSTRATION BY CHRISTOPHER GUTSCHE AND KATHLEEN SMITH.

foundation, wrap it with one of the many foundation drainage mat or panel products—dimpled plastic sheets that create a free-draining air space between fill and foundation walls. Backfill using free-draining material, including granular topsoil, and finish with a minimum 5 percent (1 in 20) grade away from the foundation for 10 feet if possible.

Wide overhangs tend to help keep rainwater off the foundation, but make sure your downspouts are led well away from the building as soon as the roof is on; once your project is complete, the path of water should be down grade to an infiltration trench, or preferably to a rain garden or cistern. (Note: If you install rain barrels or cisterns close to your house, make sure that overflows are properly plumbed and piped away, rather than drip, drip, dripping into

your foundation.)

If you build using a slab-on-grade foundation, ensure you have adequate, free-draining subbase to provide a capillary break—which prevents soil water from wicking its way up beneath the slab—and a properly taped and sealed, adequately heavy (10-mil polyethylene) moisture barrier.

Plan for water intrusion.

Good design and installation can deflect up to 90 or 95 percent of rainfall. That still leaves 5 to 10 percent that will hit your walls and may penetrate your exterior. Some will; it's a fact of life. A green home is designed so that whatever water does enter the roof and wall assemblies has a clear drainage pathway to get back out.

A key example of this approach is the use of a rain screen or drainage plane wall assembly, a method considered mandatory by building materials and wood technology researcher Paul Fisette (2001, 3). In a typical framed wall assembly, sheathing is attached to the outside of the stud wall. Then building paper or other building wrap is attached to the outside of the sheathing, and siding is applied directly to the outside of the wrap. The wrap is intended to protect the sheathing from bulk moisture (water) entering from the outdoors, while allowing moisture vapor (generated indoors) to pass through to the outside. In reality, with the siding in contact with the wrap, it can be difficult for the water to find a drainage pathway. Any moisture that finds its way through the siding can build up against the wrap for prolonged periods, seeping through or finding its way to places that haven't been properly lapped and taped. This is a common pathway for moisture to penetrate a wall assembly; water damage and mold can occur as a result.

This problem can be greatly diminished, if not eliminated, by including a free-draining air space behind the siding. Water that gets through the siding enters this space, where it's free to drain down and dry out before damage is done. Similarly, this freely ventilated air space generally reduces vapor pressure, helping any moisture in the wall to dry to the outside and moisture in the siding to dry into the air space.

This air gap can be achieved in many ways; one of the best is with vertical furring strips nailed to the sheathing at the studs. To be effective, according to the building science experts, the air gap should be ⅛ inch to ¾ inch wide, depending on wall assembly type and moisture load (Lstiburek 2005, 3–4). Any less and capillary action—the surface tension of water resisting the force of gravity—may prevent free drainage. The primary test of a rain screen system, whether constructed on-site or purchased on the market, should be whether it's providing an

The Harding residence (sample plans are in chapter 3) employs vertical furring strips nailed to the sheathing at the studs to achieve an effective rain screen. Shown are a corner detail and the rain screen wall assembly as installed. PHOTOS BY ROB HARRISON.

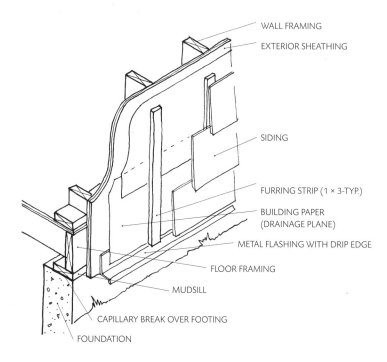

WALL FRAMING

EXTERIOR SHEATHING

SIDING

FURRING STRIP (1 × 3-TYP.)

BUILDING PAPER
(DRAINAGE PLANE)

METAL FLASHING WITH DRIP EDGE

FLOOR FRAMING

MUDSILL

CAPILLARY BREAK OVER FOOTING

FOUNDATION

This detail illustrates how a rain screen is assembled. ILLUSTRATION BY CHRISTOPHER GUTSCHE AND KATHLEEN SMITH.

adequate and consistent gap. Think like a raindrop: Would you be able to escape?

A significant weak point is at window openings, which can provide easy access into the wall assembly if not properly caulked and flashed. Window frames expand and contract with heat and cold; over time they can separate at corners and other joints, opening pathways for moisture. Windows (and doors) should be installed with proper flashing at sides, top, and bottom. Flashing on the top and sides should lap under the building wrap. Flashing below the opening will help effectively seal the wall assembly under the window and direct any errant moisture out and down. The flashing must provide a continuous waterproof barrier across the bottom of the rough opening and several inches up both sides. It should also lap over the bottom course of building wrap

so that water drains into the drainage space behind the siding, not into the wall assembly. Many building wrap systems offer products and instructions to address this.

Select all materials exposed to the elements, including the earth, with the goal of at least fifty years of service life.

Making the right choice of material(s) for your enclosure will mean less opportunity for failure and fewer requirements for replacement. Some building materials are appropriate for the Northwest climate, while others aren't. A material that works well as siding may not do as well on the roof, which is pounded by rain or covered by snow for long periods of time. Reputable manufacturers don't want to be sued and will let you know which applications are appropriate for their product.

The most durable choices for siding, roofing, and deck materials tend to hold a standard paint or stain for longer than conventional wood. This reduces frequency of reapplication, which is good because the longer-lasting paints and stains usually include problem ingredients that pollute the atmosphere or groundwater. At the O'Brien-Cunningham residence, we used two types of deck materials—a wood polymer material with a fifty-year guaranteed service life and wood. The wood polymer material has integral color and finish and has required nothing more than an occasional hosing. In contrast, in the six years since the home was built, we've had to treat the wood decks several times. We've found that water-based coatings offer lackluster performance, and we've surrendered to power washing the decks

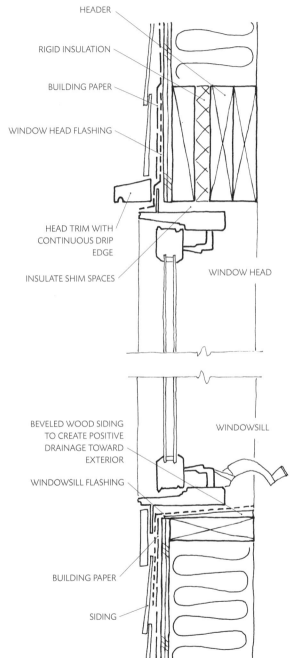

HEADER

RIGID INSULATION

BUILDING PAPER

WINDOW HEAD FLASHING

HEAD TRIM WITH CONTINUOUS DRIP EDGE

INSULATE SHIM SPACES

WINDOW HEAD

BEVELED WOOD SIDING TO CREATE POSITIVE DRAINAGE TOWARD EXTERIOR

WINDOWSILL FLASHING

BUILDING PAPER

SIDING

WINDOWSILL

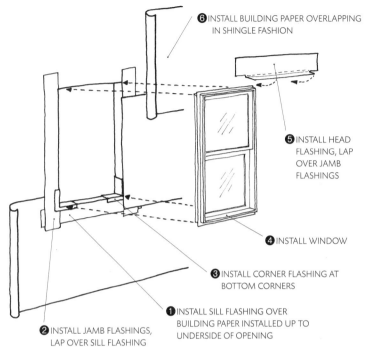

6 INSTALL BUILDING PAPER OVERLAPPING IN SHINGLE FASHION

5 INSTALL HEAD FLASHING, LAP OVER JAMB FLASHINGS

4 INSTALL WINDOW

3 INSTALL CORNER FLASHING AT BOTTOM CORNERS

1 INSTALL SILL FLASHING OVER BUILDING PAPER INSTALLED UP TO UNDERSIDE OF OPENING

2 INSTALL JAMB FLASHINGS, LAP OVER SILL FLASHING

yearly to avoid mildew buildup. When we ordered more wood polymer for the stairs up to the garage studio remodel, we ordered extra and used it to replace one of the wood decks. We plan to replace all of the wood deck material over time.

For walls, durable material choices range from fiber-cement siding to complete wall systems made from nonorganic materials that won't biodegrade. Examples of the latter include steel, concrete, masonry block, or foam-concrete composites. (Cedar siding will last fifty to a hundred years if it's properly constructed and maintained and carefully coated, but there's a lot of labor involved over the life of the product). If you use fiber-cement siding—or wood, for that matter—order it back-primed. Proper paint-

The full window detail (top) shows the order in which flashing and window elements are installed to provide proper drainage.

The window section (left) shows a closer, side view of the installation. Note that the head trim has a continuous drip edge, a groove cut from its underside that stops water from continuing on its natural path in toward the window. ILLUSTRATIONS BY CHRISTOPHER GUTSCHE AND KATHLEEN SMITH.

Across the Northwest we need to concern ourselves with moisture in wood and in the enclosed spaces of new homes we build, mainly because of the likelihood that mold spores, which are always present, might thrive. Mold can damage new structures and make them all but uninhabitable, or inhabitable only after costly remediation.

Almost all buildings get wet during construction in the Northwest. Because warm, sunny days will typically follow and dry out wood, a few showers in summer are usually not a problem. However, when it rains on new construction many times, with few or no dry and sunny days between drenchings—a situation quite common in the wetter areas of the region—kiln-dried wood may well become saturated. Even in the drier areas of the region, precipitation can pose a challenge. When winter snow melts slowly on unprotected framing for days or weeks it can cause problems.

Mold spores are everywhere looking to do their only job, which is to turn cellulose into soil. (Most species of mold in the Northwest are cellulose digesters.) When spores settle on wood that remains wet for several days or weeks, mold will start growing. You can't control the spores and you can't control the food source, so you must control the moisture content of the wood.

Following these design tips will help ensure your home or addition is less vulnerable:

- Allow generous overhangs in order to keep walls drier.
- Plan steeply pitched roofs to provide improved ventilation and access to roof sheathing at the eaves.
- Provide well-ventilated crawl spaces with more headroom than typical to prevent moisture from accumulating in the space.

- Use advanced framing (an efficient framing technique) to avoid sandwiching many studs together that take longer to dry out.
- Avoid composite materials that are vulnerable to moisture—for example, particleboard and OSB (oriented strand board, a building material made from thin strands of wood and resin formed under heat and pressure into sheets and boards).
- Use moisture- and mold-resistant woods. Cedar and redwood are the most resistant (but their long growth cycle makes them a poor choice in terms of the environmental impact of harvesting them); Douglas fir is very resistant; and hem-fir (which is mostly hemlock) is less resistant. Aspen and poplar, the woods most often used in OSB, are the least resistant to moisture, mold, and rot.
- Since moisture intrusion is likely, design in paths for water to exit quickly, such as rain screens and adequate flashing around openings in the walls and roofs.

Take these steps during framing to keep moisture out:
- Store all wood up off the ground and cover it well.
- Use closed-cell sill sealer between all concrete and wood plates. (Note that this may conflict with DfD, if that's your goal.)
- Remove all cardboard from footing forms, and other cellulose debris from the crawl space.
- Install 6-mil black poly ground cover in the crawl space and install crawl space vents right after the floor is down.
- Cut out bottom plates at door openings as soon as the walls are up.
- Sweep or vacuum standing water and wet sawdust off the subfloor every day.
- If puddles keep forming in one or two locations on the subfloor, drill a ¾-inch drain hole in the deepest part of the puddle and put

by Dan Morris, Certified Indoor Environmentalist (CIE), Healthy Buildings, Inc.

a bucket below the hole.

- Use tarps at critical times to protect the wood from getting soaked.
- When the roof is on, cover window and door openings with clear poly at once, and install building wrap, window flashing, and windows as soon as possible. Make sure installation details are complete and correct.

Beginning as soon as the roof is on, monitor the moisture content (MC) of the wood twice a week until the wood is reasonably dry. Purchase a moisture meter (we use a Delmurst BD-10 pin-type) and make a chart with rows for wood joists, subfloor, bottom plate, studs, wall sheathing, rafters, and roof sheathing, and with columns for each date you plan to test the wood for moisture. If the wood is wet (MC 20 to 40 percent), it should be dried. If the wood isn't too wet (MC 17 to 20 percent) and the weather is warm and dry, the wood may dry out on its own. To prevent mold growth, the MC should be at least below 16 percent and ideally below 14 percent.

Attempting to dry out wood is where even conscientious builders can unintentionally create a disaster. You can't just add heat to a closed-up wet building. You must add mechanical ventilation (exchanging indoor air with outdoor air) when you're drying buildings with heat. Also, gas-fired heaters can't be used to dry out a wet building because they contribute moisture of their own. Dehumidifiers are an excellent choice, however, especially in winter. With a dehumidifier you can keep the building closed up, because the dehumidifier doesn't require ventilation and adds heat to the building. Make sure the water from the dehumidifier is drained away from the building.

By measuring the moisture content twice a week, you can track how fast the building is drying out. If the drying process is progressing very slowly, more drying equipment is needed.

After your home is built, you also need to keep an eye on the relative humidity of closed spaces. Relative humidity (RH) is the ratio of the amount of water vapor actually present in the air to the greatest amount possible at the same temperature. High relative humidity in a closed space can promote mold growth. Exposed damp crawl-space soil can result in elevated humidity that affects the floor joists and subfloor. Mold can become well established by the time anyone notices that the subfloor is turning green. The best protection against humidity-caused mold is to pay attention to moisture in every part of the building. In addition to tracking the moisture in wood, keep an eye on how the wood looks in hidden spaces, such as crawl spaces, basements, closets, dormers, and attics.

Controlling moisture in your new house may seem like a lot of unnecessary work. But we've investigated dozens of still-unoccupied homes where mold-covered roof sheathing and subfloors meant that very expensive professional mold remediation was required. The closing up of wet walls can go unnoticed in quickly built spec homes; the molds that grow in such circumstances can make new occupants sick for months. An ounce of mold prevention is worth a ton of remediation grief.

This moisture meter was used to monitor the moisture levels in framing for the O'Brien-Cunningham residence while under construction. The project took place during one of the wettest winters on record—ninety straight days of rain—and required the use of a dehumidifier before the building could be closed in. PHOTO BY KATHERINE MORGAN.

ing on all six sides (including cut ends and edges) is essential for long service life.

For the roof, choose a good-quality metal or recycled rubber product. If you have more money to spend, consider concrete or clay tile or slate. For foundations, fly ash, a by-product of burning coal for electricity, is routinely used to replace Portland cement at levels of 15 to 25 percent, possibly higher if the material is good quality, the contractor experienced, and the slowed curing times acceptable. Slag cement can be substituted at levels of 25 to 50 percent for basement floors, and 30 to 65 percent for footings (Slag Cement Association 2005, 2). Quality window frames are an important factor in a longer-life exterior. Invest in fiberglass or clad wood windows for their long-term weather resistance and good looks.

For most of these materials (with the exception of fiber-cement siding, which is widely used today in midpriced housing), you may experience a cost premium. The trade-off is an exterior that requires fewer maintenance and repair expenditures (both in terms of time and money) over the life of your home.

ACHIEVING THERMAL EFFICIENCY

To achieve thermal efficiency with your building enclosure, you need to optimize the R-value (or in the case of windows, U-value) of the combined enclosure assembly, seal it up tight, and use free site resources, including solar energy and natural breezes.

How will your project resolve the natural tension between solid insulated walls and glazing for views and daylight and still achieve your green goals? Glazing is much less thermally efficient than well-insulated walls, so the more windows and skylights you add to enhance daylighting, the more you may have to heat and/or cool your home. Upgraded insulation will improve the comfort and energy efficiency of your home for the life of the building. Glazing should be limited and judiciously located to provide effective daylighting and views to the outside, particularly in areas used for activities during the daytime. More glazing will mean more cost up front for high-performance windows, and more energy to heat and cool your home, unless some of that glazing can be used to capture the sun's heat during the winter and allow natural ventilation during the summer.

Here are our *top green home picks* for enclosure choices involving thermal efficiency:

- Upgrade insulation levels to improve thermal performance of the home.
- Seal and test your enclosure.
- Select glazing to optimize thermal performance and natural light.
- Select and locate operable windows to promote natural ventilation.
- Design the enclosure to use the energy that's freely available on the site.

Upgrade insulation levels to improve the thermal performance of the home.

You can improve the thermal performance of your home by installing insulation that beats minimum (code) R-value requirements or conventional practice (whichever is higher) and, just as important, making sure the insulation has been installed properly. The amount of upgrade that's cost effective will depend on your local climate conditions. In milder climates on the West Coast, the return on investing in super high levels of insulation diminishes when compared to the return you might achieve inland where climate conditions are more extreme.

An R-value is a measure of a material's resistance to thermal conductance (the rate of heat transfer through a given surface area and thickness of a material over time, based on the temperature difference between the two sides of the material). The R-value of a material is actually the inverse of its thermal conductance (R-value = 1/thermal conductance). Thus, the higher the R-value, the more the rated material resists heat transfer. Insulation materials vary in the R-values they can provide; if they're installed improperly, the R-value is effectively decreased. The insulation performance of materials is expressed as R-value per inch, or as a gross R-value for a nominal thickness. For example, an R-19 batt is 5½ inches thick; if you compress it into a 3½-inch stud bay, it won't be R-19 anymore.

Types of insulation. Types of insulation generally include batts, blown-in insulation, spray foam, and rigid foam. The type of insulation most appropriate for your home will depend on a number of factors and may even vary depending on which aspect of the building enclosure you're thinking about— whether walls, roof, or foundation. Note that other issues may affect your choice of insulation, such as toxicity, percentage of recycled content, and longevity. Check our advice on greener choices later in this chapter. Also see the GreenSpec product directory

Spray foam (top) and recycled denim batts (middle) are installed in the Sullivan residence in Bend, Oregon. PHOTOS BY BRUCE SULLIVAN.

Formaldehyde-free fiberglass blown-in batts (bottom) are installed at the O'Brien-Cunningham residence on Bainbridge Island, Washington. Paper is stapled to studs and rafters and then loose fiberglass is blown in through holes punched through the paper, making for a very clean job. PHOTO BY JOHN CUNNINGHAM.

for an annotated listing of environmentally preferred insulation options.

Batts are long sheets of insulating material cut to fit between studs or joists. Generally made of fiberglass or rock wool (and more recently, recycled cotton), they're probably the most familiar form of insulation to the homeowner. If properly installed, they can provide good insulation. This means cutting around blocking, electrical boxes and wiring, plumbing pipes, and so on to ensure the insulation completely fills each cavity to its full depth, width, and height. Compression reduces the R-value of insulation so batts must maintain their full loft and not be squeezed behind pipes and wires.

Blown-in insulation uses loose-fill material that's blown into the bays between wall studs (behind an air-permeable fabric or mesh) and ceiling joists, fitting tightly around boxes, wires, and pipes. Typically made of fiberglass, cellulose (recycled newspaper), or mineral wool, blown-in insulation generally has a slightly higher installed cost but offers better performance, R-value for R-value, than batts because of the improved fit and some airtightness benefits, which we'll discuss later. For walls, the insulation is usually mixed with a binder to hold its structure and prevent slumping under the influence of gravity and time. Consistent, dense filling of cavities is an indication of a good installation job.

Blown-in insulation also offers a good solution for remodeling jobs because it can be more easily added to existing walls. Holes are drilled into each stud bay (through either interior drywall or exterior sheathing) and each cavity is filled using a probe to ensure complete and consistent fill. Quality instal-lation is a little harder to achieve, so it pays to use an experienced retrofit contractor. Many weatherization contractors specialize in this work, typically using blown-in cellulose as their insulation of choice. An element of quality control can be achieved by taking core samples from several early bays to ensure consistency of fill.

Spray foam insulation offers another step up in performance compared to blown-in insulation but also some additional complexity. There are several brands on the market, and it will pay to do a little research into the long-term performance of the products you're considering. Spray foams are generally polyurethane-based and use water as the spraying/blowing agent. The foam is sprayed wet into stud bays, where it expands to fill the cavity, adhering to the sheathing and studs and tightly filling the cavity and any air gaps. This offers a very airtight wall system. Cavities must be slightly overfilled, then cut back to the stud face to ensure a smooth fit for the sheetrock. Good installers keep this trimming waste to a minimum.

Rigid foam offers a higher R-value per inch than most other insulations and offers the chance to significantly reduce heat losses due to thermal bridging. R-values range from R-4 per inch for expanded polystyrene (EPS, XPS) to R-7 per inch for polyisocyanurate. Installed in sheets against the outsides of walls or roofs, rigid foam creates an effective thermal break. A one-inch layer of foam on the outside of a stick-framed wall virtually eliminates the thermal bridging effect of the studs, bringing the whole wall R-value close to the center-of-wall R-value (for example, around R-24 for a 2 × 6 wall with drywall inside, blown-in insulation, 1-inch XPS outside, and fiber-cement siding). Keep in mind you may have to use plywood sheathing or engineered shear-wall panels to meet local seismic and high wind requirements.

Also be aware that the vapor permeability of spray and rigid foams varies by brand and by density (denser foams offer higher R-values but less permeability). If you choose to use a vapor-impermeable foam, make sure you address moisture movement concerns to avoid trapping moisture in your wall or roof assembly. Generally, the product manufacturer or installer will be able to guide you on this if you ask.

Insulating walls. You can increase wall insulation by increasing the depth of your stud bays. Two framing systems that accomplish this include the Larsen Truss System and the Heslam Grid or Strapped Wall (Good 2006a, 4). Both improve whole wall thermal performance, equate structurally to a regular 2 × 4 system, and allow easy access for plumbers and electricians. But because they're different, you may need to invest at least a little money in hiring a structural engineer to work with your building officials, general contractor, framers, and other affected tradespeople to ensure these systems are permitted and installed properly. The ideal is to work with a contractor familiar with efficient framing systems.

Adding rigid foam to existing walls can be a reasonable retrofit approach if you're removing siding but not sheathing on your existing home. This can be applied as a separate layer of foam or in the form of an insulated siding product.

If you plan to use steel studs for framing, keep in

mind that studs in walls act as little thermal bridges that allow heat to bypass your insulation. A 20-gauge steel stud conducts ten times as much heat as a 1-½-inch-wide wood stud (Malin 1994, 1). A side-by-side year-long test of two similar homes (one steel framed, one wood framed) conducted by the

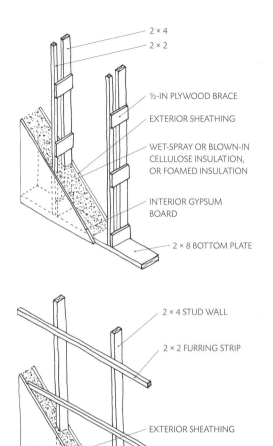

2 × 4
2 × 2
½-IN PLYWOOD BRACE
EXTERIOR SHEATHING
WET-SPRAY OR BLOWN-IN CELLULOSE INSULATION, OR FOAMED INSULATION
INTERIOR GYPSUM BOARD
2 × 8 BOTTOM PLATE

2 × 4 STUD WALL
2 × 2 FURRING STRIP
EXTERIOR SHEATHING
WET-SPRAY OR BLOWN-IN CELLULOSE INSULATION, OR FOAMED INSULATION
INTERIOR GYPSUM BOARD
2 × 4 BOTTOM PLATE
2 × 4 SHOE

The Larsen Truss System creates a 7½-inch cavity by pairing a 2 × 4 and a 2 × 2 with an air space between them, using short plywood braces. Wall panels are framed on 2 × 8 bottom and top plates. This creates a high-performing wall with a near-continuous thermal break when filled with a blown or foamed insulation product. ILLUSTRATION BY CHRISTOPHER GUTSCHE AND KATHLEEN SMITH, ADAPTED FROM ORIGINAL BY NATHAN GOOD.

The Heslam Grid or Strapped Wall, developed by Portland contractor Dave Heslam, creates a 5-inch cavity with a near-continuous thermal break by using 2 × 2 horizontal strapping on a conventional 2 × 4 stud wall with blown-in or spray foam insulation. ILLUSTRATION BY CHRISTOPHER GUTSCHE AND KATHLEEN SMITH, ADAPTED FROM ORIGINAL BY NATHAN GOOD.

National Association of Home Builders Research Center (2002) showed that energy use was higher in the steel-framed house—about 3.9 percent higher for natural gas heating in winter, and 10.7 percent higher for electric cooling / blower fan in summer. It should be noted that the steel-framed home had studs placed at 24 inches on-center, while the wood-framed home had studs placed at 16 inches on-center (2 × 6) to correlate with local practice for the given materials. If the wood-framed home had used 24-inch on-center framing, the difference would have been even greater. However, there are solutions if you want to use steel for its versatility, recycled content, and recyclability, including using continuous rigid foam insulation to effectively disconnect the steel bridge between the interior and exterior surfaces of your wall. For locations with extreme temperatures, you might want to reserve steel for interior walls.

An important point to note here is that all the materials in your wall assembly have an R-value. Putting R-19 insulation in your wall cavities (in a 2 × 6 wall) doesn't mean you have an R-19 wall. Thermal bridging across studs, gaps in the insulation, and other factors will reduce your R-value. Drywall, sheathing, and siding (especially insulated siding) will add to your wall's total R-value. A clear 2 × 6, 24-inch on-center wall with no openings, blocking, or such with an R-19 batt at the center of the wall has an actual total wall R-value of 16.4 (Christian and Kosny 1997, 3). In a real-world installation, with additional studs and headers at openings and at corners and intersections, the same wall assembly has a whole wall R-value of 13.7.

Insulating roofs. Conventional practice in the Northwest for insulating attics is to blow a loose-fill insulation (typically fiberglass, rock wool, or cellulose) onto the topside of the ceiling, between and over the joists. The 1995 Model Energy Code (International Code Council 1995) and U.S. Department of Energy insulation fact sheet (2000) provide recommended R-values for roofs. For most of the Northwest, R-38 is recommended, although some of the higher (and colder) elevations in the region call for R-49. Achieving R-38 with low-density loose-fill insulation generally requires material to be 12 or 13 inches deep. This depth covers the joists, disconnecting the thermal bridge the joists represent.

Around the roof perimeter, however, where the rafter falls to meet the joist (known as the heel), insulation effectiveness can be compromised in a couple of ways. First, the available depth for insulation tapers off, in some cases to as little as 3½ inches in roofs using trusses constructed from 2 × 4 lumber. Second, air blowing up through the soffit vents can "wash" the insulation away from the perimeter. The first problem is addressed by using a raised heel truss. By adding a vertical spacer at the truss heel, this design ensures that full-depth insulation covers all the way to the outer edge of the exterior wall. The second problem is addressed by using cardboard baffles, fixed between the rafters for the first few feet above the heel, to separate the ventilation air from the insulation. Note that raised heel roof trusses can cost more than conventional roof trusses, and because the exterior wall is extended, additional sheathing and siding will be needed. Combined, this can add as much as several hundred dollars to your

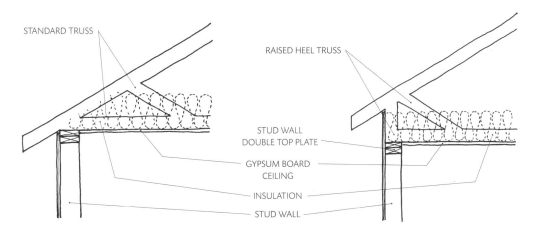

STANDARD TRUSS

RAISED HEEL TRUSS

STUD WALL
DOUBLE TOP PLATE

GYPSUM BOARD
CEILING

INSULATION

STUD WALL

A raised heel truss adds a vertical spacer at the truss heel so that full-depth insulation can extend all the way to the outer edge of the exterior wall. ILLUSTRATION BY CHRISTOPHER GUTSCHE AND KATHLEEN SMITH.

construction cost, but long-term energy savings will easily offset the initial cost.

Some designers and builders prefer to insulate under the roof deck rather than on top of the ceiling. This has the effect of creating a conditioned (or partially conditioned) attic, a useful place to locate mechanical equipment and distribution ducts.

Insulated assemblies. Structural insulated panels (SIPs), which are thick layers of rigid foam (usually expanded polystyrene) sandwiched between layers of OSB, provide the thermal benefits of rigid foam plus structural integrity in one package. SIPs can be used for floor, wall, and roof assemblies. Insulated concrete forms (ICFs), which consist of a permanent foam form (made from polystyrene) for pouring a concrete wall, offer similar performance. An alternative to the more common foam ICF system is Durisol. Durisol blocks are produced from postindustrial wood waste shreds and Portland cement; block cells are lined with rock wool insulation. Architect Nathan Good recommends this system for coastal environments, especially sites with high winds, although he

cautions that there are design implications, such as increased wall thickness and a tendency to wick moisture during winter months that must be addressed. (For more excellent field advice, see Good 2006b.)

Insulating basements. Basements should also

Structural insulated panels (SIPs) are installed by Shirey Contracting as part of a two-story addition to an existing home in Bellevue, Washington. The installation was completed in two days. PHOTO BY ANDREW BUCHANAN.

Rastra, a gridlike ICF product produced from recycled plastics, such as expanded polysty- rene, mixed with cement was used in this Seattle, Washington, construc- tion project. After the grid is set in place, its internal channels are filled with concrete. PHOTO BY GEORGE OSTROW, COUR- TESY OF VELOCIPEDE.

be properly insulated. In new construction, exterior insulation using a rigid foam product protected by a foundation drainage panel is the best solution since this arrangement creates a "warm" basement wall that can dry freely to the inside. Interior insulation is less desirable since it creates a "cold" wall that can result in condensation and other moisture problems. In a remodel, however, exterior insulation gener- ally isn't feasible. These guidelines should be strictly observed:

• The wall must be able to dry to the interior. Don't use a polyethylene vapor barrier, vapor-impermeable foam, vinyl wall covering, or vapor-retardant paint.

• The interior wall assembly must have an effec- tive air barrier to prevent warm air from contact- ing the cold basement wall. Vapor-permeable rigid foam insulation adhered to the wall is a good option, with edges caulked and seams sealed with tape and mastic.

• Any material in contact with the basement wall must be moisture tolerant. Materials that aren't moisture tolerant should be protected by a capil- lary break that's either a ¾-inch air gap or a layer of moisture-impermeable material.

• Exposed surfaces in basements must be fire resis- tant. Generally, this requires that vapor-permeable rigid foam be covered by a framed wall with drywall to provide fire protection. Additional insulation could be added in the frame wall cavity in this case.

Insulation values of windows and doors. When you upgrade the insulation values of your build- ing enclosure, don't forget windows and doors. A solid wood door has an insulating value of about R-2 and single-pane windows represent big holes in your thermal enclosure, even when they're closed. Choose insulated doors with high-performance glazing. Insulation values for windows are generally expressed in U-values, the inverse of R-values (the lower the U-value, the better the thermal perfor- mance). More extreme temperature ranges in some areas of the Northwest may justify investing in triple- glazed windows with double low-E (low emissivity) coatings and insulated frames. (Most of the thermal transfer through double-glazed windows is by ther- mal radiation from the warm pane to the cool pane. A low-E coating applied to the side of the cool pane that faces the warm pane rejects or resists that radi- ant heat transfer. Low-E2 or double low-E adds a solar control coating that limits heat gain from solar radiation.)

Conditioning your crawl space involves extending the thermal envelope down below floor level. This means fully insulating your foundation and air-sealing the crawl space from the outside (sealing all vents) and from the soil beneath, using an air- and moisture-tight membrane that's mechanically sealed to your foundation, and then circulating air from the house through the space. Conventional crawl spaces commonly cause moisture and mold problems because they create cool, still conditions with moisture from the soil; conditioned crawl spaces resolve many of these issues in most situations.

The greatest benefits appear to accrue in areas with more extreme climates, but even in the Pacific Northwest, conditioned crawl spaces offer some advantages. For example, locating your space conditioning equipment in an insulated crawl space keeps it out of your living area while still inside the thermal envelope. Heat that inevitably escapes from your equipment will still help to heat your home. It should be noted, however, that a conditioned crawl space isn't suitable for a home in a floodplain, nor can it address moisture problems that result from surface water or groundwater intruding—these must be addressed through proper drainage.

In many jurisdictions, you may run into resistance to a conditioned crawl space at the permit desk, so it pays to do your homework. Before you get too invested in this strategy, discuss it with your local building official.

A conditioned crawl space also seals out soil gases, but this shouldn't be viewed as adequate protection if you're in a location where radon is considered a potential problem. The EPA provides a map showing radon zones across the region, but your local building department should be able to give more specific information. If you're in a designated Radon Zone 1, plan to include radon-resistant construction in your project. This involves creating a sealed gas-permeable zone beneath the slab or crawl space, depressurizing that zone with a fan, and venting the resulting exhaust gases above and away from the house.

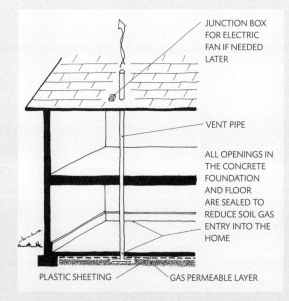

JUNCTION BOX FOR ELECTRIC FAN IF NEEDED LATER

VENT PIPE

ALL OPENINGS IN THE CONCRETE FOUNDATION AND FLOOR ARE SEALED TO REDUCE SOIL GAS ENTRY INTO THE HOME

PLASTIC SHEETING

GAS PERMEABLE LAYER

Radon-resistant construction involves creating a sealed gas-permeable zone beneath the slab or crawl space, depressurizing that zone with a fan, and venting the resulting exhaust gases above and away from the house. ILLUSTRATION BY CHRISTOPHER GUTSCHE AND KATHLEEN SMITH.

RECOMMENDATIONS FOR WINDOW AND DOOR INSULATION LEVELS

ELEMENT	ENERGY STAR NORTHWEST MINIMUMS	BETTER
Windows		
Windows	U-0.35	U-0.30 in milder climates
		U-0.18 in harsher climates
Skylights	U-0.50	U-0.35
Window Area	Up to 21 percent of heated floor area	No more than 15 percent of heated floor area
Doors	R-5	Greater than R-5

In addition to recommending U-values for windows, Energy Star Northwest suggests limiting the amount of window area. We recommend that you consider limiting window area even further to reduce heat loss even more, though you will also want to consider the need for daylight, solar gain (in winter), and ventilation (in summer).

Seal and test your enclosure.

No matter where your home is located and how much of an upgrade in insulation you decide makes sense for your location, building an airtight home with proper ventilation is essential to proper thermal performance. Insulation works by creating a thermal boundary. But if there are pathways for air to move across that thermal boundary—through leaks and holes—the thermal boundary becomes less effective, and perhaps worse, moisture problems can occur as warm moist air finds its way to cool surfaces, where the moisture can condense and create comfortable living conditions for mold.

Creating an airtight enclosure isn't costly. In stick-framed homes, it just requires a little attention to detail and judicious use of caulking and spray foam. The air boundary is generally formed by the subfloor (or the foundation or basement walls in a conditioned basement or crawl space), the wall bottom and top plates, the drywall, and either the ceiling or the roof deck (in a conditioned attic space). Every penetration into the conditioned space, such as plumbing and electrical chases, is sealed. This includes areas under stairs and behind bathtubs, which are notorious locations for air leaks.

In a typical drywall installation in a stick-framed house, most of the seams are sealed by tape and joint compound. The airtight drywall approach (ADA) uses a bead of caulk to seal the drywall to framing members, tape and mud to seal all the seams, and caulk and rubber gaskets for electrical outlets, switches, and recessed can lights, as well as plumbing penetrations. ADA has proven to be an effective strategy for reducing infiltration as well as keeping moisture, dust, and insects from entering a home.

Building wraps also contribute to airtightness, but anyone who thinks wrap alone can seal up your enclosure isn't the person you want to build your house. The same goes for the builder who believes caulk is an adequate moisture barrier. Alternative wall systems such as SIPs and ICFs tend to make the job of air sealing easier, but attention must still be paid to joints and particularly to transitions between the wall system and conventional framing, such as floors, ceilings and roofs, and bay windows and other

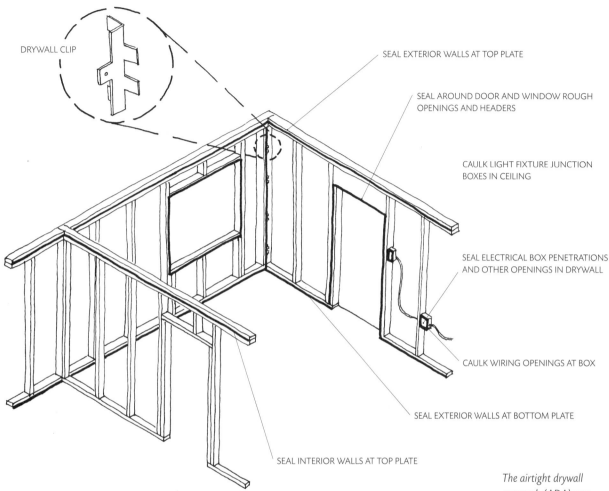

DRYWALL CLIP

SEAL EXTERIOR WALLS AT TOP PLATE

SEAL AROUND DOOR AND WINDOW ROUGH OPENINGS AND HEADERS

CAULK LIGHT FIXTURE JUNCTION BOXES IN CEILING

SEAL ELECTRICAL BOX PENETRATIONS AND OTHER OPENINGS IN DRYWALL

CAULK WIRING OPENINGS AT BOX

SEAL EXTERIOR WALLS AT BOTTOM PLATE

SEAL INTERIOR WALLS AT TOP PLATE

pop-outs (small spaces that push out beyond the main plane of the wall).

You can test the tightness of your home using a blower door test. Based on the airflow through the fan and the volume of the house, the tester can calculate the number of air changes that would naturally occur per hour (NACH). This tells you how much conditioned air you lose through leaks in the enclosure and how much natural fresh air enters the house. Losing costly conditioned air is a bad thing, but not having sufficient fresh air is worse. Energy, building science, and indoor air quality experts have determined that 0.35 NACH is a good balance point, providing sufficient ventilation while keeping energy losses moderate. This is the standard set for Energy-Star Northwest homes.

Energy performance can be improved by tightening up a house—0.15 NACH is quite achievable in new

The airtight drywall approach (ADA) uses a bead of caulk to seal the drywall to framing members, tape and mud to seal all the seams, and caulk and rubber gaskets for electrical outlets, switches, and recessed can lights, as well as plumbing penetrations. ILLUSTRATION BY CHRISTOPHER GUTSCHE AND KATHLEEN SMITH.

construction—but that house will require mechanical ventilation back up to at least the 0.35 NACH level to ensure good air quality and prevent potential moisture and mold problems. A heat exchanger will allow you to recapture the potentially wasted heat. How tight you want your house to be depends on the priority you give to energy efficiency, your contractor's willingness to make it work, and your budget for adding ventilation to your mechanical system. The tighter the house, the more comfort and energy efficiency it offers, and the more control you have over how your home performs.

The tightness of your home is an important factor in sizing the space conditioning system. You and your contractor need to be fairly confident you can achieve your goal and willing to take the time to fix the leaks highlighted by the blower door test if necessary. A contractor who's had experience with having homes tested will have a better understanding of what it will take to meet your goal. (Experiencing a blower door test is very educational; most contractors who've done so tend to do a better job supervising the sealing process.)

Caution: The rules about tightness and ventilation also apply when weatherizing and upgrading an existing home. Tightening up the enclosure can often resolve all kinds of older home quirks (like hot spots and cold spots) and improve energy performance. But your old leaky enclosure was probably very good at ventilating itself. Once you plug up those leaks, finding other ways to get the moisture out of the house will be vital. A blower door test is an important first step in most major remodeling projects. Not studying the dynamics of your older home may result in the same problems (or worse) remaining after the project is finished.

Select glazing to optimize thermal performance and natural light.

Windows aren't good thermal barriers. This can be used to our advantage, allowing free solar energy into our homes when we want it. However, windows are also pretty good at letting in heat in the summer when we don't want it, and letting out heat in the winter when we want to keep it in.

Window technology continues to improve. Double and triple glazing reduces heat loss, as do surface treatments and films, such as low-E coatings. But even top-of-the-line window technologies currently available still have insulating values only equivalent to R-5. If you have to choose between paying a premium for high-tech windows and something else, give higher priority to limiting your window area and paying careful attention to the solar and ventilation qualities of the windows you select for your project. Be aware that low-E coatings and other treatments for solar heat gain and ultraviolet control may affect how much visible light is transmitted through the windows. They may also color your worldview (blue!). Ask for samples before you buy.

The solar heat gain coefficient (SHGC) measures the amount of solar radiation the window allows through. By choosing the right SHGC for glazing in relation to its orientation in your home, you can fine-tune your home's comfort levels without touching your thermostat. You'll also want to pay attention to percentages, both of the total amount of glazing in the home, and of the total conditioned floor area. Keep in mind that window design isn't quite as simple as areas and ratios, as it needs to be coordinated with overall design, room layout, and systems strategies.

In an existing home, replacing windows can present budgetary and aesthetic challenges and may not deliver hoped-for performance gains, especially if air leakage around windows isn't taken care of. Use a blower door test to find the leaks, and, for much less than the cost of a replacement window, liberally apply caulk and weather stripping. Removable exterior storm windows can be installed cost effectively (many turn-of-the-century Northwest bungalows still have their original top-hinged storm windows in place).

If your existing home is challenged with too much solar gain in the summer from large areas of glass on the east, west, or south sides, there are several fixes. The first is to plant deciduous shrubs and trees to shade the glass. (This way winter sun isn't blocked.) If you have an attractive view (which often explains expanses of glass) and a desire to preserve it and natural light even in summer, you can use a translucent exterior sunshade. On south-facing walls, you can create horizontal shading with a vine-covered trellis or a simple overhang sized to block the summer sun from reaching the glazing from May through August.

Select and locate operable windows to promote natural ventilation.

The amount of airflow through a window is a function of the percentage of effective open area its design provides. The higher the percentage opening, the better a window is at ventilating. To admit

Translucent exterior sunshades were installed at the Luk remodel to block solar gain but preserve natural light and views from an expanse of south-facing windows.
PHOTO BY GRACE HUANG, MING ARCHITECTURE.

sufficient outside air, total openings for a given space should have a net effective opening area equal to at least 12 percent of the room's floor area (State of Hawaii Department of Business, Economic Development, and Tourism 2002, 54). The percentage of effective open area varies by window type (Warner 1995, 9):

Single hung	45 percent
Double hung	45 percent
Sliding	45 to 50 percent
Hopper	45 percent
Casement	90 percent
Awning	75 percent
Jalousie	75 percent

Locating your windows properly helps you optimize that airflow. As prevailing summer breezes blow against and across the walls of your home, slightly increased pressure will develop on the upwind side and lower pressure on the downwind side. Air will tend to move into open windows on the upwind

GLAZING CHOICES AND SOLAR HEAT GAIN

ORIENTATION	OPTIMAL PERCENTAGE OF TOTAL WINDOW AREA	SHGC	REASONS FOR RECOMMENDATION
EAST	15 to 25 percent	0.55 or less	Receives morning sun; generally beneficial for solar gain but don't overdo. A lower SHGC (such as low-E windows provide) or shading with deciduous shrubs or trees can allow you to have larger than optimal openings on this side if you have a beautiful easterly view you want to enjoy. If you exceed 12 percent of conditioned floor area, you'll have to counter that with thermal mass to manage solar gain and control nighttime losses.
SOUTH	50 to 60 percent	0.55 or higher	Receives sun most of the day, assuming it's not blocked by landscape or buildings. Putting a significant percentage of your windows on this side is part of a passive solar scheme. To achieve meaningful gain, you'll need south windows to cover at least 9 percent of conditioned floor area west of the Cascades and 8 percent of conditioned floor area east of the Cascades.
WEST	10 to 20 percent	0.40 or less	Allows wonderful sunset views but from spring through fall can cause overheating. Low-E2 is a good choice here because it both lowers heat loss (U-factor) and controls solar gain (SHGC).
NORTH	5 to 10 percent	0.55 or higher	Allows indirect light but is often exposed to the coldest winter weather. Windows should be smaller and placed high to allow good light penetration into the house.

SOURCE: Efficient Windows Collaborative fact sheet, 2006

side as long as there's a way for displaced air to move out of the house, such as an open window on the downwind side.

On walls parallel to the prevailing breezes, you can use casement windows to create the same effect. To scoop air into a room, locate the hinge on the downwind side of the window; to draw air out of the room, locate the hinge on the upwind side. Double-hung windows allow you to vent warmer air out of the top sash or to draw cool air in through the bottom sash.

Here are some techniques for placing windows for optimal airflow (State of Hawaii Department of Business, Economic Development, and Tourism 2002, 53–56):

• For rooms with openings on opposite sides, orient the room 45 degrees from wind direction. This improves airflow by 20 percent.

• Keep inlet (upwind) openings slightly smaller than outlet (downwind) openings. 1:1.25 is the recommended ratio.

• Locate inlet (upwind) windows at body level. Adapt to the kind of activity in the room (that is, if activity is happening lower down, the openings should be lower).

• For rooms with openings on adjacent walls, place windows far apart and at a diagonal. The farther apart the windows are, the better the airflow.

• For rooms with windows on the same wall, casement windows will work better than a single wing wall for setting up airflow.

Operable clerestory windows (windows set high up in walls or in a shed dormer) and skylights can be used to vent warm air from a house, using the

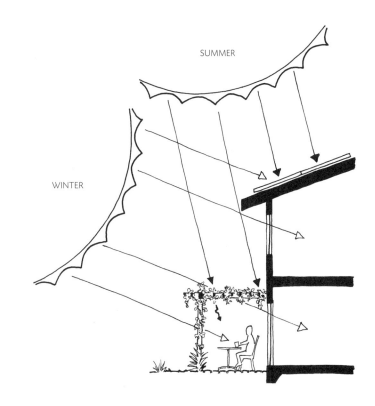

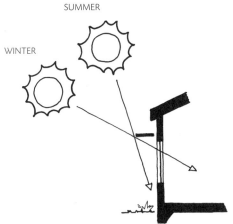

Horizontal shading can be created on south-facing walls by adding a vine-covered trellis (above) or a simple overhang sized to block the summer sun from reaching the glazing from May through August (left). ILLUSTRATIONS BY CHRISTOPHER GUTSCHE AND KATHLEEN SMITH.

For rooms with openings on adjacent walls, airflow is optimized if windows are placed far apart and at a diagonal (top row). For rooms with windows on the same wall, casement windows will work better than a single wing wall for setting up airflow (bottom row). ILLUSTRATIONS BY CHRISTOPHER GUTSCHE AND KATHLEEN SMITH, ADAPTED FROM STATE OF HAWAII DEPARTMENT OF BUSINESS, ECONOMIC DEVELOPMENT, AND TOURISM (2002, 53–56.)

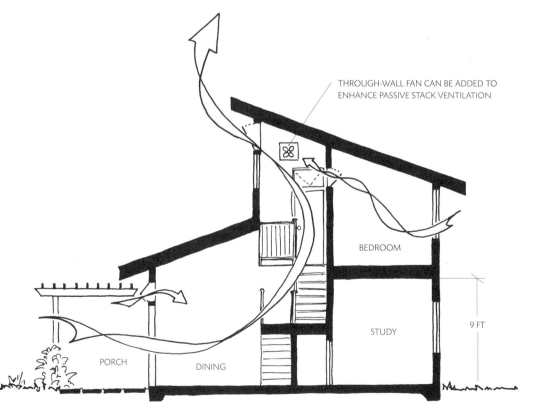

Air movement through operable clerestory windows can create a cooling effect. Rising warm air pulls air in from outside through windows or vents. ILLUSTRATION BY CHRISTOPHER GUTSCHE AND KATHLEEN SMITH.

stack effect in which rising warm air pulls air in from outside through windows or vents. If the outside air is cooler or these openings are adjacent to shade trees or on the north side, the cooling effect is enhanced. Regardless, the air movement will increase occupant comfort through what's called the sensible cooling effect.

Design the enclosure to use the energy that's freely available on the site.

With regard to enclosure design, making use of on-site free energy is a matter of ensuring that openings and overhangs properly capture or deflect the

THROUGH-WALL FAN CAN BE ADDED TO ENHANCE PASSIVE STACK VENTILATION

BEDROOM

9 FT

STUDY

PORCH

DINING

Skylights are an attractive option for bringing additional daylight and/or direct sunlight (as well as moonlight) into the core of the house. If operable, they can also help naturally cool your home. But they bring with them several challenges. Your roof is the first line of defense to keep the weather out of your house, and cutting holes in it always increases the risk of leaks. A skylight tunnel cuts a large hole through your roof insulation (R-38 or more) and replaces it with an area of glass with an R-value equivalent to about 3. Anywhere other than on a north-sloping roof, a skylight allows significant solar gain that can be difficult to control in the summer.

These aren't insurmountable challenges, as both of us, who presently enjoy skylights in our homes, can attest. In the gentler climate conditions available in some parts of our region, skylights can work quite well, as long as careful attention is paid to installation details. However, as an alternative to skylights, consider using clerestory windows or a roof monitor (a small raised area of roof, generally positioned over the ridge, with glass sides). These windows can offer almost all the light and ventilation benefits of a skylight but can be protected from high summer sun by suitable overhangs.

You might also consider solar light tubes. A solar light tube—which includes a domed collector on the roof and a highly reflective light duct—delivers daylight, but indirectly. The final effect appears much like a lighting fixture, but it's operated by the sun so it won't deliver at night. Solar light tube kits are generally easy to install as a retrofit and are especially effective in dark interior spaces and hallways.

natural resources available, as temperature, light, and prevailing breezes shift through the days and seasons. Aligning types of interior space use with the elemental directions of the structure (north, south, east, west) as well as with the elemental surfaces the enclosure offers (solid wall, fixed window, operable window, or door) is considered good design by most architects. In addition, good design will pay attention to a household's natural rhythms. For example: Are you a late riser? If so, maybe your bedroom should be located on the north. The green difference is keeping at the forefront the enclosure's role in optimizing the home's capacity to respond to and be in the site. Information about the site that you gathered as part of the site assessment—including

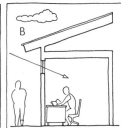

Windows can be designed to provide access to views (A), daylight (B), or both (C). A solar light tube (D) can also deliver daylight, but indirectly. ILLUSTRATION BY CHRISTOPHER GUTSCHE AND KATHLEEN SMITH.

Passive solar design utilizes the architectural features and components of the home to naturally provide for the heating, cooling, and lighting needs of the occupants. It requires no panels on the roof, no maintenance, and no outside energy (except the sun). The home itself is the collector, storage medium, and distribution system.

With a passive system, heating (and cooling) is achieved primarily through radiant transfer. This is the most comfortable form of heating and the way the sun heats the earth. Here's how it works: If we're in sight of something warmer or colder than we are, we gain or lose heat to that object through electromagnetic radiation. Radiant transfer doesn't require a transfer fluid like air or water—that's convective transfer. And it doesn't require you to be touching the heating source—that's conduction. With radiant heat, the indoor air temperature can be lower, because you act as a solar thermal collector. (It's why you can be more comfortable on the sunny side of the street on a cold day.)

Basically, a passive solar design consists of some south-facing glazing, usually glass, to collect solar gain and some form of thermal mass—typically water, masonry, or drywall—to store the solar gain. Sounds simple, but you'll want to fine-tune the design to get the most out of the solar energy available to your home space, while maintaining comfortable temperatures in your home.

According to the National Renewable Energy Laboratory, you can save up to 60 percent of your space-heating costs with a good passive solar home design in Oregon and Washington (where I live and work) and up to 70 percent in western and southern Oregon. Adjust these projected savings downward as you go north in the Cascadia region, and upward as you go south. These savings may seem optimistic, but a long mild heating season is well suited to passive solar design. In parts of the region where temperatures can soar to more than 100 degrees in summer, such as eastern Washington and Oregon, passive systems can operate in reverse to keep a home comfortable.

The amount of space-heating savings you actually achieve depends on how much you decide to invest in your passive solar design. The first step is energy conservation. It's easier and less expensive to conserve energy than to collect, store, and distribute energy. Going beyond code for insulation levels and window efficiency is a great place to start. Close attention to air sealing techniques is also very important.

The next step, which will save you roughly 20 to 30 percent, is to give the home a long south wall with minimal jogs and position the living spaces (where you spend the most time) on that side. Now put about half the windows in the house (around 12 percent of the heated floor space) on the south facade. This is called sun-tempering.

To achieve 50 percent savings, add more south glazing—up to 60 percent of the adjacent floor area. Because too much south glass can overheat a home, we add thermal mass to soak up daytime heat and provide nighttime heat. Thermal mass is most effective when directly lit by the sun. Passive strategies that work well in the Northwest include direct-gain windows (unshaded south-facing windows) and clerestories that distribute light

by Chris Herman, designer/builder, Winter Sun Design

and heat onto walls or floors acting as thermal mass; water walls (banks of water drums or other containers that hold heat); and Trombe walls (masonry walls separated from the outdoors by glass that allows solar gain). Glazing the entire south side of a home, as was often done in the 1970s, can create what I call a solar people cooker.

To get 60 percent solar savings an attached sunroom is usually required. This is a room with no auxiliary heat source that's isolated from the home by exterior-grade windows and doors (per code) and that has insulated east and west walls, and a well-insulated roof. (Overhead glass is counterproductive to passive design, as it loses a lot of heat in the winter and gains a lot of heat in the summer.) Glazing area in a sunroom can equal up to 90 percent of adjacent floor area. Setting the sunroom a couple of steps below the first floor of the home increases natural convection—air movement related to temperature differences and breezes—which is desirable because it doesn't require fans or electricity.

Double-hung windows between the sunroom and the home can help control the temperature of the air entering the living spaces. Opening the top sash of the window supplies the hottest air; opening the bottom sash supplies cooler air. Thermostatically controlled fans can also be used and may be a good idea in your situation, but then your design isn't technically passive. (Don't let that keep you from doing what makes sense in your situation.) Sunrooms are subject to large temperature swings. Water drums behind the glass will reduce overheating, provide nighttime warmth, and make a

great bench for starting plants.

A properly sized fixed overhang is recommended for most climates to reduce summer heat gain. Size the overhang for passive solar comfort in one of two ways:

1 Calculate P, the projection of the overhang from the side of the house, by dividing H (height, the distance from the bottom of the overhang to the bottom of the window) by a denominator ranging from 1.7 to 2.2, where 1.7 will give full shade on the window from May 15 to August 1, and 2.2 will give full shade on the summer solstice only.

2. Graphically use solar altitude angles for your latitude to see how much direct sun or shading is hitting your south wall. These angles can also be used to determine how far back into the home the sun will penetrate at different times of the year.

A properly sized overhang will admit all of the winter sun and block solar gain in the summer. The clerestory and south wall of this home designed by Winter Sun is fully shaded on this summer solstice afternoon. PHOTO BY CHRIS HERMAN.

The table indicates maximum solar altitude angles for selected Northwest cities. The solar altitude angle is the angle between the horizon and an imaginary line connecting to the sun. At sunset and sunrise the solar altitude angle is 0; the maximum angle occurs when the sun is at its zenith. The altitude angle relates to the latitude of the site, the declination angle, and the hour.

Night insulation and reflectors increase the performance of any passive heating system. Exterior night insulation can also act as summer heat-rejecting shades. Shading windows on the inside increases the temperature between the panes of glass in a double-pane window and can lead to premature failure of the seals. A good specular (shiny) reflector can bounce 30 to 40 percent more solar gain into the collector glazing. It can also act as night insula-tion and summer shades when closed up. If you're designing a specular reflector, locate it outside and below the glazing, tilted downward at a 5-degree angle. You can also rely on snow, water, white sand, or even white-painted exterior plywood to perform this function.

Passive solar cooling is achieved by keeping the home's thermal mass shaded during the day so it can soak up heat from the occupants and furnishings. At night the mass is exposed to the night sky (which is extremely cold) and it radiates the collected heat out at 186,500 miles per second (the speed of light). By morning the mass is cool and ready to soak up unwanted heat inside the house again. This works best where the diurnal swing is significant.

Night flushing helps this process by cooling off all the other heat sinks in the home, and it can be accomplished without fans. This is done by exhausting hot air high up on the warm sides of the building (south and west) and pulling in cool air from the shady sides of the house (north and east). Prevailing winds may alter this strategy. Opening clerestory windows take advantage of the solar chimney

Maximum solar altitude angles for selected Northwest cities

CITY	DEC. 21	MARCH/SEPT. 21	JUNE 21	LATITUDE
Vancouver, BC	17.2°	41.0°	64.1°	49° 15'
Bellingham, WA	17.8°	41.5°	64.6°	48° 45'
Seattle, WA	19.0°	42.7°	65.7°	47° 36'
Spokane, WA	18.9°	42.8°	65.7°	47° 30'
Boise, ID	22.3°	45.3°	67.7°	43° 36'
Missoula, MO	19.3°	42.6°	65.4°	46° 52'
Portland, OR	21.1°	44.7°	67.8°	45° 31'
Eugene, OR	22.5°	46.2°	69.2°	44° 03'
Arcata, CA	25.6°	49.2°	72.2°	40° 52'
San Francisco, CA	28.8°	52.5°	75.5°	37° 46'

SOURCE: U.S. Naval Observatory 2006.

or stack effect. Hot air rising and exiting is replaced by cool air from outside after the sun goes down and the air temperature drops. In extremely hot, dry climates burying the north side of the home can also help a lot.

One of the biggest challenges in designing passive solar homes is satisfying a desire for views when it conflicts with the desire for passive solar heating and cooling. Orienting the home 20 degrees off of true south will lose only about 5 percent of the possible gain, but facing the home southwest will make overheating more likely. True south is about 20 degrees east of magnetic south in western Washington. For other locations, you can determine your true south declination by looking in the newspaper and finding out when sunrise and sunset are, and at the moment halfway between them—which is solar noon—putting a stick in the ground. The shadow will be pointing true north. (You can also check with your local solar association.)

Another challenge occurs in the swing months of March and September. The sun's angle above the horizon is identical on the spring and fall equinoxes (42 degrees in Seattle). In March we want the sun's warmth and in September we probably don't. Moving shades and opening windows will help alleviate this issue. People have likened living in a passive solar home to sailing. You can set a course and let it go, or you can trim sails and adjust heading to achieve the highest performance. Being active with your passive home can save money, increase comfort, and connect you to nature.

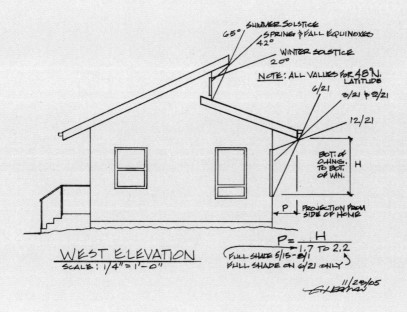

This schematic illustrates the use of both methods of determining the proper overhang size for the home in the previous photo—graphically using solar altitude angles and calculating P, the projection of the overhang from the side of the house.

ILLUSTRATION BY CHRIS HERMAN.

access to sunlight and aesthetic views, wind patterns, ambient noise—should be useful as you try to achieve this goal.

CHOOSING MATERIALS FOR SUSTAINABILITY

Your choices about materials for the building enclosure have to do first with using less, then with using materials that will be durable and that can be reused later, and finally with how green a material is in terms of the environmental impacts of its manufacture and what kind of maintenance it will require. Here are our *top green home picks* for selecting and using enclosure materials:

- Don't overbuild.
- Make greener choices for exterior products.
- Choose materials with deconstruction in mind.
- When deconstructing, preserve what you can.

Don't overbuild.

How much material is actually needed to meet your project's structural requirements? Maybe not as much as conventional practice suggests. Although there are some great alternatives out there, wood is the clear favorite for home building in the Pacific Northwest. Several decades ago, engineers at the National Association of Home Builders Research Center identified efficient framing techniques that use just enough wood to provide structural integrity. Wood is an excellent material, and while it makes sense here in the Northwest to rely on this local and, in ideal circumstances, renewable resource, it makes no sense to use more than we need.

Many designers and builders worry that if they conserve materials used to create the structure they might be sacrificing structural integrity. Obviously the latter outcome is the antithesis of our suggestion to build a long-lived building. But the fact is that wood-framed homes are frequently overbuilt and use more lumber than is actually required to carry the load. Our builder friend Steve Loken has for years demonstrated the use of resource-efficient alternatives to overbuilding. He encourages anyone who will listen to use engineered wood (such as finger-jointed lumber) and panelized systems such as SIPs, and suggests we "use the 'pretty' solid wood for places it can be enjoyed—for trim or mantle, for example" (personal communication, 2006).

Finger joints enable the use of shorter pieces of wood to manufacture longer members. Finger-jointed lumber tends to be straighter and stiffer than the lumber generally available and is a resourceful use of what was once seen as waste. Trusses use less wood than conventional joists or rafters to span the same distance, and they leave space for running ducts and wiring. Trusses were used in the Kerby

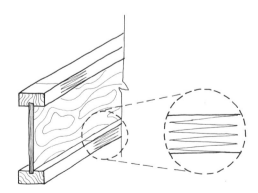

Finger joints such as the one highlighted in the illustration of an I-joist enable the use of shorter pieces of wood to manufacture longer members. ILLUSTRATION BY CHRISTOPHER GUTSCHE AND KATHLEEN SMITH..

Trusses use less wood than conventional joists or rafters to span the same distance, and they leave space for running ducts and wiring. PHOTO BY ANDREA NELSON.

Street homes in Portland, Oregon, and are frequently seen on construction sites. Even if you don't go for these engineered wood alternatives, there are some simple ways to reduce the amount of wood used in a stick-framed home (a home built from dimensional lumber):

Design with standard dimensions. Use a 2-foot module for layout so that you can use whole or half widths of sheet goods to minimize unusable offcuts. Size and position window openings so they don't need additional framing members. (Standard dimension windows can save you money, too.)

Make the most of every stud. Use a takeoff list and a central cutting area with an offcut pile so that the right framing members are cut from the right studs, and so that offcuts, instead of long sticks cut up to make short ones, are used for blocking.

Use advanced framing. This technique uses an approach called optimal value engineering to ensure that you use the most material-efficient approach to meeting the structural loads of your frame. In areas that have seismic upgrades to structural requirements, there may be a need for some additional engineering (such as installing shear panels to preserve structural rigidity in a seismic event) but most advanced framing strategies can be applied to save lumber.

Besides reducing the amount of wood used to frame the home, advanced framing improves energy performance by reducing thermal bridging, since less dimensional lumber means more wall area is fully insulated. Advanced framing also helps to improve durability by minimizing the use of multiple studs sandwiched together. Such solid blocking is notoriously resistant to drying out in the event of moisture penetration and is a common place for mold to grow. Although all of these benefits are available from advanced framing, significant material savings are practically available only if you take an aggressive approach and apply most (if not all) of these advanced framing techniques:

- spacing 2 × 6 studs at 24 inches on center instead of 16 inches on center
- stack framing (so trusses, studs, and joists align vertically)
- using single top plates
- using two-stud corners (with drywall clips instead of a third stud to nail the drywall to)
- using ladder blocking for interior wall intersections
- using appropriately sized headers for door and window openings (for example, no headers in non-load-bearing walls)
- using metal hangers in place of jack and cripple studs at window openings

The house design will affect whether you can use advanced framing or not, so your designer should be in sync with you on this if you want to do it. Two

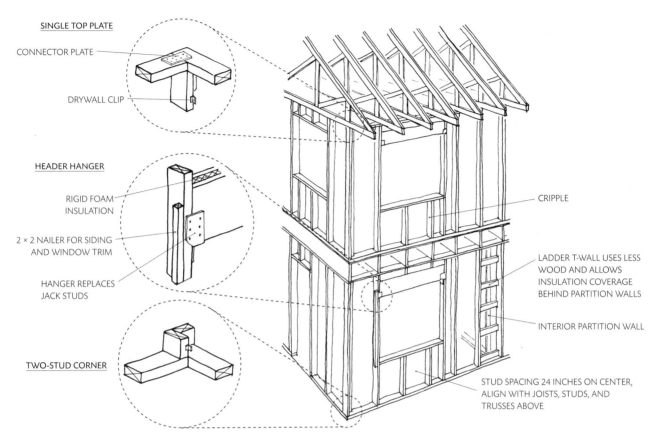

SINGLE TOP PLATE

CONNECTOR PLATE

DRYWALL CLIP

HEADER HANGER

RIGID FOAM
INSULATION

2 × 2 NAILER FOR SIDING
AND WINDOW TRIM

HANGER REPLACES
JACK STUDS

TWO-STUD CORNER

CRIPPLE

LADDER T-WALL USES LESS
WOOD AND ALLOWS
INSULATION COVERAGE
BEHIND PARTITION WALLS

INTERIOR PARTITION WALL

STUD SPACING 24 INCHES ON CENTER,
ALIGN WITH JOISTS, STUDS, AND
TRUSSES ABOVE

Advanced framing can include all of the techniques illustrated here. ILLUSTRATION BY CHRISTOPHER GUTSCHE AND KATHLEEN SMITH.

other potential barriers include the building code official and the builder, if neither has previously been exposed to this framing approach. In either case, you can educate them by providing drawings from respected sources, such as those listed in "Resources," or through crew training sessions.

Make greener choices for exterior products.

We've suggested aiming for a fifty-year exterior. Although thermal performance and durability are the most important aspects of products you may choose for your home's exterior, you can throw other considerations into the mix as well. If you're

like most people, including us, you'll be making your choices based on a number of characteristics, not the least of which are cost and environmental impact. The three big-ticket items for the building enclosure—wood, steel, and/or concrete—each have environmental advantages and disadvantages. You'll need to decide what's appropriate for your project and which material will give you the performance you want.

How are the significant materials you're considering using to construct or upgrade the building enclosure produced?

Significant materials typically include wood, steel,

and concrete. As discussed in chapter 3, FSC certification is the best guarantee that a wood product has been produced in a sustainable manner. For reasons of economy, there are still many owners of sustainably managed wood lots who haven't pursued FSC certification; if you're looking at purchasing from these sources, you'll need to do your homework to assure yourself of appropriate levels of management.

Some of the structural wood products produced in the Northwest include dimensional lumber as well as highly engineered products that provide greater strength and thus allow more flexible designs, quicker construction, and more efficient use of the timber resource. Structural engineered wood products are generally formed using moisture-resistant glues and binders that contain no urea-formaldehyde, a known respiratory irritant and suspected carcinogen. Many of these glues do contain phenol-formaldehyde, however, which is more stable and therefore less likely to off-gas. New binders that are formaldehyde-free are currently in development; they may be available for your project.

Our research has revealed that pretty much all steel sold in the United States includes a minimum of 25 percent recycled content; some manufacturers will have more. For example, structural steel can include upward of 95 percent recycled content. It helps to check product information if this is your passion. Steel is also highly recyclable. Although there are some issues with thermal performance when steel framing is used, comparisons by researchers between wood and steel used for building enclosures to determine which material has the greater overall environmental impact turn out to be inconclusive.

Concrete, which is a mixture of aggregate (sand and gravel), Portland cement, and water, generally contains additives that provide the concrete with specific desired characteristics. Portland cement is made by heating limestone and clay to high temperatures. The fine powder resulting reacts with water to form a matrix that binds the aggregate into a rock-hard material. Since most Portland cement is imported these days, and because its production tends to use large quantities of energy, methods to reduce the proportion of cement have been developed, including using fly ash and blast furnace slag to replace some of it. Fly ash was once landfilled as waste but is now considered a valuable additive by most green-minded engineers and designers. Using it results in a longer cure time and also, typically, in a higher concrete strength. Ground granulated blast furnace slag (GGBFS) is scraped from the inside of blast furnaces used to smelt steel. When processed and crushed, it makes a good substitute for Portland cement. It's becoming a popular alternative to fly ash because it can be added to concrete in much higher percentages and doesn't have a significant slowing effect on curing times yet still results in concrete with a high finished strength.

Typically, an efficient cement plant will release about 0.56 ton of CO_2 for each ton of cement produced; if carbon fuel is used to burn the clinker, an additional 0.35 ton of CO_2 is released. Taking into account all U.S. cement plants, at an average of nearly a ton of CO_2 per ton of cement, some 80 million tons of CO_2 is emitted into the atmosphere each year. GGBFS typically replaces 35 to 65 percent

All of the wood used for the Rivas-Scott remodel, featured in chapter 6, was either certified (if newly purchased) or salvaged during the renovation. Here, salvaged lumber is being used for formwork; later it will be used again, for floor framing. PHOTO BY ALAN SCOTT.

of the Portland cement in concrete. A 50 percent replacement of each ton of Portland cement would result in a reduction of approximately 0.5 ton of CO_2 for each ton of concrete produced (Hogan, Meusel, and Spellman 2001).

In addition to good durability, concrete has the advantage over steel and wood of providing significant thermal mass. This can enhance the building's ability to utilize solar gain in a passive system.

Where are the significant materials you're considering using to construct or upgrade the building enclosure produced? We're very lucky in the Northwest in that many wood, steel, and concrete products are available locally. Unfortunately, despite a significant local timber resource, wood frequently comes from elsewhere. Many woodlots in the region are being managed in a sustainable fashion, and

more and more are undergoing the rigorous third-party FSC certification process discussed in chapter 3. The greenest option in the Northwest would be to choose wood products that are third-party certified *and* harvested locally.

With concrete and steel, although some ingredients for the production process may be extracted regionally, others are imported from outside the region. The local advantage is at the manufacturing or fabrication stage. Slag cement used in the Pacific Northwest typically comes from Asia, but because it does such a good job of reducing greenhouse gas emissions, a major reason for buying local is removed. Still, the Northwest has an established infrastructure for supplying fly ash produced at local coal-fired power plants.

Now that we've discussed the environmental impacts of the big-ticket items, here are some things to consider as you select materials for particular uses:

Framing. For wood framing, use FSC-certified sustainably harvested, salvaged, and/or engineered wood products. The cost differential for these options ranges from zero to up to 30 percent. With FSC-certified wood, you may run into availability issues, although this is becoming less the case as more and more timber lots in the region are certified with this more rigorous rating. If you plan to use steel for framing, specify high levels of recycled content.

Sheathing. Use FSC-certified sustainably harvested plywood. If you opt for oriented strand board (OSB), choose OSB products that use nonformaldehyde binders and nontoxic borate pest treatments, and/or have achieved FSC certification. (Although the woods used in OSB are the least resistant to moisture, mold, and rot, OSB is generally appreciated for its efficient use of limited wood resources.)

Insulation. Some fiberglass batt and blown-in products include recycled glass; you can also get fiberglass insulation that's formaldehyde free. For rigid foam, EPS is generally preferred because it doesn't contribute to ozone depletion. (XPS manufacturers are expected to eliminate use of ozone-depleting HCFCs by 2010.) Another green alternative is cotton insulation made from recycled denim blue jeans—somehow perfect for the Northwest.

Building wrap. Wrap options are building paper and poly. In a 2001 article, Paul Fisette compared felt paper (frequently called tar paper because the product is impregnated with asphalt) to a number of poly wrap products and found that the wrap products' performance varied considerably, and only a few of the more than a dozen on the market passed his muster. He also says that either house wrap or felt will provide an adequate secondary drainage plane, and what's most important is to get the flashing details right and to be careful installing the building paper. From an environmental perspective, both options are petroleum based—definitely a negative when taking the larger environmental view, but one at this point that seems unavoidable. Perhaps a better alternative will be developed in the future, but even the rain screen approach described earlier requires use of a wrap.

Siding. Fiber-cement siding, made from Portland cement, sand, clay, and wood fiber, is a popular resource-efficient choice because it's durable and

Fiber-cement siding comes in large sheets, making installation pretty easy.
PHOTO COURTESY OF JAMES HARDIE BUILDING PRODUCTS, INC.

looks and installs like wood. It's available in vertical, lap, and shingle forms. Both lap and shingle siding were installed on the O'Brien-Cunningham residence in 1999 and to date show no sign of degradation, nor have they needed repainting. Vinyl is also a popular choice because of its longevity (although some vinyl siding products last longer than others) and general affordability, but as pointed out earlier, the product is manufactured from PVC, a controversial material from an environmental standpoint.

Roofing. Asphalt shingles are used for most homes because of their affordability. They're a petroleum product, however, so if you go this route, minimize the impact by opting for one of the better-quality versions available (with better than the fifteen-year life typically offered.) Wood shake roofs are still idealized in the Northwest but they're flammable, don't do well if not maintained, and are either made from lower quality wood than they should be to last or are made with wood that shouldn't be cut. A good-quality steel roof generally comes with a fifty-year warranty, is less friendly to moss growth because of its smooth finish, will include recycled content, and is highly amenable to deconstruction. There will be a cost premium, the size of which

Opening off the second-story master bedroom, the green roof garden installed on the Built Green Idea Home reduces and buffers rainwater runoff. The construction method included laying down an elastomeric membrane and then concrete architectural tiles (on top of plastic pedestals to protect the membrane). Preplanted recycled plastic containers were placed on top of the tiles along one side of the roof area. PHOTO BY MIKE SEIDL, COURTESY OF FUSION PARTNERS LLC.

Screws, bolts, and other forms of "dry" assembly, such as this ridge rafter screw-in connector, as opposed to friction nails or adhesives, allow for ease of disassembly. PHOTO COURTESY OF SIMPSON STRONG-TIE.

depends on how fancy your rooflines are. Concrete tiles are expensive and are energy intensive to manufacture but can't be beat for durability. There's also the option of a green roof, as demonstrated by the Built Green Idea Home.

Decks. Wood polymer decking (commonly known as plastic lumber) is our top choice for decks. As noted earlier, it lasts longer and doesn't require power washing (with or without chemicals) to be presentable.

Choose materials with deconstruction in mind.

What will happen to your house when its life is over? The goal is to build or remodel your home so it lasts for many generations. But what happens after that? Or what if the home is forced into early retirement? If adapting the building (or moving it as a piece) isn't an option, it should be deconstructed. Structure is the longest-lasting and, from

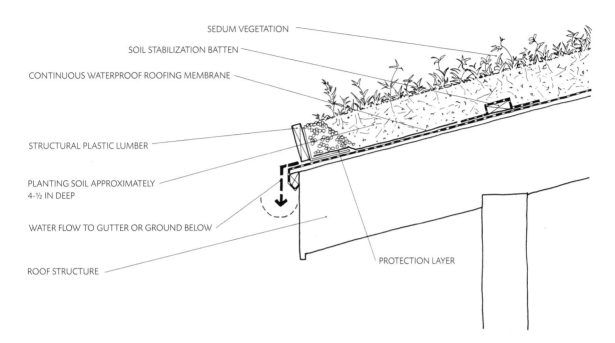

SEDUM VEGETATION

SOIL STABILIZATION BATTEN

CONTINUOUS WATERPROOF ROOFING MEMBRANE

STRUCTURAL PLASTIC LUMBER

PLANTING SOIL APPROXIMATELY 4-½ IN DEEP

WATER FLOW TO GUTTER OR GROUND BELOW

ROOF STRUCTURE

PROTECTION LAYER

the perspective of design for disassembly, the least flexible aspect of a building. As already pointed out, durability of the materials providing your home's structure is critical. This is even more true if you want them to be available for postdeconstruction use. The ability to easily separate those elements is also important. Designing so disassembly is self-evident to future deconstructors is recommended by specialists in DfD (Guy and Ciarimboli 2006, 29).

When deconstructing, preserve what you can.

Sometimes an existing home is in such poor shape that it's not even worth remodeling. In this case, deconstruction should be considered. When considering saving all or portions of the enclosure, consider two things: Will the existing structure contribute to the long life, thermal comfort, and other environ-mental attributes you're seeking? Can it do so within a reasonable budget? With the Scheulen home in Seattle, Washington, builder Jon Alexander reports that he initially intended to deconstruct the home to the first floor platform, preserving it and the existing foundation. His construction plans included excavat-ing beneath the existing foundation to allow for a full basement. Alexander notes, "I thought it would save money and conserve materials. When I was getting estimates from my concrete and excavation subs I was proven wrong. Starting from bare ground saved several thousand dollars, was faster, and surprisingly, would use less new concrete" (personal communica-tion, 2006). In the end, Alexander deconstructed the entire house, salvaging nearly all materials for reuse in the project or resale. Remaining materials were recycled.

A more committed approach than that of the Idea Home is the exten-sive green roof design shown here, meant to be quite shallow and light. Note that green roofs with deeper soil (called "intensive") require signif-icant structural support and generally aren't used for residential applica-tions. ILLUSTRATION BY CHRISTOPHER GUTSCHE AND KATHLEEN SMITH.

Fifty percent of the CO_2 emissions present ten years from now will result from the purchasing decisions made regarding appliances and equipment starting right now. If we switched to Energy Star choices, we could put this country on an entirely different path.

Kathleen Hogan, U.S. Green Building Council Federal Summit, 2002

10: Operating Systems for Your Home

IN ADDITION TO PUTTING A ROOF over our heads, we look to our homes to provide thermal comfort, good-quality fresh air, lighting at night and on those dark days of winter, and a comfortable and healthy place to prepare food, bathe, and do the laundry. The systems we use to achieve these goals can be simple or complex, but they typically use two resources: energy and water. The availability of cheap fossil fuel energy and water and our preoccupation with technology have unfortunately led to an overreliance on fancy equipment and an underreliance on good design. This has generally translated into using more resources than actually required to do the job, more money spent over the long term, and more risk in an uncertain future.

Energy conservation has been in the public's awareness for some time. It's only recently, with fast-paced growth, endangered species protections, and changing climate patterns that include lengthening drought periods, that water conservation has captured our attention in the Northwest. Water conservation is good not only for the environment but also for your pocketbook. Water conservation

pays back in three ways: savings on water you don't use, savings on sewage you don't produce, and, since a significant proportion of the water we use is heated, savings on water you don't heat.

We've discussed the importance of designing a site-responsive enclosure to reduce your heating, cooling, and lighting needs. In this chapter, we focus on choosing systems that reflect smart up-front design integrated with what nature freely provides, rather than systems that compensate for design and construction deficiencies. We'll be looking at three major systems: space conditioning (the technical term for systems that heat and cool your space), electric lighting, and plumbing.

Here's a summary of the positive environmental impacts that can result from your operating systems choices, and the general approach to achieving them:

Energy independence. Use renewable energy available on-site and systems equipment that uses energy efficiently.

Human health. Mechanically ventilate your home to provide a consistent supply of fresh air. Provide

These are the important questions to consider when making operating systems choices:

- Do the site and home design lend themselves to using on-site energy resources?
- Do the site and home design lend themselves to using on-site water resources?
- How much system do you need?
- How simple or complex should the system be?
- Are there health concerns related to the system you're considering?
- Which type of HVAC system fits your schedule?
- Does the HVAC system allow you to use a heat exchanger or recover waste heat in some way?
- How much space does the HVAC system require?
- Does the HVAC system require complicated and frequent maintenance or special servicing?
- Does your home design take full advantage of daylighting?
- Have you designed your plumbing system to minimize use of both energy and water?

good-quality electric lighting that enhances the quality of your environment.

Water conservation. Use water-efficient appliances, fixtures, and equipment. Substitute nonpotable for potable (drinking) water where possible.

ALL SYSTEMS GREEN

Do the site and home design lend themselves to using on-site energy resources? The sun provides an unending supply of clean energy, free of charge.

Even here in the Northwest, we get enough sunlight to justify reliance on it for comfort and household services. Many of the same techniques used to create a well-performing passive solar design lend themselves to active solar energy systems. For homes, this generally includes photovoltaic (PV) systems for generating electricity and solar water-heating systems. In addition, there are solar thermal collectors that deliver warm air, and for very specific conditions, micro wind turbines and hydroelectric systems for generating electricity.

If you think you can't afford to install active solar technology, explore financial incentives such as those mentioned in chapter 5 that might be available to help fund renewable energy projects. If the budget still won't stretch far enough, at least include the infrastructure to take advantage of on-site energy in the future, when the technology is more affordable, energy prices make it more cost effective, or you have more money to spend. Futureproofing for solar means ensuring you have an area where you can install solar panels (for producing hot water, space heat, or electricity). It also means running conduit from the potential solar panel location to the location where the inverter will be and/or to the electric panel, and for solar hot water, stubbing in plumbing to carry the water from where it will be heated to where it will be used. For example, homes in the Kerby Street project—the affordable home project in Portland, Oregon, featured in chapter 1—were prewired and plumbed for PV and solar water heating to ease future installation, which has since taken place.

Do the site and home design lend themselves to using on-site water resources? Many parts of the

FUTUREPROOF YOUR HOME

Over the lifetime of your home, many things may change: how much space you need, uses of the space, cost of different fuels, and availability of new technologies. A thermally efficient envelope is always the first step to futureproofing your home. When considering system options, make choices that

- are expandable to meet future needs
- allow you to switch fuels in the future as price and availability change
- are likely to be competitive with whatever the conventional technology is in five years' time, if you have to sell your home

Northwest are known for rain. Why not use this free source of water to meet domestic water needs? Just as with solar collection systems, the design of a rainwater harvesting system will depend on how much water is available and when (patterns of precipitation), as well as budget, aesthetics, and household habits.

Another on-site source of water is the wastewater from your home. There are various ways to design gray water systems that are efficient, unobtrusive, and cost effective. Gray water systems collect the wastewater from sinks, showers, and/or laundry

In the Kerby Street project in Portland, Oregon, a self-contained PV-powered exhaust fan was installed in each unit. The homes were also prewired and plumbed for PV and solar water heating. PHOTO BY ANDREA NELSON.

appliances and clean it for reuse for irrigation or toilet flushing.

With rainwater harvesting and gray water systems—and sometimes with solar collection systems—you may run into permitting issues or covenant restrictions. Working with a professional who can design a high-performance, good-looking system and is familiar with navigating the policy "narrows" can help. See "Resources" for chapter 4 for ideas on how to locate individuals who design and/or install solar energy, rainwater harvesting, and gray water systems.

How much system do you need? Systems need to be appropriately sized to meet the actual loads of your home. We most often think of this in terms of heating, ventilation, and air conditioning (HVAC) systems, but it applies equally to water heating, lighting, and plumbing systems. Even your clothes washer should be sized appropriately to meet your needs.

If you're interested in using active solar energy systems, you'll want to first reduce your load as much as possible with good passive solar design and an effective building enclosure, then reduce it further by installing energy-efficient equipment, and then size your PV, solar hot water, and/or solar thermal system to serve that load. (If you're dealing with an existing home, you can do most of this; the one constraint is the difficulty of improving your solar orientation if it isn't optimal—even then, a creative and experienced solar energy system installer can help you make the most of what you have.)

If you decide to install PV, your options for using the electricity will vary, depending on whether you're connected to the utility grid, and if so, whether your electric utility offers net metering. With new construction, it's best to bring in the solar energy system installer during the design phase of the project to determine whether it makes sense to connect with the grid, as well as the best location and appropriate inclination for PV arrays (or for a solar thermal collector, if you go that route). This way you can avoid a roof design that later restricts access to the solar energy that falls on your site—or a PV array that's shaded by a chimney, a mature tree, or the house next door.

Some solar collectors are more sensitive to inclination than others; the manufacturer can provide optimum ranges for your latitude. How you plan to use the collectors makes a difference. For example, a grid-tied PV array with a net metering facility should be oriented to produce the highest gross output over the year. A solar thermal system designed to be used for space heating will likely require a steeper inclination to optimize cold season performance with the secondary advantage of clearing snow more quickly. If you size this system to meet your winter space-heating load you're likely to have more than you need in summer. You'll need to plan for shading or shutting down the system in summer to reduce the output (which may cause operations and maintenance concerns), or shedding the excess heat in a swimming pool or hot tub.

How simple or complex should the system be? This depends a lot on you and what your preferences and tolerances are for thermal and lighting variation, maintenance requirements, technology, and cost. Simple systems generally offer lower cost and easier maintenance but also require you to be more flexible and to invest a little more time managing them. Adding complexity (usually in the form of electronic controls) allows you to tailor your home environment to more specific needs, potentially making it more efficient, but it also adds cost and maintenance requirements.

For example, a programmable thermostat will allow you to set different temperatures for different times of the day and days of the week and can reduce heating bills up to $100 per year (Energy Star 2006), but you have to know how to use it. Stepping up to zoned controls allows you to vary settings for different areas of the house. Stepping up further to an automated home operating system offers you even more control. Heating, cooling, ventilation, lighting, security, audio-visual systems, and others can be tied into a central control pad and can even be adjusted remotely via the Internet or a cell phone. When you come home a day early from your vacation, you can warm the house and turn on the driveway lights before you arrive. An automated system can also offer the advantage of managing things we're less adept at sensing than lighting and heating, such as relative humidity and CO_2 levels.

Are there health concerns related to the system you're considering? Some systems can present health concerns, while others offer benefits. For example, forced-air heating and cooling systems have a reputation for producing inferior air quality. This can be mitigated, but not eliminated, through sealing ducts properly, providing proper filtration, and balancing the system.

Ductless heating and cooling systems, such as radiant floor or wall radiator systems (hydronic

systems), are often considered healthier. However, they may not be appropriate in some situations, such as where lots of particulates tend to be suspended in the outside air (as in a windy, dusty location) or when a family member suffers from extreme sensitivities to particulate allergens. In such cases, you might want to install a balanced mechanical ventilation system, which draws outdoor air into the house and expels an approximately equal amount of indoor air to the outdoors, or a supply-based mechanical ventilation system, both of which will allow you to control ventilation and filter outside air being brought into the home, and both of which require ducts to distribute the air. (You can also minimize the presence of particulates and chemicals in the home by making adjustments in how you furnish and maintain your home.)

With open-loop hydronic systems, the same water that heats your slab can come out of your bathroom faucet or showerhead. When heating

A programmable thermostat like the one installed in the Built Green Idea Home in Issaquah, Washington, can reduce heating bills up to $100 per year (Energy Star 2006). PHOTO BY MIKE SEIDL, COURTESY OF FUSION PARTNERS, LLC.

loads are lower, the water may stagnate in the space-heating loop for long periods, increasing the risk of microbial growth. Regular purging with fresh water is recommended, but if you're anxious about this, you probably want to go with a closed-loop system.

A drinking water supply system that relies on rainwater will need to incorporate some means of treating the water, such as UV. Health districts are a little skittish about such systems for this reason. But plenty of folks in the Northwest have been tenacious enough to get such systems permitted and report no health problems.

The bottom line is that any system that's not properly maintained may cause health concerns, so if you tend to be casual about maintenance routines, you want to either budget for outside help or keep your system really simple.

SPACE CONDITIONING

Space conditioning is provided by your heating, ventilation, and air conditioning (HVAC) system, which is probably the most significant systems choice you'll make. It can also be the most expensive. Your HVAC system consists of four components:

Fuel. The origin of the thermal energy to heat or cool your home. For the purposes of this chapter, we'll consolidate the selections into electricity (whether from the grid or from on-site sources) and fuels combusted on-site, including wood/biomass and fossil fuels (such as oil, natural gas, or propane).

Source. The mechanical appliance that converts your fuel into heat or cooling. These include combustion appliances such as furnaces, water heaters, boilers, and solid fuel stoves, as well as heat pumps and condensers that use electricity to move heat from the air or ground outside the house to the inside (or vice versa for cooling).

Distribution. The method of carrying the heat or cooling from the source to the spaces that need to be heated or cooled. This includes ducts that carry conditioned air, pipes that carry heated or cooled liquid (known as hydronic distribution), and wiring that carries electricity.

Delivery. The way in which the heat or cooling is actually delivered into those spaces. This includes but isn't limited to forced-air registers, radiant floor or wall panels/radiators, fan coils that blow air across an electric or hot/cold water coil, and electric resistance heaters.

If your primary concern is environmental impact, you should first pay attention to fuel choice. Here in the Northwest, where a significant percentage of our electricity is generated from renewable sources, an electricity-based HVAC system can be a sound and sustainable choice. It has a small carbon footprint under the current regional mix, and it offers the opportunity to buy "green" power from your local utility and to utilize on-site renewable energy now or in the future. From an economic perspective, however, at least in the near term, grid-supplied electricity is more expensive than natural gas per Btu of energy supplied to your site (although a high-efficiency heat pump may offset that difference in terms of actual heat provided).

If your primary concern is comfort and health, your focus should be on the distribution and delivery systems. Many people appreciate the quiet, comforting heat and dust-free environment of a hydronic system with radiant delivery. Others prefer the flexibility and quick response of a forced-air system, one that uses high-efficiency filtration to remove airborne allergens. Electrical distribution is quiet, clean, and inexpensive to install and expand, but the delivery options (resistance-based board, wall-mounted convection and fan coil, and electric radiant panels) aren't everyone's preference. To clarify which type of distribution and delivery system is better for you, you'll want to ask yourself a few questions.

Which type of HVAC system fits your schedule? Some HVAC systems, such as forced air, are more responsive and can warm a house quickly. These systems are easier to run efficiently if you don't have a regular schedule, if you like things to be "just right" all the time, or if you need the home heated or cooled at different times every day. With these systems, you choose set points, and when the temperature goes either above or below these temperature settings, your HVAC system automatically turns on or off as needed to maintain the desired temperature.

Other types of systems, such as radiant floor heating, are slower to respond. Such systems function better with an even set point, or a regular daily cycle with small differences in temperature—warm during the day, cooler at night in the heating season, for example. These systems are less efficient if the set point is changed frequently, so a sophisticated programmable thermostat may be unnecessary and even counterproductive. With these systems, you may choose to use zonal controls to vary living and sleeping room temperatures. The Gutsche-Smith home on Bainbridge Island has an in-slab radiant

system on the ground floor and radiant baseboard heaters on the second floor that can be operated individually. In the winter, the ground floor is kept at a constant low setting to provide even and consistent heat. Upstairs, the baseboard heaters, which respond almost instantly but require more energy to operate, are kept off except on really cold nights when they are turned on for a short period to heat up only the room being occupied. In the summer the entire system, upstairs and downstairs, is turned off.

Does the HVAC system allow you to use a heat exchanger or recover waste heat in some way? The most efficient furnaces and water heaters are designed to condense exhaust gases and recover heat—that's one of the ways they gain efficiency. In a very tight home, where mechanical ventilation is required, a heat recovery ventilator (HRV) can be an excellent means of recovering even more waste heat. An HRV provides a balanced ventilation system that pulls stale air out of the house and simultaneously blows fresh air into the house, retaining some of the waste heat in the process. With appropriate filtration, this system can provide you with fresh, near–particulate-free air with a minimal energy penalty.

An HRV can most easily be incorporated into a forced-air system, typically using dedicated ducts to pull stale air from bathrooms or living spaces, while blowing fresh, preconditioned air into the return side of the main system's air handler. This fresh air is then distributed to the house through the main duct system. In a hydronic or otherwise ductless house, you'll need to install a dedicated, small-diameter duct system for both supply and return air.

HRVs can be pricey. A smaller home with an open

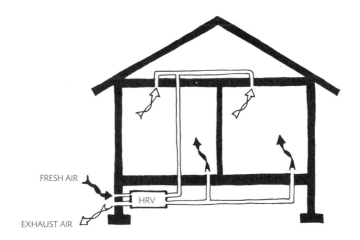

Heat recovery ventilators (HRVs) recover energy from exhaust air and use it to prewarm fresh air as it enters the home. ILLUSTRATION BY CHRISTOPHER GUTSCHE AND KATHLEEN SMITH.

FRESH AIR

EXHAUST AIR

HRV

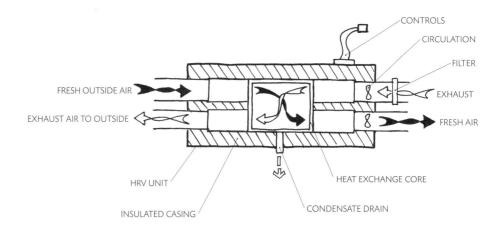

CONTROLS

CIRCULATION

FILTER

FRESH OUTSIDE AIR

EXHAUST AIR TO OUTSIDE

EXHAUST

FRESH AIR

HRV UNIT

INSULATED CASING

CONDENSATE DRAIN

HEAT EXCHANGE CORE

plan will allow for simpler, less costly options, including preheating your ventilation air using a simple heat exchanger to capture some of the waste heat from a combustion flue, locating your makeup air register behind the refrigerator to capitalize on the heat being shed from that appliance (simultaneously making your fridge more efficient), or installing a simple solar thermal plate collector on a south-facing wall or roof. An example of the latter is the Solarwall transpired solar collector, which has been used in commercial applications for some time and is now available in a do-it-yourself kit for homeowners. The perforated metal collector is mounted on a south-facing wall or roof. Fresh inlet air is drawn up into the panel, where it's preheated and ducted directly into a room or into a warm-air furnace. Energy savings, which range from 2 to 4 therms (each equal to 100,000 Btus) per year (BuildingGreen 2006), are dependent on the volume of air passing through the panel and the degree of sunshine during use (heating season)—so less sunny spots in the region (for example, along the coast) would reap savings at the lower end of the range. The kit is relatively inexpensive, however, so it might be worth exploring as an inexpensive method of preheating fresh air that's easily retrofitted into an existing home.

How much space does the HVAC system require? For greatest energy efficiency, you should locate both your heating and your cooling source and the distribution system inside the conditioned space, the area of the house that's protected by insulation, to minimize thermal losses to the outside. This means locating the furnace or boiler in a mechanical room or closet somewhere in the house. Generally it's preferable to locate it as centrally as possible to minimize distribution runs, but locating a combustion appliance too far from its exhaust location can mean a long, costly run of vent pipe.

Mechanical room/closet options can include a storage closet, laundry room, or utility room; an area that's boxed out into the garage with an air (wrap and caulking) and thermal (insulation) barrier that can be accessed from the living space or from outside; or the attic, crawl space, or basement, as long as the latter are contiguous with the conditioned space and located inside the air and thermal barrier. (More on using the attic for this purpose later.)

When space is limited, you might not want to give up precious real estate to your HVAC system. However, a small, highly efficient home may not need a distribution system at all. A centrally located heat source, such as a gas or wood stove in the main

The Solarwall thermal plate collector mounted on this south-facing wall draws fresh air up into the panel, where it's preheated and ducted directly into a warm-air furnace. PHOTO COURTESY OF SOLARWALL.

living area, with a ceiling fan to ensure effective heat distribution, may suffice. A small electric radiator or convection heater can provide supplementary heat to bedrooms and bath.

Does the HVAC system require complicated and frequent maintenance or special servicing? As system designs are optimized for efficiency, there's generally less tolerance for underperformance, so proper maintenance becomes more critical. When investigating a system, find out what the maintenance schedule is—frequency, time for each visit, materials required and average cost, how many local vendors are able to provide the service, and whether you can do it yourself. It's also useful to understand what the implications of deferred maintenance might be—are we looking at a reduction in performance, or a significant impact on air quality or system functionality? For example, air filtration media can require cleaning or replacement somewhere between once a month and once a year, depending on the type of filters you use. Failure to adhere to this schedule will reduce the efficiency and effectiveness of your HVAC system and may result in damage to the fan motors if they have to work too hard to try and move air through clogged filters.

Here are our *top green home picks* for getting the most efficient and effective space-conditioning system for your money:

- Size it right.
- Futureproof and optimize the distribution system.
- Choose the right HVAC system for your home.

Size it right.

HVAC contractors generally oversize the equipment they install. They frequently size systems using a rule-of-thumb approach, based on past experience. But this past experience generally doesn't include designs that capitalize on solar energy and have airtight, thermally efficient envelopes. In addition, a larger system can bring a home up to temperature more quickly, thus avoiding customer complaints and those pesky callbacks.

This approach has several problems. First, oversized systems cost more to install and take up more space in your home. They also operate less efficiently because of what's known as short-cycling—they shut off before reaching their most efficient operating state. This wastes energy and increases wear and tear on the equipment. In a climate that's warm and requires cooling, it can also cause moisture problems if the system doesn't adequately reduce the humidity as it cools the air.

Find an installer who's willing to do a proper load calculation for you using the Air Conditioning Contractors of America (ACCA) Manual J, *HVAC*

Residential Load Calculation, or equivalent accredited software. This will calculate your heating and cooling loads based on your house location, design, and specification for every day of the year based on averaged climate data. Equipment can then be sized to meet peak loads using ACCA Manual S for system sizing.

Keep in mind that HVAC design generally plans for the worst day of the year. You may want to design for the conditions that represent the worst for most of the time and accept that you may be uncomfortable for a couple days of the year. This may mean wearing a sweater in winter or drinking lemonade in summer.

Futureproof and optimize the distribution system.

Heating and cooling equipment will last from ten to twenty-five years and is generally easy to switch out. Distribution systems (such as hydronic piping and forced-air ducts or wiring), in contrast, are generally more integral to the structure of the house and are more difficult and costly to change. So the distribution system is a more critical choice than the equipment itself when we're planning for the future. In general, choose a high-quality system that has some built-in flexibility. The distribution system isn't the place to scrimp, since if a repair is needed down the road, it may be very costly and disruptive to your home, and life, to fix. Imagine trying to fix a leak in an in-slab radiant system.

Here are some things to think about when selecting or designing the three most common forms of distribution system—forced air, hydronic, and electrical.

Forced-air distribution. While forced-air ducts appear to be the most popular type of distribution system at the beginning of the twenty-first century, the typical installation isn't very energy efficient. According to field testing performed by energy experts in the Northwest and elsewhere, the average forced-air system is far from airtight, losing up to 30 percent of its conditioned air to the outside (Oikos 1993). That is to say, almost one-third of the energy used goes to waste. Properly sealing and insulating ducts can prevent these losses. There are very few opportunities to gain a 30-percent improvement in performance so easily!

An even better approach, particularly in new construction, is to install ducts inside the thermal envelope so that any heat leakage (it's best to assume that some will occur, even if you seal and insulate) stays where it's most useful. Soffits for ductwork can eat up valuable space, especially in a small home, so you may want to consider providing a conditioned attic to enclose the ducts and even the heat source. Another option is to put equipment in a conditioned crawl space.

In the future, as needed, forced-air systems can be switched from one fuel type to another. But when it's time to invest in the switch, the duct system should be checked for tightness and thermal performance; otherwise distribution losses will make the system less cost effective as energy prices increase.

Conditioned-air registers are generally located adjacent to windows or exterior walls to counteract heat losses or gains at those locations. In a thermally efficient envelope with high-performance windows (especially with small windows) this isn't necessary.

PROVIDING A CONDITIONED ATTIC FOR YOUR FORCED-AIR SYSTEM

Finding space to keep both heat source and distribution system within the thermal envelope can be challenging. One solution, applicable to new construction and remodels, is to put them in the attic. Instead of insulating the ceiling lid, you insulate the roof deck, providing a large conditioned space for your mechanical system.

There are several ways to create an insulated roof deck, including structural insulated panels (SIPs), rigid foam insulation between rafters or trusses, and spray foam insulation under the roof deck. Be aware that some roofing product manufacturers won't warranty their products if applied to an insulated roof deck if the deck isn't also ventilated, due primarily to concerns about overheating. This isn't generally true for manufacturers of high-quality roofing products, however.

Even with high-quality roofing products, some jurisdictions may require that you provide a flow of ventilation air over or under the roof deck to allow for drying and cooling. Check with your local building department. If they're skeptical, provide them with backup information from respected building science organizations, such as the Energy and Environmental Building Association (EEBA), or a recognized building science expert. (See "Resources" for chapter 4.)

If registers can be placed adjacent to interior walls—and closer to the equipment, so higher on the wall if equipment is in the attic, lower on the wall if equipment is in the basement—the amount of ducting required can be reduced, as well as associated cost, space requirements, material use, and energy losses.

In addition, most forced-air distribution systems use large cross-section (6 to 10 inches in diameter or more) sheet-metal or insulated-plastic flexible

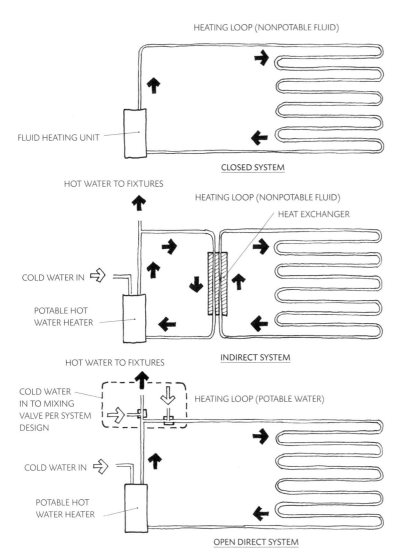

HEATING LOOP (NONPOTABLE FLUID)

FLUID HEATING UNIT

CLOSED SYSTEM

HOT WATER TO FIXTURES

HEATING LOOP (NONPOTABLE FLUID)

HEAT EXCHANGER

COLD WATER IN

POTABLE HOT WATER HEATER

INDIRECT SYSTEM

HOT WATER TO FIXTURES

COLD WATER IN TO MIXING VALVE PER SYSTEM DESIGN

HEATING LOOP (POTABLE WATER)

COLD WATER IN

POTABLE HOT WATER HEATER

OPEN DIRECT SYSTEM

Hydronic systems are either closed-loop, indirect, or open-loop. In a closed-loop system, the fluid is in a sealed system with its own heat source. An indirect system shares a common heat source with the domestic hot water system but has separate piping. In an open-loop system, the heating loop is connected to the domestic hot water system. ILLUSTRATION BY CHRISTOPHER GUTSCHE AND KATHLEEN SMITH.

ducting to deliver large volumes of air at low velocity (and correspondingly low pressure). An alternative is to use a high-velocity system, in which a high-pressure air handler moves air through small-diameter (generally 2- or 3-inch) plastic ducts. The main advantage of this approach is that the small-diameter ducts are easier to install inside the thermal envelope.

From an energy-efficiency perspective, proponents argue that high-velocity air provides better mixing and less stratification (cool air settling near the floor, warm air near the ceiling), which results in maintaining comfort using less conditioning energy. Critics argue, though, that the high-velocity air can be drafty and noisy, and that it takes more energy to move the air through the system (because of drag and pressure in the ducts). High-velocity systems may be an attractive approach in a retrofit situation, since the smaller ducts are generally much easier to install than the larger conventionally sized ducts.

Hydronic distribution. Hydronic systems use water to distribute the heat around the home in narrow-gauge pipes, usually made of PEX (cross-linked polyethylene). Water has a higher specific heat capacity than air, which means that it takes more energy to heat it up, but it also retains that heat better, making it a better medium for heat distribution. The small-diameter plastic pipe used by hydronic systems is easy to install inside the thermal envelope, keeping energy losses to a minimum. Solar hot water can be used to preheat water for a hydronic floor system. For an existing home, it's possible to install radiant baseboards or radiant heating in the wood subfloor or stapled to floor joists. Hydronic distribution carries heat from a heat source—solar thermal collector, boiler, or domestic water heater—and sheds the heat in a radiant slab, fan coil, radiator, or hot water baseboard the same way as the heating system in your car takes heat from the engine cooling system and sheds it into the passenger compartment.

A hydronic space-heating system is either closed-loop, indirect, or open-loop, differentiated primarily by its relationship with the domestic water heating system. In a closed-loop system, the fluid that distributes the heat around the house is in a sealed system with its own heat source, totally separate from the domestic hot water system. An indirect system shares a common heat source with the domestic hot water system but has separate piping; heat is passed from one system to the other via a heat exchanger that allows transmission of heat but not of liquid. In an open-loop system, the heating loop is connected to the domestic hot water system. The advantage of this approach is that a single heating unit can be used to provide both domestic hot water and space heating without a heat exchanger, saving on installation, maintenance, and replacement costs, as well as space. A mixer valve is generally installed in the system to ensure safety. Since the space-conditioning loop also provides storage for the domestic hot water, storage losses are essentially eliminated. As mentioned earlier, there are health considerations related to stagnation when heating loads are lower. Advocates recommend flushing the system regularly with fresh water.

With both indirect and open-loop systems, some consideration has to be given to water temperature, since the temperature set point for space heating water (SHW) is generally higher than the tempera-

PRIMARY AND SECONDARY SUPPLIES AND TEMPERATURE SET POINTS FOR DIFFERENT TYPES OF HYDRONIC SYSTEMS

TYPE OF SYSTEM	PRIMARY SUPPLY / °F	SECONDARY SUPPLY / °F
Radiant slab floor	DHW / 120°	SHW / 90°–100°
All other delivery methods (radiant heating in the wood subfloor or stapled to floor joists, or shed by way of fan coil units, radiant wall radiators, or hot water baseboards)	SHW / 120°–160° (depending on delivery type, system sizing, and floor assembly, including the R-value of underfloor insulation and finish floor materials)	DHW / 120°

ture set point for domestic hot water (DHW). In these systems, the supply requiring the higher operating temperature (SHW or DHW) is the primary supply, meaning heat is applied directly to this supply. The other supply is the secondary supply; the water temperature here is modified via a heat exchanger (for an indirect system) or a cold water mixer valve (for an open-loop system).

Electrical distribution. Electrical distribution uses wiring to distribute the energy as electricity, rather than as heat. This system has almost no distribution losses. Wire takes up very little space and is relatively easy to install and replace. Generally, it doesn't leak, is clean, and requires little maintenance. Within the house, it's very efficient—most appliances give almost one kilowatt of heat for every kilowatt of electricity consumed.

Electrical distribution can be used only with electrical systems, conveying electricity to the heating and/or cooling delivery equipment, such as radiant or convection heaters, or an air coil cooling system (for example, a window air conditioner). Of course, that electricity can come from one or more renewable sources—PV panels, wind turbines, small-scale hydro, and/or the utility grid (which one day may be powered by fuel cells). In addition, the electricity can come from coal-fired or nuclear power stations, and might do so increasingly as time goes on.

The disadvantage with electricity is that while it's inexpensive to install, it's not inexpensive to operate, and this is getting more and more true as the energy picture changes.

Summing it up. Hydronic and electrical distribution offer clear efficiency advantages over forced-air

distribution, since they both offer minimal distribution losses without requiring significant time and money spent on the sealing and insulation required for forced-air systems. However, forced-air distribution can perform very well in a thermally efficient home, as long as it's sealed properly and (even better) in a conditioned space. It's really a matter of personal preference. Regardless, it's important to plan well to avoid costly retrofits down the road and to allow for future modifications to power source. Aim for a distribution system that's durable, flexible, and accessible.

Choose the right HVAC system for your home.

As is probably clear at this point, a whole range of factors should go into designing—or redesigning, in the case of a major overhaul—your HVAC system. Here we'll describe four different scenarios that we think offer a great combination of benefits for particular circumstances. Even if none of these is just right for your situation, you'll have a starting place to work from.

Most of the envelope requirements for these systems are the same:

- passive solar orientation
- walls ≥ R-23 with reduced thermal bridging
- ceiling/roof ≥ R-38 with 12-inch raised heel trusses
- floor = R-30 over crawl space
- moderate area of glazing

The all-electric scenario and the small-and-simple scenario require a slightly smaller area of glazing (≤ 15 percent of conditioned floor area, average

U = 0.30, compared to ≤ 20 percent of conditioned floor area, average U = 0.32 for the gas hydronic and gas forced-air scenarios). The all-electric and the gas forced-air scenarios require slightly more airtightness (infiltration ≤ 0.2 air changes per hour at natural atmospheric pressure, or NACH, compared to 0.35 to 0.2 NACH for the gas hydronic and small-and-simple systems).

The all-electric scenario. In this scenario we start with a super-efficient ground-source heat pump. A forced-air distribution system consisting of ducts inside the thermal envelope is sealed with mastic to Energy Star standards. The air handler and the heating and cooling coils are centrally located to minimize duct runs. Balanced mechanical ventilation uses an energy recovery ventilator supplying fresh air to the HVAC return, as well as dedicated exhaust from bathrooms and bedrooms. The focus here on load minimization and system efficiency will maximize return on investment in the system. Ground-source loops are a major cost component of this system; horizontal loops, or loops situated in a pond, are less expensive, whereas vertical loops will have less impact on-site. This system can use an air-source heat pump if the site precludes ground loops.

Consider this approach if you

- don't have access to natural gas
- don't want any combustion equipment in your house (for health and safety reasons, for example)
- live in a location where summertime cooling loads may require air conditioning for comfort
- speculate that fossil fuel shortages and carbon taxes will make renewable electricity the most cost-effective energy choice within the next decade

- are hoping to meet all your energy needs with on-site generation solutions (PV, wind, small-scale hydro, and such) now or in the future
- believe that responsible action with regard to climate change demands a "carbon-neutral" home (defined in chapter 5)

If you're generating your own electricity and on the grid, and your electric utility offers net metering, you have the potential to "bank" your surplus kilowatts during the summer (assuming your cooling needs are small or none), which you can then "withdraw" in the winter to meet your space-heating needs. To do this, you'll need to choose a space-heating system that can use electricity, such as this one. This may be an air- or ground-source heat pump, using either forced-air or hydronic distribution, or an electric resistance system with radiant, fan coil, or convection heaters.

The gas hydronic scenario. For the near future, natural gas may remain the lowest-cost fuel for space and water heating. In this scenario, an on-demand water heater or boiler (EF ≥ 0.81) supplies space heating and domestic hot water. (EF is the energy factor, a measure of the overall efficiency of a water heater based on the model's recovery efficiency, standby losses, and energy input, with a bigger number being better.) Radiant loops in a gypsum concrete slab operate at 100 to 120 degrees F, depending on the floor covering, and distribute the heat quietly and evenly. (Gypsum concrete is a combination of gypsum and concrete that's less prone to cracking than conventional concrete. A slab of gypsum concrete 1½ to 2 inches deep is typically poured over the installed hot water tubes attached to the subfloor, creating a radiant panel with high thermal mass that allows a lower operating temperature and thus greater efficiency.) The system is minimally zoned for daytime living and sleeping spaces. Balanced mechanical ventilation uses a heat recovery ventilator and dedicated ducts. It's easy to add solar thermal preheat to this system or to switch to electric in the future.

This system is worth considering if you

- have access to natural gas
- live in an area where summertime cooling loads are minimal (such as on the coast)
- like warm hard-surface floors
- have some constraints on space for HVAC equipment
- plan to install sufficient solar thermal capacity to meet both domestic hot water needs and some percentage of your space-heating needs, either now or in the future

The gas forced-air scenario. This scenario calls for a centrally located, high-efficiency gas furnace (EF ≥ 94) with a dual-stage burner and an electrically commutated variable-speed fan. This furnace reduces the effective capacity of the system, which improves efficiency while accommodating possible future expansion. The distribution system consists of ducts inside the thermal envelope that have been sealed with mastic to Energy Star standards. There are transfer ducts in all bedrooms. Multistage MERV 12 filtration provides improved air cleaning without pressure drops or increased fan loads. (The MERV—standing for minimum efficiency reporting values—rating system was developed by the Association of Space Heating and Refrigeration and Air Conditioning Engineers. The higher the MERV rating, the more efficient the filter.) Balanced mechanical ventilation uses a heat recovery ventilator supplying fresh air to the HVAC return, plus dedicated exhaust from bathrooms and bedrooms. The system is switchable to electric in the future.

Forced-air systems are relatively inexpensive to install, and experienced installers and maintenance technicians can generally be found in every community. This system may be the right one if you

- have access to natural gas
- have put most of your available budget into your envelope, eliminating more costly HVAC system options
- think you might want to add air conditioning in the future by switching to an electric heat pump
- like the rapid response of forced-air heating because it fits your lifestyle
- have found it difficult to locate HVAC installers who offer anything else
- are unable to consider any on-site renewable energy generation in the near future

The small-and-simple scenario. In smaller homes (800 to 1400 square feet) central heating may be an unnecessary expense. Instead, this scenario calls for a simple central heat source in the main living area, such as a gas or wood pellet stove. A heat exchanger in the flue can be used for space conditioning or domestic hot water. Some form of supplemental heating, such as electric panel convection heaters with thermostatic and timer controls, is used in the disconnected rooms. Exhaust ventilation is integrated

If not installed or maintained properly, forced-air heating and cooling systems can perform poorly, creating air quality problems and unnecessary expense. To optimize your system, you need to design it to prevent pressure imbalances, protect it properly during construction, and use the right filter.

Preventing pressure imbalances

Leaks in the distribution system, or obstructions to free airflow from supply registers to return registers such as closed bedroom doors, can cause pressurization of some spaces and depressurization of others. These pressure imbalances can cause back drafting of some gas- or oil-fired combustion appliances, as well as wood-burning stoves and fireplaces. The negative pressure sucks flue gases into the living space instead of letting them exhaust to the outside—not a good situation.

Pressure imbalances can also cause poor-quality air to be drawn into the house from attics and crawl spaces or force warm, moisture-laden indoor air through leaks into wall cavities, where it may condense against the cooler surface exposed to the outside and cause serious moisture problems. You can mitigate small imbalances by installing return ducts in each bedroom, by installing transfer grills (a small duct often installed above a door connecting it to the next room or hallway) or jumper ducts (a duct that runs over the top of a partition wall, bypassing a bedroom door, for example), or by undercutting doors to allow some air to pass from room to room or to return ducts in each bedroom.

Protecting the system during construction

During construction, protect the system from particulate pollutants by sealing supply and return registers and not storing ducts in the construction area before installation. Periodically inspect and clean registers and ducts if necessary.

Using the right filter

Use the highest efficiency filter appropriate for your system, preferably a filter with a MERV rating of 10 or higher. When interviewing your HVAC contractor, make sure the equipment takes medium- or high-efficiency filters. Filters must be cleaned or changed according to manufacturers' instructions to maintain performance and minimize wear and tear on the equipment.

Filters with the lowest first cost, such as pleated media, require regular replacement (four times per year), amounting to considerable cost over time and making it worth investing in more expensive bag-type filters. This type of filter places less load on fan motors and can generally be replaced annually with little loss in performance. Although electrostatic air filters enjoy a PR buzz, green designers generally don't recommend them. They should be cleaned as often as once or twice per month, and people forget. When they're dirty, their filtration performance drops dramatically, and they may generate and introduce ozone—a significant respiratory irritant—into your indoor air.

COOLING SYSTEMS

Cheap energy and mechanical refrigeration have made air conditioning an attractive prospect for new homeowners, even in the temperate maritime zones. In general, a home design should strive to avoid the need for mechanical air cooling. Minimizing summer heat gain through proper orientation and envelope design and optimizing natural airflow (through open layout, good window placement, and Energy Star ceiling fans) should go a long way toward keeping you cool in summer.

There are locations (noisy or polluted) or special health circumstances, however, where air conditioning is necessary. Although not inexpensive, a geo-exchange system (such as a ground-source heat pump) can be a greener way to provide mechanical cooling. The temperature of the ground or groundwater a few feet beneath the earth's surface remains relatively constant throughout the year, even though the outdoor air temperature may fluctuate greatly with the change of seasons. Geo-exchange systems rely on the stable temperature of the earth to act as either a heat source in winter or a heat sink in summer.

If a geo-exchange system isn't appropriate for your situation because of budget or site constraints but you absolutely must have air conditioning, other options include an air-source heat pump (not as efficient as a ground-source heat pump) or installing an Energy Star room air conditioner where needed. Some of the Energy Star room conditioners have timers to help you optimize use. Proper sizing is important. Air conditioners remove both heat and humidity from the air. If the unit is too large, it will cool the room quickly but remove only some of the humidity, leaving the room with a damp, clammy feeling. A properly sized unit will remove humidity effectively as it cools.

into the kitchen or bathroom exhaust. Makeup air is ducted to the flue heat exchanger. The installed cost of this system is low compared to a central system, allowing the budget to be focused elsewhere, such as on renewable generation for other electrical needs. In this system, thermal upgrades to the envelope are beneficial because of the high exterior wall–to-volume ratio of a small structure. This system facilitates fuel switching.

Consider a small system if you

- are keeping life simple in a smaller home with an open floor plan
- are interested in meeting your minimal electrical loads with a small PV system, now or in the future

ELECTRIC LIGHTING

Roughly 10 to 15 percent of residential electricity consumption can be attributed to electric lighting. While we've made significant strides toward increasing the efficiency of building envelopes, space conditioning systems, and water heating systems, progress on efficient lighting has been slow. Consequently, lighting represents an area with great potential for improvement. After all, we have access to free lighting for roughly half of each day (averaged over the year). For those hours when the sun isn't shining, proven technology that reduces energy consumption by up to 75 percent *and* lasts longer already exists and is commonly available in the form of compact fluorescent lamps.

Here are our *top green home picks* for making the most efficient and effective use of electrical lighting in your home:

- Integrate electric lighting with daylight.
- Use dedicated compact fluorescent light (CFL) fixtures with stab-in lamps.

Integrate electric lighting with daylight.

Does your home design take full advantage of daylighting? For efficiency, and for healthy living, daylight is the best and cheapest way to light your home. Quality lighting design will integrate electric lighting into an overall design that emphasizes natural light, not the other way around (or worse, a design that ignores natural light). Windows, skylights, and light tubes should be incorporated (either in new construction or in remodels) to deliver appropriate levels of light into as many indoor spaces as possible.

Where daylight doesn't suffice, as in locations where you'll be doing detailed work or be active during evening hours, electric lighting should be designed for efficiency and visual comfort. For do-it-yourself or small remodeling projects, many big-box retailers and specialty lighting stores have staff who can work with you to identify appropriate selections given your home layout and needs. Many such stores now offer a full line of Energy Star lighting products, including sconces, light fixtures combined with ceiling fans, and dedicated compact fluorescent fixtures. If you're building a new home, your builder or lighting contractor will supply most of your lighting. You'll get an allowance that includes cost plus profit. However, most allowances only cover standard (and inefficient) lighting. You can arrange with your builder to pay the difference to get more efficient lighting. If you choose this route, be prepared to do some shopping around, as you'll have to specify which fixtures you want.

While we're discussing lighting, it's important to take a moment to talk about full-spectrum lighting, since it's frequently touted as part of a natural or earth-friendly home. The term full-spectrum was coined by photobiologist John Ott in the 1960s to describe electric light sources that simulate the visible and ultraviolet (UV) spectrum of natural light. Unfortunately, it's now used quite loosely by lighting manufacturers and credited with some pretty incredible benefits to justify charging more. Research shows that full-spectrum light tends to provide excellent color rendering (the color you see) and may have some psychological benefits (which aren't actually fully explained by science). Research also shows that the light sources generally don't have physical health benefits (unless they're specifically designed to treat seasonal affective disorder) and tend to provide reduced lighting and energy performance.

Use dedicated compact fluorescent light (CFL) fixtures with stab-in lamps.

In the early days, CFLs gave off cold, flickery illumination and were an eyesore as they poked out of fixtures designed for conventional incandescent lamps. Now they come in a range of color temperatures, sizes, and styles to meet almost every need.

CFLs provide these benefits:

- Consume 70 to 80 percent less energy than an incandescent producing the same light output.
- Last five to eight times longer than incandescent lamps (bulbs), reducing replacement chores and meaning that only one lamp instead of five to

eight must be manufactured and disposed of—we can hope that in ten years there will be better recycling options for lamps.

- Generate less heat, thereby reducing cooling loads and helping homes cool more quickly on summer nights.

With rebates commonly available from local utilities, CFLs often cost only one or two dollars each. A CFL equivalent to a 75-watt standard incandescent will save nearly $22 over its lifetime, based on an average rate of $0.7 kWh (Energy Star Northwest 2006).

CFLs come in two basic forms: screw-ins, which have the same Edison-type screw-in base as incandescent lamps and thus are compatible with most conventional fixtures, and stab-ins, which have a pin base that plugs into a socket in a dedicated CFL fixture. The electronic ballast for a screw-in lamp is built into the base, which can make it larger than the incandescent it replaces. Since ballasts generally outlast lamps, when you dispose of a screw-in CFL you're throwing away a serviceable ballast. This problem is eliminated with dedicated CFL fixtures, since the ballast is separate from the lamp. Perhaps more important, dedicated fixtures are designed to make the best use of the more diffuse light CFLs produce—so by using them, you get the best-quality output from your CFLs.

When you're selecting CFLs, keep these things in mind:

- Purchase CFLs with Energy Star labels—they're quality tested for color temperature (warm or cold), service life, and other features.

- Colors do vary slightly, so be cautious about using CFLs in multiple arrays, where color differences will be noticeable. Be prepared to try several lamps to find a set that matches—low-voltage halogens may be a better choice in these situations.

- CFL ballasts generally don't tolerate high operating temperatures well, so don't put them in an enclosed space or fixtures. Check with your lighting supplier about compatibility with recessed cans.

- If using screw-in CFLs as a retrofit in recessed can lights, use a light-colored or mirrored reflector behind the lamp to direct more light downward.

PLUMBING

Have you designed your plumbing system to minimize use of both energy and water? Making your plumbing system as green as possible means finding ways to heat and use water efficiently, reduce overall indoor water consumption, and supplement or reduce your consumption of potable or drinking water for nonpotable uses. Here are our *top green home picks* for heating, using, and conserving water in your home:

- Let the sun supply your hot water.
- Consider an on-demand water heater.
- Recapture energy before it goes down the drain.
- Capture heat from the air to preheat your water.
- Reduce waste from running the water until it's warm enough.
- Install low-flow fixtures and toilets.

Appliances aren't technically considered part of home operating systems, but they do use both water and energy (either electricity or gas). Here are a few things to consider as you sort through the options for your green construction or remodeling project.

Cooking

There are no accepted standards for energy efficiency in stoves, so the choice between gas and electric depends to a large extent on personal taste. Be aware, however, that a gas stove can produce potentially hazardous combustion products, so it needs adequate exhaust venting. It also poses a slightly higher risk of accidental fires. The most energy-efficient way to cook indoors is in a microwave oven, but some people are concerned about how microwaves affect the nutritional value of food. Solar ovens are a green substitute for backyard grills during summer months when sunshine is available.

Cleaning (central vacuum)

If you're concerned about indoor air quality, and especially if you plan to carpet a significant portion of your home, you should seriously consider a central vacuum cleaner. The advantage of a central vacuum is that the dust bag or container is generally located in the garage, and the exhausted air is blown to the outside. In contrast, a mobile vacuum cleaner, however efficient it is, blows its exhaust air back into the room you're cleaning, carrying fine particles with it.

Food storage

Energy Star rates refrigerators and freezers for energy efficiency. Energy Star refrigerators use at least 15 percent less energy than current federal standards, and 40 percent less energy than a refrigerator purchased in 2001, so think about trading out that old appliance. Energy Star freezers consume at least 10 percent less energy than nonrated models. (Note: A manual-defrost freezer will consume slightly less energy than a frost-free unit, as long as you keep it free of frost). The best way to improve the performance of any refrigerator or freezer is to keep it full and open the door as little as possible.

Laundry

Energy Star clothes washers use at least 50 percent less energy and water, on average, than conventional washers (Energy Star Northwest 2006). If you're looking for the best performance gains in energy and water conservation, choose a front-loading model. A front loader uses 15 to 18 gallons per wash, compared to 40 to 50 gallons for a similar-capacity top loader. It does this by tumbling the clothes through a pool of water rather than fully immersing and agitating them. Because front loaders use less water, they heat less water (unless you choose cold wash for 90 percent of your loads, as we do). They also use less detergent, are kinder and gentler to your clothes, and have higher spin speeds so less energy is needed to dry your clothes.

A solar-powered clothes drier (that is, a clothesline) is the most energy-efficient solution for drying your clothes (and causes less wear to your clothes). If you plan to use a mechanical drier, gas should be the choice from an energy-efficiency standpoint, but be sure to vent it properly and clean the vent regularly.

You can find performance details for Energy Star–rated appliances at the U.S. EPA Web site (see "Resources").

In the Northwest, we're beginning to see more evacuated tube systems for solar water heating, like this one installed on a home in Seattle. PHOTO BY JON ALEXANDER.

- Reduce water consumption indoors and outdoors.
- Use on-site water sources.
- Consider water filtration as an alternative to bottled water.

Let the sun supply your hot water.

Solar water systems consist of a collector and a storage tank. The most common system for residential applications uses flat plate collectors. Mounted on the roof, a flat plate collector generally consists of copper tubes fitted to a flat absorber plate enclosed in an insulated box and covered with tempered glass. This type of system works well in areas with long periods of uninterrupted sunlight and is quite affordable.

In the Northwest, we're beginning to see more evacuated tube systems. The collector design is significantly more sophisticated than for flat plate collectors. The thermal collector itself is a metal tube containing water or a volatile liquid, running down the center of a 4-foot-long double-walled glass tube. The space between the walls of glass contains a vacuum, eliminating conductive heat losses, and the glass has low-emissivity coatings to reduce radiant heat losses, just like a double-glazed window. The sun's rays enter the glass tube and heat the collector directly or are re-reflected within the tube by the coatings, whatever angle they enter at. A typical system for a house consists of twenty tubes, each connected to a manifold at one end, covering a total area of 30 or 40 square feet. These systems are much more effective in all climate and site conditions, and are particularly suited to areas with intermittent sun or even regular periods of light overcast. These collectors are also more tolerant of imperfect orientation and inclination, and of being shut down in the summertime.

As mentioned earlier, hydronic space-heating systems should be compatible with solar thermal collection, though you'll need to incorporate storage in your collection system, since you'll be generating hot water during the day but needing to use the heat after dark. This may take the form of a hot water storage tank or some type of thermal mass.

If you use an on-demand water heater or boiler as your primary source of hot water, you can preheat the water with a solar water system so that it takes less energy to bring it up to temperature. Keep in mind that you'll need a storage tank large enough to meet your supply needs for the evening. Sizing your equipment will take normal factors into consideration (such as heating requirements) as well as solar access to determine energy supply.

Consider an on-demand water heater.

The storage tank water heater has been the standard fixture in American houses for decades.

This model is simple, reliable, and inexpensive. Yet it requires considerable space, can waste energy, generally doesn't last much more than ten or twelve years, and can cause moisture damage problems when it fails. Granted, not all tank water heaters are alike. The American Polaris features a complex flue–heat exchanger that enables it to reach a thermal efficiency of 95 to 96 percent, and a dense foam insulating jacket that keeps storage heat loss to a minimum.

But there is an alternative. Elsewhere in the world, and with some builders in the Northwest, the on-demand water heater has become popular. These gas-fired or electric appliances use a high-output heater and heat exchanger to heat water. Supply water reaches service temperature as it flows through the heater to the faucet, shower, or appliance where it will be used. Since there's no storage or insulation required, these heaters are a fraction of the size of a tank heater and can more easily be installed inside the thermal envelope of the house in a closet or utility room (although the special concentric venting needed for closed combustion units can be costly, making an exterior wall location preferable). One danger with on-demand water heaters is that the supply of hot water is endless. If you have teens, you may not want to go this route!

On-demand water heaters can serve the entire house or be installed at the point of use. You can install a small on-demand water heater close to a point of use that's more than 20 feet from your main water heater to reduce the amount of cold water you run off waiting for the hot water to reach the faucet or shower.

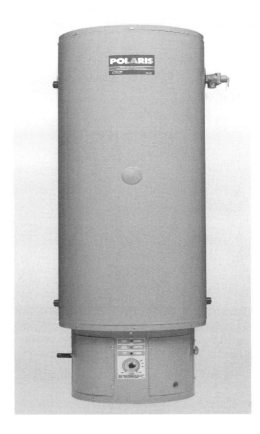

The American Polaris water heater features a complex flue–heat exchanger that enables it to reach a thermal efficiency of 95 to 96 percent. Its dense foam insulating jacket keeps storage heat loss to a minimum. PHOTO COURTESY OF AMERICAN WATER HEATER COMPANY.

The Takagi Flash T-K1S tankless water heater (below), occupying just 2.2 cubic feet of space and weighing only 45 pounds, generates hot water as needed. The first-hour flow rate is more than 240 gallons, and the unit provides 190,000 Btus of continuous heat. Thermal efficiency reaches 85 percent using natural gas and 87 percent with propane. PHOTO COURTESY OF TAKAGI INDUSTRIAL CO. LTD.

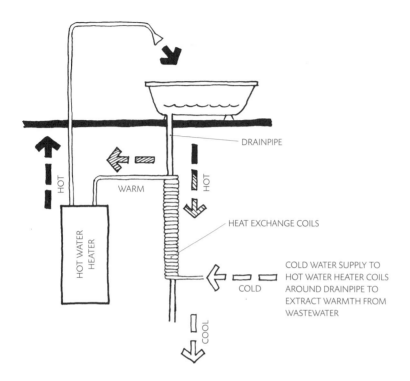

DRAINPIPE

HOT

WARM

HOT

HEAT EXCHANGE COILS

HOT WATER HEATER

COLD

COLD WATER SUPPLY TO HOT WATER HEATER COILS AROUND DRAINPIPE TO EXTRACT WARMTH FROM WASTEWATER

COOL

Incorporating a heat exchanger into the drain line recaptures most of the heat from drain water and uses it to preheat either the water in the hot water heater or the fresh water that's moving toward the same point of use. ILLUSTRATION BY CHRISTOPHER GUTSCHE AND KATHLEEN SMITH.

Recapture energy before it goes down the drain.

Just as heat recovery ventilators capture energy from heated stale air as it's exhausted, drain water heat recovery (DHR) captures heat energy from shower water before it goes down the drain. The temperature of the drain water is generally close to 80 or 90 degrees F. Incorporating a heat exchanger into the drain line recaptures most of that heat and uses it to preheat either the water in the hot water heater or the fresh water that's moving toward the same point of use. For example, in a shower, you might precondition the cold water flowing to the shower so that you use less hot water to achieve a comfortable temperature.

DHR should be well insulated to retain waste heat after drain flow stops. Cold wastewater (from toilet flushing, for example) should be plumbed downstream of the DHR to preserve the heat. Payback improves as you run more drain water through the system, so it's best to connect as many showers to the system as possible. DHR is more effective with flows of 3 gallons per minute (gpm) or more, thus less effective with very efficient shower fixtures (< 2 gpm).

Capture heat from the air to preheat your water.

Another system that's similar in concept to the heat recovery ventilator is the exhaust air heat pump (EAHP) used to preheat water. An EAHP heats water using a small compressor about the size of a window air conditioner. A duct connected to the EAHP draws stale house air through the unit. The EAHP strips the stale air of much of its heat, then blows that air outside at a temperature between 45 and 50 degrees F. The recovered heat is used to preheat domestic hot water. Branched collection ducts are often used to pick up stale air from bathrooms, so bath fans aren't needed. When the EAHP is connected to a properly installed duct system, the airflow rate is about 150 cubic feet per minute (cfm). Long or convoluted duct runs could reduce the flow rate.

Houses need regular ventilation. The EAHP is a way to get adequate ventilation while reducing the amount of heat that escapes. Since some people don't operate bath and kitchen fans as much as they should, the enforced ventilation of the EAHP guarantees at least a minimum level of ventilation.

In the Gutsche-Smith remodel on Bainbridge Island, Washington, an EAHP system is used to heat the domestic hot water. Ducts collect air through registers mounted near the ceiling in both bathrooms and the kitchen; the heat from this air is used to preheat the hot water supply. The system is incredibly efficient.

Reduce waste from running the water until it's warm enough.

Letting water run until it has reached a tolerable temperature is a common practice in most households, but it doesn't have to be. By either keeping the distances heated water has to travel to 20 feet or less or by recirculating hot water before it goes down the drain (by installing a recirculation pump, a good option in an existing home), you can cut both energy and water consumption. Also, hot water runs should be well insulated and kept inside the conditioned thermal envelope.

Shortening plumbing runs can be done by centralizing or stacking runs. Another method is "home run" plumbing, which basically means you run a dedicated, small-diameter pipe from the water heater directly to the furthest point of use. A version of this approach is manifold distribution, which takes hot water from the heater to a nearby manifold, from which small-diameter pipes run direct to each fixture. This type of distribution is becoming popular as the use of flexible PEX piping for indoor plumbing becomes more accepted. The material comes on a reel and can be pulled in continuous lengths like wire. In addition to saving water and energy, manifold distribution allows greater control of your plumbing system, isolating individual fixtures when you have a leak, for example.

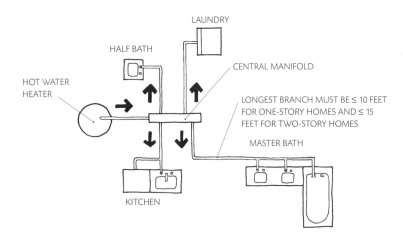

A. CENTRAL MANIFOLD DISTRIBUTION SYSTEM

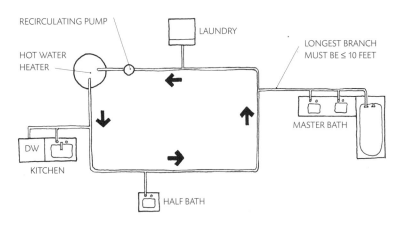

B. STRUCTURED PLUMBING SYSTEM WITH RECIRCULATING PUMP

A central manifold distribution system (A) takes hot water from the heater to a nearby manifold, from which small-diameter pipes run direct to each fixture. With a structured plumbing layout (B), a recirculating pump can be used to pull hot water through the loop, displacing cooler water back into and through the water heater before the faucet is turned on. ILLUSTRATION BY CHRISTOPHER GUTSCHE AND KATHLEEN SMITH.

Delta used the science of fluidics to design a new showerhead that has a pattern of wetting and water droplet size that maintains comfort and saves water, according to Peter Yost of 3D Diagnostics, who tested the prototype shown here in his own shower. PHOTO BY PETER YOST.

With a structured plumbing layout, where a main hot water loop serves the house and fixtures and appliances are connected by short (maximum 10 feet) small-diameter spurs, a recirculating pump can be used to pull hot water through the loop, displacing cooler water back into and through the water heater (instead of down the drain). A switch at each point of use (manually operated, or a motion or pressure sensor) activates the pump and charges the system so that the cold water in the spur to that fixture is run off and replaced with hot water before the faucet is turned on.

Install low-flow fixtures and toilets.

Use low-flow aerators on all faucets. These should be pressure-compensating so that they deliver the rated flow, whatever your water pressure:

- Bathroom faucets—0.5 to 1.0 gallons per minute (gpm).

- Kitchen faucets—1.5 to 2.0 gpm. This actually isn't much beyond code (2.2 gpm), but that's because the kitchen faucet is used to fill pots. Flow regulators can be attached to the sink faucet; these can be flipped up to stop the flow of water and flipped down to resume flow without turning knobs or readjusting temperature. They cost a few dollars, are available at most hardware stores, and can be easily installed.

- Bathtub faucets—Unrestricted, because generally people fill the tub, and the quicker it fills, the less heat you waste while it's filling.

- Showerheads—1.6 to 2.0 gpm with a manual shut-off so you can shut off the water to soap up without adjusting the temperature setting. Ask around for recommendations—a poorly performing shower is a disappointing experience you won't tolerate for long.

After your clothes washer, toilets generally consume more water than any other appliance or fixture in the home. Standard code-compliant toilets use 1.6 gallons per flush (gpf). Older toilets may use 3.6 gpf or more, so there's lots of opportunity for improvement here. Be aware, though, that many toilets rated at 1.6 gpf don't perform well (and unfortunately, performance doesn't correlate to cost), resulting in double-flushing and wasted water. At a minimum, you should select a well-performing toilet—and there are plenty. (See "Maximum Performance Testing of Popular Toilet Models" by Gauley and Koeller, listed in "Resources.")

A better alternative is a dual-flush and/or ultra-low-flush toilet. Dual-flush toilets have a standard 1.6 gpf flush option, but they also offer a "liquids only" flush option of 0.8 gallons. Averaged out over time, they consume about 1.1 gpf, a 31 percent improvement. Ultra-low-flush toilets use a pressure tank to achieve a reliable flush at just 1.0 or 1.1 gpf. Again, performance varies, particularly where flush button and valve service life is concerned, so ask around for recommendations. Substituting a 1.0 gpf for a code-compliant 1.6 gpf toilet can save roughly 2950 gallons per year in an average (2.7-person) household (Wilson and Piepkorn 2004, 7).

Even better are composting toilets. As taxpayers, we spend significant amounts of money to store water, treat it to ensure it's safe to drink, and distribute it to people's homes, then we put it in the toilet and use it to convey human waste. Where's the sense in that? Instead of using drinking water to convey human waste to some remote treatment facility, a composting toilet composts the waste right there in a bin below the toilet. If you're not familiar with the idea of a composting toilet, you may be conjuring up memories of your last visit to a pit toilet in a state park, but you should erase that thought. Properly functioning composting toilets are clean and odor-free, incorporating small fans to create negative pressure so odors don't return into the house. They break down and recycle human waste very similarly to the way your yard or food waste compost bin works, converting it into good-quality organic matter that can be returned to the soil in your yard.

Composting toilets come in many forms. In the simplest systems, the waste is collected in a sealed chamber in the toilet base, upon which the toilet bowl sits. The simpler systems generally require more active management by the homeowner. In the more

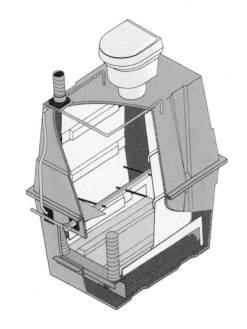

In the Phoenix Composting Toilet System, rotating tynes turn the compost in the large bin below, and sensors make sure it's operating efficiently. This "automation" means less work is required by the homeowner. The bin illustrated can serve one or two toilets. ILLUSTRATION COURTESY OF ADVANCED COMPOSTING SYSTEMS.

sophisticated systems, less work is required by the homeowner. For example, in the Phoenix Composting Toilet System, rotating tynes turn the compost in the large bin below, and sensors make sure the system is operating efficiently. A small power supply or a PV system provides the energy.

Considering cost, user resistance, or permitting challenges, a composting toilet may not be at the top of your list if your home is in a sewer-served urban or suburban location—although the truly dedicated among us are installing them in-town. But if your home site isn't sewer-served, composting toilets (in combination with a gray water system with some kind of subsurface infiltration field) may be a very cost-effective and environmentally responsible alternative to a new or replacement septic system.

Planning for composting toilets must be included in the predesign phase, and you'll need to do enough research to be confident you'll get them permitted before you get too far into the design phase of the project, particularly if you're taking this approach as an alternative to a septic system. Failure to get a permit can mean a lot of costly and time-consuming redesign work. If your site is sewer-served, permitting can be simplified by installing conventional toilets as a redundant (and somewhat costly) backup system, even if you plan to never use them.

Reduce water consumption indoors and outdoors.

The biggest factor in water savings in a home is how household members tend to operate water fixtures and appliances. The best water-conserving faucet isn't going to help if you run the water while you brush your teeth. Patterns of usage matter in all areas of green but especially in the realm of water consumption and conservation. Besides installing water-conserving fixtures and appliances, and developing water-conserving usage habits, here are three things you can do to conserve precious drinking water:

Fix leaks. In an existing home, and after installation in new homes, check for and eliminate leaks in faucets and toilets. Use food coloring in the toilet cistern to spot small leaks there; color will appear in the bowl. While this measure is simple, the payback on it is usually tremendous.

Don't install a permanent irrigation system. If you follow our recommendations in chapter 8 on putting together a landscape that requires minimal watering to look great, you shouldn't need to irrigate once plants are established. However, if you insist on putting in an irrigation system, install an efficient one. Timers, moisture sensors, micro-spray nozzles, and drip irrigation devices all aim at saving water. Work with an expert, such as a licensed irrigation contractor, when planning to install a permanent system.

Don't install a sink drain–mounted garbage disposal unit. These appliances take high-quality drinking water and nutrient-rich organic material and send them to the sewage treatment plant. Some alternatives include purchasing a compost or worm bin.

Use on-site water sources.

Another effective approach to reducing consumption of potable water is to look for other sources of water you can use for nonpotable purposes, such as irrigation and toilet flushing, whether you're on the water "grid" or on a well. Rainwater harvesting is one such source. Gray water reuse is another.

Our climate kindly delivers a certain amount of water direct to each home site every year. If you live in Forks, Washington, it might be 90 inches of rain per year, whereas in the Tri-Cities area of Washington it may be closer to 10 inches. This rainwater may represent a viable resource to help you reduce your consumption of potable water. (It can even be put to potable uses when properly treated. If you go this route, be ready for some work to get it permitted, however.)

When designing your rainwater harvesting system, think about what your water needs are, how much rainwater is available to you, and how much storage you'll need. As with energy, we can calculate water loads, based on the efficiency of our water fixtures, our lifestyle, and the number of home

occupants. The average person in Seattle consumes around 100 gallons of water per day (Seattle Public Utilities 2004). That's 146,000 gallons per year for a family of four—a lot of water. A very water-conscious family we'll call the Frugals can probably reduce that to around 50 gallons per person per day, or 73,000 gallons per year.

To put these figures into context, one inch of rainfall on 1000 square feet of roof will generate 623 gallons of water (catchment area in feet × rainfall in feet × 7.48 = gallons of runoff) so even in Forks, you would need 1300 square feet of catchment area (such as a roof) to meet the water requirements of the Frugals (73,000 gals / 7.5 feet of rainfall × 7.48 = 1301 square feet). In much of the Northwest, precipitation isn't evenly distributed throughout the year; most of the state experiences a dry spell of eight

to twelve weeks during the summer, so you'll need a way to store enough water for this period. That's about 14,000 to 18,000 gallons for the Frugals—a huge volume of water. Thus, storing it probably isn't cost effective for a single-family home.

While getting a permit to use rainwater harvesting for potable water is currently still challenging, using it for toilet flushing is less difficult. The Frugal family's dual-flush toilets use about 9000 gallons of water per year for flushing, 2250 gallons during a three-month dry summer. Storing 2500 gallons of water is more manageable. A concrete or plastic cistern underground or perhaps in a properly drained basement or crawl space, with appropriate filtration and sterilization, is feasible.

We've been conditioned to think of all the water that goes down drains in our homes as wastewater.

Rainwater can be stored in a small cistern in a tight urban location (left) or a larger cistern in a rural location (right). PHOTOS BY ANDREA NELSON (LEFT), TIM POPE (RIGHT).

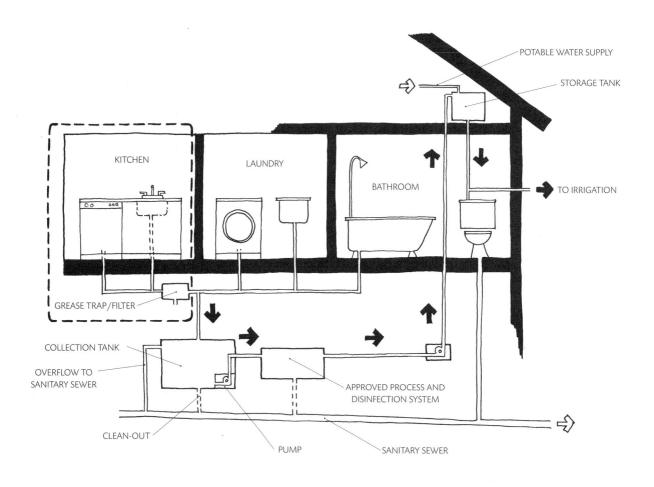

POTABLE WATER SUPPLY

STORAGE TANK

KITCHEN

LAUNDRY

BATHROOM

TO IRRIGATION

GREASE TRAP/FILTER

COLLECTION TANK

OVERFLOW TO
SANITARY SEWER

APPROVED PROCESS AND
DISINFECTION SYSTEM

CLEAN-OUT

PUMP

SANITARY SEWER

Systems for indoor gray water use generally include a collection tank, pump(s), filtration, and sterilization devices. Kitchen water should be treated separately. ILLUSTRATION BY CHRISTOPHER GUTSCHE AND KATHLEEN SMITH.

But with a little rethinking, some or all of this water could become a valuable on-site water resource to help us reduce consumption. In plumbing terms, the waste water from our homes consists of gray water, which is the water from bathroom sinks, showers, and laundry; and black water, the water from toilets and, generally, kitchen sinks and dishwashers because it may have high organic content. In conventional plumbing systems, these two types of water are mixed together, effectively making it all black water, which

is sent to the sewer line or septic tank. However, gray water can easily be salvaged and reused for irrigation. With a little treatment, gray water can also be used for toilet flushing. Its big advantage over rainwater is that it's available consistently all year, so storage requirements are minimal. You'll only need enough to serve as a buffer between the generation of gray water and the demand for irrigation or flush water.

The physical steps to setting your home up to use salvaged rainwater and/or gray water are fairly straightforward and involve only moderate cost if properly integrated in the design phase and during initial construction. One scheme for harvesting rainwater was described in the Snyder remodel case study in chapter 6. To recap, in a typical rainwater harvesting system there's a collection surface, such as a metal roof; storage, typically a cistern that may be above or below ground; a method of filtration, such as a filter pump; and distribution to a point of use, such as a toilet.

A system that recovers gray water for indoor use includes a collection tank, a pump or pumps, and filtration and sterilization devices to prevent buildup and/or discoloration of water in the toilet tank and bowl. Gray water from the kitchen sink may contain food scraps, grease, and other suspended solids, so it may pay to separate and pretreat this source before combining it with other gray water sources for final treatment—or to not include the kitchen gray water in the system at all.

A larger hurdle than setting up a rainwater or gray water system is getting the permits—a challenge that's becoming easier but that still requires some tenacity in most jurisdictions. The good news is that gray water reuse is slowly gaining acceptance in the face of increasing concern about potable water demand. For this reason, you might choose to install the equipment for your system but wait to hook it up until the permitting process gets easier. Regardless of whether you decide to wait, move forward cautiously, or move full speed ahead, you should use an expert in such systems to help you both decide which alternative to pursue and to help you get it done.

Consider water filtration as an alternative to bottled water.

Many of us now purchase bottled drinking water because of concerns about city or well water quality. Trace levels of chlorine are common in utility-supplied water, below (legal) minimum health thresholds but enough to affect flavor and possibly influence living systems. In some communities, the water is also fluoridated to improve everyone's dental health, whether you want it or not. If your water comes from a well on your site, you may have concerns about microbial or mineral contaminants that may affect taste, color, and even health. But the energy involved in the alternative of extracting, bottling, and transporting water to our homes in small or large plastic bottles is significant. One way to address these concerns and avoid this energy consumption is to employ point-of-use and whole-house water filtration systems—now commonly available and increasingly affordable. The scale of filtration you choose will depend on the specifics of your water and how concerned you are about it.

A kitchen faucet water filter is quick and easy to install but generally requires frequent filter replacement, which can be costly and involves your participation. A more cost-effective option is to use an under-sink filtration system. This type of system uses a larger carbon or ceramic filter, which can be replaced, recycled, or cleaned and reused. These systems offer the greatest environmental benefit since they use neither water nor energy to operate. Some issues to consider with under-sink systems include ease of cartridge replacement and amount of pressure drop at the faucet caused by the filter. (For more information on available water treatment, see H2ouse Water Saver Home Tour in "Resources.")

An alternative that's growing in popularity is reverse osmosis (RO) filtration, which uses physical pressure to move water across a semipermeable membrane. The semipermeable membrane allows water molecules to pass through it but not the larger contaminant molecules, leaving you with more concentrated contaminants on one side and pure water on the other. The process is slow but can produce very high levels of purity with less-frequent filter replacement. These systems are often installed at point of use for drinking water and at a bathroom sink for oral hygiene. They generally require an energy source and do produce wastewater with concentrated impurities in it.

If you choose to install a whole-house system, it should be installed downstream of the takeoff for all outdoor water fixtures, such as hose bibs and irrigation systems, in order to reduce the filtration load and extend filter life.

> Actually we believe that the perfect environment is outdoors, perhaps on a spring day, under the varied light of trees, with plant fragrances carried on light breezes. Since we can't live outdoors all the time, we can make the indoors something like the outdoors.
>
> David Rousseau, Archemy Consulting Web site, 2006

11: Interiors

MANY OF THE SIGNIFICANT GREEN choices we've been discussing up to this point become all but invisible once your home is complete, whereas the care you take in selecting the finishes for your home will be quite apparent. In this chapter, we focus on creating a green interior—one that can speak volumes about your commitment to green living. Speaking for ourselves, it's frequently an interior finish that catches the attention of visitors to our homes, inevitably leading to a larger conversation about green building and the environment, as well as about the less visible but important choices we made.

In addition to offering our top picks for interior choices, this chapter provides a checklist of materials and strategies to consider when building or remodeling specific rooms. We also invited Sandy Campbell, a designer specializing in green interiors, to offer some tips for you to follow when shopping for case goods, upholstered furniture, window treatments, and area rugs. It's too easy to build a healthy, green home and interior and inadvertently introduce furnishings that offset your good work, especially in the realm of indoor air quality.

Here's a summary of the positive environmental impacts that can result from your choices regarding interior finishes, and the general approach to achieving them:

Human health. Choose materials that don't degrade the quality of your indoor air as part of being installed or maintained, or by their mere presence in your home. Reduce day-to-day upkeep duties by keeping it simple.

Ecosystem health. Take less and take wisely from habitats that are the source of your finish materials.

Materials efficiency. Use materials that are reused or manufactured using recycled or rapidly renewable materials. Use finishes only where you need them or as an aesthetic accent.

Energy independence. Choose fewer exotic finishes from far away to save transportation energy and associated pollution.

INTERIOR CHOICES FOR HUMAN HEALTH

Does the finish you're considering introduce possible air quality problems into your home? Indoor air

Velocipede Architects of Seattle, Washington, created a green oasis for a client's master bedroom. Nontoxic finishes and uncarpeted floors are better to sleep with than the alternative. The room is compact, but the raised ceiling (painted a reflective white) and natural light from doors and windows provide a sense of spaciousness during the day and on moonlit evenings. PHOTO BY MICHAEL MOORE.

quality can largely be dealt with through carefully planned ventilation, but it's best to avoid problem materials in the first place. This includes, for example, paints, coatings, or adhesives with high amounts of volatile organic compounds (VOCs). Products with a high VOC rating can off-gas significantly, causing odors that sometimes persist over a long period of time. For some, this isn't simply an annoyance, but a serious health problem. Another area of concern includes fuzzy finishes, such as carpet or fabric wall coverings, which attract dust mites, collect dirt and particulates, and irritate individuals with allergies, and in particular, with asthmatic conditions.

Here are our *top green home picks* for choosing materials and finishes to maintain the air quality in your home and ensure that the place is healthy for all inhabitants:

- Use low- or no-VOC, formaldehyde-free water-based interior paints, stains, sealers, and coatings.
- Use low- or no-VOC adhesives.
- Limit or eliminate carpet in your home.
- Use formaldehyde-free cabinets, doors, and trim.
- Design in self-cleaning.

Use low- or no-VOC, formaldehyde-free water-based interior paints, stains, sealers, and coatings.

The VOC content of products you use should be given right on the can and/or in the product literature. If it isn't, don't purchase the product. Green Seal certification standards are generally accepted as the green building standard for coatings. For interior coatings, the pertinent Green Seal standard (GS-11)

requires that flat coatings have no more than 50 grams per liter (g/l) of VOCs, and that nonflat coatings have no more than 150 g/l of VOCs (Green Seal 1993).

The GreenSpec product directory publishes a good list of coatings that beat these VOC standards, including some that meet the more rigorous needs of individuals with multiple chemical sensitivities. Note that the VOC amounts listed by manufacturers are based on the base or neutral color. Adding color to the base neutral tone will add VOCs—generally, the darker and bolder the color, the more VOCs. The same is true for gloss—the higher the gloss, the more VOCs. Many products in the directory offer other environmental attributes, including fewer or no toxins (such as biocides, thinners made from

Especially in choosing interior finishes, the issue of making choices that don't compromise good air quality comes up. The choices discussed in this chapter are for the general population and not intended as advice for individuals who suffer from serious and multiple chemical sensitivities (MCS) or serious allergies. A product labeled as nontoxic or natural may be harmless for most people but may cause problems for particularly sensitive individuals. If you fall into this category, we urge you to consult with a qualified health professional as you choose your materials. The "Resources" listing for this chapter, as well as for chapter 3, includes some books that focus on this topic in depth. The process of material selection for someone with MCS generally includes testing of each component of a product. This is typically done by small exposures over time, to see if there's a reaction. The process of material installation frequently includes isolating and/or sealing offensive materials.

Perhaps most important for this discussion is for us to say that we believe multiple chemical sensitivities are symptomatic of a general problem that all of us are more or less vulnerable to. Individuals suffering from MCS are canaries in the coal mine, not anomalies. Anyone can become chemically sensitized if exposed to the right material for the right amount of time. Thus our emphasis in this chapter is on eliminating problem chemicals to the maximum degree possible.

petroleum-based ingredients, or other chemical additives) and recycled content.

If the concept of using recycled-content paint appeals to you, understand that because these are remanufactured from a mix of paints, they may have higher VOC levels than the greenest options. These paints may be better used on the exterior, where they will have less impact on air quality inside your home. A new Green Seal standard (GS-43) for recycled-content latex paint provides guidance for your selection; look for recycled-content paints with the Green Seal label (Green Seal 2006).

Low-VOC paints are applied like conventional paints and also vary in performance like conventional paints. Your painting contractor can help you check out the options. The issues are primarily hiding power (that is, how many coats it takes to cover the surface), scrubbability (abrasion resistance), washability (ease of stain removal), and ability to touch up easily. To meet Green Seal standards, paints have to meet minimums for each of these characteristics.

Even if a product is touted as odorless or VOC-free, we recommend that you ventilate the space well when applying it. This goes for any coating,

WHAT'S A VOC AND WHY SHOULD WE CARE?

Volatile organic compounds (VOCs) are emitted as gases from solids or liquids. They include a variety of chemicals, some of which may have short- and long-term adverse health effects, and can be found in literally thousands of products including many building-related materials and products (such as synthetic carpet, kitchen cabinets, wall paneling, paints, lacquers, glues, adhesives, and strippers) as well as furnishings. Concentrations of many VOCs are consistently higher indoors—up to ten times higher—than outdoors, according to the U.S. EPA (1994), even in locations with significant outdoor air pollution sources, such as petrochemical plants. Formaldehyde is probably the best-known VOC and, as pointed out in chapter 3, is considered a serious health risk. Relevant to this chapter, the chemical is found in preservatives in some paints, coatings, and composite wood products.

It's important to note that the VOCs the EPA regulates (and that must be listed in manufacturers' safety data sheets) are actually those responsible for producing smog outdoors. Levels of these VOCs, since they're regulated and known, have become somewhat of a proxy for the other VOCs that are found in materials. It's important also to point out that VOCs aren't the only issue with interior products. For example, coatings may include biocides, fungicides, or other toxic chemical additives that can be quite problematic. Research typically focuses on the adverse effects of these substances acting alone. Unfortunately, not much is known about the impact of multiple chemicals acting on humans and the atmosphere at the same time, so it's best to use the precautionary principle and eliminate what you can. The bottom line is to ask for and get as much information as you can about materials you plan to live with inside your home.

adhesive, or other interior product that's applied wet and goes through a drying process. Drywall and soft goods, such as carpet and drapes, act as excellent sinks (collectors of odors, gases, VOCs, and such); that's why you can always tell when you've entered the home of a smoker, even after the smoker is long gone. Exhausting the gases or odors released during the drying process and immediately afterward—when off-gassing is at its highest levels—is a good precaution. If you're remodeling and you're working in a furnished space, make sure you protect furnishings with sheets of plastic.

Use low- or no-VOC adhesives.

As with paint, the drying of adhesives can release VOCs. There are products available that meet the relevant Green Seal VOC standard (GS-36). Here are the maximum recommended VOC levels for a variety of adhesive types and applications (Green Seal 2000):

Carpet pad installation	150 g/l
Ceramic tile installation	150 g/l
Indoor floor covering installation	150 g/l
Multipurpose construction	150 g/l
Perimeter bonded sheet vinyl flooring	100 g/l
Wood flooring adhesive	150 g/l
Flexible vinyl substrate	250 g/l
Metal to metal	30 g/l
Other substrates	250 g/l

For carpet adhesives, you can also refer to the Carpet and Rug Institute's industry certification program (2004). There are now two levels: Green Label and the more stringent Green Label Plus. The latter was developed for independent testing of carpets and carpet adhesives installed in schools in California; by the time this book is published we anticipate that the label will be available for residential applications. (Ask for it—it will help bring the product to market faster.)

Performance is an important issue. Adhesive failures can be extremely disappointing, and sometimes costly to repair. The best way to avoid such failures and be green is to start with an environmentally friendly finish with proven performance. Manufacturers of green finishes requiring adhesives for installation will generally make specific recommendations for adhesives to be used (if they don't actually supply the appropriate adhesive themselves). They also have requirements for proper installation, which you

should follow to the letter to prevent failures and protect your warranty. Some manufacturers of green products—for example, Forbo, the maker of Marmoleum (a linoleum flooring product)—offer two certifications (associate and master mechanic) to installers to ensure proper procedures are followed. Use only approved installers of a given product if they exist.

Limit or eliminate carpet in your home.

Carpet can be one of the worst offenders in terms of off-gassing. This is particularly a problem when it's new and up to a year after installation. If it's glued down, the adhesive can irritate those with allergies or sensitize those who are vulnerable. Carpet also acts as a highly effective reservoir for allergens such as dirt, pollen, mold spores, dust mites, and other toxins carried into the house on shoes. Moreover, as carpet wears out, the yarn breaks down and becomes house dust. If you do select carpet for the home, tack it (don't glue it) and make sure it bears the CRI indoor air quality Green Label or better yet, Green Label Plus.

Area rugs are a great substitute, because you can remove and clean them. But this only works if you actually clean them! Some other tips if you decide to get carpet:

Purchase natural fiber carpet or all-nylon carpet, which is less attractive to dust mites and mold. The processed materials used in recycled carpet tend to be less toxic than virgin synthetics. Avoid dark colors; more dye may mean more problems for those who are sensitive.

Never use wall-to-wall in wet or moist areas like kitchens, baths, basements, and attics, unless you like mold and mildew. For the same reason, never apply carpet to a concrete slab unless provisions for a moisture/vapor barrier or insulation have been made to keep the carpet warm and dry.

Air out carpet before installation—roll it out and let it off-gas for as long as possible. (This can be done in your garage or at the installer's shop.)

Protect ducts and other rooms from cross-contamination when removing old carpets during a remodeling job. The removal process can stir up and spread all that dust and such. A sales representative in the carpet renewal business once told us that more than half the weight of an average carpet being removed is dirt, dust, mites, and the like. Yuck!

Use a fan to flush out your home with fresh air after carpet installation.

Use formaldehyde-free cabinets, doors, and trim.

Since it's especially costly to purchase cabinets made entirely from solid wood, for most of us these items will be assemblies that include a mix of solid wood, particleboard or fiberboard, and plastic. It's the particleboard or fiberboard that's the primary cause of concern for indoor air quality, since it's generally manufactured with a formaldehyde-based binder. The GreenSpec product directory lists fiberboard and particleboard products that are formaldehyde-free or manufactured with phenol-formaldehyde binders that result in lower formaldehyde off-gassing. For custom cabinetry, you might want to think about having coatings (stains, clear finishes) applied in the factory, where it's easier to control and ventilate the process adequately.

Doors are another place where composite wood is often used. Interior doors are typically made with wood, molded hardboard, and/or composite wood or agrifiber products. Solid wood doors are beautiful, but finding clear stock wood is difficult and when you do find it, it may have come from old-growth forests. Molded hardboard is a composite wood product often made with some recycled content but held together with a binder that conventionally has been formaldehyde based. Some manufacturers are starting to use formaldehyde-free binders, and this is what you should look for. Doors made with plywood veneer are common. Luan plywood is most often used and typically comes from non–sustainably harvested rainforests. More manufacturers are now offering doors using FSC-certified, sustainably harvested wood for the veneers, core, and structure of the door. These are good choices and can be combined with urea-formaldehyde-free agrifiber cores to make a door that's more solid and soundproof. You may also be able to find doors made with salvaged materials or better yet, salvaged doors. Some homeowners have used old barn doors or carved entry doors throughout their home to great effect.

Trim pieces are typically solid wood or composite wood. If you use solid wood, look for finger-jointed lumber that makes use of smaller pieces of wood to make the longer pieces and/or FSC-certified wood. If you use composite wood, look for formaldehyde-free and recycled-content products. Also be sure to properly seal against moisture.

Design in self-cleaning.

Install a bench and a shoe cubby at your home's entry to encourage folks to take off their shoes—and

To encourage folks to take off their shoes at the Scheulen home in Seattle, Washington, a box-bench (where visitors' shoes can also be stored) is built into the stair landing next to the front door. PHOTO BY JON ALEXANDER.

Built-in shelves on a stair landing and in a small bathroom use space efficiently. PHOTOS BY GEORGE OSTROW (LEFT), GRACE HUANG (RIGHT).

use a walk-off or interior door mat. This will keep your floors cleaner—especially important if you install carpet—and will also protect your health. Another option is to install a slotted grate in your porch or mudroom. Dirt and debris fall through the grate into a collection area, which can be emptied periodically.

INTERIOR CHOICES FOR LIVABILITY

Your choice of interior details can make a big difference in your home's livability. Here are our *top green home picks* for designing spaces and choosing finishes for livability:

- Design in space savers and other details to improve livability.
- Choose lighter, reflective colors.

Design in space savers and other details to improve livability.

Built-ins and other space-saving details help you keep the overall square footage of your new or remodeled home within reasonable limits, which is where we started in chapter 2, while making your home more livable. Other details, such as solar tubes

and interior glazing, can help transfer light into interiors that would otherwise be dark and make them seem larger.

Choose lighter, reflective colors.

Lighter colors enhance a natural lighting scheme, create spaciousness, and generally introduce fewer VOCs. They also save energy since lighter, more reflective colors bounce more daylight and artificial light into and around rooms, thus making it comfortable to use no or less artificial light.

INTERIOR CHOICES FOR DURABILITY AND SUSTAINABILITY

Like all building materials, interior finishes make dents in the earth's natural capital account along the way to your job site that might be harder to see unless you're looking. One way to reduce the environmental impact of the finishes you use is to reuse materials (in the case of a remodeling project) or purchase reclaimed or salvaged materials. Reusing materials gives new life to what might otherwise become waste without extracting or harvesting any raw materials from the environment or using energy to produce. Recycled-content materials also turn waste into resource and conserve raw materials, but they generally use energy in the manufacturing process.

Here are some questions to ask yourself as you consider the environmental impact of your interior choices:

Is the surface actually required? An open interior can offer benefits including a lighter, airier, and potentially more energy-efficient home. Eliminating

A solar tube in a hallway (top) and an interior glazed door (bottom) allow light into an interior space to help the smaller space seem larger.
PHOTOS BY GRACE HUANG (LEFT), BRUCE SULLIVAN (RIGHT).

The balustrade added during remodeling of the Olivé-Mortola residence in Seattle, Washington, consists of a railing made with reclaimed wood, and salvaged wood balusters.
PHOTO BY ANNA STEUCKLE.

interior partition walls also reduces material used to build the home and provides greater flexibility as your household changes. Portable room dividers, such as your grandmother's hutch, contemporary shelving, or an attractive antique chest, can be moved as needed to rearrange the space.

Does the surface really need a finish? More and more, homeowners are opting to use structural materials that don't require additional finishes. An example is a concrete slab floor with integrated color or incised to look like Spanish tile. (An exposed concrete floor with radiant heat built in makes for a toasty warm home.) Generally, structural materials are more durable than typical finishes, so they have the added advantage of providing a longer service life.

How is the finish material produced? Consideration should be given to which materials are used, how much energy is consumed, and how much pollution or waste is produced during manufacturing.

How does the finish material need to be maintained? By choosing materials that don't require topical applications of toxic substances or regular maintenance with cleaning products that include problem chemicals, you eliminate or reduce the potential harm to the environment where the cleaning products or topical applications are produced and disposed of. You're also less likely to introduce problematic volatile chemicals into your home.

Here are our *top green home picks* for choosing materials and finishes to ensure durability and minimize environmental impact:

- **Choose durable, easy-to-clean countertops.**
- **Use wood to show it off, not use it up.**
- **Use exposed concrete as a finished floor.**
- **Use appropriate finishes in high-traffic areas or areas subject to moisture.**
- **Use recycled, reclaimed, or reused materials for large interior surfaces.**
- **Use innovative green materials to accent your home and create fun counters, floors, and cabinets.**

Choose durable, easy-to-clean countertops.

Countertops need to be durable and easy to clean and maintain. Kitchen countertops in particular are among the hardest-working surfaces in your home. There are many wonderful green options available, including FSC-certified butcher block; terrazzo-like countertops made with recycled glass; recycled paper countertops, some of which are infinitely recyclable and don't use binders; concrete; linoleum; recycled

tile; and solid surfaces with recycled content. Where you're using the countertop will help determine which material to use—special care should be given, in particular, to selecting countertops for places where water will be present, like bathrooms and kitchens. In wet situations, avoid or minimize seams as much as possible to protect against water damage and mold growth. Where seams exist, look for low- or no-VOC water-based caulks and invest in a high-quality one. It will be much cheaper in the long run if you can avoid water damage and limit replacement. If you choose a silicone caulk, look for one that's additive-free and aquarium grade.

Countertops tend to be expensive, so in remodeling situations, give serious thought to whether the countertop really needs to be replaced. Perhaps it can be repaired or refinished. For example, tile countertops can be regrouted and sealed, wood counter-

tops can be refinished, and laminate surfaces can be reglued or perhaps resurfaced.

Use wood to show it off, not use it up.

Although in theory a renewable resource, trees are often overharvested, causing great environmental damage. Trees are a precious natural resource and a vital part of many ecosystems, so wood should be judiciously used where it will have the biggest impact. Most people enjoy the look, feel, and warmth of wood—qualities you won't enjoy when wood is sealed inside a wall or under a floor. Specific examples of where it works well to use wood for maximum enjoyment include wood for windowsills, not entire frames; for cabinet faces, not interior shelves; and for door veneers, not cores. For the wood you use, check out sustainable alternatives, such as FSC-certified or reclaimed options. Interior finish use is

Two green countertop ideas include the concrete kitchen counter with integrated food compost bin (right) designed by Velocipede Architects for a home in Seattle, Washington, and the Richlite countertop installed in the Luk kitchen galley (left). (Richlite is a natural-looking material made from recycled paper and plastic resins.) PHOTOS BY DAVID H. ERICSON (LEFT), GRACE HUANG (RIGHT).

In the Cunningham-Pinon home in Portland, Oregon, wood is used judiciously for sills but not frames (left). In the Sullivan home in Bend, Oregon, the stairs were constructed with salvaged and FSC-certified wood (right). PHOTOS BY ANDREA NELSON (LEFT), BRUCE SULLIVAN (RIGHT).

The eating nook at the Sullivan residence has a concrete tabletop, as well as a solid concrete floor, scored to emulate tile and selectively colored with a green stain. PHOTO BY BRUCE SULLIVAN.

an especially good option for salvaged, refurbished, or remilled wood that was originally used for structural purposes but no longer meets structural or code requirements.

It may be possible to mill wood harvested from the project site itself (from downed trees or demolition debris), reducing transportation-related impacts considerably. Believe it or not, that weedlike alder makes a great trim source if it's mature enough and harvested before it rots! Buying seconds helps build

a market for less-than-perfect products, making sure the wood is used at its highest value. The antithesis of these green choices is to use exotic woods harvested by conventional means from a distant location.

Use exposed concrete as a finished floor.

Exposed concrete is durable, attractive, easy to clean, and can be a part of your thermal comfort scheme. Remember that thermal mass works best when it's hit directly by the sun. In winter, spring, and fall, a concrete floor can soak up the heat from the sun and then radiate it into the space. (In summer, you'll want to shade the floor to keep it cool underfoot, following the principles of passive solar design.) Because it allows a direct transfer of heat, concrete is also a great surface over radiant heat.

You'll need to apply a clear finish, but this can be applied over an integral color or stain. Tilelike or

mosaic patterns are fun, as is an acid wash stain. You can minimize cracking by installing a topping slab over the structural slab. It's best to assume some cracking will occur as part of the character of the surface, however.

Use appropriate finishes in high-traffic areas or areas subject to moisture.

Resilient flooring (in either tile or sheet form) provides a durable choice for high-traffic areas or areas subject to moisture, such as bathrooms or laundry rooms. Avoid vinyl for reasons explained earlier in the book. There are some vinyl flooring products made without chlorine that incorporate recycled content; these are definitely preferable. Even better would be nonvinyl plastic flooring (frequently available with recycled content) or bio-based material such as linoleum. (Take care—some salespersons or installers refer to all resilient flooring as linoleum, but that's not accurate.)

If you have the budget, install a tile floor made of ceramic, glass, or concrete or install hardwood, cork, or bamboo floors. The material and installation cost more, but they provide a good long service life. A variety of tiles are now available with recycled content. (See the GreenSpec product directory and your local green material supplier for the latest options.)

Use recycled, reclaimed, or reused materials for large interior surfaces.

Many products with recycled, reclaimed, or reused content are available in the region. This includes drywall with recycled-content gypsum for your walls and ceilings, and reclaimed wood or recycled-content tile for floors and bathroom walls.

Use innovative green materials to accent your home and create fun counters, floors, and cabinets.

Too many of the early versions of environmentally responsible products looked clunky and like they were manufactured in garages (some were). Today there are some very elegant-looking bio-based

The master bathroom in the Luk residence in Seattle, Washington, makes attractive use of recycled tile (left). The home also used reclaimed wood for the stairs (right). PHOTOS BY GRACE HUANG.

Materials chosen for the master bathroom in the Peterson residence in Pasco, Washington, provide a geological theme—the natural granite counter shown in the photo, skipping stones used for the floor of the shower, and small basalt rocks serving as soap dishes and shower shelves. PHOTO BY KEITH PETERSON.

materials. Some great options are bamboo, cork, biocomposites made with soybean and sunflower seed by-products, and wheatboard. Color-integrated concrete makes a nice working counter you can brag about, as does linoleum.

If you use your imagination, your material choices can also serve as conversation pieces, providing a focal point to talk about your green home. For example, the Peterson residence in Pasco, Washington, subject of the case study in chapter 4, includes a master bath that's fun and green. Materials chosen provide a geological theme—a natural granite counter, stones just right for skipping used for the floor of the shower (many of them collected on-site over the course of construction), and a half-ton chunk of Canadian basalt that serves as a bench in the shower. Smaller basalt rocks serve as soap dishes and shower shelves.

Green Materials and Design Strategies Checklist

To help you think about and plan for your green interior design, we've prepared a room-by-room checklist. If you're remodeling a particular room, this can help you get started.

All rooms

- ❏ Choose energy-efficient windows. Use options with an Energy Star rating at a minimum.
- ❏ Maximize daylight and natural ventilation. Use operable windows, skylights, solar tubes, vents, and fans as appropriate. Consider room usage and your daily patterns to help locate and size windows (for example, east-facing windows in a bedroom for early risers).
- ❏ Landscape for shading as appropriate.
- ❏ Choose energy-efficient lighting. Use compact fluorescent stab-in lamps where possible, and integrate with a natural daylighting scheme.
- ❏ Opt for blinds instead of drapes or curtains. Blinds are easier to clean and help control dust as well as absorption and re–off-gassing of VOCs
- ❏ Use low- to no-VOC adhesives and sealants.
- ❏ Use low- to no-VOC water-based finishes.
- ❏ Use low- to no-VOC nontoxic paint. Avoid wallpaper, which is often made with vinyl and can provide a place for mold to grow behind it.

Kitchen

- ❏ Opt for durable, nontoxic, easy-to-clean counters. A solid surface is easier to clean and keep clean than tile. The surface must be water

The kitchen and the dining room in the Olivé-Mortola residence in Seattle, Washington, take a minimalist approach to materials use yet achieve a very rich feel. PHOTOS BY ANNA STUECKLE.

resistant.

- ❏ Use urea-formaldehyde-free cabinets made with recycled or natural materials. All wood has naturally occurring formaldehydes that may be problematic for some; seal all wood or composite wood products

The open living room in the Ziophirville project in Seattle is inviting and uses simple materials.
PHOTO BY MICHAEL MOORE.

to minimize off-gassing.

❏ Opt for durable, nontoxic, water-resistant, easy-to-clean flooring. For example, choose linoleum and/or tile.

❏ Choose energy-efficient and water-efficient appliances. Look for Energy Star approved appliances.

❏ Install a flow regulator on the kitchen faucet. Low-flow faucets don't always make sense in the kitchen (especially if you cook a lot). A flow regulator can be flipped up to stop the flow of water and flipped down to resume the flow without requiring you to turn knobs or readjust the temperature.

❏ Install a gray water collection system. Gray water from kitchens must be carefully treated

to remove grease and such.

❏ Install an on-demand water heater. Locate it at the source or for the whole house.

❏ Install a water filter. Locate it above or below the sink, or install a whole-house system.

❏ Insulate hot water pipes.

❏ Install built-in recycling containers.

❏ Install built-in composting chutes/containers. Use instead of a garbage disposal, which wastes water and the nutrients present in food scraps.

❏ Ensure good exhaust to the outside with an insulated vent. This should vent air from directly over the cooking surface (especially important with gas appliances). Combine it with an exhaust air heat pump where appropriate.

❑ Design the kitchen to avoid leaks and water damage that can cause mold and mildew. Fix leaks and mitigate any mold problems before doing any remodeling.

Bathroom

❑ Opt for durable, nontoxic, easy-to-clean counters. A solid surface is easier to clean and keep clean than tile. The surface must be water resistant.

❑ Choose urea-formaldehyde-free cabinets made with recycled or natural materials. All wood has naturally occurring formaldehydes that may be problematic for some. Seal all wood or composite wood products to minimize off-gassing.

❑ Opt for a durable, nontoxic, water-resistant, easy-to-clean floor. For example, use linoleum and/or tile.

❑ Choose recycled-content tiles.

❑ Use low-flow fixtures for sink.

❑ Use a high-performance, low-flow showerhead with a chlorine filter.

❑ Install a water-conserving toilet—low-flow or dual-flush.

❑ Install a gray water or rainwater system to flush toilets. Gray water can be collected from bathroom sinks and showers, laundry rooms, and in some cases kitchen sinks.

❑ Install an on-demand water heater. Locate it at the source.

❑ Install a wastewater heat recovery system for the shower. This only works when there's an adequate drop below the shower drain, and

Use of an antique corner vanity in this bathroom in the Scheulen residence in Seattle means that newly manufactured materials didn't need to be employed to finish the room.
PHOTO BY JON ALEX-ANDER.

thus it's only for showers on the second floor or above a basement.

❑ Install a water filter. Locate it above or below the sink, or install a whole house system.

❑ Insulate hot water pipes.

❑ Ensure good exhaust to the outside with an insulated vent. Combine this with an exhaust air heat pump where appropriate. Operable windows can also help ventilate.

❑ Design the bathroom to avoid leaks and water damage that can cause mold and mildew. Fix any leaks and mitigate any mold problems before doing any remodeling.

Living areas

❑ Choose urea-formaldehyde-free bookcases and built-ins made with recycled or natural materi-

The Huppert's entryway in Seattle features a pond fed with rainwater.
PHOTO BY MICHAEL MOORE.

als. All wood has naturally occurring formaldehydes that may be problematic for some. Seal all wood or composite wood products to minimize off-gassing.

- ❏ Use FSC-certified wood for finish carpentry. Use wood sparingly to conserve this resource. Use it where it will have the most impact or effect.
- ❏ Choose resilient or hard flooring made with recycled or natural materials—for example,

cork, bamboo, FSC-certified hardwood.

- ❏ Choose area rugs instead of wall-to-wall carpeting, or avoid rugs altogether.
- ❏ Design lighting to emphasize area/task lighting.
- ❏ Don't rely on general lighting for tasks. Design so it's easy to turn off general lighting when you're performing tasks.
- ❏ Landscape for privacy as needed. Integrate with landscape for shading.
- ❏ Avoid combustion stoves and fires. Properly exhaust when used.

Entryway/mudroom

- ❏ Choose urea-formaldehyde-free cabinets and built-ins made with recycled or natural materials. All wood has naturally occurring formaldehydes that may be problematic for some. Seal all wood or composite wood products to minimize off-gassing.
- ❏ Opt for durable, nontoxic, water-resistant, easy-to-clean flooring. For example, use linoleum and/or tile.
- ❏ Provide abundant storage for jackets, mittens, tools, and the like. Ensuring that the storage space is naturally ventilated (with a screen in the door of a storage cabinet, for example) is important in winter.
- ❏ Provide shoe storage. Encourage a no-shoe policy to minimize dirt and particulates entering the house.
- ❏ Provide entry mats. Choose options that are easy to clean and maintain. Minimize dirt and particulates entering the house.

- ❏ Install an insulated and sealed entry door. This minimizes heat loss and infiltration.
- ❏ Provide a covered area outside the door. This minimizes water penetration.
- ❏ Provide a ventilated area in which to hang wet clothes. Combine with an exhaust air heat pump where appropriate.

Bedroom

- ❏ Install resilient or hard flooring made with recycled or natural materials. For example use cork, bamboo, and/or FSC-certified hardwood.
- ❏ Use area rugs instead of wall-to-wall carpeting, or avoid rugs altogether.
- ❏ Minimize electrical appliances and keep them away from the bed.
- ❏ Avoid forced-air systems if possible. This is true for all rooms of the house, but especially the bedroom, where many spend a third of their day. If your house uses a forced-air system consider closing the vent to the bedroom and using a supplemental heat source when needed (radiant panel or portable heater).
- ❏ Minimize furnishings and clutter to help control dust.
- ❏ Opt for low- to no-VOC nontoxic furniture and furnishings.
- ❏ Store clothes in a closet or in furniture that closes. This helps control dust and lessens clutter.
- ❏ Use organic bedding that's easy to clean.
- ❏ Maintain a peaceful view from the bed. The view can be to the inside and/or the outside.
- ❏ Design lighting to emphasize area/task light-

The bedroom in the Olivé-Mortola residence in Seattle, Washington, minimizes furnishings and clutter to help control dust. PHOTO BY ANNA STUECKLE.

ing, not general overhead lighting.
- ❏ Landscape for privacy as needed. Integrate with landscape for shading.

A note about nurseries: Special care should be taken when designing or remodeling a room to serve as a nursery or child's room. Babies and young children are particularly vulnerable to the effects of chemicals and particulates. As parents we want to provide a healthy, safe, and secure environment for our children. While we can't completely eliminate exposure, we can limit it by carefully selecting products and materials and being conscientious in the design and construction process.

The impact of furniture on our health and environment is often taken for granted. We try out a chair or a bed in the local department store and make our purchase based primarily on cost and comfort. However, many of the same questions we ask ourselves in designing our green home apply:

- Where does the material to make the furniture come from?
- Does harm to others or the environment occur in the process of production?
- Does the furniture introduce health risks to you and other members of your household while you're using it?
- How long can you expect the furniture to serve you?
- Does harm to others or the environment occur once you're finished using it?

In general, store salespeople won't have the answers to all of these questions at their fingertips. You have several courses of action to choose from. For store-bought furniture, you might want to shop at the growing number of stores that specialize in selling natural or environmentally friendly furniture. This will generally cost more than generic purchases at your local department store, but you'll know what you're getting. Another (more) pricey option is to have your furniture custom-made.

Most of us shop at stores that sell a variety of products that may or may not meet our desire to have a healthy and green lifestyle. An interior designer specializing in green interior design or a conscientious salesperson can be of help here. You can also do the homework yourself by reviewing any technical information the store may have, or more likely, by getting contact information for the manufacturer and requesting the information directly. If you take the latter course, make sure you're talking to someone knowledgeable about the technical specifications for the furniture, and not the marketing department. Even if you don't get all the information you need, or the modifications you'd like, you'll have provided both the manufacturer and the supplier with a clue that consumers care about these things.

In considering your purchase, keep in mind that as with building materials in general, when you purchase furniture made with locally derived materials you reduce the amount of transport energy and its associated impacts required to get the goods into your home.

Now I'll discuss some major furniture purchases and the issues related to each.

Case goods

Case goods include furniture with wood as its main component. Examples of case goods include end tables and other bedroom furniture, coffee tables, and dining room furniture. There are three main issues with case goods. For solid wood, is the wood certified by the FSC or reclaimed? There are beautiful examples of furniture made with wood reclaimed from

By Sandy Campbell, interior designer, 1Earth1Design

The dining set pictured at left was produced using wood from a tree removed by an arborist because it was dying from weather-related damage. The hutch shown at right was produced using wood salvaged from a barn deconstructed in Ellensburg, Washington. PHOTOS BY JOHN GRANEN, COURTESY OF MEYER WELLS, INC. (LEFT), ALAN VOGEL (RIGHT).

old barns, fences, and floors. Just make sure any reclaimed material isn't painted with lead paint. For composite wood, such as particleboard, does the material contain added urea-formaldehyde? For any finishes used, including paints, do they contain urea-formaldehyde, petroleum-based solvents, defoamers, fire retardants, plasticizers, preservatives, or fungicides? Any of the latter may contain VOCs that introduce a health risk to your home. You might be able to ask the manufacturer to use water-based finishes with low or no VOCs.

Upholstered furniture

Chairs, couches, and mattresses are another area of concern. Green alternatives in this area are still hard to find. Components that might cause health problems include synthetic foams, fabrics, and protective coatings. The foam used is typically polyurethane, which is petroleum-based and will continue to release chemicals into your home interior. It's difficult to determine the length of time chemicals will off-gas and not much information is available. Urea-formaldehyde and polybrominated diphenyl ethers (PBDEs), for example, off-gas for the life of the product.

PBDEs are commonly used as fire retardants in foams and plastics used in upholstered furniture. PBDEs build up in the environment and are absorbed into our bodies. The Washington State Department of Ecology reports that in North America, levels of PBDEs in humans are increasing rapidly and are now forty times higher than in humans on other continents (Washington State Department of Ecology 2006). If this rate continues to increase, the levels in humans could reach those known to cause problems in laboratory rodents, including memory and learning impairments as well as effects on other bodily functions. Out of concern over this threat, in April 2007 Washington became the first state to ban the use of Deca PBDE in household goods. The measure passed by the state legislature prohibits the manufacture, sale, or distribution of items treated with the suspected neurotoxin. Other PBDEs, Octa and Penta, had previously been phased out voluntarily.

Stain-resistant and wrinkle-resistant coatings frequently contain urea-formaldehyde and other chemicals. Ask the manufacturer to produce the pieces you want with natural latex foam, wool, and cotton batting, preferably organic.

Fabrics are an area where there's been a lot of progress. Several choices of durable commercial-grade fabrics that are safe for the environment and for people are generally available through interior designers. Natural fibers that don't contain finishes and coatings are also a great choice.

If the material is dyed, find out if the dyes are vegetable based or low-impact; if so, they use less water and energy and expel cleaner wastewater. If a fabric is bleached, look for a chlorine-free method.

Window treatments

Use the same guidelines for fabric selection as just mentioned for upholstered furniture. Plasticizers and vinyl plastics may be present in all types of window treatments (as well as furniture). Both should be avoided for reasons discussed elsewhere in the book. An alternative is wood blinds; they're easier to clean and won't harbor hard-to-see dust and grime.

Area rugs

Area rugs are a good option to use instead of wall-to-wall carpeting. They can be more thoroughly cleaned than carpeting, lessening the risk of dust and dust mites building up. Choose area rugs made with natural, untreated fibers and backings. Be aware that imported wool rugs and carpeting may have chemical mothproofing. Try to find wool rugs produced in the United States or from manufacturers that use alternative mothproofing methods.

> Nature is the infrastructure of our communities, and we must meet our obligation as a generation, as a civilization, as a nation, to create communities for our children that provide them with opportunities for dignity and enrichment and good health.
>
> Robert F. Kennedy, Jr., Sierra Summit, 2005

12: Operations and Maintenance

THIS CHAPTER ADDRESSES AREAS related to operating and maintaining your green home—house cleaning, lawn and garden care, and moss control. In addition, we've invited Dan Morris, the indoor air specialist who earlier provided tips on designing to prevent mold, to offer pointers on how to deal with mold when it occurs. His discussion focuses primarily on the cleanup of mold on wood components in new or newly remodeled homes, but the measures he suggests can apply to any household mold outbreak. First we'll look at three simple rules to guide you as you operate and maintain your green home.

THREE SIMPLE RULES

If you've instituted many of the ideas discussed in the previous chapters, you now have a green home surrounded by a healthy green landscape. The key to continued enjoyment of the benefits your green home can offer—such as energy and water savings, a healthier indoor environment, and longer service life—is following three simple rules:

❏ Pay attention to how your home works and address problems right away.

❏ Set up and keep a routine of regular maintenance of your home's new systems and materials.

❏ Make green choices as you maintain, repair, clean, and operate your home.

Pay attention to how your home works and address problems right away.

It's easy to be excited about your green home but to be so busy with your life that you don't notice a problem. Pay attention to your home's performance and keep on top of needed repairs. Don't wait so long that the installer's warranty on the work lapses.

Pay attention to energy and water bills. If they seem higher than anticipated, don't hesitate to ask why. If the air is stuffy when it should feel fresh, investigate. If a finish doesn't seem to hold up the way you expected it to, say so. If you smell or see something that might indicate a mold problem—yes, even in your new home—follow up on it. If particulates are puffing out of the exhaust from your brand

The Cunningham-Pinon residence with its attractive landscape was featured on the City of Portland's 2005 Build It Green home tour as an example of simple, afford-able design. PHOTO BY ANDREA NELSON.

be. Most contractors understand that building systems frequently don't operate perfectly from the get-go and will conscientiously honor agreements that establish periods (usually one to two years) for callbacks to repair defective equipment or installation.

Even after the contractor's responsibility has expired, continue to pay attention for problems that can be nipped in the bud. Look for these red flags:

- sharp spikes in utility bills
- signs of moisture damage, including stains or musty odors
- strange sounds when systems are operating
- cracks in the foundation or other signs of extreme settling
- physical discomfort of household members
- significant physical degradation of materials

Set up and keep a routine of regular maintenance of your home's systems and materials.

Earlier in the book, we discussed the importance of a final walk-through of the project when it's completed. This walk-through will help you start out on the right foot. It should include a thorough orientation to your home's systems and materials, whether you've directly participated in the construction process (as with a new home project or remodel) or not (as with a production home purchase).

The orientation should include information about preferred service routines, service providers, and what you can do to get the best performance out of installed equipment and systems. This should cover individual systems and also how the home's systems work together and should optimally perform for health, comfort, and efficiency. The goal is to get

new hot water heater, don't just hope the problem will work itself out.

The symptoms you observe may indicate something significant, such as a mistake in the way an exhaust fan is installed, or something more incidental, such as a misplaced bird's nest. Regardless of the cause, the problem is probably resolvable and the sooner it's fixed the less serious the consequences will

the information you need to keep the systems in your home operating at peak performance for the longest time possible.

If you're moving into a new residence, the final walk-through or orientation should also point out any places on your site or in your neighborhood that are environmentally sensitive—for example, a salmon-bearing stream or a wetland. These areas may require special protection and maintenance practices.

You should learn—either from the supplier you obtain them from or the contractor who installs them—how to maintain the following products or equipment in your home:

- HVAC (heating, ventilation, and air conditioning) systems, including furnace filters, chimneys, fans, and timers
- water-heating systems
- floors of all kinds, including wood, linoleum, tile, and carpet
- wood decks, concrete patios, and other outdoor wood structures or furniture
- appliances, including gaskets and hoses
- plumbing fixtures and systems
- on-site renewable energy systems
- lighting sensors and systems
- smoke detectors, CO_2 monitors, and fire extinguishers
- gutters, heating ducts, dryer vents, and fireplaces
- irrigation systems
- landscapes
- any specialized equipment such as programmable thermostats or security systems

Developing a checklist of routine maintenance tasks with a schedule for performing them can help you stay on track. Ideally your contractor or the sales office in the case of a production home has prepared a maintenance checklist for you that's specific to your home and its features. If not, you can also generate your own checklist. Maintenance ideas for systems commonly included in homes can be found in "Resources." You'll want to include items relevant to the more innovative systems or materials installed in your home. For a start, here are some ideas for your checklist:

This wetland in the Longfellow Creek neighborhood of Seattle, Washington, requires special consideration from homeowners in decisions that may affect its health.
PHOTO BY SUE NICOL.

Routine Maintenance Checklist

❏ If you have a forced-air heating system, have a professional inspect it before winter arrives. This should include inspecting the chimney or vent piping to make sure it's not blocked, servicing the burner and fan units, and determining whether the ductwork needs a thorough cleaning.

❏ Change the filters in your heating system according to the manufacturer's recommendations. If recommendations aren't readily available, change the filters once every month or two during periods of use. Proper maintenance is important even for new furnaces, because they can also corrode and leak combustion gases, including carbon monoxide (U.S. Environmental Protection Agency 1995).

❏ Inspect chimneys and vents associated with fireplaces or stoves annually and clean them as inspections indicate. The National Fire Protection Association (NFPA) has set a standard—NFPA 211—for home heating appliance inspections, and professionals certified by the Chimney Safety Institute of America (CSIA) are trained to meet this standard. The inspection should include the readily accessible exterior and interior portions of the chimney, the heating appliance, and connections between the two. An inspector will look for obstructions, soundness, and any combustible materials needing removal.

❏ Make sure your home is ventilated properly. Most homes ventilate through the use of dedicated exhaust fans in the bath, laundry, and kitchen range hood. The airflow of exhaust fans in your home should be strong enough to hold a piece of tissue in place. If it isn't, the fan(s) may need maintenance or to be replaced. Like most things with a motor, if a fan is getting really noisy, it's about to bite the dust. If your home has a whole house fan, follow the inspection and maintenance routine suggested by the manufacturer.

❏ Monitor the moisture in your home by noting whether condensation is occurring on the inside of double-paned windows or cold water pipes. You can also purchase a relative humidity (RH) gauge (about $30) and check regularly to make sure the RH of your home's interior stays within a healthy 30-to-50-percent range. If your home is having problems staying at 50 percent or below, consider flushing your home regularly during the winter months (by opening all the windows for a short period of time and then reheating to 70 degrees). Using a dehumidifier in basements can also help, but note that dehumidifiers should only be used when the room temperature is 65 degrees or warmer (Northwest Clean Air Agency 2005). Keep an eye out for leaks where they occur most often—basements, under windows, through roofs, and around dishwashers, ice-making refrigerators, showers, and toilets.

❏ If you own a photovoltaic array, periodically wash accumulated dust and debris off of panels and check mounting hardware and conduit connections to assure tightness. Maintenance is more complicated if your PV system is hooked up to batteries. Industry technicians recommend checking terminal connections and wiring regularly to ensure terminals are kept free of debris, and adding distilled water to lead-acid batteries on a quarterly basis (EC&M magazine 2006).

❑ If you own a solar water heating system, regularly inspect and maintain it to keep it operating efficiently. Your owner's manual should suggest a maintenance schedule. The U.S. Department of Energy recommends that the following items be inspected periodically (note that some of these are best done by a qualified technician):

- collector, for shading from debris or vegetation growth
- collector glazing and seals
- plumbing seals and wiring connections
- piping and wiring insulation
- roof penetrations and support structures
- pressure relief valve (on liquid solar heating collectors)
- dampers (in solar air heating systems)
- pumps or blower fans
- heat transfer fluids (such as antifreeze)—replace periodically
- storage tanks and systems

❑ If you have a rainwater collection system, maintain it periodically to operate at full efficiency. For rainwater systems hooked up to indoor plumbing, you should receive and follow maintenance guidelines from your installer. Texas A&M University offers these tips on

maintaining a rainwater collection system dedicated to landscape irrigation:

- Keep debris out of holding areas.
- Clean and repair channels.
- Clean and repair dikes, berms, and moats.
- Keep debris out of gutters and downspouts.
- Flush debris from storage container bottoms.
- Clean and maintain filters, especially those on drip irrigation systems.

❑ Maintain your washer and dryer. Regularly remove lint from your dryer's lint trap, because it's a fire danger and likely reduces the performance of your machine. Also remove the dryer's vent hose from its connection to the appliance twice a year to check for lint for the same reason. Use your regular inspection to make sure the appliances are level so they operate properly and wear and tear are reduced.

❑ Maintain your dishwasher. Check for small kitchen items that occasionally fall to the bottom of the dishwasher and end up under the heating element or clogging a drain. Keep door gaskets and spray arms clean by wiping them down with a cleaning agent. Be sure to inspect the bottom part of the door gasket, since this is where leaks are likely to occur. Check rubber supply and drain hoses once a year for cracks or hardening and replace if needed.

❑ Maintain your refrigerator. Vacuum the condenser coils at least once a year to remove dust, more often if you have pets. Check the gasket seal by closing the door on a dollar bill. If the bill is easily pulled out, replace the rubber gasket. Use petroleum jelly or household oil on the gasket to keep it soft and pliable and thus extend its life. If your refrigerator requires manual defrosting, do this as soon as the frost is ¼-inch thick. Replace water filters on ice makers or water dispensers twice a year, remembering to close the water valve before disconnecting the hose.

❏ Maintain your stove top and oven. Clean burners regularly. Inspect your gas oven to make sure that burners run blue and not yellow. If yellow, have a professional adjust them immediately. Clean any clogged gas burner holes with a pin, not a toothpick. Every ten years, replace electric oven heating elements.

❏ Clean your gutters in fall.

❏ Check proper functioning of fire extinguishers monthly. The gauge should read "full" with the pin inserted. "Spank" the extinguisher every six months by turning it over and patting the bottom with the pad of your hand as you rotate it around. This helps ensure that the powder inside hasn't caked and that the extinguisher will work most effectively if needed. Check the hose to make sure it's intact, well connected, and pliable, and that nothing is obstructing the nozzle. If the extinguisher has been discharged, it must be replaced.

❏ Maintain CO_2 monitors according to the manufacturer's recommendations.

❏ Check smoke detectors monthly. Replace batteries annually.

❏ Turn on and inspect your irrigation system each spring. Check for leaks and/or clogs and replace broken parts. Preferably this can be part of the contract with the irrigation company that installed your system.

❏ Inspect your landscape for dead or dying plants every spring. This is an opportunity to prune, divide perennial plants, and eliminate winter annual weeds. After weeding, mulch with an inch or two of organic mulch. Give lawns a light application of a slow-release organic turf fertilizer, such as sulfur-coated urea.

❏ Inspect the exterior of your home every spring. Check for foundation cracks, moisture damage at the connections between decks and exterior walls, and moss and algae growth on walkway and deck surfaces, which can make them slippery. If you have a wood deck made of lumber pressure-treated with chromated copper arsenate (CCA), you should know that CCA is no longer available for purchase because of concerns about arsenic leaching into the soil (U.S. Environmental Protection Agency 2005). Pressure washing or sanding such wood isn't recommended. To clean outdoor wood structures, use an oxygen-bleach (not chlorine-bleach) solution and then seal with a synthetic resin water repellent.

A green cone can aerobically decompose a variety of food scraps. The plastic rodent-proof unit comes with an attached underground basket. PHOTO BY SUE NICOL.

Municipalities frequently distribute green cleaning kits, such as this one. You can also make your own cleaning products using ingredients such as baking soda and vinegar. PHOTO BY KATHERINE MORGAN.

Make green choices as you maintain, repair, clean, and operate your home.

As you care for your new or remodeled green home, make sure you don't introduce problem substances into the environment. It's easy to unwittingly purchase a product for the home or yard that compromises your good intentions. When making minor repairs to your home, follow the same guidelines for material selection provided in this book for new construction and remodels.

As the owner of a green home, you can make choices in your home and community that exemplify environmental stewardship and good common sense. Recycling waste rather than sending it to the landfill is one example. It's possible to recycle most waste from a green home if recycling systems are designed into it. A well-designed recycling center will include bins convenient to you but not to pests.

Worm bins and/or food waste compost bins can be installed near the kitchen door and produce compost for the garden. Many Northwest communities now require homes and businesses to recycle tin, aluminum, glass, paper, and some plastics. In some communities, such as Seattle, vegetable food scraps and paper food containers can be placed in yard waste containers. Check with your municipality to see what's possible where you live.

GREEN CHOICES FOR CLEANING AND MAINTAINING YOUR HOME

Here are our *top green home picks* for cleaning and maintaining your green home:

- Clean green.
- Use a nature-based approach to plant and lawn care.
- Use fish-friendly methods of moss control.

Clean green.

The cleaning cupboard of a typical home contains more than a dozen chemicals considered hazardous to humans and the environment. In your

Instituting a no-shoes policy is a simple way to keep your green home clean and healthy. PHOTO BY SUE NICOL.

green home, you can easily opt for less-hazardous cleaning products and save money at the same time. Traditional household cleaning products such as dishwasher detergent, glass cleaner, floor wax, and scouring powder contain dangerous chemicals. Effective substitutes that are much safer and cheaper are available (Davis and Turner 1995).

Many companies sell eco-friendly cleaning products for the home. General-purpose cleaners, window cleaners, and other cleaning products have been certified by Green Seal and are listed on the Green Seal Web site. Use microfiber cleaning cloths to reduce the amount of cleaning product needed.

You can also make your own cleaning products using ingredients such as baking soda, vinegar, borax, cornstarch, isopropyl alcohol, and other items easily purchased in the grocery store. Here's a recipe for a great all-purpose window cleaner: Combine ¼ cup vinegar, ½ teaspoon liquid soap or detergent, and 2 cups of water in a spray bottle. Shake to blend. Use a good-quality squeegee and place a towel on the windowsill to catch drips.

Invest in a pressure washer as a way to avoid using chemicals when cleaning algae, moss (more on that later), and dirt from concrete driveways and patios, wood decks, outdoor furniture, and, occasionally, your home's siding.

And think about keeping your home cleaner in the first place. For example, one way to keep your home clean (and healthy) is to initiate a no-shoes policy. According to Terry Brennan, a nationally recognized indoor air quality expert, shoes are the source of up to 80 percent of airborne particulates in the average home (personal communication, 2002). Some of that stuff can be pretty nasty, depending on where you walk—pesticides, fertilizers, tire fragments, and even lead dust.

Use a nature-based approach to plant and lawn care.

Creating and maintaining healthy soil, selecting the right plant for the right spot, and following organic plant-care practices make up the foundation of a healthy and cost-effective landscape. Once you've alleviated soil compaction after construction, brought in good topsoil or amended existing soil, selected drought-tolerant plants appropriate for your site, and planted them correctly, you won't need chemical fertilizers and pesticides.

A plant-care program that's nature-based emphasizes plant health over pest management, works with nature, and considers the ecosystem as a whole. This five-step plant-care program is adapted from suggestions made by Washington State University (Bobbitt et al. 2005):

1. Know your plants, their needs, and their vulnerabilities. The majority of plants brought into Master Gardener plant clinics aren't suffering from insects or diseases but from cultural and environmental problems such as drought stress, lack of fertilizer, or winter damage.

2. Determine the key problems of your site including poor drainage, wind speed and direction, pest-prone plants already growing in your garden, and the pests and diseases your plants are likely to get.

3. Study your landscape ecosystem including your soil type, minimum and maximum temperatures, sun and shade aspect, and surroundings. (If you built your own home using green principles, you've already done this.) This can help you determine appropriate plant types and best locations. Monitor your landscape regularly to evaluate how well plants are growing and adapting to site conditions.

4. Optimize your plants' health by making planting location choices based on their needs. Some plants, like roses, are pest prone. Instead of using fungicides to reduce black spot on roses, find a rose cultivar that resists this fungus, or another plant that blooms in summer. Most rhododendrons don't do well if planted in the sun. Moving a rhody to a shadier spot will help it stay healthier. Lavender likes well-drained soil, so if your garden has a slow-draining clay soil, don't plant lavender in your garden.

5. Employ the principles of integrated pest management (IPM) if, after taking the previous four steps, you still have a pest problem.

This healthy lawn, perfectly brown in summer, turns bright green when the winter rains return. PHOTO BY JACQUELINE JAMES.

IPM uses cultural, biological, and mechanical control of pests before chemical control. Monitoring of plants and pest problems is important to IPM, as well as determining when a problem is severe enough to deal with. IPM emphasizes using the least-toxic pest control solution first. If you're having trouble with a particular pest or plant condition, contact your local extension agent, consult the Master Gardeners, or consult organic gardening guides. Don't go to the hardware store looking for a solution—unless, of course, the Master Gardeners are there.

More and more municipalities in the Northwest are requiring their public parks and school lands to be managed organically. They're able to do this while still maintaining sports fields and grassy areas

The moss garden at the Japanese Garden in Seattle's Washington Park Arboretum is an example of working with instead of against nature. PHOTO BY SUE NICOL.

in parks, demonstrating that it's entirely possible to eliminate pesticides and herbicides from your turf care practice. Instead of making a seasonal application of weed and feed, aerate your lawn and then top-dress with well-aged compost, fertilize sparingly with organic fertilizer, and mow with a mulching mower to leave grass clippings to decompose and provide nitrogen.

Fighting dandelions? Grass can outcompete lawn weeds if well cared for. Aerate and sprinkle grass seed over your lawn each spring and fall. To reduce the number of weed seeds (and maintain moisture) keep the grass at the longest length possible (ideally 2½ to 3½ inches).

Water your lawn deeply but infrequently. If you've amended your soils adequately, grass roots will grow deeply and need less water. The conventional wisdom that turf needs an inch of water a week may be appropriate for sports fields and golf courses, but your grass can certainly survive on a great deal less than that in summer if you choose the right grass seed, provide a good soil base, and fertilize during fall to help roots grow deeply. Consider the brown of summer to be part of your seasonal aesthetic, and water only the areas that function as outdoor rooms. Do your planting in the fall and you may be able to avoid watering altogether after the first growing season.

Use fish-friendly methods of moss control.

Moss is a fact of life in large areas of the Pacific Northwest. When it grows on rooftops, decks, and walkways, it can be hazardous and damaging. It can also be quite tenacious. Many commercial de-mossing solutions available are considered harmful to fish swimming in waterways adjacent to homes—a common situation in our bioregion. The good news is that cost-effective, environmentally friendly ways to deal with moss are available. They take some thought and care, but they can help you and all of the species that depend on water. Here we discuss what to do about moss in lawns, and moss on roofs and decks.

Moss thrives in shady, damp areas with poor drainage, just the areas where lawns do not thrive. Unless these physical conditions are changed, moss will always outperform your lawn in these areas. Lawns need sunlight to thrive. In areas where lawn is desired, first evaluate the current condition of the soil and turf, and then increase direct sunlight. If more than 50 percent of your lawn is filled with moss, you may have to renovate it, which involves a process of de-thatching, aeration, overseeding (with a 50-50 mix of fine fescue and perennial rye), and establishment with fertilizer and water. If you want to pursue this route, you'll need more details (see "Resources")—and a fair amount of patience.

There are lawn products on the market that are effective moss killers, including ferrous compounds and complete fertilizers with iron. Check your local nursery. You may also consider surrendering. If moss is thriving in your lawn, consider nurturing it. It can be an especially attractive ground cover and nicely complements a shady hosta or fern garden.

Moss can shorten the lifespan of roofs and decks. Especially vulnerable to moss are cedar shake or shingle roofs, shady areas, and surfaces that retain moisture from leaf and needle debris. Here are several chemical-free and/or less-toxic ways to deal with moss in these areas:

• Periodically clean your roof, decks, patios, and walkways of moss and other organic debris (leaves, needles, branches) with a stiff brush, broom, or power washer. Make sure to remove foreign matter from the spaces between individual shingles.

• Remove overhanging branches to allow direct sunlight, good aeration, and faster drying of your roof and outdoor surfaces.

• Use nontoxic moss-control products. Soap-based products meet this goal. They're biodegradable and noncorrosive, and pose minimal hazards to people and animals. Be sure to thoroughly rinse overspray.

• Don't use moss-control products that include copper and zinc. While very effective in killing moss, they're corrosive and have been linked to harming fish in nearby waters. Specifically avoid copper sulfate and zinc sulfate. Table salt is sometimes used, but it's also corrosive, can damage plants it lands on, and isn't very effective. Local environmental agencies and homeowner associations can provide information about local chemical-control regulations and covenants that might prohibit the use of certain moss-control products. For example, the Issaquah Highlands development in Washington, which is located above an important aquifer, bans the use of toxic fertilizers and pesticides and prohibits installing zinc-galvanized ridge caps, copper flashing, and copper wires.

• Whatever you choose to use, follow all application directions.

KEEPING YOUR COMMUNITY GREEN

As we complete this journey with you, we encourage you to extend your effort to green your own home to greening your community. There are lots of ways to contribute to a greener community—including staying out of your car, contributing time or money to local environmental advocacy groups, and participating in beach clean-up days and stream restoration projects. Another way you can contribute that dovetails and builds on the principles you've undertaken in your new green home or remodel is to participate in neighborhood planning. When you do this, you help to shape a more sustainable vision for your community, which can make it even easier for you and your neighbors to live green. Walkable

What do you do when you find mold growing in your new or newly remodeled house? It depends on how much area it covers, what material it's growing on, and how long it's been growing. But in any case, don't panic. A small amount of mold on solid wood isn't a big deal and can easily be cleaned. On the other hand, a large amount of mold growing for months on particleboard or oriented strand board (OSB) is a big deal.

We're constantly inhaling mold spores and particles outdoors and in the built environment. All mold species can be allergenic, some mold species produce irritating chemicals, and a few produce toxins. Also, mold growth can be detrimental to a building, causing dry rot. It can also cause particleboard and OSB to lose its structural integrity.

Any indoor environment has a fungal ecology. When a house has a moisture problem, this fungal ecology changes and the growth of certain species is amplified. This amplification can produce visible and/or destructive and dangerous mold colonies.

It can be particularly disturbing to find significant mold growth on the wood in a brand new home, but it happens all too frequently. When it does, all visible mold growth should be removed from framing and sheathing before it's covered with drywall or insulation. It's irresponsible to dry out wood framing and leave substantial visible mold anywhere in a new or old house.

You may ask why you can't just dry out wet wood and leave dried-out mold in the wall, crawl space, or attic. Dry or dead (nonviable) mold can cause the same allergic reactions in people as fresh, live (viable) mold. Microscopic mold spores have evolved to spread to new locations via air currents, just as easily as dandelion seeds. Air moves around in even the tightest buildings due primarily to wind, stack effect, people, and mechanical appliances. Another risk of just covering up moldy materials is the possibility of future moisture intrusion that will allow the existing spores to start growing again rapidly.

In one new, not-yet-occupied home I was consulted about, several types of mold were already well established in the crawl space. The house had been rained on many times before the roof and windows were installed and the wet soil in the crawl space hadn't been covered with a plastic moisture barrier. Mold was also found growing on the attic sheathing. It cost more than $20,000 to remediate this problem.

Most of the published mold remediation guidelines divide mold cleanup into three categories: small, medium, and large amounts. All guidelines direct us to stop the moisture source before cleanup is started.

Cleaning up small amounts of mold

Almost all houses built in the Pacific Northwest will have a small amount of mold on the framing lumber. If you see a few long, narrow streaks of black (or dark blue) mold on the light-colored sapwood, it's most likely "lumber mold" (*Ceratocystis*). A few square inches of this can just be vacuumed or sanded off; wear an N-95 dust mask while doing this.

When the moldy area takes up several square feet, it needs to be removed in a way that protects the workers and the house. A containment area must be set up to prevent mold

by Dan Morris, Certified Indoor Environmentalist (CIE), Healthy Buildings, Inc.

from spreading to other parts of the building.

Cleaning up medium amounts of mold

EPA guidelines (2006a) and City of New York guidelines (2006) say areas of roughly 10 to 100 square feet need more careful cleaning. Remember that published guidelines are similar to building codes in that they specify the absolute *minimum* that needs to be done. Three general principles apply to all mold remediation jobs:

- Workers must use personal protection equipment. This should include a half face respirator with HEPA and organic vapor cartridges, goggles, and gloves.
- The rest of the house must be protected. This includes erecting containment (6-mil poly barriers), establishing negative air pressure (at least a fan in the work area in a window blowing out), and covering all vents, ducts, or other appliances.
- The mold must be removed effectively. Don't just bleach or paint over it.

Cleaning up large amounts of mold

When the area covered with mold is well over 100 square feet, trained and certified professionals should remediate it. Whenever mold is discovered in a house, the water source should first be found and blocked. Drying shouldn't be started until a professional indoor environmental consultant or a professional mold remediation firm is consulted. Never just add fans or heat to a closed building with visible mold growing. This can turn the indoor environment in your house into a Mississippi swamp

In this crawl space under a new, not-yet-occupied home, several types of mold are already well established. Gray and translucent young molds are easy to detect in flash photographs. PHOTO BY DAN MORRIS.

and make the mold problem much worse. Containment, negative pressure, and ventilation must be employed but aren't well understood by many architects, builders, and homeowners. If you think you have a serious problem with mold, it's best to hire a professional to deal with it.

Materials that need extra work

All of what's been said so far assumes the mold has grown on solid wood or exterior-grade plywood (CDX). CDX is as good as or better than solid wood in terms of resisting mold growth because it's made of moisture-resistant fir and glued with waterproof phenol adhesive. On the other hand, some engineered materials are much more vulnerable to microbial attack because they're made of chopped-up wood with little or no mold resistance.

Industry consensus is that moldy drywall, insulation, and particleboard must be replaced. OSB can be salvaged only if the moisture and mold weren't there for more than a few days and didn't start growing within the material. Moisture causes OSB to swell and lose strength. Mold can grow throughout the entire core of OSB in a few months.

The test for OSB is whether it has expanded in thickness and whether the mold has grown into the core. This is often a tough call, with huge cost implications if completed roofs or walls need to be replaced. The only sure way of knowing is to drill out a 1-to-1½-inch plug of the moldy material. Test the core with a pin moisture meter. If it's wet, it should probably be replaced. To find out for sure, send the plug to a mycology lab for analysis. Ask the lab to separate the strands and examine the core for mold. If mold has penetrated past the surface, the material should be replaced. A professional indoor air quality firm should be consulted to minimize the risk of inadequate remediation and to do clearance testing after the work is done.

Some final words

The bottom line is that mold spores (which are everywhere) plus food (the organic materials with which you build your home) plus moisture add up to mold in your home. By using more durable materials (such as solid wood and exterior-grade plywood) and keeping them dry through good design, good construction practice, and proper whole-house ventilation and diligence in checking for leaks once the house is up and running, you minimize the risk of mold growth in the first place and make it easier to deal with it if it occurs.

and bikeable streets and available transit services can help you leave your car at home, reducing pollution and boosting your health at the same time. Working for zoning changes so that businesses and services can be built closer to homes also helps reduce trips and improve walkability. Connecting your wildlife friendly yard to other yards, greenways, and open spaces gives animals the contiguous habitat they need to thrive as development encroaches into wild areas.

You can be an ambassador for a greener lifestyle by holding a green open house, by participating in a green home tour or community eco-fair, and by supporting local conservation groups or community outreach programs such as Master Composters. If your neighborhood is in transition or lacks a collective organization, you might find inspiration in "Share-It Square" in Portland, Oregon. Neighbors in Portland's Sellwood neighborhood took over an intersection and created a gathering place, complete with a twenty-four-hour tea stand, a children's library, and a children's playhouse with games and stuffed animals for neighborhood kids. Neighbors paint the center of the intersection annually with a colorful design. Keeping the neighborhood vibrant helps reduce the urge to move out of town to more auto-dependent locations.

Whatever you choose to do, we wish you luck with greening up your home and neighborhood. In a very concrete way, you'll be contributing to the Cascadia region's overall sustainability.

NOTE: Internet links change frequently. If a link no longer works, try using the organization's name in your web browser or contact the organization by telephone or snail mail.

1: THE CASE FOR GREEN BUILDING

Green projects featured in this chapter

Issaquah Highlands, Issaquah WA, (425) 427-8736. ww.issaquahhighlands.com/LG_Home.html. Community outside Seattle with Built Green and Energy Star certified homes.

Kerby Street Townhomes, Reworks, Inc., and City of Portland Office of Sustainable Development, Portland OR, (503) 823-7725. www.portlandonline.com/osd/index.cfm?c=ecfgh. Innovative development in north Portland with Energy Star verification and eco-roof (rainwater harvesting) technology.

Living Homes, Santa Monica CA, (310) 581-8500. www. livinghomes.net. Construction firm with a specific focus on modern, green, affordable homes. Designed and built first LEED Platinum certified home in August 2006 (Santa Monica).

McStain Neighborhoods, Louisville CO, (303) 494-5900. www. mcstain.com. Company located outside Denver that focuses on sustainable development and promotes livable communities.

New Columbia, Housing Authority of Portland (HAP), Portland OR, (503) 802-8300. www.hapdx.org/newcolumbia/sustainability.html. Project exemplifying location efficient design (LED), permeable storm water systems, and sustainable materials.

Sustainability

Architecture 2030, Sante Fe NM. www.architecture2030.org. Movement to first slow, then reverse the growth rate of greenhouse gas emissions by 2030.

David Suzuki Foundation, Vancouver BC. Sustainability within a Generation. www.davidsuzuki.org/WOL. Campaign to bring Canada to sustainability by the year 2030.

Hawken, Paul, Amory Lovins, and Hunter Lovins. 1999. *Natural Capitalism.* Boston: Little, Brown. An alternative to traditional economics; how businesses can be profitable by adopting environmental policies.

Rocky Mountain Institute (RMI), Snowmass CO, (970) 927-3851. www.rmi.org. Research and information on economic and environmental solutions to a broad variety of issues.

Sightline Institute (formerly Northwest Environmental Watch), Seattle WA, (206) 447-1880. www.sightline.org. Research, insight, and information about the Cascadia region, particularly in relation to leading factors of sustainability.

Green building certification programs—regional

Built Green Washington. www.builtgreenwashington.org. Web portal to all Built Green programs in Washington State.

Earth Advantage, Portland OR, (888) 327-8433. www.earthadvantage.com. Standard for homes, covering indoor environmental quality, resource and energy efficiency, and environmental responsibility.

Energy Star Northwest, Portland OR, (888) 373-2283. www.northwestenergystar.com. Regional division of the national Energy Star program. Provides verification for products, as well as homes that are at least 15 percent more efficient than local and/or state standards.

Green Building Design and Construction, California BIA, Sacramento CA, (916) 341-6489. www.ciwmb.ca.gov/GreenBuilding. California's state program and standards.

Santa Barbara Built Green, SB Contractors Association, Santa Barbara CA, (805) 884-1100. www.builtgreensb.org. Certification program for green building projects.

Green building certification programs—national

American Lung Association (ALA) Health House program, St. Paul MN, (877) 521-1491. www.healthhouse.org/index.asp. Note: Washington State ALA has its own Healthy House program, but it doesn't certify homes; see www.alaw.org/master_home_environmentalist/home_health_assessment. html.

Energy Star and IAQ Star, U.S. Environmental Protection Agency / Climate Protection Partnerships Division, Washington DC, (888) STAR-YES. www.energystar.gov. Joint government program from U.S. EPA and Department of Energy to promote energy efficiency in homes and businesses.

Environments for Living, Daytona Beach FL, (386) 763-7638. www.eflhome.com and www.eflbuilder.com. Certification program for building energy efficient homes, with a particular focus on HVAC systems.

LEED for Homes, U.S. Green Building Council (USGBC), Washington DC, (202) 82-USGBC or (202) 828-7422. www.USGBC.org. Green building rating system and product phase information.

Green building programs and organizations—regional

Build It Green, Alameda County, Oakland CA, (510) 845-0472. www.builditgreen.org. Membership and training organization for California green building professionals and consumers.

BuildSmart, Greater Vancouver Regional District, Vancouver BC, (604) 451-6575. www.gvrd.bc.ca/buildsmart. Vancouver's green resource for local design and construction professionals.

Cascadia Region Green Building Council, Portland OR, (503) 228-5533. www.cascadiagbc.org. Cascadia Chapter branches of the GBC are active in a number of cities in Oregon, Washington, and British Columbia. Other U.S. and Canada Green Building Council chapters active in the Pacific Northwest can be contacted through the national organizations: USGBC at www.USGBC.org and Canada GBC at www.cagbc.org

Global Green USA, Santa Monica CA, (310) 581-2700. www.globalgreen.org. Global focus, particularly addressing climate change through greening communities.

G-Rated Program, City of Portland Office of Sustainability, Portland OR, (503) 823-7725. www.portlandonline.com/osd/index.cfm?c=42133. Local program information for Portland area residents and businesses.

Northwest EcoBuilding Guild, Seattle WA, (206) 575-2222. www.ecobuilding.org. Professional membership organization with several branches throughout the region.

SeaGreen: Greening Seattle's Affordable Housing, Seattle WA, (206) 684-0721. www.ci.seattle.wa.us/housing/SeaGreen. Seattle's guide to creating sustainable, affordable housing through multifamily building projects.

Green money resources

Canada Housing and Mortgage Corporation, Vancouver BC, (604) 731-5733. www.cmhc-schl.gc.ca/en/corp/about/hi/index.cfm. In 2005, CMHC introduced a 10 percent green refund on mortgage loan insurance premiums for homeowners who buy or build an energy-efficient home.

Countrywide Home Loans, Calabasas CA, (818) 225-3000. www.
countrywide.com. Some Countrywide offices (particularly in
Washington State) offer special discounts on construction
loans for green buildings. Worth inquiring at Countrywide in
your area.

Fannie Mae Regional Office, Seattle WA, (206) 839-1540.
Energy-efficient mortgages, an option available with all Fannie
Mae products: www.fanniemae.com/homebuyers. Location
Efficient Mortgages: www.locationefficiency.com.

Federal Housing Administration and Federal Office of Veterans
Affairs, Washington DC, (202) 708-1112. Energy Efficient
Mortgage Home Owner Guide: www.pueblo.gsa.gov/cic_
text/housing/energy_mort/energy-mortgage.htm.

Residential Energy Services Network (RESNET), Oceanside CA,
(760) 806-3448. www.natresnet.org. Information on home
energy rating systems and energy-efficient mortgages.

2: STARTING OUT WITH GREEN IN MIND

Green projects featured in this chapter

Ericksen Cottages, Bainbridge Island WA. The Cottage Company,
(206) 525-0835. www.cottagecompany.com//ccEricksen.
html.

Gutsche-Smith remodel, Bainbridge Island WA. Eco-Smith Design
and Consulting, (206) 780-7913, kathleen@ecodesign.org.
Winslow Cohousing, (206) 780-1323. www.winslowcohous-
ing.org.

Higgins Residence, Portland OR. The Living Smart Project. Plans
and specifications, www.livingsmartpdx.com/home/higgins.
asp.

O'Brien-Cunningham residence, Bainbridge Island WA. Built
Green case study, www.builtgreenwashington.org/study.
php?id=9.

Olivé-Mortola residence, Seattle WA. The Compact Home Project. Built Green case study, www.builtgreen.net/studies/1061.
html. Also contact GreenLeaf Construction, (425) 712-9014.

Ecological footprint

Built Green Washington. Case study: Honey, I Shrank My Ecological Footprint! Daley-Peng Residence. www.builtgreenwashing-
ton.org/study.php?id=10. Case study showing the differences
green design can make in a building's footprint.

Chambers, N., C. Simmons, and M. Wackernagel. 2001. *Sharing
Nature's Interest: Ecological Footprints as an Indicator of Sustainability.* London UK and Sterling VA: Earthscan Publications.
Using case studies and practical measurement, provides
further insight into calculating ecological footprints.

Inforain: A Project of EcoTrust, Portland OR, (503) 227-6225.
www.inforain.org. EcoTrust's GIS portfolio and interactive
mapping applications.

Norwood, Ken, and Kathleen Smith. 1995. *Rebuilding Community in
America: Housing for Ecological Living, Personal Empowerment, and
the New Extended Family.* Berkeley CA: Shared Living Resource
Center.

Redefining Progress, Oakland CA, (510) 444-3041. www.Rede-
finingProgress.org. Ecological Footprint Quiz and Office
Footprint Calculator available, as well as information on their
projects and programs. Also, calculate your own footprint at
www.myfootprint.org.

Small house design

Built Green case study: Centex Homes, Mukilteo WA, (425) 216-
3400. www.builtgreen.net/studies/1071.html. Small home
green design elements from design inception through each
part of the construction. Centex Homes, www.centexhomes.
com.

City of Portland Bureau of Development Services. Living Smart:
Big ideas for small lots. www.livingsmartpdx.com/home.
Plans and specifications.

Editors of Fine Homebuilding. 1998. *More Small Houses (Great
Houses).* Newtown CT: Taunton Press. Examples and images
of small home designs.

Editors of Fine Homebuilding. 2003. *Small Homes: Design Ideas for
Great American Houses.* Newtown CT: Taunton Press. Examples
of a handful of small houses, as well as tips for design.

Kodis, Michelle. 2003. *Blueprint Small: Creative Ways to Live with Less.* Salt Lake City UT: Gibbs Smith. Various ways that small spaces can fulfill different lifestyles and budgets.

Metz, Don, et al. 2004. *The Big Book of Small House Designs: 75 Award-Winning Plans for Your Dream House, All 1,250 Square Feet or Less.* New York: Black Dog and Leventhal Publishers. More than five hundred drawings of seventy-four small homes in a wide variety of styles and locations.

Susanka, Sarah, Not So Big. www.susanka.com, www.notsobig.com. Information and sources for designing homes to fit the individual, as well as ways to identify what needs should be met. Books, www.notsobighouse.com/books.asp. Plans, www.notsobighouse.com/plans/index.asp. Home professionals directory, www.notsobighouse.com/directory.asp.

Tolpin, Jim. 2000. *The New Cottage Home: A Tour of Unique American Dwellings.* Newtown CT: Taunton Press. Thirty small homes, highlighting the unique characteristics and advantages of living in smaller spaces.

Wetland sensitivity

Bigley, Richard, and Sabra Hull. Washington State Department of Natural Resources, Olympia WA. Wetland Field Guides for Washington State Forest Lands. Available for download: *Recognizing Wetlands* and *Managing Wetlands.* http://dnr.wa.gov/htdocs/lm/field_guides.

Washington State Department of Ecology, Olympia WA, (360) 407-6000. Wetlands page, www.ecy.wa.gov/programs/sea/wetlands/index.html. Information on Washington's wetland policies and regulations.

3: MANAGING YOUR GREEN HOME, PART 1

Green project featured in this chapter

Harding residence, Woodinville WA. http://harrison-architects.com/projects/new_homes/harding_home. Also contact Harrison Architects, (206) 956-0883, info@harrisonarchitects.com.

Project management and general green building resources

Oikos: Green Building Source. www.oikos.com. News, products, and resources (including a comprehensive bookstore) all related to green building.

Partnership for Advancing Housing Technology (PATH). www.pathnet.org/sp.asp?id=14053. Tech Sets designed to encourage a systems approach to technology integration to improve one or more of the PATH building priorities: durability, energy efficiency, environmental performance, disaster resistance, and safety.

Ruiz, Fernando Pages. 2005. *Building an Affordable House: Trade Secrets for High-Value, Low-Cost Construction.* Newtown CT: Taunton Press. Ideas and insider techniques for cutting cost throughout the building process without cutting value.

Smith, Carol. 2005. *Building Your Home: An Insider's Guide.* Washington DC: National Association of Home Builders. A good primer on the design and construction process, though not focused on green home building.

Design specialties

Elizabeth, Lynne, and Cassandra Adams, eds. 2005. *Alternative Construction: Contemporary Natural Building Methods.* Hoboken NJ: Wiley. Modern construction methods using alternative materials.

Guy, Brad, and Nicholas Ciarimboli. 2006. *Design for Disassembly in the Built Environment: A Guide to Closed-Loop Design and Building.* Hamer Center for Community Design, Pennsylvania State University, (814) 865-5300. www.hamercenter.psu.edu. Prepared on behalf of King County WA and Resource Venture, Inc. Download from www.lifecyclebuilding.org/resources/DfDseattle.pdf.

King, Bruce, and Mark Aschheim. 2006. *Design of Straw Bale Buildings: The State of the Art.* San Rafael CA: Green Building Press. The architectural and design aspects of straw bale buildings.

Resource Venture, Inc., Seattle WA, (206) 343-8505. www.resourceventure.org. Provides information as well as financial and technical assistance to Seattle businesses.

Eco-labels and verification services

Canadian Standards Association (CSA) Group, Toronto ONT, (866) CSA-WOOD. www.csa-international.org. Independent nonprofit accredited for chain-of-custody verification. The CSA Forest Products Marking Program signifies compliance with Canada's National Standard for Sustainable Forest Management (CAN/CSA Z809).

Energy Star Northwest, Portland OR, (888) 373-2283. www.northwestenergystar.com. Regional division of the national Energy Star program. Provides verification for products, as well as homes that are at least 15 percent more efficient than local and/or state standards.

Forest Stewardship Council (FSC), Washington DC, (202) 342-0413. www.fscus.org. International forest management standards and chain-of-custody certification through third-party verifiers.

GreenGuard Environmental Institute, Atlanta GA, (800) 427-9681. www.greenguard.org. Independent certification organization that establishes indoor air quality standards. Works exclusively with the Air Quality Sciences (AQS) laboratory, www.aqs.com.

Scientific Certification System (SCS), Emeryville CA, (510) 452-8000. www.scscertified.com. Green Cross label: third-party evaluation and certification for FSC chain-of-custody, environmentally preferable products (EPP), recycled content, life-cycle assessment (LCA), and the like.

Sustainable Forestry Initiative (SFI), Washington DC. www.sfiprogram.org. Forestry program managed by the Sustainable Forestry Board of the American Forest and Paper Association.

Material selection and evaluation

Athena: Environmental Impact Estimator Version 3.0.2, 2005, (866) 520-6792. www.athenasmi.ca/ (free demo available). Software used for performing a life-cycle analysis (LCA) of building design and components.

BEES Version 4.0, 2007, (202) 566-0799. http://bfrl.nist.gov/oae/software/bees.html. Free software used for comparing environmental attributes of building products, available from the National Institute of Standards and Technology.

GreenSpec Directory, (802) 257-7300. www.buildinggreen.com. Information on nearly two thousand green building products carefully screened by the editors of Environmental Building News and BuildingGreen, Inc.

Northwest Green Directory. www.nwgreendirectory.com. Online tool maintained by the City of Portland's Office of Sustainable Development. Green building products available in Idaho, Oregon, Washington, and British Columbia.

4: MANAGING YOUR GREEN HOME, PART 2

Green projects featured in this chapter

Peterson residence, Pasco WA. PEX Technology case study (pdf), www.pathnet.org/si.asp?id=2760.

Scheulen residence, Seattle WA. www.builtgreen.net/studies/1041.html. Also contact Sunshine Construction, (206) 782-4619.

Green building professionals

Building Concerns: Northern California Resource Directory. www.buildingconcerns.com. Online directory of building professionals in Northern California.

Built Green Washington. www.builtgreenwashington.org. Built Green programs in Washington State, along with lists of builders and allied professionals participating in the programs.

Energy and Environmental Building Association (EEBA), Bloomington MN, (952) 881-1098. www.eeba.org. A respected nonprofit that offers education and resources to industry professionals. Two credential programs certify professionals with a level of understanding and expertise in building science: the Institute of Building Technology Certification and the more comprehensive Institute of Building Technology MasterBuilder Designation.

Energy Star Northwest, Portland OR, (888) 373-2283. www.northwestenergystar.com. Regional division of the national Energy Star program. Listings of Energy Star builders as well as performance testing and verification specialists can be found at www.northwestenergystar.com/index.php?cID=264.

Environments for Living, Daytona Beach FL, (386) 763-7638. www.eflhome.com and www.eflbuilder.com. Listing of participating builders.

Green Building Blocks. www.thebeam.com/find_a_professional.go. Listing of green design and building professionals. Detailed company profiles and networking opportunities.

Green Pages. Northwest EcoBuilding Guild, Seattle WA, (206) 575-2222. www.ecobuilding.org. Local directory of sustainable services, published annually.

Northwest Green Directory. www.nwgreendirectory.com. Online tool maintained by the City of Portland's Office of Sustainable Development. Green building services available in Idaho, Oregon, Washington, and British Columbia.

Green materials

Environmental Building Supplies (EBS), 819 SE Taylor Street, Portland OR, (503) 222-3881. 550 SW Industrial Way, Unit 32, Bend OR, (541) 317-0202. www.ecohaus.com.

Environmental Home Center (merged with EBS in June 2004), 4121 1st Avenue South, Seattle WA, (206) 682-7332, (800) 281-9785. www.environmentalhomecenter.com.

Green Building Pages, San Luis Obispo CA, (805) 782-9431. www.greenbuildingpages.com. Sustainable materials database and design tools.

Rate It Green. www.rateitgreen.com. Database of resources for green building, with information for consumers, manufacturers, and service providers.

Resource Venture, Inc., Seattle WA, (206) 343-8505. www.resourceventure.org. Provides information as well as financial and technical assistance to Seattle businesses.

Site-assessment resources

Association of American State Geologists. www.stategeologists.org. Links to each state's Geological Survey.

Google Earth. http://earth.google.com. Satellite imagery and 3D data from across the globe. Free version available to download.

Municipal Code Corporation, Tallahassee FL, (850) 576-3171. www.municode.com. Searchable database for local codes (more than 1600 municipalities).

National Resource Conservation Service (NRCS), (202) 690-2197. www.nrcs.usda.gov/technical. Soil, water, and climate information, as well as the National Resource Inventory (NRI), Geospatial Data Gateway, aerial photography, and such.

U.S. Army Corps of Engineers. www.usace.army.mil. Maps and information on major water resources, including flood control and disaster response.

U.S. Census Bureau. www.census.gov. Population and demographic statistics, as well as reference and thematic maps.

U.S. Fish and Wildlife Service, Washington DC, (703) 358-2161. National Wetlands Inventory. www.fws.gov/nwi. Wetlands data and maps for many regions across the United States and Puerto Rico.

U.S. Geological Survey (USGS), (888) 275-8747. www.usgs.gov. Various maps and resources, including topographical maps.

5: GREEN ENERGY CHOICES FOR THE NORTHWEST

Green power and incentives for renewable energy systems and energy efficiency

Bonneville Environmental Foundation (BEF), Portland OR, (866) 233-8247. https://www.greentagsusa.org/GreenTags. Purchase Green Tags (also known as renewable energy certificates), supporting renewable energy production in the United States and Canada.

Canadian Solar Technologies. www.canadiansolartechnologies. ca/incentives-grants. Solar technology alternatives.

Cascade Solar Consulting, (503) 655-1617. www.cascadesolar. com. Cascade Solar operates the Northwest Solar Cooperative, which sells and purchases Green Tags (in concert with BEF).

Database of State Incentives for Renewables and Efficiency (DSIRE), North Carolina State University. www.dsireusa.org/. Comprehensive information on federal, state, and local incentive programs for renewable energy systems.

Ministry of Small Business and Revenue, British Columbia Provincial Sales Tax Exemption program. www.rev.gov.bc.ca/ctb/ publications/bulletins/sst_011.pdf.

Natural Resources Canada, Office of Energy Efficiency. http:// oee.nrcan.gc.ca/residential/personal/index.cfm. Information about residential systems, as well as the national Energy Star and EnerGuide programs.

Northwest Power and Conservation Council. 1998. How the Northwest Can Lead an Energy Revolution. www.nwcouncil. org.

Solar Hot Water Acceleration Project, British Columbia. www. solarbc.org.

Off-the-grid planning

Kemp, William T. 2006. *The Renewable Energy Handbook: A Guide to Rural Energy Independence, Off-Grid and Sustainable Living.* Tamworth ONT: Aztext Press. Solutions for Sustainability, www.aztext.com.

Schaeffer, John. 2005. *Real Goods Solar Living Sourcebook, 12th Edition: The Complete Guide to Renewable Energy Technologies and Sustainable Living.* Gabriola Island BC: New Society Publishers.

Wind and renewables mapping

BC Hydro, Burnaby BC, (604) 224-9376. www.bchydro.com/ environment/greenpower/greenpower1761.html. Information about wind mapping for British Columbia (from TrueWind Solutions' MesoMap system).

Energy Foundation, San Francisco CA, (415) 561-6700. Renewable Energy Atlas of the West. www.energyatlas.org. Detailed interactive maps and links to other relevant mapping Web sites.

Gipe, Paul. 1993. *Wind Power for Home and Business: Renewable Energy for the 1990s and Beyond.* Post Mills VT: Chelsea Green. Comprehensive look at wind power technology and systems.

——. 1999. *Wind Energy Basics: A Guide to Small and Micro Wind Systems.* White River Junction VT: Chelsea Green. Introduction to wind power and how systems work.

Northwest Sustainable Energy for Economic Development (SEED), Seattle WA, (206) 328-2441. www.nwseed.org. Local project information as well as technical assistance and mapping for potential community projects. The Northwestern U.S. Wind Mapping Project can also be viewed at http:// windpowermaps.org/.

U.S. Department of Energy (DOE), Wind and Hydropower Technologies Program. Wind Powering America: State Wind Resource Maps. www.eere.energy.gov/windandhydro/windpoweringamerica/wind_maps.asp.

6: PLANNING A GREEN REMODEL

Green projects featured in this chapter

Rivas-Scott remodel, Portland OR. Office of Sustainable Development case study, www.portlandonline.com/osd/index. cfm?a=bbcdbd&c=ebjdh. Also contact Craftsmen Unlimited, (503) 238-1895.

Snyder remodel, Portland OR. www.snyderhouse.net. Also contact Ground Up Developers, (503) 888-3445.

Ziophirville remodel, Seattle WA. Sunnyside Up. www.builtgreen. net/studies/1081.html. Also contact BLIP Design, (201) 501-8746.

Material recovery resources

Building Materials Reuse Association (BMRA). www.buildingreuse.org. Nonprofit organization that encourages building deconstruction and reuse/recycling of materials. Comprehensive directory of resources by state.

CalMax (California Materials Exchange), California Integrated Waste Management Board, Sacramento CA, (877) 520-9703. www.ciwmb.ca.gov/calmax. Listings and exchanges for businesses and consumers in the state of California.

Freecycle Network. www.freecycle.org. Nonprofit network for donating and receiving free goods within communities.

Habitat for Humanity, Americus GA, (229) 924-6935. www.habitat.org. Resources for getting involved, as well as contact information for local programs.

Industrial Materials Exchange (IMEX), Seattle WA, (206) 296-4899. www.govlink.org/hazwaste/business/imex. Free service for businesses to find new ways to recycle their surplus materials and waste.

Montana Material Exchange, MSU Extension Service, Bozeman MT, (406) 994-3451. www.montana.edu/mme. Statewide materials exchange listing run through the MSU Extension Service Pollution Prevention Program.

Recycling Council of British Columbia (RCBC) Materials Exchange, Vancouver BC, (604) 683-6009. www.rcbc.bc.ca. Listings and exchanges for British Columbia.

Sonoma County Waste Management Agency, CA. www.recyclenow.org/. Commercial and residential resources, including local listings for recyclable materials.

2Good2Toss. www.2good2toss.com. Washington State online materials exchange program with several counties across the state participating.

Hazardous material mitigation

U.S. Environmental Protection Agency. www.epa.gov/asbestos. Information about health effects and best management practices for handling asbestos and vermiculite.

Remodeling resources

City of Seattle, Department of Planning and Development. Green Home Remodeling Guides. www.seattle.gov/dpd/ GreenBuilding/SingleFamilyResidential/Resources/RemodelingGuides/default.asp. Series of guides focused on common remodeling topics: kitchen, roofing, paints and finishes, bath and laundry, landscape materials, hiring a pro, salvage and reuse.

Johnston, David R., and Kim Master. 2004. *Green Remodeling: Changing the World One Room at a Time.* Gabriola BC: New Society Publishers. Simple green renovation solutions for homeowners, focusing on key aspects of the building.

Partnership for Advancing Housing Technology (PATH). Green Kitchen Remodel Tech Sheet #8. www.pathnet.org/sp.asp?id=20081.

Rooney, E. Ashley. 2005. *Spectacular Small Kitchens: Design Ideals for Urban Spaces.* Atglen PA: Schiffer Publishing. Designs for working with small kitchen and home spaces.

Venolia, Carol, and Kelly Lerner. 2006. *Natural Remodeling for the Not-So-Green House: Bringing Your Home into Harmony with Nature.* New York: Lark Books. Techniques for using green solutions to remodel a conventional home.

7: PURCHASING A NEW GREEN HOME

Green projects featured in this chapter

Daley-Peng residence, Seattle WA. Built Green case study: Honey, I Shrank My Ecological Footprint! www.builtgreenwashington.org/study.php?id=10.

Idea Home, Issaquah Highlands, Issaquah WA, (425) 427-8736. www.issaquahhighlands.com/ideahome/buildspecs.html. Specs for the Built Green Idea Home.

Green home buying

EcoBroker, Evergreen CO, (800) 706-4321. www.ecobroker.com. Certified real estate EcoBrokers, listed by state.

EcoBusiness Links: Environmental Directory, Sustainable Real Estate. www.ecobusinesslinks.com/green_real_estate.htm. Homes and neighborhood sites, listed by state.

GreenHomesforSale.com, Santa Barbara CA, (805) 898-0079. www.greenhomesforsale.com. Existing green homes for sale.

Home Builders Association of Kitsap County. How to Shop for a "Fish-Friendly" Home. www.kitsaphba.com/pdf/BGfact-sheet5.pdf. Also available at www.obrienandco.com. Potential water and site impacts of homes, as well as ways to avoid those issues.

U.S. Department of Housing and Urban Development (HUD), Homes and Communities. Buying a Home. www.hud.gov/buying/. Step-by-step process for purchasing a home, particularly focusing on programs and mortgage options.

Building inspection

American Society of Home Inspectors (ASHI), Des Plaines IL, (800) 743-2744. www.ashi.org. Listing of ASHI-certified home inspectors, as well as a virtual home inspection and other resources.

National Association of Certified Home Inspectors (NACHI), Boulder CO, (877) FIND-INS. www.findaninspector.us. Directory of NACHI-certified home inspectors.

Green modular homes

Living Homes, Santa Monica CA, (310) 581-8500. www.livinghomes.net. Construction firm with a specific focus on modern, green, affordable homes. Designed and built the first LEED Platinum certified home in August 2006 (Santa Monica).

Michelle Kaufman Designs. www.mkd-arc.com. Sustainable design firm with specially designed "package" homes, such as the Glidehouse, Sunset Breezehouse, and mkSolaire.

8: SITE CHOICES

Green projects featured in this chapter

Sullivan residence, Bend OR. Earth Advantage Builder Wins National Award at the NAHB's Green Building Conference. www.earthadvantage.com/news/item/?key=14. Also contact

SunTerra Homes, Inc., (541) 389-4733, http://sunterra-homes.com.

Solar orientation and passive solar design

Akbari, Hashem, ed. 1992. *Cooling Our Communities: A Guidebook on Tree Planting and Light-Colored Surfacing.* Lawrence Berkeley National Laboratory Report LBL-31587. Washington DC: U.S. Government Printing Office. Methods to reduce the heat island effect in our cities.

Brown, G. Z., and Mark DeKay. 2000. *Sun, Wind and Light: Architectural Design Strategies,* 2nd ed. New York: Wiley. Options for passive heating, cooling, and lighting design.

Chiras, Daniel. 2002. *The Solar House: Passive Heating and Cooling.* White River Junction VT: Chelsea Green.

Jones, Leslie. 1998. *Tap the Sun: Passive Solar Techniques and Home Designs.* Ottawa ONT: Canada Mortgage and Housing Corporation.

Kachadorian, James. 2006. *The Passive Solar House: The Complete Guide to Heating and Cooling Your Home.* White River Junction VT: Chelsea Green. Techniques and options for all climates, budgets, styles.

Mazria, Edward. 1979. *The Passive Solar Energy Book: A Complete Guide to Passive Solar Home, Greenhouse, and Building Design.* Emmaus PA: Rodale.

Site preparation and site water management

Council of Tree and Landscape Appraisers. 2000. *Guide for Plant Appraisal,* 9th ed. Champaign IL: International Society of Arboriculture (ISA). Purchase from ISA, www.isa-arbor.com. Assistance in evaluating plants worth saving and salvaging.

International Society of Arboriculture (ISA), Champaign IL, (888) 472-8733. www.isa-arbor.com. Wealth of information about trees, including a database of certified arborists.

Pacific Northwest Trees Online, PNW Chapter of ISA, Silverton OR, (503) 874-8263. www.pnwisa.org/. Local chapter of ISA, includes list of area certified arborists.

U.S. Environmental Protection Agency. Surf Your Watershed. www.epa.gov/surf. Nationwide searchable database for locating area watersheds, with information for local protection organizations, maps, and USGS data.

Erosion control

O'Brien & Company. 1999. Keep It On Site! Residential Builder's Guide to Small Site Erosion Control and Stormwater Management. www.obrienandco.com/pdfs/KIOS.pdf.

U.S. Environmental Protection Agency. 1997. Innovative Uses of Compost Erosion Control, Turf Remediation, and Landscaping. www.epa.gov/epaoswer/non-hw/compost/erosion.pdf.

Low-impact development

Dunnett, Nigel, and Andy Clayden. 2007. *Rain Gardens: Managing Water Sustainably in the Garden and Designed Landscape.* Portland OR: Timber Press.

Dunnett, Nigel, and Noël Kingsbury. 2004. *Planting Green Roofs and Living* Walls. Portland OR: Timber Press.

Hinman, Curtis. 2007. *Rain Garden Design Handbook for Western Washington Homeowners.* WSU Extension, Pierce County. Sizing for Western Oregon will be fairly similar.

Puget Sound Action Team (PSAT). 2005. *Low Impact Development: Technical Guidance Manual for Puget Sound.* www.psat.wa.gov/Publications/LID_tech_manual05/lid_index.htm. Detailed information about site assessment and planning for low-impact development projects.

Permaculture

Earle, Dan, and Sue Hutchins. *A Permaculture Primer.* home.klis.com/~chebogue/PermacultureIndex.html. Information on permaculture.

Holmgren, David. 2004. *Essence of Permaculture.* Holmgren Design Services, Victoria AUS. www.holmgren.com.au/DLFiles/PDFs/EssenceofPC3.pdf. Description of how permaculture is used and designed, as well as guiding principles.

Mollison, Bill, with Reny Mia Slay. 1994. *Introduction to Permaculture.* Tyalgum NSW, Australia: Tagari.

Plant selection and landscape design

Robson, Kathleen A., Alice Richter, and Marianne Filbert. 2008. *Encyclopedia of Northwest Native Plants for Gardens and Landscapes.* Portland OR: Timber Press. Comprehensive reference to ferns, conifers, and flowering plants native to the Pacific Northwest that are beautiful garden ornamentals and important natural components of habitat diversity.

U.S. Department of Agriculture, Forest Service, Center for Urban Forest Research, Davis CA. ecoSmart Design Software. (530) 752-7636. www.ecosmart.gov. Free Web-based software that can help homeowners determine the best landscape designs to save energy and water, and to protect homes from fire.

Washington Department of Fish and Wildlife. Backyard Wildlife Sanctuary. http://wdfw.wa.gov/wlm/backyard. Information on creating a backyard wildlife habitat.

Soil

Diver, Steve. 2002. Notes on Compost Teas. ATTRA National Sustainable Agriculture Information Service. http://attra.ncat.org/attra-pub/compost-tea-notes.html. Methods and instructions for brewing compost tea.

Soils for Salmon Oregon. www.soilsforsalmonoregon.org/. Web site for both homeowners and contractors, highlighting the importance of soil conservation, composting, and restoration.

Washington Organic Recycling Council, Longview WA. Soils for Salmon Project. (360) 556-3926. www.compostwashington.org/soilss2.asp. Web site for Washington's project for addressing soil issues and salmon recovery. *Guidelines and Resources for Implementing Soil Quality and Depth,* www.soilsforsalmon.org/pdf/SoilBMP_Manual-2005.pdf.

9: THE BUILDING ENCLOSURE

Green projects featured in this chapter

Harding residence, Woodinville WA. http://harrison-architects. com/projects/new_homes/harding_home. Also contact Harrison Architects, (206) 956-0883, info@harrisonarchitects.com.

Luk remodel, Seattle WA. Contact Ming Architecture and Design, (206) 272-9900, grace@mingad.com.

Rivas-Scott remodel, Portland OR. Office of Sustainable Development case study, www.portlandonline.com/osd/index. cfm?a=bbcdbd&c=ebjdh. Also contact Craftsmen Unlimited, (503) 238-1895.

Sullivan residence, Bend OR. Earth Advantage Builder Wins National Award at the NAHB's Green Building Conference. www.earthadvantage.com/news/item/?key=14. Also contact SunTerra Homes, Inc., (541) 389-4733, sunterrahomes.com.

Advanced framing

Integrated Building and Construction Solutions (IBACOS). Best Practices, Optimum Value Engineering. www.ibacos.com/ pubs/OptimumValueEngineering.pdf. Detailed description of OVE framing techniques.

International Code Council. 2003. International Residential Code, Panel Box Headers. Table R602.7.2: p. 123, and Fig. R602.7.2: p.124. www.iccsafe.org. Your builder or designer should have a copy of the code.

Morley, Michael. 2000. *Building with Structural Insulated Panels (SIPs): Strength and Energy Efficiency Through Structural Panel Construction.* Newtown CT: Taunton Press. Advantages of and construction methods for SIPs, particularly in relation to the environment.

National Association of Home Builders Research Center. Advanced Framing Techniques. www.nahbrc.org/greenguidelines/advancedframing.pdf. Detailed framing techniques and instructions.

Oregon Building Codes Division, OSU Extension Service. Oregon Residential Energy Code: Advanced Framing for Walls and Ceilings. www.oregon.gov/ENERGY/CONS/Codes/docs/ res10.pdf.

Thallon, Rob. 2000. *Graphic Guide to Frame Construction: Details for Builders and Designers.* Newtown CT: Taunton Press. Visual reference, including topics such as better energy efficiency, use of modern materials, and construction in hazardous areas.

WSU Energy Program. Washington State Energy and Ventilation Codes, Builders Field Guide. www.energy.wsu.edu/code/ code_support.cfm. Residential construction guide for the WA State Energy Code.

Building science

Building Science Corporation (BSC), Westford MA. www.buildingscience.com. Architecture and building science consulting firm with focus on moisture dynamics, indoor air quality, and forensic investigations. Also see: Conditioned Crawlspace Construction, Performance and Codes. www.buildingscience. com/resources/foundations/conditioned_crawl.pdf

Energy and Environmental Building Association (EEBA), Bloomington MN, (952) 881-1098. www.eeba.org. A respected nonprofit that offers education and resources to industry professionals. Offers an educational series called Houses that Work, as well as other resources and educational programs.

NAHB Research Center, Toolbase Services, Upper Marlboro MA. www.toolbase.org. Detailed information on building systems, design and construction guides, and best practices.

3-D Building Solutions, Bexley OH, (614) 231-9330. www.3-d-buildingsolutions.com. Building diagnostics, architectural design review, and technical training and writing.

U.S. Department of Energy, Building America, Washington DC, (202) 586-9472. www.eere.energy.gov/buildings/building_america. Research on energy-efficient solutions that can be implemented on a large scale, particularly in relation to systems engineering.

U.S. Department of Energy. Insulation Fact Sheet. www.ornl.gov/sci/roofs+walls/insulation/ins_16.html. Includes an interactive tool to help you determine what R-value to aim for, as well as good information on types of insulation and both new and existing home applications.

U.S. Department of Energy, National Renewable Energy Laboratory (NREL), Washington DC and Golden CO. www.nrel.gov.

U.S. Environmental Protection Agency. Radon (Rn): Map of Radon Zones. www.epa.gov/radon/zonemap.html. *Building Radon Out: A Step-By-Step Guide on How to Build Radon-Resistant Homes,* EPA Publication 402-K-01-002. www.epa.gov/radon/construc.html.

Steel framing

Waite, Tim. 2002. *Steel-Frame House Construction.* Carlsbad CA: Craftsman Book Company. Good information if you're considering using steel framing, although the publication tends to minimize thermal considerations.

Weatherization

Harley, Bruce. 2002. *Insulate and Weatherize: Expert Advice from Start to Finish.* Newtown CT: Taunton Press. Part of the Build Like a Pro series, enabling readers to understand and execute energy-efficient designs.

Myers, John H. 1981. The Repair of Historic Wooden Windows. U.S. National Park Service Preservation Briefs. www.cr.nps.gov/hps/tps/briefs/brief09.htm#Weatherization. Part of a larger article on historic preservation.

Shapiro, Andrew M., and Brad James. 1997. Creating Windows of Energy-Saving Opportunity. Home Energy Magazine Online. www.homeenergy.org/archive/hem.dis.anl.gov/eehem/97/970908.html. Weatherization and preservation of historic windows, as well as cost and material comparisons.

10: OPERATING SYSTEMS FOR YOUR HOME

Green projects featured in this chapter

Cunningham-Pinon remodel, Portland OR. Contact Greg Acker, Architect, (503) 735-9192.

Idea Home, Issaquah Highlands, Issaquah WA, (425) 427-8736. www.issaquahhighlands.com/ideahome/buildspecs.html. Specs for the Built Green Idea Home.

Kerby Street Townhomes, Reworks, Inc., and City of Portland Office of Sustainable Development, Portland OR, (503) 823-7725. www.portlandonline.com/osd/index.cfm?c=ecfgh. Innovative development in north Portland with Energy Star verification and eco-roof (rainwater harvesting) technology.

Ziophirville remodel, Seattle WA. Sunnyside Up. www.builtgreen.net/studies/1081.html. Also contact BLIP Design, (201) 501-8746.

Space conditioning

Oikos. 1993. Duct Losses Hurt Forced Air Heating System Performance. http://oikos.com/esb/28/duct_losses.html. Efficiency loss in standard ducted air distribution systems.

Lighting

Energy Star, Life Cycle Cost Estimate for Energy Star Qualified Compact Fluorescent Lamp(s). http://energystar.gov/ia/business/bulk_purchasing/bpsavings_calc/Calc_CFLs.xls. Comparison of life-cycle cost of CFLs versus conventional lamps.

Energy Star. www.energystar.gov. Search for products to find lists of appliances, heating and cooling products, lighting, and such.

National Association of Home Builders Research Center, Toolbase Services, Tech Set 4: Energy-Efficient Lighting. www.toolbase.org/TechSets/energy-efficient-lighting.

National Lighting Product Information Program (NLPIP), Rensselaer Polytechnic Institute, Lighting Resource Center. Lighting Answers, Full Spectrum Light Sources. www.lrc.rpi.edu/programs/nlpip/lightingAnswers/fullSpectrum/lightSources.asp.

Northwest Energy Efficiency Alliance, LightingPlans.com. www.lightingplans.com. General design tips as well as downloadable lighting plans and specs for different room types with lots of variations.

Household water systems

Advanced Composting Systems, Whitefish MT, (406) 862-3855. www.compostingtoilet.com. Information about the odorless, waterless Phoenix composting toilet system.

Banks, S., R. Heinichen, and T. Arenz. 2004. *Rainwater Collection for the Mechanically Challenged.* Dripping Springs TX: Tank Town Publications. Easy-to-understand and detailed book on setting up a rainwater catchment system.

Del Porto, David, and Carol Steinfeld. 2000. *The Composting Toilet System Book.* EcoWaters Projects (formerly the Center for Ecological Pollution Prevention), www.ecowaters.org. Composting and wastewater management alternatives.

Gauley, William, PE, and John Koeller, PE. 2003. Maximum Performance Testing of Popular Toilet Models Final Report: A Cooperative Canadian and American Project. www.cwwa.ca/pdf_files/freepub_6Ltoiletreport04.pdf.

H2Ouse Water Saver Home Tour, California Urban Water Conservation Council and U.S. Environmental Protection Agency. www.h2ouse.org/tour/index.cfm. Excellent information on water-using activities in the home, including details on consumption, savings, energy and other environmental benefits, costs, regulations, research, as well as tips on purchase, installation, maintenance, and end-of-life issues (recycling and such).

Kourik, Robert, and Heidi Schmidt. 1993. *Drip Irrigation for Every Landscape and All Climates.* Santa Rosa CA: Metamorphic Press. Great resource on drip irrigation and specific installation details.

Ludwig, Art. 1998. *Builders Greywater Guide: The Guide to Professional Installation.* Santa Barbara CA: Oasis Design. Specific information about building codes when constructing gray water systems.

——. 2006. *The New Create an Oasis with Greywater: Choosing, Building and Using Greywater Systems.* Santa Barbara CA: Oasis Design. Detailed information about gray water systems and uses.

Ramlow, Bob, and Benjamin Nusz. 2006. *Solar Water Heating: A Comprehensive Guide to Solar Water and Space Heating Solutions.* Gabriola Island BC: New Society Publishers. History of solar water and space heating systems, current methods, and how to make the appropriate choice.

Solar cooking

Anderson, Lorraine, and Rick Palkovic. 2006. *Cooking with Sunshine: The Complete Guide to Solar Cuisine.* New York: Marlowe & Company. Comprehensive overview of solar cooking and solar ovens, with recipes as well as plans for building box and panel ovens.

11: INTERIORS

Green projects featured in this chapter

Huppert remodel, Seattle WA. City of Seattle case study (search for Huppert case study), www.seattle.gov. Also available from Velocipede Architects, (206) 529-9356, www.velocipede.net/houses/Huppert.html.

O'Brien-Cunningham residence, Bainbridge Island WA. Built Green case study, www.builtgreenwashington.org/study.php?id=9.

Olivé-Mortola residence, Seattle WA. The Compact Home Project. Built Green case study, www.builtgreen.net/studies/1061.html. Also contact GreenLeaf Construction, (425) 712-9014.

Peterson residence, Pasco WA. PEX Technology case study (pdf), www.pathnet.org/si.asp?id=2760.

Sullivan residence, Bend OR. Earth Advantage Builder Wins National Award at the NAHB's Green Building Conference, www.earthadvantage.com/news/item/?key=14. Also contact SunTerra Homes, Inc., (541) 389-4733, http://sunterra-homes.com.

Finishes and furnishings

Ecobaby Organics, San Diego CA, (800) 596-7450. www.ecobaby.com. Organic and other green goods for young children (and their parents).

Environmental Building Supplies (EBS), 819 SE Taylor Street, Portland OR, (503) 222-3881. 550 SW Industrial Way, Unit 32, Bend OR, (541) 317-0202. www.ecohaus.com.

Environmental Home Center (merged with EBS in June 2004), 4121 1st Avenue South, Seattle WA, (206) 682-7332, (800) 281-9785. www.environmentalhomecenter.com/

Green HomeGuide Northwest. http://northwest.greenhome-guide.com/. Community-based resource for reliable green products and services, as well as articles and case studies.

Northwest Green Directory. www.nwgreendirectory.com. Online tool maintained by the City of Portland's Office of Sustainable Development. Lists green building products available in Idaho, Oregon, Washington, and British Columbia.

1Earth 1Design, 14300 Greenwood Ave N, Suite A, Seattle WA, (206) 418-8120, (888) 270-7005. www.1earth1design.com. Sustainable home products store and interior design firm.

Suite Baby Furniture, (800) 770-6250. www.earthfriendlyinteriordesign.com/suite_baby_furniture.php. Healthier options for baby furniture and furnishings.

Wilson, Alex, and Mark Piepkorn, eds. 2006. *Green Building Products: The GreenSpec Guide to Residential Building Materials,* 2nd ed. Gabriola Island BC: Building Green, Inc., and New Society Publishers. Information on many green building products for the home, carefully screened by the editors of *Environmental Building News* and BuildingGreen, Inc.

Health and indoor environments

American Lung Association of Washington, Master Home Environmentalist (MHE) Program. www.alaw.org/air_quality/master_home_environmentalist. Trains volunteers to conduct home environmental assessments.

Baker-Laporte, P., E. Elliot, and J. Banta. 2001. *Prescriptions for a Healthy House: A Practical Guide for Architects, Builders, and Homeowners.* Gabriola Island BC: New Society Publishers.

Building Materials for the Environmentally Hypersensitive. Markham, ONT: CMHC Publications. A 238-page assessment of materials suitable for occupants with chemical sensitivities. Available at www.cmhc-schl.gc.ca/en/inpr/bude/heho/index.cfm.

Hobbs, Angela. 2003. *The Sick House Survival Guide: Simple Steps to Healthier Homes.* Gabriola Island BC: New Society Publishers.

Leclair, Kim, and David Rousseau. 2004. *Environmental by Design, Professional Edition.* Vancouver BC: Hartley and Marks. Notebook publication with symbols representing various criteria, including recycled content, renewable resource, in-plant energy efficiency, low emissions in plant, minimum packaging, minimum transportation, minimum installation hazards, low toxic emissions, durability, simple nontoxic maintenance, reusable, recyclable, fair business practices, research and education programs.

Thompson, Athena. 2004. *Homes That Heal (and Those That Don't): How Your Home Could Be Harming Your Family's Health.* Gabriola Island BC: New Society Publishers.

12: OPERATIONS AND MAINTENANCE

Green project featured in this chapter

Cunningham-Pinon remodel, Portland OR. Contact Greg Acker, Architect, (503) 735-9192.

General maintenance

Abundance Center, Home Maintenance Schedule. www.abundancecenter.com/Forms/Excel_Forms/Home Yearly Maintenance Schedule.xls. Requires Microsoft Excel to open and can be adapted once downloaded.

Chimney Safety Institute of America (CSIA). 2006. Chimney Inspections Explained. www.csia.org/homeowners/inspections-three-levels.htm.

Shuker, Nancy, ed. 1999. *Householder's Survival Manual: How to Take Care of Everything in Your Home.* Pleasantville NY: Readers Digest Association. Comprehensive manual for fixing almost any household problem.

Tenenbaum, David. 2004. *The Complete Idiot's Guide to Home Repair and Maintenance Illustrated.* Indianapolis IN: Alpha Books. Step-by-step guide to common home repairs.

Gardening and lawn care

Morris, Ciscoe. How to Have a Dynamite Lawn. www.ciscoe.com/lawns/lawnout.pdf. Popular garden expert provides information on turf renovation.

Seattle Tilth, Seattle WA, (206) 633-0451. www.seattletilth.org. Natural Lawn and Garden Hotline, as well as classes and other information.

Washington State University, (206) 296-3900. http://gardening.wsu.edu. Lawn and garden care in the Northwest.

Washington Toxics Coalition, Seattle WA, (206) 632-1545. www.watoxics.org/homes-and-gardens. Weed management for the lawn and garden, and links to green gardening programs.

Green cleaning and household products

Berthold-Bond, Annie. 1999. *Better Basics for the Home: Simple Solutions for Less Toxic Living.* New York: Three Rivers Press. Hundreds of alternatives to traditional household products.

Green Guide. www.thegreenguide.com. Consumer guide focusing on green living.

Green Seal, Washington DC, (202) 872-6400. www.greenseal.org/findaproduct/index.cfm. Listings of Green Seal certified products.

Seventh Generation, Burlington VT, (802) 658-3773. www.seventhgeneration.com. Information about household hazards and alternatives, as well as Seventh Generation product information.

Siegel-Maier, Karyn. 1999. *The Naturally Clean Home: 121 Safe and Easy Herbal Formulas for Nontoxic Cleansers.* Pownal VT: Storey Books. Recipes for alternative home products, focusing on healthy and economical solutions.

Simple Green, (800) 228-0709. http://consumer.simplegreen.com. Product information and comparisons, as well as cleaning tips.

Worldwatch Institute, Washington DC, (202) 452-1999. www.worldwatch.org/pubs/goodstuff/cleaningproducts/. Research about sustainable and toxic cleaning products.

Food composting

Washington State University. Composting with Green Cones / Food Digesters. http://gardening.wsu.edu/stewardship/compost/kitchen/grncone/greencon.htm. Information about the Green Cone composting process.

Mold

Washington State Dept of Health (WADOH). Got Mold? Frequently Asked Questions About Mold. www.doh.wa.gov/ehp/ts/iaq/got_mold.html. Basic information on and removal methods for mold in the home.

Moss control

Home Builders Association of Kitsap County. How to Maintain a "Fish-Friendly" Home. www.kitsaphba.com/pdf/BGfactsheet4.pdf. Also available at www.obrienandco.com. Ways to control erosion, manage storm water runoff, conserve water, and protect water quality.

Oregon State University, Extension Service Garden Hints. Why You Might Have Moss in Your Lawn and What to Do. http://extension.oregonstate.edu/news/story.php?S_No=533&storyType=garden.

References

Akbari, Hashem, ed. 1992. *Cooling Our Communities: A Guidebook on Tree Planting and Light-Colored Surfacing.* Lawrence Berkeley National Laboratory Report LBL-31587. Washington DC: U.S. Government Printing Office.

Alexander, Christopher, Sara Ishikawa, and Murray Silverstein, with Max Jacobson, Ingrid Fiksdahl-King, and Shlomo Angel. 1977. *A Pattern Language: Towns, Buildings, Construction.* New York: Oxford University Press.

American Lung Association. 2005. Trends in Asthma Morbidity and Mortality. www.lungusa.org/atf/cf/%7B7A8D42C2-FCCA-4604-8ADE-7F5D5E762256%7D/ASTHMA1.PDF.

Anderson, Ray C. 2005. Rethinking development: Local pathways to global well-being. Keynote address, Second International Conference on Gross National Happiness, June 2005, Halifax NS.

Bobbitt, V. M., A. L. Antonelli, C. R. Foss, R. M. Davidson, R. S. Byther, and R. R. Maleike. 2005. *Pacific Northwest Landscape Integrated Pest Management (IPM) Manual,* rev. ed. Cooperative Extension Publication MISC0201. Pullman WA: Washington State University.

Bower, John. 2000. *The Healthy House: How to Buy One, How to Build One, How to Cure a Sick One,* 4th rev. ed. Unionville IN: Healthy House Institute.

BuildingGreen. 2006. Solarwall Transpired Solar Collector. www.buildinggreen.com.

Carpet and Rug Institute (CRI). 2004. Green Label Plus: Carpet and Adhesives. www.carpet-rug.org/pdf_word_docs/CRI_GLP_factsheet.pdf.

Christian, Jeffrey, and Jan Kosny. 1997. Wall R-Values That Tell It Like It Is. Home Energy Online. www.homeenergy.org/archive/hem.dis.anl.gov/eehem/97/970308.html.

City of Corvallis OR. 2005. Erosion Prevention and Sediment Control Manual. www.ci.corvallis.or.us/downloads/cd/erosioncontrol/manualchapter1.pdf.

City of New York. 2006. Guidelines on Assessment and Remediation of Fungi in Indoor Environments. www.nyc.gov/html/doh/html/epi/moldrpt1.shtml.

Davis, Gary A., and Em Turner. 1995. Safe Substitutes at Home: Non-Toxic Household Products. http://es.epa.gov/techinfo/facts/safe-fs.html.

Devine, John. 1999. *Washington State Ventilation and Indoor Air Quality Code Whole House Ventilation Systems Research Report.* Olympia WA: Washington State University.

EC&M magazine. 2006. Empower Your Customers to Perform Their Own PV Maintenance. http://ecmweb.com/mag/electric_empower_customers_perform.

Efficient Windows Collaborative. 2006. Fact Sheets. www.efficientwindows.org/factsheets.cfm.

Egan, Timothy. 1991. *The Good Rain: Across Time and Terrain in the Pacific Northwest.* New York: Vintage Books.

Energy Bulletin. 2006. Peak Oil Primer. www.energybulletin.net/primer.php.

Energy Star. 2006. Programmable Thermostats. www.energystar.gov/index.cfm?c=thermostats.pr_thermostats.

Energy Star Northwest. 2006. Energy Star Homes and Consumer Products: Call Center Frequently Asked Questions. www.northwestenergystar.com/files/6241Call_Center_Scripts_FINAL.doc.

Environment Canada. 2006. Incentives and Rebates. http://incentivesandrebates.ca.

Ewing, Reid, et al. 2003. Relationship between urban sprawl and physical activity, obesity, and morbidity. *American Journal of Health Promotion* 18: 54.

Fisette, Paul. 2001. Housewraps, Felt Paper, and Weather Penetration Barriers. www.umass.edu/bmatwt/publications/articles/housewraps_feltpaper_weather_penetration_barriers.html.

Fisk, William. 2000. Health and productivity gains from better indoor environments and their relationship with building energy efficiency. *Annual Review of Energy and the Environment.*

Franklin Associates. 1998. *Characterization of Building-Related Construction and Demolition Debris in the United States.* U.S. Environmental Protection Agency, EPA 530-R-98-010. Washington DC: U.S. Government Printing Office.

Go Northwest! 2006. Cascadia: Pacific Northwest Bioregion. http://gonorthwest.com/Visitor/about/bioregion-map.htm.

Good, Nathan. 2006a. Alternative wall-framing systems. *NGA Newsletter,* Spring 2006. www.nathangoodarchitect.com/news.htm.

———. 2006b. The Durisol ICF wall-forming system. *NGA Newsletter,* Summer 2006. www.nathangoodarchitect.com/news.htm.

Green Seal. 1993. Paints (GS-11). Green Seal Standards and Certification. www.greenseal.org/certification/standards/paints.cfm.

———. 2000. Commercial Adhesives (GS-36). Green Seal Standards and Certification. www.greenseal.org/certification/standards/commercialadhesives.cfm.

———. 2006. Green Seal Environmental Standard for Recycled-Content Latex Paint. www.greenseal.org/newsroom/GS-43_Recycled_Content_Latex_Paint.pdf.

Gronbeck, Christopher. 2006. Climate responsive building design, energy unit. Presentation at the Sustainable Building Advisor Course, Olympic Community College, Poulsbo WA.

Guy, Brad, and Nicholas Ciarimboli. 2006. *Design for Disassembly in the Built Environment: A Guide to Closed-Loop Design and Building.* Hamer Center for Community Design, The Pennsylvania State University. www.lifecyclebuilding.org/resources/DfDseattle.pdf.

Harrison, Rob. 2005. The Harding Home: Woodinville, WA. http://harrison-architects.com/projects/new_homes/harding_home/.

Hawken, Paul, Amory Lovins, and Hunter Lovins. 1999. *Natural Capitalism: Creating the Next Industrial Revolution.* Boston: Little, Brown.

Healthy Building Network. 2005. Sorting Out the Vinyls—When Is Vinyl Not PVC? www.healthybuilding.net/pvc/SortingOutVinyls.html.

———. 2006. PVC in Buildings: Hazards and Alternatives. www.healthybuilding.net/pvc/HBN_FS_PVC_in_Buildings.pdf.

Helfand, Judith, and Daniel B. Gold. 2002. *Blue Vinyl.* www.bluevinyl.org.

Hogan, Frank, Jerry Meusel, and Lou Spellman. 2001. Breathing Easier with Slag Cement. *Cement Americas* magazine. http://cementamericas.com/mag/cement_breathing_easier_blast.

Hogan, Kathleen. 2002. Presentation at U.S. Green Building Council Federal Summit, Washington DC.

Horowitz, Michael. 2006. Size Matters (a Lot): The Mistreatment of House Size in Green Rating Systems. Unpublished paper.

International Code Council. 1995. Model Energy Code. Replaced by the International Energy Conservation Code, or IECC, in 1998 and revised every three years, with IECC 2004 being the most current version. www.energycodes.gov/implement/pdfs/modelcode.pdf.

Kennedy, Robert F., Jr. 2005. Speech at the Sierra Summit, Sierra Club National Convention, San Francisco CA. www.sierraclub.org/pressroom/speeches/2005-09-10rfkjr.asp.

Kusnierczyk, E. R., and G. J. Ettl. 2002. Growth Response of Ponderosa Pine to Climate in the Eastern Cascade Mountains: Implications for Climatic Change. *Ecoscience* 9: 544–51.

Lawrence Berkeley National Laboratory (LBNL), Environmental Energy Technology Division, Heat Island Group. 1999. Evapotranspiration. http://eetd.lbl.gov/HeatIsland/Vegetation/Evapotranspiration.html.

Leopold, Aldo. 1949. *A Sand County Almanac: and Sketches Here and There.* New York: Oxford University Press.

Lowry Miller, Karen. 2006. Will we hit $100? *Newsweek* International Edition, msnbc.com, May 15–22, 2006. www.msnbc.msn.com/id/12667616/site/newsweek.

Lstiburek, Joseph. 2005. Understanding Drainage Planes. www.buildingscience.com/resources/walls/drainage_planes.pdf.

Malin, Nadav. 1994. Steel or wood framing: Which way should we go? *Environmental Building News* 3 (4): 1.

McDonald, David. 2005. Soil Strategies for Stormwater Management, Erosion Control, and Landscape Success. www.epa.gov/epaoswer/non-hw/green/pubs/asla-soil.pdf.

Mote, Philip. 2002. Global Regional Climate Change: An Update on the Science. www.seattle.gov/environment/ICLEImote_distr/index.htm.

Mullen, Joe. 2006. Hatchery strives to recover from flooding. *Seattle Times,* November 22, B2.

NAHB Research Center. 2002. Steel vs. Wood Long-Term Thermal Performance Comparison: Valparaiso Demonstration Homes. http://pathnet.org/si.asp?id=487.

National Association of Home Builders. 2004a. Building Greener Neighborhoods: Trees as Part of the Plan. www.nahb.org.

——. 2004b. Remodeling vs. Moving. www.nahb.org/generic.aspx?genericContentID=319.

——. 2006a. Housing Facts, Figures and Trends for March 2006. www.nahb.org.

——. 2006b. What 21st Century Home Buyers Want. www.nahb.org.

Natural Resources Defense Council. 2005. Dangerous Chemicals in the Home: A "Most Wanted" List of Five Common Household Contaminants. www.nrdc.org/health/home/fchems.asp.

Northwest Clean Air Agency. 2005. Mold in Your Home: Causes, Prevention, and Cleanup. Video available at www.nwcleanair.org/aqPrograms/indoorAir.htm.

Northwest Environment Watch. 2002. *This Place on Earth 2002: Measuring What Matters.* Seattle WA: Northwest Environment Watch.

Oikos. 1993. Duct Losses Hurt Forced Air Heating System Performance. http://oikos.com/esb/28/duct_losses.html.

Oregon Department of Energy. 2003. Energy Use in Oregon. www.oregon.gov/ENERGY/CONS/docs/EnergyUseOR.pdf.

Pacific States Marine Fisheries Commission. 1991. The 44th Annual Report of the Pacific States Marine Fisheries Commission. www.psmfc.org/files/Annual%20Reports/1991.pdf.

Puget Sound Action Team (PSAT). 2005. *Low Impact Development: Technical Guidance Manual for Puget Sound.* www.psat.wa.gov/Publications/LID_tech_manual05/lid_index.htm.

Renewable Northwest Project. 1999. Solar Energy Technology. www.rnp.org/RenewTech/tech_solar.html.

Roberts, Jennifer. 2003. *Good Green Homes: Creating Better Homes for a Healthier Planet.* Salt Lake City UT: Gibbs Smith.

Romm, Joseph J. 1994. *Lean and Clean Management: How to Boost Profits and Productivity by Reducing Pollution.* New York: Kodansha International.

Roodman, David, and Nicholas Lenssen. 1995. Worldwatch Paper #124: A Building Revolution: How Ecology and Health Concerns Are Transforming Construction. Williamsport PA: Worldwatch.

Rousseau, David. 2006. Archemy Consulting Web site. http://archemyconsulting.com/healthy-. buildings.html.

Schurke, Joel. 1996. Presentation at Building with Value Workshop, Seattle WA.

Seattle Public Utilities. 2004. Demographics and Water Use Statistics. www.ci.seattle.wa.us/util.

Slag Cement Association. 2005. LEED Guide: Using Slag Cement in Sustainable Construction. Sugar Land TX: Slag Cement Association. http://slagcement.org.

Smith, David, et al. 1997. A national estimate of the economic costs of asthma. *American Journal of Respiratory and Critical Care Medicine* 156: 789.

Snoonian, Deborah. February 2006. How architects can reverse global warming: A conversation with Ed Mazria. *Green-Source: The Magazine of Sustainable Design.* http://archrecord. construction.com/features/green/archives/060201mazria. asp.

Spirn, Anne. 1985. *Granite Garden.* New York: HarperCollins.

State of Hawaii Department of Business, Economic Development and Tourism (DBEDT). 2002. *Field Guide for Energy Performance, Comfort, and Value in Hawaii Homes.* Honolulu: State of Hawaii with AIA.

Steingraber, Sandra. 2004. Update on the Environmental Health Impacts of Polyvinyl Chloride (PVC) as a Building Material: Evidence from 2000–2004. www.healthybuilding.net/pvc/ steingraber.pdf.

Susanka, Sarah. 2006. The not so big green house. Keynote address, Built Green Conference, Seattle WA.

Texas A&M University. nd. Rainwater Harvesting: System Maintenance. http://rainwaterharvesting.tamu.edu/system.html.

Urban Horticulture Institute. 2005. Using CU-Structural Soil in the Urban Environment. Ithaca NY: Cornell University.

U.S. Census Bureau. 2004. American Housing Survey for the United States, 2003. Washington DC: U.S. Government Printing Office.

U.S. Department of Energy. nd. Solar Water Heating System Maintenance and Repair. www.eere.energy.gov/consumer/ your_home/water_heating/index.cfm/mytopic=12950.

——. 2000. Technology Fact Sheet: Ceilings and Attics (Insulation and Ventilation). www.eere.energy.gov/buildings/info/documents/pdfs/26450.pdf.

——. 2001. How to Buy an Energy-Efficient Ground-Source Heat Pump. Federal Energy Management Program (FEMP). www1. eere.energy.gov/femp/pdfs/groundsource_heatpumps.pdf.

——. 2006. Overview of the Electric Grid. www.energetics.com/ gridworks/grid.html.

U.S. Environmental Protection Agency. 1989. Indoor Air Facts # 6: Report to Congress on Indoor Air Quality. Washington DC: U.S. Government Printing Office.

——. 1994. Indoor Air Pollution: An Introduction for Health Professionals. www.epa.gov/iaq/pubs/hpguide.html.

——. 1995. Inside Story: A Guide to Indoor Air Quality. www.epa. gov/iaq/pubs/insidest.html.

——. 2005. Chromated Copper Arsenate. www.epa.gov/ oppad001/reregistration/cca.

——. 2006a. Indoor Air–Mold. www.epa.gov/mold.

——. 2006b. An Introduction to Indoor Air Quality–Formaldehyde. www.epa.gov/iaq/formalde.html.

U.S. Geological Survey. 2006. WaterWatch–Current Water Resources Conditions. http://water.usgs.gov/waterwatch.

U.S. Naval Observatory. 2006. Sun and Moon Altitude / Azimuth Table for One Day. http://aa.usno.navy.mil/data/docs/ AltAz.html.

Van der Ryn, Sim, and Stuart Cowan. 1996. *Ecological Design.* Washington DC: Island Press.

Venetoulis, J., D. Chazan, and C. Gaudet. 2004. Ecological Footprint of Nations 2004. Oakland CA: Redefining Progress. www.redefiningprogress.org/newpubs/2004/footprintnations2004.pdf

Wackernagel, Mathis, and William Rees. 1996. *Our Ecological Footprint.* Philadelphia PA: New Society Publishers.

Walker, Christopher. 2006. Green finance: Accelerating global green building investment to stop dangerous climate change. Presentation at U.S. Green Building Council GreenBuild Conference, November 16, Denver CO.

Warner, Jeffrey. 1995. Selecting windows for energy efficiency. *Home Energy* magazine. http://homeenergy.org/archive/ hem.dis.anl.gov/eehem/95/950708.html.

Washington State Department of Community Trade and Economic Development. 2006. Fuel Mix Disclosure 2005. http://cted.wa.gov/portal/alias__cted/lang__en/tabID__ 539/DesktopDefault.aspx.

Washington State Department of Ecology. 2006. PBDE Flame Retardants: A Fast-Growing Concern. www.ecy.wa.gov/ programs/eap/pbt/pbde.

Werner, J. A., R. M. Lyman, and N. R. Jones. 2005. Case Study of Current Domestic Energy Deficit in the United States and Simulated Solutions for Filling the Deficit by Utilizing Renewable Resources and Other New Technologies. Wyoming State Geological Survey Coal Section, University of Wyoming. www.wsgs.uwyo.edu.

Wilson, Alex. 1999. Small is beautiful: House size, resource use, and the environment. *Environmental Building News* 8: 2, 11.

Wilson, Alex, and Jessica Boehland. 2005. Small is beautiful: U.S. house size, resource use, and the environment. *Journal of Industrial Ecology* 9: 279. http://mitpress.mit.edu/journals/ JIEC/v9n1_2/jiec_9_1-2_277_0.pdf.

Wilson, Alex, and Mark Piepkorn. 2004. All about toilets. *Environmental Building News* 13: 7. www.buildinggreen.com/auth/ article.cfm?fileName=130101a.xml.

Wilson, Alex, and Nadav Malin, eds. 2003. *GreenSpec Directory: Product Directory with Guideline Specifications.* Brattleboro VT: BuildingGreen.

Wilson, A., J. Thorne, and J. Morrill. 2003. *Consumer Guide to Home Energy Savings,* 8th ed. Washington DC: American Council for an Energy Efficient Economy.

TRADEMARKS

Aglaia® is a registered trademark.

AtticWrapTM is a trademark.

Built GreenTM is a trademark.

CU-Structural SoilTM is a trademark.

DupontTM is a trademark.

Durisol® is a registered trademark.

Earth AdvantageTM is a trademark.

Energy Star® is a registered trademark.

Environments for Living® is a registered trademark.

LEED® is a registered trademark.

Living MachineTM is a trademark.

Location Efficient Mortgage® is a registered trademark.

Lyptus® is a registered trademark.

Marmoleum® is a registered trademark.

1Earth1DesignTM is a trademark.

PaperstoneTM is a trademark.

Parallams® is a registered trademark.

Rastra® is a registered trademark.

Richlite® is a registered trademark.

Simpson Strong-Tie® is a registered trademark.

Solarwall® is a registered trademark.

Terragren® is a registered trademark.

Velocipede Architects, 238, 247
ventilation
    during construction, 75
    mechanical, 133, 134,
        140, 168, 174–175, 181,
        184–185, 186, 209, 212,
        215, 219–220, 222, 229
    natural, 58, 89, 100, 121,
        130, 139, 146, 176, 188,
        191, 175, 186, 209, 239,
        262
verification (home), 27, 75,
    77–78, 130, 133
Vineyards (Bainbridge Island),
    129–130
vinyl flooring, 88, 242
volatile organic compounds
    (VOCs). See chemicals

Wackernagel, Mathis, 30, 38
walkable, 131, 269, 272
walk-through, 75, 78
washing machine, front-loading,
    133, 225
Washington Organic Recycling
    Council, 162
Washington State Department
    of Ecology, 257–258
Washington State University
    Energy Extension Office,
    130
waste heat, 113, 186, 212, 228
water
    black, 159, 234
    conservation, 122, 205, 225
    domestic hot water (DHW),
        35, 121, 126, 139, 217,
        219, 220, 228, 229
    -efficient, 69, 87, 252

filtration, 235, 235–236,
    252
filtration (rainwater), 88,
    159, 121,
gray, 80, 160, 164, 207–
    208, 232, 234–235,
    252–253
intrusion, 169–173
nonpotable, 158, 159, 164,
    232
potable, 159, 232
recirculation, 219–230
reverse osmosis (RO)
    filtration, 236
rights (legal), 159–160
space heating water (SHW),
    217–218
surfacewater management,
    75, 151, 156
storm runoff, 36, 151
supply, 160
treatment (rainwater), 210
treatment (wastewater), 80,
    84
withdrawals (freshwater),
    17
watershed, 165
WaterWatch, 155
Wells, Kim, 85
West Nile virus, 155
wetland, 17, 43, 131, 137, 142,
    144, 148, 165, 261
wheatboard, 250
Willamette River, 120
Wilson, Alex, 35
wind, 100
    farms, 104–105
    turbines, 100, 206

window
    clerestory, 190–191, 195
    design, 58, 145, 172–173,
        176, 184, 188–189, 191
    double-hung, 126, 188, 189,
        193
    glazing, 186, 188
    insulation value, 182–184
    overhangs, 62, 88, 169, 170,
        174, 187, 189, 191, 194
    skylights, 191
Winslow Cohousing (WCG),
    49–50
wood
    certified, 72, 200, 243, 247,
        254, 257
    energy, 100, 105
    polymer (decking), 45, 173,
        202
    treatment, 54, 164
Woodside, Doug (Woodside
    Construction), 44
wood stove, 100
worm bin, 265

xeriscape. See landscaping

Yost, Peter, 230

Ziophirville remodel, 112–113,
    207, 252
zoning, 33, 66, 89, 142, 272